MW00450998

Larry's SalesGame methodologies and strategies have been integrated into to our firm culture, which has been a business-development game changer for us.

—Dan Soukup, Soukup Bush, Colorado CPA firm

Identifying and nurturing new clients who are both enthusiastic and loyal is the lifeblood of a practice and requires a truly consultative approach. It is the result of following and executing a deliberate and repeatable process focused on truly understanding each client's unique needs and tailoring solutions to ensure those needs are addressed. The SalesGame has provided our team with a practical and repeatable roadmap for doing just that, making our business-development efforts more focused and productive.

—David Graham, wealth management executive

SalesGame:

A Guide to Selling
Professional Services
Second Edition

J. Larry White

with Diane Brown and Tom Porter

Project Advisor: Stacy Hiquet

Project Editor: Kate Shoup

Copy Editor: Kate Shoup

Interior Layout: Shawn Morningstar

Cover Designer: Mike Tanamachi

Indexer: Kelly Talbot Editing Services

Proofreader: Kelly Talbot Editing Services

©2015 J. Larry White and SalesGame LLC

ALL RIGHTS RESERVED. No part of this work covered by the copyright herein may be reproduced, transmitted, stored, or used in any form or by any means graphic, electronic, or mechanical, including but not limited to photocopying, recording, scanning, digitizing, taping, Web distribution, information networks, or information storage and retrieval systems, except as permitted under Section 107 or 108 of the 1976 United States Copyright Act, without the prior written permission of the publisher.

All SalesGame vocabulary and terms are copyrighted by J. Larry White.

All trademarks are the property of their respective owners.

All images © J. Larry White and SalesGame LLC unless otherwise noted.

Image ID 216549799 (front cover): ©Edyta Pawlowska

Image ID 12869758 (back cover): ©Hurst Photo

Library of Congress Control Number: 2015916576

ISBN-13: 978-0-9967515-0-6

Printed in the United States of America

To my family: Susan, Dana and Ryan.
My heart, my soul and my spirit...
you give my life meaning and purpose.

To my sister, cousins, nieces, nephews, and friends.
You have all enriched my life.

To my many clients and colleagues.
You have given me a wonderful career
and the opportunity to make a difference in your lives.

J. Larry White

To Steve, Alec, and Dana for your patience, love, and support in all that I do.

To Tom and Larry for being the best partners and mentors one could ask for.

To my network of business colleagues and friends who have helped me grow.

To my clients for allowing me the privilege of serving you.

All of you inspire me daily!

Diane Brown

To those who have influenced me most in business development
which has led to the revision of this book:

Dave Donaldson, who first impressed upon me the value of business
development in a professional services organization;

Steve Strelsin, who showed me how to do it effectively and led me to
the learning model we follow today;

Diane Brown, who put the "meat on the bones" of our teaching/coaching approach;

And most influential of all, Larry White, who created the SalesGame process and
allowed us to become collaborators with him in further enhancing the SalesGame.

On the personal side, to Jane Ann Porter for her support of me as well as
Diane and Larry in everything we do related to SalesGame.

Tom Porter

Acknowledgments

I have been fortunate to have had five mentors over my career, each of whom played an important role. First and foremost was my father Gene, who sold everything from candy bars to refrigeration equipment, which he eventually manufactured in his own factory. He gave me advice and counsel from my childhood until he left us at age 95. Then there was John Mahoney, who was dean of LSA at the University of Detroit. He afforded me the opportunity to grow when he took a chance and made me the chairman of the Department of Communication Studies at age 23. Pete Burgher, an outstanding rainmaker and managing partner at a Big Eight accounting firm, lured me away from academia when he hired me as the firm's first director of marketing. Dick Connor helped me make the transition from employee to consultant. Finally, Jim Smith, a CPA, was another outstanding rainmaker, head of a Big Eight firm's national business-development function, and, most of all, one of the classiest gentlemen I have ever met. Jim opened my eyes to my own potential and started me on the road to entrepreneurial success.

Although these five individuals played the most significant role in my development, I have always been able to learn from people in all walks of life, whether a cab driver or a captain of industry. Every client and prospect with whom I have talked, every professional who participated in my workshops, every employee I have hired has in his or her own way contributed to this book and my success. Of course, some have contributed more than others. My two colleagues, Tom Porter and Diane Brown, with whom I started working as clients in the 1990s and as colleagues in 2000, energized and motivated me. Without them, the second edition of SalesGame would never have been written, and I probably would have retired long ago. I also greatly appreciate the many clients who have shared their business-development experiences with me. They will hopefully recognize their stories, even though the names have been changed to protect everyone's confidentiality. Thank you all for a most rewarding and enjoyable career!

—J. Larry White

We have many people to thank for this second edition coming to fruition. First, we must thank Larry White. We have been privileged to work with Larry and the SalesGame for more than 15 years to make a difference for our clients, and that has been immensely rewarding. Second, we must thank the team that helped us on the book. When we first conceived updating the book, Stacy Hiquet served as a sounding board and coach and helped us better understand how to navigate the waters of the publishing industry. She could not have been more positive and encouraging. Stacy also got us to the right cadre of professionals, which included an extraordinary quarter-back, Kate Shoup, our editor. Kate has shepherded us with patience, support, "gentle reminders," and cheerleading, and helped us through decisions at every step. In addition, she has been our primary interface with the rest of the team on the project and has been an absolute joy as a collaborator. Finally, we too have had great mentors, colleagues, and clients who have invested in us, created with us, challenged us, and most importantly, inspired us. We hope this edition of the book makes them proud.

—Diane Brown and Tom Porter

About the Authors

J. Larry White, SalesGame Founder

J. Larry White has worked exclusively with professional services firms in business development for more than 30 years. His engagements have included assignments with law firms, accounting firms, consulting organizations, wealth advisory firms, and investment bankers in the U.S., Canada, Europe, Asia, South America, and Africa.

Larry founded Services Rating Organization (SRO), which served more than 1,000 professional service firms in 75 cities before being acquired by an international publishing company, Wolters-Kluwer. In addition to consulting, Larry is an entrepreneur involved with real estate and other businesses, and is the author of *SalesGame: A Guide to Selling Professional Services*.

After receiving his undergraduate degree in communications from the University of Michigan, Larry went on to earn three graduate degrees in business and communications from Northwestern University, the University of Detroit, and the University of Michigan. Before beginning his career serving professional service firms, Larry taught at the University of Notre Dame and the University of Detroit, where he was the chairman of the Department of Communication Studies.

Diane Brown, SalesGame Coach

Diane Brown has worked with both individuals and teams within CPA firms, law firms, and wealth management firms to strengthen their business-development discipline and results. With experience in organization effectiveness, performance consulting, executive coaching, communication, facilitation, and training, Diane brings a unique blend of knowledge and expertise to promote behavior change, skill building, and improved execution. Diane has been a SalesGame coach, trainer, and consultant since 2003.

Tom Porter, SalesGame Coach

Tom Porter has been a SalesGame Coach for more than 10 years. Serving clients in the professional services arena, Tom coaches and advises senior executives and owners, with special expertise in business development, succession management, leadership development, partner relationship building, client relationship management, and growth and personal development. As a retired partner in a professional services firm, Tom knows what it takes to build a practice in that environment.

For more information and resources about SalesGame, visit www.salesgame.com.

Table of Contents

Introduction xvii

Part 1
An Overview of the SalesGame 1

Chapter 1   The Goal of the SalesGame 3

The Client's Enthusiasm Is More Important Than
    Getting the Work 4

Qualified Leads Are Decision-Makers Who Recognize a Need 6

Understand Your Mission 7

Don't Just Sell Work—Build the Practice of Your Dreams 8

Satisfied Clients Aren't Enough 8

True Value Is Personal 9

Chapter 2   The Players: Who's Involved in the SalesGame? 11

The Decision-Maker 13

The User 14

The Influencer 14

The Coach 15

Analyzing the Network of Relationships 16

Chapter 3   The SalesGameProcess 19

Chapter 4   Stage One: Create and Identify Leads **21**

Build Relationships First 23

Start with a Vision for Creating the Practice of Your Dreams 24

Don't Sell in Stage One 26

The Role of Marketing Is to Create Leads 28

Don't Wait...Initiate! 29

Chapter 5   Stage Two: Qualify and Track Leads **33**

Qualification Means Exploring the Opportunity, Not Selling 34

When Selling, Bigger Is Not Better 36

Positioning Leads Versus Qualified Leads 37

Position by Building Relationships and
Demonstrating Selling Points 38

Track Leads for the Long Term 39

Chapter 6   Stage Three: Shape the Service **43**

Get to the Decision-Maker to Find the True Source of Value 45

Meet More, Write Less 46

Chapter 7   Stage Four: Trial Close **49**

Ask for the Business 51

Extend Stage Four to Improve Your Success Rate 52

Chapter 8   Stage Five: Final Close **57**

Ask the Tough Question 58

Continue to Close 59

Confirm the Financial Arrangement 61

**Chapter 9   Stage Six: Assure Enthusiasm
(or Determine the Reason for Loss)** **63**

Make Time for Assuring Client Enthusiasm Meetings 65

How to Win When You "Lose" 67

Close by Positioning for the Future 69

Chapter 10   The Importance of Preparation **73**

The Will to Prepare 73

Best Practices in Planning 74

Part 2
Best Practices for Setting Up the Game 81

Chapter 11   The Sales Matrix: Four Types of Stage Two Leads 83

Opportunities Are Often Won or Lost Early in the Game 84

Respond Mode 86

Initiate Mode 86

If a Client or Prospect Starts the Process, It Is
   Probably a Qualified Lead 87

When Initiating in Stage Two, Set Realistic Goals and Next Steps . . 88

Why Initiate at All? 90

Chapter 12   Best Practices for Quadrant One:
               Responding to Prospects 93

Respond Quickly 94

Get the Right Information 95

   Who Is Calling? 96

   How Did the Prospect Get Your or the Firm's Name? 97

   What Is the Prospect Trying to Accomplish? 98

   What Is the Time Frame? 99

   What Is the Next Step? 100

Go for a Creative Close 102

Build Relationships First 104

Responding to Prospects You Already Know 106

Chapter 13   Best Practices for Quadrant Two:
               Responding to Clients 109

Responding Quickly and Getting the Right Information 110

Beware of the Easy Sale 111

Clients: A Natural Starting Place to Initiate Contact 115

Chapter 14   Best Practices for Quadrant Three:
               Initiating Contact with Clients 115

Focus on Issues, Not Products 116

Build Awareness of Resources 117

Chapter 15   Best Practices for Quadrant Four:
              Initiating Contact with Prospects 119
              Prospecting with Unknown Targets 120
                   Choose the Right Situation 120
                   Sell the Meeting, Not the Service. 123
                   Be Prepared for the First Objection. 126
                   Follow Up, Follow Up, Follow Up 128
              Prospecting with Known Contacts 130
                   Exploring Your Contact Base. 130
                   Prospecting: Dealing with Friends and Relatives 137

Part 3
The Scorecard: Add Value, Differentiate
Your Service, and Build Strategy 145

Chapter 16   What Is the Scorecard? 147
              Focus for the Future. 149
              Keep It Short. 150

Chapter 17   Why Use the Scorecard? 153
              Make It Fun. 154
              Make It Tangible. 155

Chapter 18   Start with the Heart of the Matter. 157
              Recognize the Difference Between Service and Value 158
              Getting to the Heart of the Matter When the Client
                   or Prospect Calls. 160
                   Establishing What They Really Want: It's a Dialogue 161
                   Ask and Ask Again 164
              Getting to the Heart of the Matter When You Initiate Contact ... 164
                   Start Broad. 166
                   Know How Your Service Might Benefit the
                        Client or Prospect 167

Chapter 19   Shaping the Service: Features, Benefits, and
              Conditions of Satisfaction 171
              Find the Right Scorecard Factors 176
              Don't Believe the RFP 177
              Shape the Service, Even If the Work Is Sold. 178
              Know Your Selling Points. 179
              Find Your Style 180
              Few Are Better Than Many 181

Chapter 20   Differentiating Your Service and Developing a Strategy . . 183
              Start Developing a Strategy Early 184
              Use the Power of Three 186
              Implement a Strategy by Making Scorecard Factors Real. 187
              Building a Strategy for the Long Term 188
              Don't Forget Negative Factors on the Scorecard 189
              Be Prepared: Negative Factors Lead to Objections 190
              Let Sleeping Dogs and Negative Scorecard Factors Lie. 190
              Sell Responsibly 192
              Make the Scorecard Part of the Permanent File 193

Part 4
The Ground Rule: Improve Communication,
Handle Objections, and Define Scorecard Factors. 197

Chapter 21   Understanding the Ground Rule. 199
              Achieving Win-Win Communication with the Ground Rule 200
              The Basic Elements of the Ground Rule 201

Chapter 22   Ground Rule Step 1: Listen for Value. 205
              Focus on Agreement. 206
              Feelings Are the Most Important Source of Value. 206

Chapter 23   Ground Rule Step 2:
              Feed Back Value and Agreement First. 209
              How to Connect with Clients and Prospects. 211
              Use Client or Prospect Words 212
              Smile 213
              Communication Is a Two-Way Street. 215

**Chapter 24   Ground Rule Step 3: Provide Information
and End with a Question** **215**
Provide "Stage-Appropriate" Information 216
Watch Out for the Danger Zone 218
Don't Interrogate Your Client or Prospect 219
End with a Question to Keep Control 219
Focus on Using Open-Ended Questions 221
Practice Even When You Are Not Selling 221
Getting to the "Real" Heart of the Matter 223

Chapter 25   Refine the Heart of the Matter and Scorecard Factors . . . **223**
Responding to Positive Scorecard Factors 224
Slow Down and Peel Back the Onion 225
Provide Information to Position Your Service When
Dealing with Positive Factors 227

Chapter 26   How to Handle Objections **231**
Don't Handle the Wrong Objection 232
Explore Offsetting Benefits 235
Don't Be Stopped by Any Negative Factor or Objection 237

Chapter 27   Handling Price Objections **239**
Do Not Discuss Price Until You Know What You're Selling 240
Establish a Frame of Reference 241
Don't Lose an Opportunity Because of a
Small Price Difference 242
Show Them You Really Can Be More Valuable 243
Don't Let Their Budget Get in the
Way of Working Together 244
Determine the Scope of Service 245
Establish Offsetting Benefits 247
Explore Gaps in Coverage 249

Chapter 28   Handling Objections from a Satisfied Prospect or Client . . **249**
Find Out What They Like—and Don't Like—
About Their Current Firm 251

Chapter 29   Handling Objections Phrased Like Questions 255

Always Be Prepared for "Why You?" 256

Use the Rule of Three. 257

Distance. 259

Chapter 30   Tips for Handling Other Objections 259

Depth. 260

Too Little Experience 261

Too Much Experience 261

Resistance to Using a Firm in a New Area 262

You Are All the Same 263

Part 5
The Opening: Start the Game 269

Chapter 31   Creating a Favorable Impression 271

Dress for the Game You Are Playing. 272

Create an Air of Confidence 274

Be on Time 274

Contact the Client or Prospect If You Will Be Late 275

Chapter 32   Building Rapport 277

Introduce the Players First. 278

Keep It Simple. 278

Keep It Short. 279

Have a Plan 281

Chapter 33   Making the Transition to Business 281

Don't Make a Pitch. 282

A Universal Meeting Tool: TEPE. 283

T: Thank the Client or Prospect 283

E: Express Interest. 283

P: State the Purpose of the Meeting 285

E: End with an Easy-to-Answer, Open-Ended Question. 287

Make TEPE Your Routine 289

Simple, Isn't It! 290

Part 6
Questioning Technique **293**

| Chapter 34 | Questions: A Fundamental Tool in the SalesGame . . . . . . 295 |

Start Broad and Easy 296

Emphasize Open-Ended Questions 297

   The Risks of Asking a Closed-Ended Question 298

   People Like to Talk 298

Use Closed-Ended Questions to Confirm or Verify 299

Ask BIG Questions First 300

| Chapter 35 | Choose Three to Five Areas of Inquiry . . . . 303 |

Use Areas of Inquiry to Get a Vision for the Meeting 304

Start with Easier Areas of Inquiry 305

Identify the BIG Questions 306

Use the Ground Rule to Drill Down 307

Developing Questions for a Specific Meeting 308

Using POGO for Stage Two Meetings 309

What Is a Must-Ask Question? 311

| Chapter 36 | Ask the Must-Ask Question . . . . **311** |

Identifying the Must-Ask Question 313

Part 7
Closing: Establish Next Steps and Advance Your Cause . . . **317**

| Chapter 37 | The Closing Process and Best Practices . . . . **319** |

Best Practice #1: Be Prepared with Two Next
   Steps to Close Every Meeting 321

Best Practice #2: Set Up the Close with a Must-Ask Question 324

Best Practice #3: Avoid the Yes/No Question 325

Best Practice #4: Use the Ground Rule to Respond to a Rejection . . 326

Best Practice #5: Close as Soon as Possible 328

Best Practice #6: Avoid Writing Whenever Possible 330

Closing for Promotional Seminars 333

| Chapter 38 | Stage One: Close to Set Up Qualification . . . . 333 |

Closing for Other Marketing Activities 335

The Positioning Close 337

Chapter 39   Stage Two: Close to Shape the Service or
Position for Another Day **337**

Closing to Advance the Cause in Stage Two................... 339

Get to the Decision-Maker 340

Don't Position When You Can Advance..................... 340

Chapter 40   Stage Three: Close to Build Relationships,
Implement Strategy, and Differentiate **343**

Relationships: The Key to Winning 344

Implement a Strategy to Differentiate Your Service 345

Example 1 345

Example 2 346

Example 3 347

Better Understanding Means a More Enthusiastic Client 348

Chapter 41   Stage Four: Close to Ensure Client Satisfaction
and Surface Hidden Objections **349**

Use a Draft Proposal to Improve Your Success Rate 350

Gain Permission for Contact Beyond the Beauty Contest 352

Use a Trial Close Even When You Know the Work Is Sold 352

Use the Trial Close to Surface Hidden Objections 353

Always Close, Even in Formal Situations..................... 355

Chapter 42   Stage Five: Close to Start the Work or
Position for Another Day **355**

With Some RFPs, Winning Is Just the Beginning 356

Closing in Stage Five When You Lose....................... 357

Stay Proactive, Even in Stage Five 358

When the Trial Close Is Accepted, Ask for the Business 359

Close with Enthusiastic Clients to Build Bridges for the Future .. 363

Chapter 43   Stage Six: Close to Create Future Qualified Leads **363**

Close with Lost Opportunities to Build Relationships
and Position for the Future 366

Part 8
Appendixes 373

Appendix A   Marketing and Lead-Generation Activities 375

Examples of Stage One Marketing Activities 378

Networking 378

Prospecting 379

Internal Marketing 379

Friends and Family 380

Promotional Activities 380

Present Clients 381

Following the Sales Planning Checklist 383

Appendix B   The Planning System 383

Creating a Play Diagram 385

Execute Your Plan 387

Index 389

Introduction

How to Use the SalesGame

The SalesGame is based on the assumption that selling professional services is much more like a game than a science. Webster's defines a game as "a contest based on strength, skill and chance." When selling professional services, strength can be based on any number of factors, such as experience, credentials, or depth of the team. Strength often dictates who will win a "contest" for new work, whether the competition is another professional, internal personnel, or simply a decision to proceed with a given project. Banks frequently choose accounting firms that have the most experience in their industry. Law firms may be hired because their attorneys are alumni of the Environmental Protection Agency or some other governmental institution relevant to the matter at hand. A Fortune 500 company is more likely to hire consultants who come from a large organization and have the depth to tackle a given problem quickly.

The SalesGame will not change the relative strength of various professional competitors in the short term. If you have the weakest credentials or experience, you are not as likely to win a business-development contest. However, if you use the skills and best practices described in this book, you will improve your chances of winning even when the competition is more experienced or has more credentials or depth. More importantly, you will improve your chances of achieving the ultimate goal of the SalesGame—ending up with an enthusiastic client—even in sole-source situations such as an opportunity to expand services to a present client. By playing well, you also learn how to develop your own strengths so you are not at a competitive disadvantage in the future and win more in the long term.

As with all games, the discipline to work at getting better and a passionate belief in what you're doing also contribute to a player or team's strength. This is certainly true for professional services. After more than 10 years of watching individuals, practice groups, and firms use the SalesGame, it has become very clear that those who have the discipline to practice and embrace the fundamentals described in this book achieve much greater and more sustainable success. In other words, don't just read this book, but have the discipline to use the tools, especially with your teammates (if you have them).

Good Skills Can Overcome Weaknesses in Strength

Skill is a function of talent, knowing the fundamentals, and practicing them. Sometimes playing a game with skill can overcome weaknesses in strength.

A basketball team with short players might have a good understanding of fundamental passing skills, develop them through practice, and be able to use them to beat a much taller group of players. Professionals can overcome weaknesses in strength as well. A small professional firm might overcome the reputation and depth of a larger competitor by using their skills to find out what the client or prospect needs and build relationships with important members of the decision-making team. One of the comments I hear most when interviewing those who are not rainmakers in their professional service firms is that Bill or George or whoever "is just naturally good at selling" and they are not. Certainly, talent plays a role in how effective someone will be at business development. However, it is also true that anyone can improve at any game—including the SalesGame—if they take the time to learn the fundamentals and have the discipline to practice.

Understand the Game Before You Play

If anyone wants to improve at a particular game, the first thing that person should do is understand the fundamentals of the game he or she is playing. The opening part of the SalesGame provides an overview of business development in a professional service environment. It will help you understand the true goal of the game, the players, and the framework that provides direction and measures progress. Reading Part 1, "An Overview of the SalesGame," is required for you to gain the foundation needed to use the skills and best practices described in the sections that follow. After you have read Part 1, you may choose to use this book as a reference manual. The remaining parts cover the following topics:

- **Part 2, "Best Practices for Setting Up the Game":** This part shares best practices for handling the start of the sales process (for example, how to approach leads) by reviewing the concepts of responding and initiating. It also discusses the differences in approach for each of these for prospects and clients (for example, responding to requests for proposals versus discussing new services with a present client).

- **Part 3, "The Scorecard: Add Value, Differentiate Your Service, and Build Strategy":** This part describes a fundamental tool for playing the SalesGame and ensuring clients feel they are being well served. This tool is useful even when there is an ongoing relationship, such as an accounting firm providing audit services or a law firm handling employment work for a large corporation. In fact, in the years since the first edition of the SalesGame was published, literally hundreds of professionals have told me that this fundamental tool is as important to being a great professional as it is for being good at business development. The Scorecard is used for qualifying leads, finding the true source of value, developing a strategy, differentiating service, and measuring satisfaction.

■ **Part 4, "The Ground Rule: Improve Communication, Handle Objections, and Define Scorecard Factors":** This part describes a second fundamental tool for playing the SalesGame: the Ground Rule. The Ground Rule is used to develop relationships, gather information, define buying criteria, handle objections, respond to a rejected close, discuss a client's satisfaction level, and so on. In other words, it's a tool that is useful in every stage of the buying and delivery process. I have had many clients tell me that the Ground Rule has been useful way beyond the world of business—for example, for having easier, more productive, and less argumentative conversations with family and friends.

■ **Part 5, "The Opening: Start the Game":** This part describes a fundamental that everyone uses but that few have broken into the individual elements, making it reliably replicable and easily taught to others, especially those who participate in team sales meetings. Most professionals are capable of establishing a good impression and making small talk, but making the transition from small talk to the business part of the meeting or telephone conversation tends to be more problematic. This is the essence of this SalesGame fundamental. Many of those with whom I've worked have told me that they use this skill for every meeting, regardless of whether they are in "business-development mode."

■ **Part 6, "Questioning Technique":** This part describes the best practices for maintaining a dialogue with clients and prospects, including preparing areas of inquiry and asking the right questions to advance in the SalesGame. Although we all have spent our whole lives asking questions, the fundamentals described in this part will ensure that questions are asked using the right structure and order.

■ **Part 7, "Closing: Establish Next Steps and Advance Your Cause":** This part describes another fundamental that everyone has heard of but professionals rarely understand. A *close* is simply an agreement for a next step in an ongoing process. Because the sales cycle for professional services is usually long—often stretching over months or years—professionals must understand and be skilled at closes that position them for a future contact and advance their cause. I've often said in workshops that every meeting has a close.

This is a bit of an exaggeration, but failing to have an effective close is one of the real weaknesses in most professionals' game. Far too often, they end a meeting with no next step or one they can't control—for example, when the client or prospect says, "Let me think about that," or "We'll give you a call if something comes up." This part will help you prepare and execute the fundamental skill of closing to avoid these pitfalls and help you understand the best way to close in every stage of the SalesGame.

Appendix A, "Marketing and Lead-Generation Activities," and Appendix B, "The Planning System," tie all the fundamentals together, much like a football team weaves fundamental skills like blocking and tackling into a play. It matches steps in the planning process with the contents described in each section of the book. You can use the Sales Planning Checklist in Appendix B to develop a Play Diagram as you pursue a specific business-development opportunity. I've found these tools to be extremely valuable when professionals are involved in team selling situations. As with any team game, it's critical that everyone has the same vision for the play they are about to make.

Luck Plays a Role in Any Game

Everyone recognizes the role chance or luck can play in any game. A soccer or football hits the goal post and bounces in or out. A golf shot goes into the woods and bounces back into the fairway, while another lands in the fairway only to take a bad bounce off a sprinkler head and end up behind a tree. I have worked with professionals whose largest revenue client came into their lives because the right decision-maker just happened to move in next door. I have also seen situations when the competition lived next door to a desirable prospect and that relationship cost my client the business.

The professionals with whom we work—whether they are accountants, attorneys, wealth advisors, consultants, bankers, or engineers—are used to performing at very high levels. I often work with larger firms, and the professionals they hire have outstanding academic careers and have usually demonstrated their technical expertise for several years before they end up in a SalesGame workshop. They are used to taking on an assignment, following procedures, and ending up with the "right answer" whether it's an opinion on a financial statement or a legal contract to protect a client. In short, professionals are not accustomed to luck playing much of a role in their performance. When these same professionals become involved in business development, they often have the same expectations for success as they had competing on an exam or delivering a work product. I have heard many professionals who fail to understand the business-development process say to a colleague who is going to a lunch with a prospect, "Bring us back some work!" Of course, this only heightens the expectation for quick success and leads to disappointment if the world follows its normal course and the lunch simply leads to another meeting.

Using the analogy of a game for business development hopefully helps professionals understand that they cannot control the outcome. They can only control how well they play. We all know losing is much more painful if we do not play well. Conversely, there is no shame in not winning if we have done our best. The mission of the SalesGame is very simple. It should help professionals improve their game and avoid "if onlys," like the following:

- "If only I would have asked for a meeting with the decision-maker. I would have known the real issue was confidentiality!"

- "If only we would have reviewed a draft of the proposal. We would have been aware of how far off we were on the fee quote!"

- "If only we would have invited the prospect to our offices so he could see the depth of our team. We wouldn't have been looked at as being too small for this engagement!"

You can use the SalesGame to play as well as possible so you can walk away from an opportunity with a feeling of a job well done regardless of whether you won or lost or how much Lady Luck chose to smile on you.

Good Preparation Improves Your Luck

Although luck plays a role in any game, solid preparation has a way of creating its own good fortune, as most professional athletes will testify. Successful football coaches plan for the opponent's strengths and weaknesses, for weather conditions, for fan noise, for potential injuries to key players, and on and on. Tiger Woods once spent weeks practicing a single shot he thought he would need on the 15th hole of the Masters tournament. His preparation paid off when he hit the shot perfectly on Sunday's final round to clinch the victory.

Unfortunately, preparation is one the most glaring weaknesses in the way most professionals play the SalesGame. Professionals often plan business-development interviews on the car ride out to the client or prospect, on the elevator ride up, or in a two-minute discussion walking down the hall to an important business-development conference call. I once worked with a partner who told me he had been positioning with his hottest prospect for several years. When I asked what he did to prepare for the first meeting to discuss an actual piece of work, he responded by saying, "I was so busy that I just didn't have a chance to plan." Chase a prospect for years and then not plan an important meeting. This does not make much sense, does it?

To get the most out of this book, you should use the SalesGame to better plan and prepare for your business-development meetings, whether they're in person or on the phone. The Sales Planning Checklist and Play Diagram mentioned earlier should be useful for this purpose. The more you use these tools, especially in a team setting, the more likely you are to achieve sustainable improvement in your business-development performance. As one of our favorite clients likes to say, "Learning is not an inoculation, it is a process."

Have Fun

I believe the most important reason professionals in our workshops respond well to the SalesGame is that using the analogy of a game makes this responsibility seem more like fun and less like work. Professionals who see business development more like work than fun project this feeling in sales meetings. Unfortunately, this feeling does not serve them well because clients and prospects want to work with professionals who enjoy what they do. Professionals who read the SalesGame will hopefully find that business development can and should be fun.

Games are always more fun if you feel like you are getting better. The way you improve at any game is to practice and play. The SalesGame does not provide any magical answers, only "best practices" to use when you are playing this important game. To improve results, you should use the SalesGame as a foundation to improve your performance through good preparation, practice, and, of course, making sure you play the game as much as possible. The pleasant irony is that the more you play, the more you will find that business development is a lot more fun than you ever would have imagined!

Part 1

An Overview of the SalesGame

The Goal of the SalesGame

In almost every game, the goal is pretty clear: End up with a higher score (or lower, depending on the game) than your competitor. There's a winner and a loser. How many times have you heard a sports announcer say after a dramatic and well-played contest, "It's a shame there has to be a loser in this game..."?

The SalesGame is different. In the SalesGame, there doesn't have to be a loser. If professionals play well, they win—and so do their clients. Prospects and clients are not adversaries. They are more like fellow players in your quest to solve a problem or capitalize on an opportunity. This certainly applies when pursuing sole source situations, which professionals often don't even think of as selling—for example, when a client calls for an additional service. When it's a competitive situation, such as responding to a request for proposal, the real issue isn't being chosen but making sure that both the client *and* the professional end up feeling like the work that was done served both parties well. Even the firm that isn't chosen can profit from these situations if it plays well by building relationships, learning how it can improve, and positioning for the future.

Most professionals fail to grasp this important concept. In workshops, when I ask them what they are trying to achieve, the usual response is, "Get the work!" But as I have said many times, the goal of the game is not just to get the work, but to have an enthusiastic client when the work is done.

If professionals "get the work" but their client isn't pleased with the result, they may have generated some revenues—but at the cost of damaging their reputation. On the other side of the coin, if professionals get the work but go way over budget to deliver what's been promised, they set up false expectations for the future and diminish their own and their staff's job satisfaction.

The true goal of the SalesGame, then, is to convert qualified leads into enthusiastic clients who generate rewards commensurate with the value received. These words have been carefully chosen. They express the basic concept that underlies all the fundamentals described in this book.

> Convert qualified leads into enthusiastic clients who generate rewards commensurate with the value received.

The Client's Enthusiasm Is More Important Than Getting the Work

The chief goal of the SalesGame—to convert qualified leads into enthusiastic clients who generate rewards commensurate with the value received—should also serve as a guide to professionals in their efforts to develop business. Most importantly, professionals—that is, you—must realize that the goal is *not* to simply obtain work, but to sell and deliver services in such a way that the client is an enthusiastic buyer. Any action that an accountant, lawyer, consultant, wealth manager, engineer, banker, or any other professional takes when playing the SalesGame should be with this ultimate goal in mind. Why? Because enthusiastic clients are more fun to work with, pay better, rarely switch providers, usually buy additional services, and provide opportunities to leverage their enthusiasm to get more work such as generating referrals.

> Enthusiastic clients are more fun to work with, pay better, rarely switch providers, usually buy additional services, and provide opportunities to leverage their enthusiasm to get more work such as generating referrals.

I am often asked by workshop participants to share any sales tricks or gimmicks that I find useful. My response is simple: If your goal is to end up with a happy client, there are no such things as tricks or gimmicks.

In the world of professional services, it is far better to not acquire the work if the outcome will not please the client or prospect.

Of course, ending up with an enthusiastic client is more difficult in some situations than others. For example, if a company is being sued and hires an attorney to defend it, the outcome is obviously uncertain and may not be what the client wants. It is far easier to end up with a happy client if the engagement is to represent a company that is being acquired by a large conglomerate, thus making the client wealthy. Nevertheless, an attorney assisting a client in either of these situations must be careful to manage expectations on the front end to ensure an enthusiastic client when the work is done.

The importance of this point was driven home to me recently when a lawyer with whom I'd been working sent me the following e-mail (on a Saturday night, no less):

> I am so excited about some incredible meetings I had this week that I had to share this with you. One was a phone call with a woman who was referred to me by another attorney. It was one of those calls where a few months ago it would have lasted five or ten minutes. We talked for well over an hour, and I was able to listen, ask questions and really get to the "heart of the matter." I was able to steer the conversation away from rates to showing her the value I can bring. She brought up rates in the first five minutes, but I was able to steer the conversation by using the "ground rule." I didn't mention my rate until the last five minutes, and by then I was in a position that I was able to give her some good business advice and guide her to ask the right questions with the other side in the deal. It hit me that this was as much about being a better lawyer—i.e., really focusing on what the client wants to accomplish from our services —as it was about "selling." Lots of thanks to you for this.

The last sentence speaks volumes about why the SalesGame resonates so well with professionals. They are extremely motivated to provide great advice and valuable assistance to their clients. We've all heard the old adage that the best way to generate more business is to do good work. Doing good work starts before the engagement. It involves using the tools and skills described in this book to manage expectations and to make sure you know what the client or prospect thinks is "good"—or, better yet, "outstanding."

Qualified Leads Are Decision-Makers Who Recognize a Need

The goal of the SalesGame is to convert "qualified" leads. A *lead* is anyone with a role in the buying process (decision-maker, user, influencer, or coach, as described in Chapter 2, "The Players: Who's Involved in the SalesGame?") who can open the door to a potential new business opportunity. An example of a lead might be an old college roommate or an alumnus at a firm that interests you. *Qualified leads* are those who have something they want to accomplish through the use of professional services—for example, a problem to solve or an opportunity to pursue. You must identify these people and build relationships with them.

Qualified leads are almost always decision-makers because they have the resources to take action. For example, suppose an accountant has a strong relationship with a CFO who knows his growing company needs a new accounting firm to help it manage its growth. The company's CEO is the decision-maker—that is, he or she holds the purse strings and has veto power—but does not perceive such a need. In this situation, the accountant has a lead, but not a qualified lead. The accountant must work with the CFO to convince, persuade, or in some way educate the CEO that such a need exists. Only then will the accountant have a qualified lead. This may take months or even years, during which time professionals must maintain and build the relationship by what I like to call *positioning*.

Just being a decision-maker does not make someone a qualified lead, however. A need must also exist. For example, suppose a commercial bank loan officer has a great relationship with attorney A, who has been drafting his loan agreements for years. The loan officer is very satisfied with attorney A and has no interest in changing providers. As a result, a competing attorney, attorney B, cannot consider the loan officer to be a qualified lead, even though the loan officer decides which provider to use. For the loan officer to become a qualified lead for attorney B, a problem that attorney B can solve must exist. For example, attorney A must retire, make a mistake, move out of town, have a conflict of interest in a deal, or lack the requisite industry experience for a particular deal. Without such a problem, attempts by attorney B to solicit work from this loan officer will be ineffective. Talk of credentials—for example, why attorney B's firm is better than attorney A's—will be perceived as pushy. This does not mean that attorney B should do nothing, however. He should initiate contact with the loan officer to build a relationship, position himself, and wait for the right opportunity. But until that opportunity arises, no selling should occur.

Understand Your Mission

When learning how to develop their business, perhaps the biggest obstacle for professionals is their image of selling. That is, they perceive the act of selling as simply convincing or telling people why a particular service or product is better than another, regardless of need. But in the world of professional services, selling should be seen as listening to people to identify problems or opportunities act upon them in the way that is best for the client.

> In the world of professional services, selling should be seen as listening to people to identify problems or opportunities act upon them in the way that is best for the client.

Let me illustrate this point with one example. The owner of a successful business that needed capital to take it to the next level was introduced to an investment banker. They discussed options ranging from seeking funds through a venture capitalist to selling the business to reap the rewards of his hard work over the past decade. The investment banker recommended a sale because of all the problems he'd seen in the past when venture capital was part of the equation. The owner ended up not working at all with the investment banker because he perceived him as "pushing" the option to sell the business for his own selfish motivations—that is, the commission he would make from a transaction. In other words, he saw the investment banker as a pushy salesman, not a trusted advisor. The investment banker would have been far better served by listening more and talking less so he really understood what the business owner wanted to accomplish and advise him accordingly, even if this approach didn't result in revenues.

Participants in my workshops feel a great sense of relief when they realize their mission in business development is *not* to convince someone to buy something whether they need it or not. It is much easier to have fun in the SalesGame if you remember that your mission is to work with clients and prospects *if* you can provide true value by helping to solve a problem or take advantage of an opportunity. Stating the goal of the SalesGame early in the business-development process by saying something like the following takes the pressure off both the professional and the client or prospect:

> We really would like to work with your company *if* there is a way we could really make a difference, be truly of value.

As in any game, each of you will have your own style of communicating this message. However, understanding the real goal of the SalesGame and communicating it to clients or prospects will make everyone more comfortable!

Don't Just Sell Work—Build the Practice of Your Dreams

One of my early mentors was a managing partner of a North Carolina accounting firm. When his partners wanted to discount work, he loved to say, "You can sell as much work as you want to if it's free!" You only truly win at the SalesGame—that is, you only achieve your goal—if you are fairly rewarded for the work you perform. Of course, discounting is permissible in certain situations. But you must earn a fair return on your time and, more importantly, your intellectual property, built through years of education and experience.

That being said, you should view rewards as being more than merely financial in nature. Everyone wants to get up in the morning and

> Do not play the SalesGame just to sell more hours. Instead, play it to build the practice of your dreams.

be excited about the project at hand. Too many people, however, sell their time to meet some chargeable hour quota. This is a mistake! Do not play the SalesGame just to sell more hours. Instead, play it to build the practice of your dreams. Every hour you spend doing work that does not reward you financially or in terms of job satisfaction is an hour that you could be spending creating the practice you really want.

Satisfied Clients Aren't Enough

If you recall, the goal of the SalesGame is to convert qualified leads to enthusiastic clients, not just satisfied ones. Having clients who are merely satisfied is just not enough to generate the lifelong relationships that you will find most rewarding in terms of financial and personal gain. As a partner in a Midwest accounting firm put it, "I don't want clients, I want apostles!" Apostles are clients who buy more and different services and send referrals. They're the best kind of public relations tool a professional like you can have.

Research by my company, the Services Rating Organization (SRO), found that fewer than 20 percent of our 150,000 respondents were "very satisfied" with their current firm. In other words, there seems to be plenty of room to develop more apostles! On the other side of the coin, clients who are merely "satisfied" rather than "enthusiastic" are much more vulnerable to switching providers due to minor fee variations or service problems. According to Frederick F. Reichheld, author of *The Quest for Loyalty: Creating Value Through Partnerships* (Harvard Business Review Press, 1996), more than 50 percent of executives who switched providers said they were "satisfied" with them before they switched. Along a similar vein, SRO found fewer than 3 percent of the companies contacted were dissatisfied with their current accounting, law firm, or bank, yet the turnover of service firms in follow-up studies was much greater than that number would suggest. In fact, it often ran as high as 25 percent!

For both offensive and defensive reasons, the goal of the SalesGame clearly must be more than to convert qualified leads to "satisfied" clients. You need apostles!

True Value Is Personal

Sometime during the 1990s, it seemed like almost every accounting and law firm started using the word "value" in their promotional material and mission statements. Professionals pledged to provide more than a service; they were going to provide real value to their clients. The problem was that most professionals did not really understand what the word "value" means. Often, they confused it with the word "quality."

We have all heard the phrase "Beauty is in the eye of the beholder." The same could be said for the value of a professional service. These services must be considered from the perspective of what they do for the individuals who buy them. An estate plan should be of high "quality"—that is, it should make correct use of the law. But the true "value" of that estate plan is a function of what it does for the client. That is, it should do the following:

■ Ensure a legacy will be passed on.

■ Provide future generations with good educational opportunities.

■ Reduce the chance of family disputes.

■ Help someone sleep better at night.

In other words, the true value comes from changing someone's life, not from the quality of the service being delivered.

Finding the source of true value is not always easy. At the very least, it requires a dialogue with the client or prospect. Clearly, what's important to one client might not be the

> True value comes from changing someone's life, not from the quality of the service being delivered.

same as what's important to another. For example, most of the firms I work with provide some form of due diligence service to help clients who are acquiring a new business. In one case, the value of this service might come from protecting the reputation of the executive who is driving the acquisition. In another case, the value of the same service might be to assure the owner of the acquiring company that the acquisition will be a good marriage. The goal of the SalesGame should remind you that you are in the business of making a difference for each individual client you serve because value, like beauty, is in the eye of the beholder.

One final thought on value with respect to the SalesGame: I cannot think of one situation of the thousands I have studied in which true value came from a professional service being less expensive. Lowering fees and discounting rates might induce someone to use a service, but it does not create real value. Professionals who use this strategy to get work are vulnerable to even deeper discounts that might be—and almost always are—offered by others.

2

Chapter

The Players:
Who's Involved in the SalesGame?

W hen you walk into almost any major sporting event, one of the things you will see is someone selling a program. The program enables you to identify who's involved in the contest. This chapter serves as a program of sorts for the SalesGame. The professionals pursuing the opportunity—such as attorneys, accountants, consultants, engineers, or bankers (those who both sell and deliver the service) are one set of players. The other set of players consists of those professionals who have a role in the buying process in the client or prospect organization.

Building relationships between these two sets of players is absolutely critical for success in business development. When my company conducted syndicated research for accounting and law firms, the interviewers asked more than 150,000 respondents why they chose the professional service firms they did. By far the most common answer was "relationships." This was true whether the respondent lived in China, Germany, Los Angeles, Indianapolis, or Miami. Quite simply, an overwhelming number of people want to hire people they like.

In my experience, professionals generally have too little information and too narrow a focus when they start to analyze relationships in client or prospect organizations.

> An overwhelming number of people want to hire people they like.

When professionals call me for advice on how to pursue a particular opportunity, I typically start by asking them to identify key personnel. They usually name one or two contacts but are not able to identify others, much less define their role in the buying process. This is a problem!

It's critical that you identify who's who in an organization before pursuing business there. To that end, this chapter provides you with a way to analyze relationships so you can better strategize your business-development efforts. Specifically, it divides people in buying organizations into four categories, each of which is discussed in more detail in the following sections:

- The decision-maker

- The user

- The influencer

- The coach

Categorizing people in this way is a useful way to analyze the network of relationships at client or prospect organizations. Teams in most sports have a common vocabulary because it facilitates communication; the same is true for teams playing the SalesGame.

Note

It's just as important to identify who's who in an organization in your efforts to retain clients as it is in your efforts to bring in new clients. In recent years, one of the biggest challenges I have seen in business development is to transition service personnel for a client from a senior attorney or accountant who is nearing retirement to a younger professional, or from a senior executive to the next generation of management. Doing this the right way requires a plan to identify and build relationships between current and future players, just as should be done when pursuing a prospect. I recently heard an attorney say he was transitioning work by making sure he was not accessible so clients had to call other attorneys in the firm. This plan might work in some respects, but it certainly won't help create an enthusiastic client!

The Decision-Maker

The decision-maker is the person (or people) who makes the final decision. He or she controls the purse strings and has veto power. The decision-maker must not only recognize a need, but also have the resources and authority to do something about it. The decision-maker in any given organization can change depending on the scope or type of service, but there is almost always only one decision-maker for a given opportunity. The decision-maker for an audit might be the owner of the company, while the decision-maker for a smaller special project might be the controller. When an organization is involved in "bet the company" litigation, you can be sure the owner or board of directors will make the call. For a routine contract, the in-house counsel or business person will probably be the decision-maker.

One of the most common mistakes professionals make is to sell to those who are users rather than decision-makers. Selling to users without getting to the real decision-maker wastes time and money. If proposals are written to someone who cannot buy, it could create even more serious problems—for example, successfully selling a service to a user that does not respond to the needs of and create value for the decision-maker. If the player at the client or prospect organization can not authorize payment without approval, that person probably is not the decision-maker.

> The decision-maker is the person (or people) who makes the final decision.

Note

Be cautious of people who talk and act like they are the decision-maker but are not, particularly if they start talking about an "approval process," no matter how routine it might be.

I am often asked how to find the decision-maker. The answer is simple: Ask! You'll read about a variety of ways to tactfully ask this question later in this book. In the meantime, a straightforward question like "How exactly will ABC go about making a decision on this project?" should get you moving in the right direction. Remember, however, that sometimes even the client or prospect does not know or understand the decision-making process. Asking questions should help both the professional and the client or prospect clarify the best way to move forward.

The User

The user is the person (or people) who will be using whatever services are provided. The user works most closely with the professional after the professional has been engaged to provide a particular service. The user generally plays a significant role in decision-making and gets a vote in the selection process.

> The user is the person (or people) who will be using whatever services are provided.

There can be one or multiple users, depending on the particular opportunity. For tax services, the user might be a CFO, but for a software consulting project, the users might include all those who use the software. For legal services, the commercial loan officer might be the single user for documentation on a transaction, while several VPs might be users for assistance to improve outplacement procedures.

There can also be layers of users. For example, a VP of HR might be the immediate user for expatriate tax services done by an accounting or law firm, but the expatriates themselves are also users of the service. I have seen situations in which building relationships with any of these people has made the difference between winning and losing a particular engagement.

The Influencer

The influencer is a person (or people) inside or outside the organization who usually does not get a vote in the decision-making process but can significantly influence the outcome. All decision-makers and users have influence, of course, but their impact is much more direct. That is, they usually get a vote in the selection process if one exists. In contrast, an influencer has a more indirect role in the buying process because decision-makers and/or users trust the influencer's judgment and listen to his or her opinion. Referral sources obviously fit in this category. An influencer might be someone like a bank loan officer if accounting services are the issue or an attorney if wealth management or investment banking services are involved. An influencer can also be a lower-level employee at the client organization, such as a bookkeeper or paralegal.

> The influencer is a person (or people) inside or outside the organization who usually does not get a vote in the decision-making process but can significantly influence the outcome.

The line between influencers and decision-makers or users can sometimes be difficult to distinguish. For example, the in-house counsel at an insurance company might be the decision-maker for choosing outside counsel. But sometimes, this decision-maker role would belong to the insured, in which case the insurance company's in-house counsel's role might be limited to that of user or influencer. Even a secretary or family member without any official status in the buying process can and often does have some influence in the buying process.

While all professionals face time pressures and probably would not be able to contact everyone they would like to when attempting to secure business, identifying and building relationships with influencers is important. Not only can such relationships affect the outcome of current situations, these relationships can also pay off in the future. The influencers of today are often the users or decision-makers of tomorrow, whether at their current company or at some future place of employment. Much like asking a question to determine the real decision-maker, you should ask questions to identify all those who might have influence in choosing service providers.

The Coach

The coach is a person inside or outside the organization who can guide the professional by providing useful "insider" information—for example, company politics, culture, terminology, etc. The coach is someone who wants to see you, the professional, succeed and therefore is willing to help in the sales process by providing advice. The coach could be a decision-maker, user, or influencer. Or, the coach could be a person who has no real role in the buying process, such as someone in an entirely different division of a company who might know useful information about the organization's culture or preferences. Consequently, the coach is the only person in the buying process who might have a dual role. When I sold research, I often found the managing partner of an office (the decision-maker) "coaching" me on how to sell the marketing committee (the users). He or she wanted the research package, but also wanted the marketing committee to buy in to the process instead of seeing it solely as the managing partner's initiative.

I've often said that it's hard to win without a coach. When professionals find themselves in requests for proposal (RFP) situations in which they have had no previous contact with the prospect, they are usually unsuccessful.

> The coach is a person inside or outside the organization who can guide the professional by providing useful "insider" information.

This is because they do not have a coach in the organization. Odds are, one of their competitors *does* have a coach, and it's this competitor who usually gets the work. (Never believe a prospect when he or she says, "We want everyone on a level playing field.") If professionals do not have a coach, they need to develop one by building a relationship and asking for advice. While this may not help you win in the short term, building this relationship is important for the long term. The next time you receive an RFP, you will already have a coach in place.

Analyzing the Network of Relationships

One of the first things you should do when developing a strategy for a new business opportunity with a client or prospect is to analyze the current network of relationships with those who have a role in the buying process. The preceding categories can be used for this purpose. To analyze the current network of relationships, ask the following questions:

- Who is the decision-maker?

- Who are the direct and indirect users of the service?

- Beyond the decision-maker and user(s), who might have influence in the buying process?

- Who do you know who would be willing to help you develop business with the client or prospect? Who could be your coach?

When answering these questions, I find it useful to list the relationship and then place some kind of value rating on it. For example, you could rate each relationship with a number between one and ten, with one being weakest and ten being strongest. Or, you could use my favorite system which is a bit simpler. Mark each person with a role in the buying process with a plus sign (denoting a good relationship between the professional and this person), a minus sign (indicating a negative relationship—for example, an in-house counsel who is an alumnus of a competing law firm), or a zero (denoting someone you do not know). (See Figure 2.1.)

I find that most professionals do not know enough about those with roles in the buying process to answer these questions. Or, if they do, their list features many more zeroes than plusses. This can even be true when dealing with current clients, particularly when pursuing a new area of service or looking for ways to transition relationships on either side of the table. If you cannot answer these questions, then one of the goals for the next contact should be to identify and clarify the roles in the decision-making process. If the list of contacts is fairly complete but has a lot more zeroes than plusses, any additional step that creates a plus where there was a zero is a valuable way to move closer to obtaining work and increases the odds of you ending up with an enthusiastic client. Any relationship rated as a zero or minus represents an opportunity for a next step. You can measure your progress in the SalesGame by tracking your improvement in building relationships with those who have roles in the buying process at client or prospect organizations.

Decision Maker	Rating	Influencers	Rating
Kate Jackson, CEO	0	Joe Conrad, CPA	+
		Jennifer Smith, CFO	+
		Jack Wilson, In-house Counsel	−
User(s)	Rating	Coach	Rating
John Westwood, COO	0	Jennifer Smith, CFO	+

Figure 2.1 Analyzing the network of relationships.

Note

The SalesGame can be a very long game indeed. That means measuring progress, and not just results, is very important. I once worked with an audit partner at a Big Four firm in London who estimated that he had built relationships with more than 60 individuals at a target company over a three-year period. While many opportunities would not justify this investment of time, in this case the prize was the acquisition of a £2 million annual audit, which was awarded without a competitive proposal. He labeled his strategy "penetrate and radiate." While this usually gets a laugh in a workshop, it's a good phrase to remember at any stage of the business-development process because it quickly communicates a best practice and is easily remembered. It's one of those terms that almost always becomes part of the common vocabulary of most of the business-development teams with whom I've worked.

The Six Stages of the SalesGame

Y ou "win" the SalesGame by working with clients or prospects to move through six separate stages of the SalesGame. Together, these six stages represent an overview of the business-development process. The six stages are as follows (see Figure 3.1):

- **Stage One:** Create and identify leads

- **Stage Two:** Qualify and track leads

- **Stage Three:** Shape the service

- **Stage Four:** Trial close

- **Stage Five:** Final close

- **Stage Six:** Assure enthusiasm (or determine the reason for loss)

The SalesGame Process

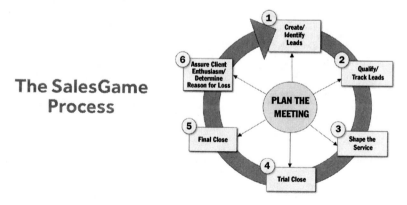

Figure 3.1 The six stages of the SalesGame.

One of the most beneficial aspects of this framework is that it is universal. That is, it can be applied to all new business opportunities, whether you are an attorney, accountant, consultant, engineer, or any other professional pursuing a major prospect or handling a simple request for additional services from a long-time client. If pursuing a prospect, it may take you years to move through these six stages. When dealing with a client that you have served several times before, however, a 30-minute phone call may be all you need to progress from Stage Two to Stage Five. The universal nature of the six-stage process makes it perhaps the most important of the SalesGame fundamentals. One of my Irish clients once likened it to a GPS in a car or on a smartphone, noting, "If you know where you are and where you want to go, it's a lot easier getting there!" Regardless of the type of opportunity or the time involved, you will be more effective and efficient if you know where you are in the SalesGame and what you have to do to move ahead or "advance the ball," as one of my clients once put it.

When you respond to an RFP, for example, you often move directly from Stage Two (handling the initial request) to Stage Five (writing the final proposal and awaiting a decision). Even if you are lucky enough to get the

> You "win" the SalesGame by working with clients or prospects to move through six separate stages of the SalesGame.

work, this approach will make it difficult to achieve the ultimate goal: creating an enthusiastic client. By comparison, if you use the SalesGame's six-stage process to make sure you take the time to "shape the service" (Stage Three) and perform a "trial close" (Stage Four), you will experience a higher percentage of success and generate more enthusiastic clients.

The following sections of this book describe each of the six stages, including best practices and pitfalls.

4

Chapter

Stage One:
Create and Identify Leads

The purpose of Stage One is to build relationships with potential leads to develop a practice that is rewarding both financially and personally. Your task in this stage is to generate as many quality leads as possible. A relationship or lead remains in Stage One until you express interest in working with the contact—that is, until you and the contact start a dialogue about potentially working together. Stage One ends when the lead changes from something on a list to an actual meeting with a person (telephone or face to face).

The process of building relationships and identifying leads starts on day 1 and continues throughout your career. Of course, more senior professionals should have a more defined vision

> The purpose of Stage One is to build relationships with potential leads to develop a practice that is rewarding both financially and personally.

of the type of practice they want to build and, consequently, a more targeted approach to building relationships than younger professionals. For their part, younger professionals should look at building relationships for the future, like putting money in the bank.

Most accountants, attorneys and consultants understand that their success in business development will be a function of a simple equation:

# of Quality Opportunities (Marketing)
× Percentage of Success Rate (Sales)
= Total New Revenues

Stage One deals with the first part of this equation: the marketing element of the SalesGame. There are a myriad of ways to develop and build relationships to create opportunities. Most of them are normally part of a strategy, but some opportunities happen by chance. This book is designed primarily to assist professionals with the second part of the equation— that is, improving their success rate when they have an opportunity—so I won't go into a comprehensive list of the many ways to create leads. Instead, the following list summarizes the six major areas of activity that professionals can employ for this purpose, and more specific ideas for each area are included in Appendix A, "Marketing and Lead-Generation Activities."

- **Networking:** Building and maintaining relationships with other professionals like bankers, attorneys, accountants, friends, family, and so on. Examples of networking include attending lunches, mixers, and the like.

- **Prospecting:** Identifying and contacting targets through mutual connections, electronic media, telephone calls, direct mail, and so on with whom you may or may not have a previously established relationship. This might include approaching clients who are not using a particular service area of the firm—for example, employee benefits for litigation clients or wealth management for audit clients.

- **Internal marketing:** Building relationships and learning about practice areas of other professionals to find mutually beneficial areas for cross serving clients.

- **Friends and family:** Making sure present, personal, and often long-standing relationships know what you and your firm do should a relevant problem or opportunity arise.

- **Promotional activities:** Getting out into the community or marketplace, whether business related (for example, trade groups, chambers of commerce) or tied to personal interests (groups related to children, colleges, recreation, church, and so on). These activities also include firm efforts such as public relations and advertising.

- **Present client activities:** Finding ways to leverage off of enthusiastic clients, such as staying in touch with former client personnel, obtaining direct referrals, meeting other professionals who serve the client, and meeting the client's customers, outside board members, or network.

Regardless of the type of marketing activity, you must invest time in Stage One throughout your career to create and build relationships with those who have current or potential roles in the buying process. An attorney I worked with likened it to dating: "It's hard to find someone to date if you sit at home and watch TV." The most important point to remember when developing a combination of the right marketing activities is that one size does not fit all. Each professional must come up with his or her own plan based on factors like age, experience, type of practice, and personal inclination.

The value of Stage One activities is often hard to quantify. As in the example about the partner in the regional accounting firm, luck plays a role. There's a scene in *Any Given Sunday* when Al Pacino, who plays the head coach of a professional football team, delivers an emotional talk to his players about how the game of football is a game of inches, and the inches are all around them. Creating business relationships is very similar. They are all around us. We all know they are in trade and professional associations, banks, and other professional firms. While these are certainly "target rich" environments, I have also worked with professionals who have developed leads from their next-door neighbor, standing in line at a supermarket, coaching their child's little league team, starting a hang-gliding club, or participating in a cooking class. The key is to be active doing something you enjoy. Building relationships will follow.

Build Relationships First

The most important aspect of Stage One is to build genuine relationships with individuals you like. This is true regardless of whether you are a seasoned employee benefits consultant who is active in a professional group for HR directors or a young attorney embarking on your career. Earlier, I suggested that young attorneys stay in touch with fellow law school alums. But staying in touch with them solely with the aim of developing business is not what I mean. This kind of targeting rarely works. Rather, you should stay in touch with them because you enjoy their company and have good chemistry with them. Similarly, the seasoned employee benefits consultant should focus on building relationships with those HR directors with whom he or she has chemistry.

This is a paradox of sorts: If you build relationships with people because you like them, not because they can generate business opportunities, you will develop more work. As an example, professionals often develop strong relationships through involvement in various churches. In fact, it is not uncommon for these relationships to become qualified leads and generate good business opportunities. But few professionals would say they joined a church to get business.

Different professionals will have different styles when playing the SalesGame. For example, some may be more aggressive than others. Regardless of your own personal style, you must remember that the purpose of Stage One is to build relationships, not sell work. This is a best practice that will lead to long-term success.

This approach will also make you feel more comfortable when engaged in marketing activities. I once worked with an attorney who admitted to me that he hated going to the annual conference of gaming companies—his area of specialty—because it made him feel like a "shill." I suggested he go to the upcoming conference and focus on getting to know the people he was meeting rather than looking for work—for example, asking questions about their family, their background, where they lived, their hobbies, etc. When I saw him a month later, he said he'd had a much better experience this time around. Even better, he had met a few people with whom he knew would develop a relationship thanks to mutual interests that were revealed as they spoke. These gave him an easy and natural way to follow up.

One problem for young professionals in particular is that they are often encouraged to join civic or social activities as a way to get started in business development. This suggests that these young professionals might actually develop work by participation in these organizations, leading to disappointment when the desired result does not occur. The message must be clarified: Get into these organizations to build relationships, and opportunities will come later—sometimes much later. Relationships are a little like fine wine: They become better with age. I've often counseled young professionals to leave some of their relationships in Stage One—that is, don't be in a hurry to jump to Stage Two—until they "age" by growing into roles of greater responsibility.

My father always used to tell me, "Build your allies when you don't need them." This would be good to remember when operating in Stage One. Build relationships *before* the point of sale. You'll find that it's far easier to build a relationship when you're not selling something!

> Build your allies when you don't need them.

Start with a Vision for Creating the Practice of Your Dreams

One of the best practices in Stage One is to start with vision. As professionals advance in their careers or as practice groups seek a higher level of business-development performance, they need to focus on creating quality opportunities—that is, opportunities that will help them build a practice that generates the desired rewards, not just more hours.

As will be discussed later in this book, professionals move through the stages of the SalesGame by virtue of the questions they ask, not by what they say. In Stage One, the most important question for professionals to be asking is, "What kind of clients do I most want to work with?" This will be difficult to answer for an accountant in his or her first year or two of practice. However, finding a fit between what a professional likes to do and the clients he or she serves is one of the main reasons so many firms rotate professionals through several areas of practice. This enables them to get a taste of what each has to offer. Your answer to the question "What kind of clients do I most want to work with?" will go a long way toward dictating the most effective marketing strategy.

To illustrate the importance of creating a vision, consider the case of a small office of a large accounting firm that was trying to develop its client base in a large Midwestern city. The office provided services to a wide range of clients, both in terms of industry and size. To ascertain what kinds of clients they really liked to serve, a new managing partner came in, did some market research, and held a meeting with his key players. The group concluded that mid-sized manufacturing companies who were suppliers for the auto industry provided the best potential in terms of revenue, practice growth, and job satisfaction. The group translated this vision into targeted marketing activities, including the following:

■ Networking with bank loan officers and attorneys who serve the same market segment

■ Conducting client seminars on lean manufacturing

■ Using direct mail to build name recognition

■ Participating in appropriate trade organizations

They used these activities to generate and build relationships. Within a year, this office began to see the results of the group's efforts. Looking over their growing list of leads, it was obvious that they were putting themselves in position to build the practice of their dreams. All professionals must balance the need for chargeable hours with investing time in business development so they work *on*, not just *in*, their practice.

> All professionals must balance the need for chargeable hours with investing time in business development so they work *on*, not just *in*, their practice.

I'm often asked, "How much time should one invest in Stage One marketing activities?" The answer is not simple, nor does the same answer apply to everyone. Answering this question depends on what you already have in your inventory of relationships. When you are ready to start a more organized approach to this game, you should analyze your current relationship base by going through the following:

- Past client lists

- Outlook contacts

- LinkedIn connections

- Facebook friends

- Cell phone contacts

- Holiday card list

- Seminar attendees

Many professionals tell me they don't have enough contacts. When they go through these lists, however, they are often surprised by how many people they already know who might be a coach, an influencer, a user, or even a decision-maker. Starting with people you already know is always the easier way to go. However, this inventory will usually run dry at some point, so you must concoct a strategy for developing additional relationships. As noted, this is a never-ending task, so you should find ways to build relationships that are enjoyable and keep replenishing your inventory for the long term. That is, the relationships you start building today usually take at least 12 to 18 months to mature to a point where beginning to work together is a real possibility. If you are just getting started in your career, this time frame is probably much longer.

OK, so how much time *should* you invest in Stage One activities? I'd say at least three or four hours a week, on average. Some weeks might be completely devoted to business development—for example, you might be attending a conference. Other weeks might find you tied up with tax deadlines or in a trial, meaning you won't be able to invest any time in Stage One activities.

Don't Sell in Stage One

The best way to be seen as pushy is to constantly bring up business in a Stage One activity like playing golf at the country club, attending a fundraiser, or simply seeing friends socially.

I love to play golf. Every so often, while playing with a wealth manager or an accountant, that person will ask me about my investment strategy or whether I've used a new tax idea while in the middle of the round. Personally, I find this distasteful, and typically make a conscious decision not to play with these individuals again. This is not to say that business shouldn't be discussed during a round of golf. Some big deals have been closed that way. However, in such situations, those involved know they will be talking about business.

The best practice is to avoid trying to turn a relationship-building (Stage One) activity into a more in-depth discussion of needs, current providers, etc. (Remember the insurance salesman in *Groundhog Day*, who constantly tried to sell to Bill Murray?) Instead, use a Stage One activity to set up a Stage Two meeting. Here are some real examples my clients have used effectively:

- "You know, it would be interesting to see if there's anything we could do to help each other."

- "We work a lot with clients in your industry. It would be interesting to have lunch sometime and compare notes about some of the new developments going on."

- "I've sat in a bunch of meetings with you on the NFP Board and it hit me that we've never talked professionally. How about we do that sometime? I'd like to know more about what you do in your day job!"

- "We've known each other since high school and I've never really talked to you about business. Isn't that stupid? We ought to talk sometime. It would be a lot of fun to work with you!"

These are only examples that worked for others. Each professional will have to find his or her own way to make the transition from Stage One to Stage Two. Much like the Paul Simon song "50 Ways to Leave your Lover," there is no shortage of options. If you are unsure of the right words to use, I find the best approach is to share your phrasing with a colleague or two and see how they react. If colleagues like what they hear, then give it a try. If you get a favorable reaction—and you almost always will—then let the games begin. If not, back off and enjoy the relationship, knowing you've thrown your hat in the ring. If your contact feels a need to talk about business at a later date, at least that person knows you're interested in working with him or her!

> **Note**
>
> Certain Stage One activities lend themselves more to discussing business, such as a trade association meeting or a cocktail mixer with another professional firm. You can be more aggressive in these settings. The key point is to remember that Stage One is about building relationships, not selling work. Professionals should proceed accordingly.

The Role of Marketing Is to Create Leads

You can—and should—use the marketing staff to facilitate building relationships if you have this resource available. Decades ago, when I began my consulting career, I was hired by an international accounting firm to be the director of marketing. This was the first position of its type in any of the firm's 70 offices. Today, even small firms have full-time marketing assistants, while large international firms often have legions of marketing professionals. There are even trade groups that specifically serve this relatively new niche of marketing experts.

Certainly, the number and quality of strategic marketing plans, promotional brochures, newsletters, seminars, and so on have increased dramatically with the involvement of true marketing specialists. However, one problem that has arisen is the perception that marketing experts provide a substitute for an attorney's, an accountant's, or a consultant's own marketing efforts. This may be true in the sense an attorney, accountant, or other professional with a high billing rate no longer needs to spend time organizing the mechanics of a seminar or supervising the printing and distribution of a newsletter. It is certainly not true, however, when it comes to developing new business as the professional moves through the six stages of the SalesGame. If anything, the involvement of these marketing specialists has yielded more leads, thus creating more time demands on attorneys, accountants, and consultants to pursue them.

Nonetheless, employing marketing specialists can be a very valuable way to do the following:

- Conduct research to better develop a vision building the practice.

- Develop strategic and tactical marketing plans to guide the use of the firm's resources.

- Produce marketing tools like brochures, newsletters, seminars, and public relations events.

- Organize lead tracking systems.

- Gather intelligence on specific prospects.

- Coach the firm's professionals on how to approach various opportunities.

- Provide ongoing reminders of the need to follow up on important opportunities.

- Help write proposals and prepare presentations.

- Conduct and evaluate client satisfaction surveys and research.

These marketing professionals should not be looked at as a vehicle for converting leads to new business. They can only create and facilitate the pursuit of leads. Unfortunately, the gap between what managing partners think these marketing specialists can do and what they can actually deliver has cost numerous marketing directors their jobs.

Don't Wait...Initiate!

One of the ramifications of the increased involvement of marketing specialists and departments is that most firms are now practically choking on lists of leads that have been generated by marketing initiatives. These lists come from a variety of sources, which include the following:

- Attendees of client or prospect seminars

- Non-attendees who were invited to client or prospect seminars

- Trade association membership directories

- Market research on particular industry segments

- Analysis of the current client base to identify cross-selling opportunities

Most accounting, law, and consulting firms would be a lot more effective and efficient if they used the lists they already have to start moving toward Stage Two. Instead, most of them merely continue to generate more lists.

Consider the example of Janette, an attorney in the Northeast who did three seminars on a hot topic and generated a list of 250 prospects—obviously a great marketing success. She also sent out a follow-up letter and a DVD summarizing her presentation to those people on her list. When I talked to Janette, she was frustrated because only one or two small engagements had resulted from this effort. She wanted to know what to do next. I suggested she (or someone else, such as an associate) contact those prospects from the current list who were most desirable to her to determine their level of interest. Unfortunately, the firm decided it did not have the budget for such follow-up. As Janette and I discussed this unfortunate decision, she had to cut the phone call short because she was on her way to catch a flight to the West Coast to do another seminar. This is an example of great marketing, but poor follow-up. Janette did not need to initiate contact with all of the 250 seminar participants. Rather, she needed to start a dialogue and build relationships with the 25 or 30 participants who would be consistent with her vision of an ideal practice so she could build relationships before the point of sale.

Janette's situation reminded me of the time my son, Ryan, had three "prospects" for the Homecoming Dance. Despite my advice, Ryan failed to call any of these prospects far enough in advance to invite her. Instead, he waited until the last few days. Not surprisingly, his prospects were already spoken for. Ryan ended up going to the dance with someone who was not the date of his dreams. As he put it, it was more like "going out with my sister."

One of the pitfalls that professionals should avoid is over researching prospect or even client opportunities. I've seen firms gather thick files of background data, trying to decide when and how to approach a particular opportunity. While some research is a good idea—to get at least an initial read on whether it makes sense to pursue an opportunity and to be able to show that you have done your homework when a meeting does occur—too many professionals invest way too much time gathering data instead of planning and executing a meeting. As a managing partner in an accounting firm in Dublin said in a workshop, he didn't want his professionals to use the approach of "Ready…aim…aim…aim…aim…." Don't wait, initiate!

As soon as you take action to move a lead from being merely a name on a list to someone you express interest in working with, you move from Stage One to Stage Two. There are many ways to make this transition, such as the phrases mentioned earlier, in the section "Don't Sell in Stage One." You'll find other ideas in Part 2, "Best Practices for Setting Up the Game." However, the message is hopefully clear: Don't sit on the sidelines waiting for someone to call you. This does not necessarily mean you should start selling. It does mean, however, that you need to be proactive in building relationships. To a young professional, this might mean reaching out to a fellow college alum to have a few beers. For a senior accounting partner, it might mean following up after a tax seminar. In either case, don't wait…initiate!

> Don't sit on the sidelines waiting for someone to call you.

Saying you want to learn about a prospect's company or to tell him or her about your service will rarely entice a contact to meet with you. As will be discussed in Part 2, one of the most important things when initiating at any stage in the business-development process is to sell the meeting, not the service. In other words, think about how your contact will benefit from meeting with you whether by phone or in person. For example, maybe the meeting will enable the person to do one of the following:

■ Get some idea of what others are doing in their industry.

■ Find out about some new developments or trends that could affect him or her.

■ Put a face with a name.

■ Gain access to a second, backup resource.

■ Build his or her own network.

> Sell the meeting, not the service.

And of course, simply to maintain a friendship is often a good reason to meet. We all want to stay in touch with people we know and like! Regardless of the reason, remember to sell the meeting, not the service.

Stage One Recap

* Build relationships first.

* Develop a vision of the ideal practice.

* Identify and analyze current leads and develop a marketing strategy and marketing activities to generate new leads.

* Explore the opportunity, but don't overdo it.

* Move to Stage Two only with leads that will help you to build the ideal practice.

* Don't sell in Stage One.

* Set up initial contact by selling the benefits of a meeting, not the service.

Stage Two:
Qualify and Track Leads

In Stage Two, you begin a dialogue with clients or prospects to express an interest in working with them now or in the future. Relationship building continues in Stage Two as it does in every stage of the SalesGame. Note, however, that "expressing interest" does not mean "asking for the business." That comes in Stage Four, when you know what the client or prospect wants to accomplish, his or her criteria for success, and so on. Expressing interest is more like throwing your hat in the ring. Clients and prospects need to be aware of professionals who would be interested in working with them *if* the right opportunity occurs. This dialogue continues until a need is recognized by the decision-maker—that is, until the lead becomes qualified. When this need is recognized, Stage Two ends.

In Stage Two, you begin a dialogue with clients or prospects to express an interest in working with them now or in the future.

Note

Of course, you may decide a lead is no longer worth pursuing for a variety of reasons, such as your contact moving to another company or simply becoming frustrated that things are taking so long. However, my recommendation is to take a long-term approach to tracking leads. Think in terms of years, not weeks or months, when pursuing desirable opportunities that fit with the vision of your practice.

As discussed, you want to assure the client or prospect that your interest is based on finding a mutual fit—that is, that the rewards generated will be commensurate with the value delivered. In other words, you want to work with a given client or prospect only if you can really make a difference for that person or his or her organization.

Stage Two can last for years. This is because it might take that long for a client or prospect to recognize a need. Or, Stage Two might be very short in duration—for example, a client or prospect calling with a request or an RFP. In this scenario, it's likely there is already an established relationship and a presumed need, or the client wouldn't be calling. In this case, you still need to make sure what the client or prospect wants to accomplish is achievable—that is, you have to convert a service request into a definition of value. Whether it is short or long in duration, Stage Two is critical to achieving success in the SalesGame. After all, this stage is the first time the players actually discuss the possibility of working together.

Because of the importance of Stage Two, Part 2, "Best Practices for Setting Up the Game," is devoted largely to handling this stage of the process. The following pages highlight important points that should be considered when handling any type of Stage Two lead.

Qualification Means Exploring the Opportunity, Not Selling

Regardless of the type of lead, your job in Stage Two is first to qualify the lead. This means having a dialogue with someone who has a role in the buying process either in person or by phone to learn the following:

- What the client or prospect is like (is he or she someone with whom you want to work?)
- Who the players inside the client's or prospect's organization are

■ How the chemistry with these players feels

■ Whether the client or prospect will generate rewards commensurate with the value received (for example, will the client or prospect be able to pay the bills?)

Most importantly, qualifying the lead means finding out if there is something the decision-maker really wants to accomplish—for example, a problem that needs to be solved or an opportunity that needs to be seized.

Qualifying the lead is important even if you are responding to a client or prospect request. For example, a common pitfall for accountants meeting with prospective audit clients who have sent them an RFP is focusing too fast on how to approach the audit. The best practice is to focus first on what the client or prospect wants to accomplish. Far too frequently, CPAs meet with a Stage Two lead, look at the state of accounting records, and then write a proposal. Instead, the CPA should remember that the first meeting with a client or prospect—regardless of how it comes about—should be dedicated to asking questions and listening. This will allow the CPA to learn more about the client or prospect as well as give the CPA an opportunity to qualify the lead—that is, to find the true source of value. Proposing on an audit without first finding out what the decision-maker wants to accomplish puts the accountant back in the game of selling a commodity, not providing real value.

Another reason to focus on listening and not selling or telling in a Stage Two meeting is that it enables you to build a relationship before the point of sale. This isn't an issue when dealing with clients where a relationship already exists, but it can be a problem when dealing with prospects. One of the most common mistakes professionals make is to rush to Stage Three and Stage Four when they have a request for service from someone they don't know. Ideally, your participation in Stage One activities will enable you to create relationships before requests come in, but this isn't always the case (or perhaps even the majority of cases). I recently received a request from a prospect to conduct a workshop and spent almost half of an hour-long call learning about the background—both personal and professional—of the CMO who was driving the process. After a few more contacts, I obtained the engagement for which I was competing with two other firms. When I asked the CMO what factors made the difference, he said that I was the only vendor he'd talked to in his six years on the job who actually took the time to learn about him. It's hard to believe my competitors failed to realize the importance of relationship building before they started to focus on the service at hand, but I'm glad they didn't!

When Selling, Bigger Is Not Better

When professionals get a contact that they believe to be a desirable prospect, they usually want to show that person all their resources to demonstrate all their skills, commitment, and so on. It is not uncommon to arrange a presentation to the prospect that includes several professionals, each representing a particular area of expertise. In essence, they are selling to an unqualified lead. Large meetings like this generally:

- Make it difficult to build much personal chemistry.

- Stifle a free exchange of information.

- Fail to make efficient use of time and resources.

- Make clients or prospects feel like professionals are selling before they understand what is needed.

- Bore the client or prospect, since most of what is discussed would not be relevant to the real problem he or she is facing that day.

- Make it harder to find the right next step. If the client or prospect has met everyone at the first meeting, where do you go from there?

By understanding the purpose of Stage Two, you can focus on your true objectives: to express interest, build relationships, and learn enough to qualify the lead.

I once coached a partner in a West Coast law firm, Norma, who had met the in-house counsel from a large Tennessee company at a national convention. Norma and the in-house counsel really hit it off in this Stage One activity. Norma wanted to advance her position in the SalesGame, so she suggested going on a trip to the company's headquarters with three other attorneys who possessed relevant skills based on what she already knew about the prospect. Clearly, this was a big next step that would require a lot of resources to implement. After a few minutes of discussion, we changed the next step to a one-on-one telephone conversation with the in-house counsel. In the call, Norma restated her interest in working together, further built the relationship, and learned more about the company. This was a much easier and cheaper option than the Tennessee road show. A few more phone calls involving other attorneys followed, and eventually, the company in Tennessee used the right person from Norma's West Coast firm, an IP lawyer, to meet their needs.

Positioning Leads Versus Qualified Leads

The initial contact in Stage Two generally tells you the type of lead you are dealing with and whether to move ahead in the business-development process. A lead moves from Stage Two to Stage Three only when it becomes a qualified lead—that is, when there is something a decision-maker wants to accomplish, whether it is solving a problem or seizing an opportunity. As mentioned, this may happen very quickly (for example, if a current client calls with a request for additional services) or it can take a very long time if professionals are pursuing large prospects with which they initiated the dialogue. As soon as a new opportunity or a positioning lead (that is, someone with whom you have expressed interest in serving but who has not yet presented the right opportunity or the decision-maker hasn't recognized a need) becomes a qualified lead, the job of shaping the service (Stage Three) begins. Until that time, professionals should track leads to be in position for the window of opportunity that almost always occurs.

Professionals who are good at business development look at this stage of the process like a consultant who is advising a client rather than a salesperson convincing someone to buy, even if the client is still a prospect. One of the pitfalls to avoid in this stage is assuming that because someone has called you, you have a qualified lead. I've seen many cases in which a call comes in but the timing or situation isn't right for the client or prospect to undertake a particular engagement. Perhaps management is in a state of flux or a merger needs to be completed. If you look at yourself as a consultant, you can help the client or prospect understand why the service being requested isn't appropriate at the current time. In this way, you earn credibility and trust, which will almost certainly get you work at some future point.

Once, my colleagues and I received a call from a wealth-management firm that had been referred to us by another client. We spent at least an hour planning what turned out to be an hour-long Stage Two conference call. At the end of the discussion, we agreed that this wouldn't be the right time for the assistance we could provide. The prospect was grateful not only for our candor but, as he said in a follow up e-mail, also for our questions, which helped him clarify what he needed to do next. My colleagues and I felt gratified by the e-mail because it showed us that we were of value to our contact even though we didn't actually have a chance to work with him…yet. I hope this reinforces the point that the principles of the SalesGame are as important for being a great professional as they are for being a great rainmaker.

Position by Building Relationships and Demonstrating Selling Points

In most cases, a big part of Stage Two continues to involve relationship development, particularly if the client or prospect is a positioning lead. If you don't have a coach, you must build such a relationship during this stage of the SalesGame. While there are always exceptions, you usually need to get to know clients or prospects as people before they start to generate the kind of work that truly benefits both sides of the business-development equation. As discussed, there are usually multiple roles in the buying process, and you cannot really say you have a qualified lead until you build a relationship with the decision-maker. One reason Stage Two takes so long is that relationship building takes time. Sometimes, trusting and open relationships are built in a meeting or two. Sometimes, building the right relationships can take years.

A good example comes from Troy, a partner in an accounting firm in Tokyo, who was a director of an investment banking firm in his previous life. Troy told a story in a workshop about how he was introduced by a mutual friend to a partner from another accounting firm soon after he had joined the investment banking company. He recounted how this partner expressed interest in working with him but then proceeded to spend the next six months getting to know him. Troy had recently moved to the area, so the accounting firm partner helped him find schools for his kids and a country club. He learned the kinds of deals Troy wanted to do and provided some introductions to potential customers. By the time six months had passed, Troy said that he was excited to find a deal on which he could use the accountant and generated over $1 million fees for him during the course of their relationship.

As mentioned, one phrase I use in workshops that tends to resonate with professionals is "penetrate and radiate." In other words, use your present contacts at a client or prospect to meet as many other players as possible in the organization. I first heard this phrase when I was leading a discussion of partners from a Big Four firm who came from all over Europe and had a track record of bringing in business. The partner from London who I mentioned earlier, Colin, was in attendance. Everyone wanted to know how he was able to bring in a £2 million audit without a competitive proposal. He responded that his strategy over a three-year period before the acquisition was to "penetrate and radiate." It's a good strategy for professionals to remember when operating in Stage Two.

You can also work with positioning leads in Stage Two to demonstrate what it would be like to use your services once they have a need—that is, to demonstrate selling points. Something as simple as following up at the agreed-upon time can demonstrate responsiveness. Building relations between the client or prospect and others in your firm who might be a useful resource demonstrates breadth of service. Sending relevant newspaper articles or newsletters to clients or prospects in Stage Two demonstrates a proactive approach to identifying needs.

Webster's Dictionary defines "strategy" as the "artful or ingenious use of resources." When operating in Stage Two, collaborate with colleagues in your firm to develop an effective strategy to pursue an opportunity—that is, determine how the firm can use its resources to make the benefits of hiring it at some future point more real and tangible. Start thinking strategy early. For example, it might make sense for a major law firm with a nice office to invite a large prospect to a meeting in its conference room to demonstrate it is a big-time player. Be aware that this can backfire, however. I once worked with a large accounting firm that invited a small but growing construction firm to its office during the sales process. The accounting firm lost the opportunity due in part to the fact that the owner of the construction company felt the firm was too big for them based on the visit. In particular, he was taken aback by the big-screen TV in the conference room. The accounting firm might have been better served by thinking about strategy before it set up the meeting. Going to the offices of the construction firm might have sent a message that the accounting firm was accessible instead of expensive.

In short, Stage Two is an excellent opportunity for you to actively position yourself and your service capabilities with clients or prospects. By taking the time to develop relationships and a strategy during this stage, you will find that the actual sale will be much easier when the client or prospect moves from a positioning to a qualified lead. Even more importantly, you will have a much better chance of winning the SalesGame by ending up with an enthusiastic client.

Track Leads for the Long Term

Perhaps my biggest frustration with professionals is their short-term perspective on business development. Rarely do professionals recognize that Stage Two can go on for years. I have assisted many practice groups in developing lists of leads they intend to pursue. Upon follow-up, I usually find their attention span lasted only six months before they shifted their focus and forgot to actively pursue the opportunity they were targeting.

In contrast, my first contact with what was my biggest client for more than five years came through a Stage One marketing activity (a speech for the local CPA association) early in my career. My contact was at least a user or influencer and could have been a decision-maker. He approached me after the speech and told me he wanted me to work with his firm. I met with him and the partner in charge of HR. One thing led to another, but the bottom line was that they were already working with another consultant who was doing something they perceived to be similar to my service. I continued to position this Stage Two lead by building multiple relationships—a breakfast meeting with one contact, a sporting event with another, and so on. The decision-maker changed at least four or five times during my pursuit. None of these activities took a great deal of time. Finally, seventeen years later, they recognized they had a problem: Their team was simply not good at closing the deal. It was then that I was able to do my first workshop for this client!

One other important point needs to be made with regard to pursuing leads over the long term: Have fun! Every contact with a Stage Two opportunity shouldn't be about business or "advancing the ball." After all, a big part of this stage is continuing to build relationships, and that is often best done in a non-business setting. If you are pursuing an opportunity with someone you've known for years, you should make a point of simply enjoying each other's company without necessarily adding business to the mix. Even when you *are* trying to advance the ball—trying to "penetrate and radiate"—you should do so in ways that aren't as formal or threatening. For example, a good way for a firm to introduce another professional from its organization or to meet someone from the client or prospect might be to go to a sporting event, arrange a round of golf, or participate in a fundraising event. I worked with a client in Norway that was pursuing a bank. The bank had an annual fundraising event in the summer. The partner leading the effort made sure that a number of his staff participated in the event. This facilitated relationship building and was noticed by bank executives, particularly because their current provider did not participate. In short, the best practice is to balance substantive contacts that advance the ball with informal, fun contacts that simply continue to build the relationship.

You must do two things to maintain this level of persistence:

■ Keep some form of written tracking system to easily recall all the leads you are pursuing. There are many methods for doing this, including spreadsheets, simple word-processing documents, or even computer programs. The form that this tracking system takes will depend on the situation. Regardless, it's hard for an individual or team to say they are serious about business development if they don't maintain a list. Even when situations arise when professionals don't have time to update or even look at the list, they still have a control mechanism that will make it a lot easier to restart their business-development efforts.

■ Have the discipline to keep making progress. For some, this discipline will be self-enforced. For others, it can be built by scheduling regular —for example, weekly, bi-weekly, or monthly—meetings led by a practice unit leader. I've found this best practice to be a major differentiator between firms that are successful and those that are not. Some of us stay in shape by ourselves; others hire personal trainers.

There are no easy solutions. If you want to succeed at the SalesGame, you must have both a workable list and the discipline to follow through.

Stage Two Recap

* Express interest in working with the prospect *if* you can do something that would really be of value.

* Determine whether prospect is a qualified or positioning lead.

* Listen, don't sell.

* Bigger isn't better. Start small.

* Build relationships before the point of sale.

* Penetrate and radiate to locate decision-makers, users, and influencers.

* Position for an opportunity and implement a strategy over the short *or* long term. (Remember, Stage Two can last for years.)

* Balance substantive meetings with fun and informal contacts.

Stage Three:
Shape the Service

The purpose of Stage Three is to clarify the need and shape the service. In Stage Three, you must uncover the client or prospect's *Scorecard*—the true source of value of the service (what I call the *Heart of the Matter*) and the most important requirements necessary to create an enthusiastic client (the Scorecard Factors). The Scorecard is discussed in more detail in Part 3, "The Scorecard: Add Value, Differentiate Your Service, and Build Strategy." Stage Three starts when the decision-maker recognizes a need and continues until the professional feels there is an agreement on the services required to meet that need. This stage ends when you have a clear vision of the client's need, including the Heart of the Matter, and the two or three most important Scorecard factors. Stage Three and Stage Four are usually where the action is and where the fun begins.

> In Stage Three, you must uncover the client or prospect's *Scorecard* —the true source of value of the service (what I call the *Heart of the Matter*) and the most important requirements necessary to create an enthusiastic client (the Scorecard Factors).

The late Jim Valvano, who, in 1983, coached the North Carolina State men's basketball team to an NCAA basketball championship despite being viewed as the underdog, used to say that it was all about being "in a position to win" in the last few minutes of a game. Similarly, Stage Three is all about being in a position to win the SalesGame. In Stage Three, you have the opportunity to engage clients or prospects in meaningful discussions about their problems, opportunities, vision, goals—even their hopes and dreams. This knowledge is required for a professional to not only be a trusted advisor, but to be perceived as such. It's also critical for coming up with the best solution to help the client or prospect. Unfortunately, professionals rarely take advantage of this opportunity. Instead, they move too quickly to try to "close the sale." The irony is that most professionals rush through this stage even though they may have spent years positioning for such an opportunity.

Don't shortcut the process. One of the biggest pitfalls all professionals should avoid is skipping Stage One and Stage Two when they receive a request for service. The tendency is to assume there is a need—which is understandable, since the client or prospect is making the request—and start discussing the problem and solutions right away before even a modicum of relationship building. But you must establish at least some connection with prospects to facilitate an open discussion about what is needed and why.

Another common scenario in which a professional shortcuts the process is when an opportunity comes about through a referral source—for example, a banker refers a client to a CPA. I once worked with a client in Canada who received such a referral. He called the prospect, who immediately agreed to work with him based on the strength of the banker's recommendation. When the CPA sent the first invoice for services, however, the client became concerned about the fee, which was higher than he had expected. The CPA was able to keep the client by reducing the fee, but learned an important lesson: You won't end up with an enthusiastic client if you shortcut the process. Things would have gone better if the CPA had taken more time to build the relationship (Stage One) and find out what was driving the client or prospect's desire to switch accounting firms so he could qualify the lead (Stage Two) and shape the service (Stage Three). He should have set up a meeting—maybe a breakfast or a lunch—with the banker and the prospect at the outset to discuss the opportunity. This would have taken more time, but would have increased the chances of creating an enthusiastic client who would generate better fees and possibly even referrals.

While rushing through Stage Three is particularly common when pursuing prospects, it also occurs when an existing client requests more services.

Often, when a client calls to request help on a special project or assistance on a new file, professionals often fall into a trap of simply saying "Yes, we can do that!" They fail to remember that they need to find the real value and shape the service to ensure an enthusiastic client on the new engagement.

Once, a client called me to see if I had dates available to do a workshop for an office I had not worked with before. I looked at a calendar, found some options, and agreed to conduct the session. After I learned more about the situation from talking to some workshop participants, however, it became apparent that I had not spent enough time defining the source of value and shaping the service. By then, I was already committed, so I had no choice but to conduct the program. While I wouldn't call it a disaster, the four-hour session seemed to go on forever. All I could think about was how much I wished I had followed my own advice and taken more time in Stage Three to reach an agreement on what the program was really about!

Get to the Decision-Maker to Find the True Source of Value

As discussed, a qualified lead is someone who has something he or she wants to accomplish and has the ability to retain professional services to deal with this recognized need. In Stage Three, you need to be sure you are talking with such a person—that is, the decision-maker.

> **Note**
>
> Remember, the decision-maker can change depending on the nature of the service. While an owner or CEO might be the decision-maker for a major piece of litigation, a CFO or GC might make the call on a matter of lesser importance because he or she has the economic authority—that is, the budget—to pay for the service being rendered.

In many cases, the original expression of the need may come from someone with a role in the decision-making process such as a user or influencer—for example, a referral source. Nevertheless, you must start a dialogue with the decision-maker in Stage Three if not before. Progressing to Stage Four without this dialogue is risky because you can waste considerable time pursuing an opportunity that never has a chance of being successful. I once did a study for a mid-sized accounting firm that had lost a dozen proposals in a row and wanted to find out what it was doing wrong.

I discovered that the biggest reason the firm was unsuccessful was that it was dealing with the wrong audience. Of the 12 proposals, eight of them had been requested by a controller or CFO, even though the owner or CEO was never interested in making a switch in the first place—something the firm didn't realize until the process was over because it never talked to the decision-maker.

When a CFO, GC, home office manager, or whoever is an employee of a closely held business requests services, the professional handling the requests should build a relationship with this individual during Stage Three. This is true for a number of reasons, including learning about how the organization or family will go about making a decision on who to use or whether they will use anyone at all. If the CEO or owner is the true decision-maker for the service being discussed, you should attempt to open the door for a dialogue with this individual to uncover his or her vision of what's needed—that is, the true source of value or the "heart of the matter," as I like to call it. I have seen situations in which partners of accounting firms have politely refused to go farther in the buying process unless they are granted the opportunity for such a dialogue. In one case, a partner in a Big Four firm stated that he would rather not propose on the half-million-dollar audit of a closely held manufacturer unless he could meet with the patriarch of this family business. He was the only one of three competing firms to take this position. He was granted the meeting and, predictably, acquired the engagement.

Meet More, Write Less

One of the simplest ways to achieve your goal in the SalesGame is to meet more often with clients and prospects to do the following:

- Get to know the players and procedures in the buying process.
- Clarify the need in terms of what the decision-maker wants to accomplish.
- Determine what will be required to create an enthusiastic client.
- Create and implement a strategy to differentiate yourself.
- Send a message that your firm truly wants the opportunity to work with the prospect.

Obviously, this does not apply in situations such as a current client calling with a simple request for additional assistance. In this case, all the aforementioned issues could be handled in a single discussion. And although you do not necessarily need to literally "meet more and write less" when dealing with clients, you do need to extend Stage Three by asking enough questions to understand the mission. That is, you need to steer clear of assuming you know what the decision-maker needs and how you will create an enthusiastic client. In the words of a sage managing partner I knew in Detroit, "Never let your clients hurry you into an engagement!"

This phrase also illustrates what I think is a big part of the problem: Clients are often conditioned to buy professional services in a way that doesn't serve their own interests. They are in a hurry to hire an attorney because they want to sue someone, but in fact, filing a lawsuit might be the least effective way to solve their problem. Clients use procurement departments to evaluate proposals, which make it all about the cost and not about the value. Companies who are choosing someone to sell their organization are famous for having two or three investment bankers make a "pitch" without sharing their goals for the transaction.

Considering complex opportunities with existing clients and dealing with new prospects take time. Of course, there will be situations when only one meeting with a client or prospect is allowed—for example, with certain governmental entities. However, you should strive to avoid the common pitfall of meeting just once with a client or prospect and moving immediately to Stage Four by developing a verbal or written proposal or saying "yes" too quickly to a client request. The "one and done" meeting approach is rarely effective to successfully pursue an opportunity, much less end up with an enthusiastic client. After 35 years of studying business development, I can say with certainty that one of the most reliable indicators of who will win a competitive opportunity is which firm has met more—face to face or on the phone—with the client or prospect.

Simply put, you need to do your best to slow down the process not only because it increases your odds of winning, but also because it serves your clients well. Most buyers I have interviewed have told me that they often do not fully understand what they need until they have a dialogue with the professional. In most cases, professionals have years of experience dealing with issues, which may be new and/or unique to the client or prospect. This is precisely why they *are* professionals and the reason the client or prospect eventually engages them. As an example, I once received a phone call from a client—an accounting association—who wanted to know when I would be available to conduct "sales training" (a commodity) in three major cities to which they would send CPAs from several of their member firms. I asked a few questions and learned that the idea had come out of a meeting of managing partners whose firms were part of the association. I slowed down the process by arranging a conference call with several of the managing partners and the representative from the association who had called me. This led to about three more months of interaction. In the end, we created a program that was designed to create a business-development culture (the source of true value or the Heart of the Matter) in those firms that wanted to participate. The program was two years long, generated far more fees than three "training" days, and helped me create a similar approach for other clients. Most importantly, the program made a huge difference for the participating firms and was one of the most professionally satisfying engagements of my career. Again, the SalesGame is as much about being a great professional as it is being great at business development.

Stage Three Recap

- Clarify the central issue, the source of value, or the Heart of the Matter, and identify the most important requirements. In other words, don't talk about services. Find what the prospect wants to accomplish. Uncover his or her Scorecard.

- Meet more, write less.

- Identify ways to meet client needs, expectations, and so on.

- Implement a strategy to differentiate service(s).

7

Chapter

Stage Four: Trial Close

S tage Four is a trial close. It starts when you believe you have a shared vision with the client or prospect about how a particular service can be of value and how it should be shaped and delivered. In Stage Four, you ask for the business—for example, via a written or informal (verbal) proposal. This stage continues until you and the client reach a final agreement to do the work.

The purpose of Stage Four is to confirm a mutual vision of the need and the most important factors required to fulfill that need to create an enthusiastic client—the Scorecard. As discussed in Chapter 6, "Stage Three: Shape the Service," the Scorecard is a summary of what clients and prospects want to get out of a service and how they will evaluate the quality of the service provided. In other words, it's a tool to help clients and prospects choose the best professional for their needs and manage their expectations. This confirmation usually requires a dialogue, which could go on for a couple of meetings or might be nothing more than a quick phone call. In describing this stage, I use the phrase "trial close" because you won't really know that your perception of what is needed is correct until it is confirmed by the client or prospect. When you have confirmed this mutual vision, you enter Stage Five, where you remain until you get permission to start the work.

> In Stage Four, you ask for the business.

> ## Note
>
> Many participants in my workshops ask how to get better at closing, or asking for the business. In my experience, the best way to improve in this area is not a function of using a certain skill, like closing (discussed later in this book) as much as it is a matter of purpose, timing, and understanding the overall business-development process.

If you don't share your vision of what's needed with clients or prospects in Stage Four, you might acquire the work, but you are far less likely to end up with an enthusiastic client. Unfortunately most professionals do not recognize this and move directly to a final close. For example, the professional might send a proposal to a client or prospect without any interaction such as a personal or phone review of the document. Or an attorney might agree to handle a new file for a client's HR director without verbally gaining agreement on any unique attributes of the case or the HR director's expectations for how the case should be managed.

A client of mine who was the in-house counsel in charge of employment litigation for a large West Coast grocery chain once told me a story that illustrates the importance of this stage even when dealing with clients for whom you have done extensive work. He had been in the position for five years before joining a firm as a lateral. During that five-year period, the grocery chain worked with two law firms to handle employment litigation. One was primary counsel and handled 80 to 90 percent of the cases. The second "backup" firm was used in the event of conflicts, capacity issues, and so on. By the time he left his in-house position, he told me these ratios were completely reversed. He even generated a bar graph showing the gradual shift over the five-year period. He explained that the reason for the shift was that the backup firm always took the time to learn the unique elements of any given case, while the firm that had the lion's share of the work treated every case the same. The results of the various cases reflected this difference, so he gradually started calling the backup firm more and more.

I've even suggested that associates or managers should do a trial close when partners ask them to undertake a special project such as writing a brief or preparing a cash-flow analysis. This is to make sure they understand what the partner wants out of the research—that is, what the real value of the service they are providing is, how much time the associate or manager should invest, and so on. Not only does this help younger professionals make sure they have an enthusiastic "internal" client, it's also a great way to practice using this process every day rather than waiting for a sales opportunity.

Remember, following the best practices of the SalesGame is as much about being a great professional as it is about being great at business development. Unfortunately, most professionals don't look at sole source opportunities with current clients as "selling," so they move too quickly through the process. They don't take the time to make sure client and professional are on the same page.

Ask for the Business

Most experienced rainmakers I have worked with insist that one of the keys to their success is that they ask for the business. This has certainly been confirmed by my company's research, which found that one of the top three reasons people chose their professional service firm was because that firm "wanted our business more."

Asking for the business is, of course, an effective way to let clients or prospects know you want their business, but asking too soon might create pressure and/or end up causing you to take on assignments you don't really want. The issue for most professionals is understanding how and when to actually "make the ask," as some rainmakers phrase it. As discussed, you can certainly express an interest in working with a client or prospect as early as Stage Two, but Stage Two is not the time to actually ask for the business. That's because there is no defined need and no qualified lead. Stage Three is also too early to ask for the business because you don't yet know the criteria that the client or prospect is using to measure performance. And even if there is a recognized need and a qualified lead, you usually don't know enough about the situation in Stage Three—for example, client or prospect expectations, standards for success, and willingness to pay—to know for sure that you really want the work. (If a client or prospect is only willing to pay half your standard rate or requires an impossible turnaround time for the completion of a project, asking for the business would be foolish. As a wise mentor of mine once said, "Better to turn them down then let them down.") You should express your appreciation and excitement about the potential engagement in Stage Three, but hold off actually asking for the business until you are in Stage Four.

In Stage Four, you can and should ask for the work because you believe you have a good understanding of the Scorecard based on multiple contacts (competitive proposals) or an extended phone call (sole source with a client). By asking for the business, you will either obtain permission to start the work (in which case the final close is pretty much a single sentence, like "Let's start!") or surface any issues not yet discussed.

In many cases, the most sensitive and difficult objections like age, gender, experience level, or cost will not arise until you ask for the business. Professionals often fear this part of the process. Perhaps it goes back to the dating analogy I mentioned earlier—that is, they are afraid of being rejected. Whatever the reason, you must remember that asking for the business in Stage Four is simply a step in the process that creates an opportunity for you to refine your initial ideas to better meet the needs of the client or prospect.

Of course, asking for the business doesn't necessarily mean you will get the work. But at least you will find out what obstacles need to be overcome or how the service must be reshaped to create an enthusiastic client. Either way, you will be ahead of the game if you ask for the business as soon as you think you know what's on the Scorecard.

Note

Of course, *how* you ask is also important in achieving the desired result. Various techniques for doing this will be discussed later in the book.

Extend Stage Four to Improve Your Success Rate

Stage Four offers you a great opportunity to increase your odds of success in achieving your goal of ending up with an enthusiastic client. All that is necessary is to extend this stage long enough to create a dialogue that confirms what the client or prospect wants to accomplish and to identify his or her most important performance criteria. This is true whether you are dealing with an existing client who telephones with a simple request for additional or expanded services or a major proposal for a new prospect. I am amazed how rarely professionals invest time in this critical stage of the process, instead electing to accept work from a client with little more than past experience to guide them. Or they simply mail proposals to prospects, missing a great opportunity to create a dialogue that is in everyone's best interest!

As mentioned, there are times when such a dialogue is prohibited in both Stage Three and Stage Four (for example, with many governmental RFPs), but these situations are rare in the grand scheme of professional selling. Based on my experience, these relatively few "no contact" situations rarely generate satisfying client-professional relationships anyway. The sale becomes more like a commodity or bid purchase. Of course, if there was a relationship established before the point of sale in Stage One and Stage Two, or if a professional is wise enough to circle back to Stage One, Stage Two, Stage Three, and Stage Four after he or she has "won" a competitive proposal, there is still a chance that even without any pre-proposal contact, professionals can achieve their ultimate goal of creating an enthusiastic client.

Even stranger to me are those situations when the client or prospect does not allow pre-proposal contact based on choice rather than governmental or other regulations. This has always seemed to me a little like choosing a doctor for major surgery without talking to him or her first. A word of caution to professionals who encounter these situations and hear the phrase "We want everyone on a level playing field." Almost always, everyone *isn't* on a level playing field. Odds are, a competitor has an inside track. It reminds me of the movie *Rounders*, about professional poker players, in which one of the characters says, "If you can't spot the sucker in the first half hour at the table, then you *are* the sucker."

When dealing with existing clients over the telephone, you can extend Stage Four by adding a minute or so near the end of a telephone call to summarize the discussion. This summary should include the following:

■ The client's request in terms of what he or she wants to accomplish (the value)

■ The service to be provided, including the criteria for successful delivery

■ A question like, "Are we on the same page?" or "How does that sound?"

At a minimum, this summary will crystallize the agreement between you and the client or prospect (assuming this proposal is accepted by the client and permission is granted to start the work). However, without extending Stage Four with this summary, there is always the risk that something was not covered and might lead to a disappointed client.

One of my own experiences using a professional service always seems to resonate with participants in my workshops. I had owned a piece of property for several years and had not listed it. Someone found my name on the tax rolls and made an offer on the property. The first call I made was to my accountant to ask what the "ramifications" of the sale would be. (I was trying to sound intelligent.) The tax manager who was handling my account at the time said she could take care of it but didn't ask any questions. The potential buyer called three times over the next week or so. In the third call, he told me he was looking at other properties and would like to know my level of interest. I began to wonder why I hadn't heard back from my accountant yet, so I called her and left a voicemail. An hour later,

I received a three-page, single-spaced letter from my accountant via fax. It contained lots of information about tax rules and regulations but no indication of how much I would have to pay in taxes if I sold the property—for me, the Heart of the Matter. Needless to say, I was not an enthusiastic client. All that was required was for my accountant to ask a few questions such as the ones discussed earlier, and to then extend the process by summarizing her understanding of my request. She should have said something like, "Let me get this straight. What you really want is to know how much you'd have to pay the IRS if you sold the property. You want me to give you a phone call—not a formal report—with that number by Wednesday, and you don't want me to invest more than an hour or two getting the number for you. How close am I?" If she had remembered this best practice, she would have saved herself some work and ended up with an enthusiastic client. Plus, she wouldn't have had to write off part of the bill because she spent way too much time writing a report when a phone call would have sufficed.

When dealing with prospects, you can extend Stage Four by discussing an outline or draft of a proposal or work plan to include these same elements. Or, you can extend it by establishing another contact to follow up the formal oral presentation—for example, to see what additional questions might have come up after hearing from other firms. I once extended Stage Four by discussing and revising a draft of a proposal three different times. The project started as a competitive bid situation but, after the third draft, the prospect actually said, "Let's not call it a proposal any more. Just make it into an engagement letter so I can get it in my budget and we can get started."

Perhaps the best evidence that extending Stage Four increases your odds on achieving success comes from a research project my company was hired to do several years ago for a Big Four firm. We were asked to analyze 50 consulting proposals that won and 50 that lost. We received a hard copy of each proposal, were able to interview the lead partner pursuing the opportunity, and were able to talk to the buyer in six or seven cases. When the proposals were delivered to my office, the first difference between winners and losers was obvious. The stack of losers was about three times as high as the stack of winners. Being a brilliant research scientist, I came to conclusion that short sells. (Sounds a lot like "meet more, write less" to me!) The only other significant difference I could find was that 38 of the 50 winners had been reviewed in draft form with someone who had a role in the buying process, while only three of the losers had been.

Why this very significant difference? I'm sure a lot of factors were in play, but I think the biggest one was getting the decision-maker, user, or influencer involved in the process as a coach of sorts. As soon as a buyer reviewed a draft of the proposal and made some suggestions for how it could be better —no matter how small the recommendation—he or she was invested in the proposal. It was no longer simply an outside vendor's document, but one in which the buyer had some ownership. Of course, any suggestions made also improved the final work product and better demonstrated that the consultant really understood the situation.

I've shared this research in many workshops over the years. One alumnus—an attorney named Dan—called me to tell me he was having lunch with a prospect he had known for years. The prospect had recently invited him to propose on a project in competition with two other firms. He wanted to ask my opinion as to whether he should bring a draft of the proposal to lunch and show it to the prospect. I encouraged him to do so because this follows the best practice of extending the process. He then followed this question with another: "Should I include a fee estimate in the draft that I show him?" I said that was probably a good idea as well. He called me the next week to tell me that he did bring the draft, but left a blank space for the fee. His coach/prospect asked him what he thought the number was going to be. Dan knew the quote would be in the tens of thousands of dollars, so he told him it would probably start with a three. His coach responded, "If it could start with a two, as in $29,999, I believe I can get you the work." Dan laughed and told him he didn't want to price it like Walmart, but would go in at $29,000. Dan finished the call with me by giving me the best part of the story: He won the engagement!

Stage Four Recap

- Review the Scorecard to test for accuracy.

- Ask for the business.

- Revise the Scorecard as necessary.

- Continue to implement strategy.

- Review the Scorecard again to test for accuracy.

- Extend the process to make sure there is agreement on the Scorecard between you and client or prospect—for example, review drafts of proposals and outlines of presentations before submission.

8

Chapter

Stage Five: Final Close

The purpose of Stage Five is to move from selling into service delivery. It starts when there is a final agreement on the service package and continues until permission is granted to start the work (or the offer is rejected). Stage Five is the easiest step in the SalesGame to describe: It's decision time. By this stage, little can be done to change what the client or prospect wants or to modify the service package.

When talking with present clients requesting additional or expanded service, this stage may last only a few seconds—that is, long enough for the client to say "yes" after the trial close has been offered, thus

> Stage Five is the easiest step in the SalesGame to describe: It's decision time.

granting permission to start the work. In more formal situations, the final proposal must eventually be submitted regardless of how many drafts or outlines are discussed to extend Stage Four. At some point, the client or prospect has to make a decision.

For many professionals, the frustrating part of Stage Five is that even though it may be time to make a decision, many clients or prospects do not. I recently worked with a law firm offering a lobbying package to a not-for-profit (NFP) organization. The law firm had played the game well, having written two drafts of the proposal and met with the board in a presentation setting. Nevertheless, the NFP took a little more than six months to finally grant permission to start the work. This is not uncommon. In recent years, I've even had clients respond to and "win" an RFP—that is, they were approved to provide service to the prospect—but still not get any actual assignments. The work often remains with the incumbent service provider or is given to another firm, who also "won." Needless to say, if faced with such a scenario, this is not the time for you to be passive and wait for the phone to ring or for an e-mail to arrive, any more than you should sit at your desk and hope someone contacts you with a Stage One or Stage Two lead.

What should you do in these situations? There is no easy answer, but here are a few ideas:

- Ask the tough question.

- Continue to close.

- Confirm the financial arrangement.

Ask the Tough Question

In Stage Five, you have a right—if not a responsibility—to identify whatever obstacle is preventing you from starting the work. The goal of the SalesGame is to convert a qualified lead—someone who needs to solve a problem, take advantage of an opportunity, etc.—to an enthusiastic client who receives true value. If you've made it this far in the SalesGame, then something must need to be done that benefits the client or prospect. In other words, it's not about selling more work. Sometimes, however, a client or prospect just needs a gentle push to get him or her over the hump so he or she does what is in his or her own best interest.

Both you and the client or prospect have invested time in shaping a service to respond to the problem or opportunity. If at this point you are not moving forward, it's time to summarize where you are in the process. That means asking the tough question: "What's standing between us and getting started?"

When you ask this question, one of two things will happen:

■ You might get permission to start the project. Frequently, all it takes to move ahead is to ask.

■ You might surface an obstacle to moving ahead regardless of all the dialogue in Stage Three and Stage Four. Discussing such an obstacle helps both you and the client or prospect. For example, by discussing the obstacle, you may find a way to help the client or prospect by changing some aspect of the service—say, modifying your billing procedures to ensure the client can pay from next year's budget.
In addition, the client or prospect will determine whether there is a way to accomplish the original objective in spite of any issues that still seem to be in the way of moving ahead.

No matter what, you will save yourself time and energy by finding out where you really stand. Once, I worked with a pair of attorneys in a workshop in Boston. They were pursuing an engagement to help a prospect on a real-estate transaction. After several meetings, the attorneys knew what the prospect wanted and how they could help. And yet, more than a month had gone by since the attorneys and their prospect had discussed and agreed upon this shared vision. Needless to say, the attorneys were frustrated. When we talked about it, and they recognized they had a Stage Five lead, they looked at each other as if to say, "Why haven't we asked, 'What's the holdup?'" At the next break, they left the room and called the prospect. Ten minutes later, they returned with smiles on their faces. They had permission to start the work! Even better, the prospect thanked them for their persistence. Some other issues had arisen in his business, and he felt like he had dropped the ball on the transaction in question. The moral of the story? Ask and—more often than not—ye shall receive!

> Ask and—more often than not—ye shall receive!

Continue to Close

On occasion, there may be good reasons for a delay. For example, there might be budgetary issues. Or maybe there are other events that must take place before the project can begin. Or maybe the prospect is just waiting for all those with a role in the buying process to meet so they can make the final decision. Asking the tough question will generally surface such issues.

Unfortunately, the frustration professionals feel in such a scenario may cause them to lose interest in the deal and focus on something else. After all, you've invested time and effort and shaped what seems to be a perfect service to create value for their client or prospect, but still you are not able to start the work. But you can improve your odds of success even at this late stage in the process by continuing to close.

Each contact—whether in person, by phone, or via e-mail—should end with a close that establishes a next step. This step should be something that you can control. That is, the responsibility for initiating the next step belongs to you, not the client or prospect. For example:

- If you discover that the decision-making team hasn't been able to meet for one reason or another, you can establish a time frame for the next contact.

- You can leave a voicemail saying you want to follow up as previously discussed and will check in again in two weeks.

- You can send an e-mail requesting a time to talk and note that you will follow up (be sure to say when) if there is no response.

When you follow up as required by the next step, you build trust and show your continued interest in working with the client or prospect. Remember, one of the key factors that buyers cited for choosing their professionals was "they wanted our business more." Persistent follow-up will almost always be welcomed by clients or prospects if they have something they really want to accomplish (that is, they are a qualified lead), which should be pretty obvious at this late stage in the game. In my own experience, and in that of many of my workshop participants, clients or prospects usually appreciate the follow-up to remind them it is time to move ahead. For example, one attorney told me about a hospital administrator who thanked him for calling to pursue a proposal for a review of policies to protect patient privacy. The administrator said she appreciated the attorney acting as her "conscience" and set up a meeting to begin the project.

Recently, a participant in one of my workshops—an accountant—told me a story that clearly illustrated the importance of staying proactive in Stage Five. He had submitted a competitive proposal to a prospect a month before the workshop in December and asked if I thought he should follow up. Naturally, my response was in the affirmative. The accountant followed up the next week and discovered that the CFO and owner had not yet had a chance to talk about the project. The accountant closed that call by saying he'd follow up in mid-January. When he did, he was again told that no decision had been made, so he closed again by saying he'd follow up again in early February. When the accountant talked with the CFO the next time, he was told his firm had won the work. As the conversation unfolded, the accountant asked what made the difference when it came down to their final decision. The CFO said with a chuckle, "You were the only one who kept calling!"

Look, the SalesGame is, well, a game. And as in any game, there's nothing that works every time. There are always exceptions. And the line between being persistent and being a pest can often be difficult to find. If you follow up too often, it could be counterproductive, irritating or alienating the client or prospect. But this is far more the exception than the norm, particularly if you establish a mutually agreeable time frame for the next contact. By the time you reach Stage Five, you've earned the right to be persistent. Besides, clients or prospects often need to be reminded that failing to make a decision can work against them. Continuing to close doesn't just increase your odds of success, it can be the very reason you get the work.

Confirm the Financial Arrangement

By the time you reach Stage Five, the financial arrangement is usually already established, whether it's the protocol for invoicing hours and expenses, a flat fee for the service, regular monthly charges, etc. Nevertheless, one pitfall that professionals can encounter, especially when dealing with "easy" sales—that is, responding to a request from a present client or a sole-source prospect who is in a hurry to get started with a particular engagement—is to fail to clarify the financial arrangement. Inevitably, this causes issues when the client is billed. In my own experience as well as that of my clients, there are few things that can upset clients more than receiving a bill that surprises them.

As in any game, you must make decisions based on the situation you're in and the players involved. I once worked with an accounting client who was coordinating a proposal for a company that was expanding internationally. The prospect received a full-blown proposal, including fees for various services beyond the audit, such as due diligence on a potential acquisition in Australia. The owner/CEO was very "type A" and asked that the proposal be e-mailed to him so he could review it on a plane he was about to board. He then called from the plane to tell the firm he wanted to hire them. Six weeks later, he received an invoice for the due-diligence work and was upset by the fee—even though it was the same number that had been included in the proposal. Perhaps extending the process in Stage Four by reviewing a draft of the proposal or even the final document would have helped to ensure the accounting firm had an enthusiastic client. Even if the type A prospect didn't want to take the time to complete this extra step, the professional should have asked for it to increase his odds of winning the SalesGame (that is, creating an enthusiastic client). It's all about playing the odds.

Of course, because it is a game and we are all human, anyone can make a mistake in execution. I've worked with one Midwest client for several years, doing one-day sessions for them, each focusing on a given area of need. One year, instead of working with the managing director to coordinate the program, I was asked to collaborate with another partner in the firm, named Ryan. Things went well, but as I was assembling my invoice, I realized that because Ryan was new to my program, I had invested almost twice the number of hours on it as in previous years. Worse, I had failed to follow my own best practice of confirming the financial arrangement with Ryan beforehand. Frustrated with myself for this failure, I invoiced for only 50 percent more than the previous year, feeling like I was being generous. Even so, Ryan e-mailed me almost immediately after receiving the invoice to say he was concerned about the size of the bill. Thankfully, we were able to come to a mutually agreeable compromise. Nevertheless, negotiating fees after the fact is never a good idea, and usually detracts from the glow that follows a job well done.

Confirming the financial agreement does not mean that you have to establish a fixed fee. It might be as simple as mentioning to a new client that services will be invoiced each month based on the hourly rate of the professionals involved. Or you could just review an engagement letter or proposal, or add a sentence or two in a discussion with an existing client who is calling with a new matter. The right approach will depend on the situation. But following this best practice is important if you want to achieve the goal of the SalesGame—creating an enthusiastic client!

Stage Five Recap

- Identify any obstacles to working together.
- Don't be afraid to ask what's standing between you and the starting the work.
- Keep closing!
- Confirm the financial arrangement.
- Gain permission to start work.

9

Chapter

Stage Six: Assure Enthusiasm (or Determine the Reason for Loss)

S tage Six starts when the client or prospect makes a go/no-go decision and continues until you, the professional, express interest in working together again in the future. The purpose of Stage Six depends on the outcome of Stage Five. If you are successful in obtaining permission to start the work, the purpose of Stage Six is to make sure the client is an enthusiastic buyer. If you are *not* successful obtaining permission to start the work, the purpose of Stage Six is to explore the loss to improve future business development performance. In either case, you should also use Stage Six to position for future engagements with the client or prospect. Stage Six ends when you have made sure the client is enthusiastic and have identified this client as a prospect for additional work—that is, returning to Stage Two.

> Stage Six starts when the client or prospect makes a go/no-go decision and continues until you, the professional, express interest in working together again in the future.

Win or lose, this is the stage of the SalesGame that professionals most often fail to complete. The irony is that the vast majority of professionals I have worked with say that the best way to develop business is to "do a good job." However, few of them actually take the steps necessary to make sure they have achieved this goal in their clients' eyes and to leverage their goodwill into more business. The goal of the SalesGame is to convert qualified leads into enthusiastic clients that generate rewards commensurate with the value received. The only way for professionals to know if they have achieved this goal is to talk with their clients.

The estimates I have seen from other sources about how often professionals "survey" their clients support this. A few years ago, *The American Lawyer* found that less than 20 percent of law firms surveyed their clients to determine their levels of satisfaction. From a statistical perspective, accounting firms do a little better. Yet these numbers do not even begin to get to the real problem. Even if a firm *does* conduct a survey, it rarely generates qualitative input. When my clients tell me they use surveys to make sure their clients are satisfied, I usually ask them, "How much time do you spend filling out a survey card at a hotel or restaurant you visit?" Yes, a survey can flag a specific problem or identify a client who is already dissatisfied. But it doesn't enable you to drill down with follow-up questions to really see how clients feel. Surveys don't provide an opportunity to build relationships, get a sense of what is currently on clients' minds, or better understand their future hopes and dreams. And surveys certainly can't be used to close—that is, to create a next step to position for future opportunities with the client or prospect.

When professionals end Stage Five with a "no," very few follow up with the prospect or client to find out what they might have done to improve their performance for the next opportunity. Can you imagine a serious athlete in any sport—basketball, soccer, tennis, golf—failing to review video of a lost game to see what went wrong and attempt to identify how similar problems could be avoided in the future? Large firms invest hundreds of hours and thousands of dollars in the proposal process for a Fortune 500 company, not to mention the cost of the marketing efforts that went into creating the opportunity in the first place. Smaller firms and even sole practitioners are no different—they spend countless hours networking, going to Rotary Clubs and trade associations, to create opportunities to obtain more business. But few of these professionals invest the time required to prepare and meet with the decision-maker, user, or influencer when they are not successful.

If professionals carry out this stage of the SalesGame with the same commitment they show in the earlier parts of the process, they will inevitably improve their business-development performance and their odds on achieving their ultimate goal—creating an enthusiastic client.

Make Time for Assuring Client Enthusiasm Meetings

Professionals with whom I've worked aren't usually satisfied with doing an OK job for their clients. They want to do an outstanding job. As I've said, the SalesGame is as much about being a great professional as it is being great at business development. The only way professionals can truly know if they've provided outstanding service is if they have a dialogue with their clients to learn how they're performing and how they can do better. I call these "assuring client enthusiasm meetings," or ACE for short.

Note

Remember, it's not enough to have satisfied clients. Clients who are merely satisfied generally are more likely to change because of a competitor's fee discount or a glitch in service. They also aren't as likely to use more services or generate referrals. You want enthusiastic clients!

Client enthusiasm meetings can uncover ways to turn good service into great service. Here are a few real-world examples:

- One company wanted to see the accounting firm's staff at its own place of business rather than having the staff do the field work in the firm's offices. This was revealed in a client enthusiasm meeting.

- A litigation attorney learned in a client enthusiasm meeting that his client's in-house counsel wanted to have input on even minor decisions. This level of collaboration enabled her to feel more in control and to give better progress updates to her superior.

- A wealth-management professional learned in a client enthusiasm meeting that one of the biggest concerns her client had was that her children, who were already in their early 20s, didn't understand the responsibility that money brings. The professional was able to arrange meetings with both offspring to further their education in this area.

While the purpose of client enthusiasm meetings is by definition to ensure client enthusiasm, the delightful irony is that these meetings routinely generate more work. The managing partner of a law firm I worked with made a point of arranging 50 of these meetings each year with the firm's most significant clients, whether he was the partner who managed the account or not. He did this throughout his five-year term. By his estimates, at least half these meetings generated an opportunity to serve the client in additional ways. An interesting side note is that only one of the 250 clients he contacted didn't want to take the time for a meeting, thus dispelling the commonly held notion that clients don't think these discussions are valuable. In my experience, quite the reverse is true. Clients love these discussions because they show the professionals' commitment, provide an open forum to evaluate the services they're receiving, and enable executives to focus on the future with a knowledgeable and trusted advisor.

> Clients love these discussions because they show the professionals' commitment, provide an open forum to evaluate the services they're receiving, and enable executives to focus on the future with a knowledgeable and trusted advisor.

I talked with the head of a consulting practice who estimated that he generated one qualified lead for every five ACE meetings. Unfortunately, he told me with a guilty look, he rarely conducts these meetings due to other demands on his time. Think how incredible a lead generator this technique would be if contact was made on a systematic, face-to-face basis with every significant client a firm serves. It's simple: Professionals *must* make time for client enthusiasm meetings.

There are many approaches to handling these meetings. Generally, they are best done outside the delivery of the work product. For example, at a minimum, the discussion should move from a conference room to a lunch table after the work product has been discussed. One firm I work with conducts them on a weekly basis on a golf course. Other firms take a more formal approach, spending 10 to 20 hours gathering background data and planning questions for visits with their major clients. Individual partners at accounting and law firms often take key members of client organizations to lunch, cocktails, or dinner for some honest feedback in an informal setting. While good preparation always improves performance, your approach to these meetings really is not the issue. The most important thing is to have them.

Many professionals hold client enthusiasm meetings at the end of the engagement. Others, especially when working on long and complex assignments such as a major piece of litigation, conduct these meetings throughout the process. I worked with one litigator who made it a point to conduct client enthusiasm meetings at certain milestones in a case. His reasoning was simple: If the client was enthusiastic at each milestone, they would be far less likely to blame the attorney if a judge or jury came back with the wrong decision.

Tip

If you've done your job in Stage Three and Stage Four, outlining and confirming the client's or prospect's goals and how those goals should be achieved, you should wind up with mutually agreed upon performance standards. These standards can and should be used throughout the engagement—not just at its completion—to measure performance. In the client enthusiasm meeting, you'll want to refer to these measurements to ensure the client is getting what he or she wants. If, during the course of the engagement, a gap in expectations is found, you can usually take corrective action to get everything back on track.

It's also a good idea to conduct a modified ACE meeting in the event that your firm is in the process of transitioning the responsibility for a client from a senior representative, who might be in the process of winding down his or her career, to a younger professional. This meeting can be used to convey what elements of the service provided are of greatest value to the client and how the next generation of service provider can make the overall experience even better. The same is true for any transition on the client side—for example, if a new GC, controller or director of HR has emerged.

How to Win When You "Lose"

Anyone who has been in the business world would agree that we learn more from our failures than our successes. This has certainly been true in my own career as well as my life in general. Some of my best ideas for workshops have come from some of my worst disasters.

If you have the courage and discipline, you can improve your game by talking with those who do not choose to use your services. Even better, this type of Stage Six follow-up call after a "loss" can create additional opportunities to generate revenue. While I don't know if the success rate generating new work is as high as the 50 percent cited for client enthusiasm meetings, my experience working with clients over the years would suggest that it is high. Consider the following examples:

■ An accounting firm received an RFP to perform the audit for a port authority. No one had a good relationship at the organization, and the rules for the process prohibited contact before submission of the proposal. Knowing it would probably lose, the firm decided to submit a proposal in an attempt to develop a relationship for the future. After a competitor acquired the audit, the partner leading the effort arranged a follow-up meeting to get to know the decision-maker and see what she and the firm could do differently the next time around. During the meeting, she learned of several needs the port authority had for consulting services. Within a matter of months, the firm was engaged to complete two high-value projects. These projects generated far more revenue than the firm would have earned doing the initial audit!

- A law firm lost a competitive proposal for an organization for which it was already doing substantial litigation. The lead senior associate reached out to three of his contacts in the organization to learn more about how the process unfolded and how the firm could position for the future. In these one-on-one meetings, he learned that the proposal was driven by the purchasing department, and that the fee structure had a significant impact on the outcome. These contacts also confirmed that they were pleased with the firm's past work and that they understood the disadvantages of switching to a different firm for litigation. More importantly, they were so impressed with his follow-up, they decided to override the purchasing department and continue using the senior associate's firm.

- A partner in a law firm learned that a client of his had hired another firm to handle some tax appeal projects for several of their properties. He was especially disappointed because this was the kind of work that a new lateral had been hired to do. He reached out to the CEO, with whom he had a long and good relationship. The CEO told him that the GC had already talked to another provider and was ready to move forward with him. The partner expressed his understanding and suggested the GC and/or CEO meet with the lateral so the GC would know about this resource in case anything changed. When the meeting happened, the GC and the lateral hit it off very well. They shared similar backgrounds and knew many of the same people. Even better, the GC said that he had not made a firm commitment to the competitor and decided to hire the lateral for the initial project.

The last example is of particular interest because it illustrates that using a Stage Six meeting to follow up after a loss is not only effective when dealing with formal proposal opportunities, it can also work very well with clients who've chosen another provider for specific projects.

Perhaps my favorite example involves a consultant with whom I worked in Washington D.C., the "mother lode" of RFPs, and also a place where contact during the proposal process is often prohibited (even though this protocol is rarely followed). This consultant's firm responded to an RFP for a government finance project but had no previously established relationship with the agency in question. Given the rules of engagement, the consultant and his firm were prohibited from talking to any of the players during the proposal process. Not surprisingly, his firm did not win the engagement. Afterward, the consultant asked me if I thought it would be a good idea for him to talk with one of the functionaries at the government agency in question, as post-proposal contact was not prohibited. Of course, I said yes. He met with a high-level departmental assistant, who confided in the consultant that his firm's bid had been way too high. She gave him some ideas and said she'd make sure he was on the bid list the next time around. Unfortunately, the next time ended with the same result. The consultant contacted the assistant again. They had lunch, and the assistant told the consultant that this time, his firm had underpriced the engagement. In fact, they were so much lower than the competition, the selection committee felt they must have misunderstood the assignment. The assistant reviewed how the agency evaluates pricing and gave him more ideas. The next RFP came out a few months later, and this time the consultant's firm was victorious. (By the way, the consultant never said whether there was any pre-submission contact on this third go-around, and I did not force the issue. Regardless, following up in Stage Six certainly enabled the consultant to achieve his goal of developing work from this governmental agency.)

It all comes down to relationships. If you are unable to develop a relationship before or during the pursuit of a new piece of business, then why not develop it after? My first mentor in business was a managing partner of a Big Four firm. When he was not successful, he would always ask his contact, "If we can't do this project for you, what *can* we do?" His efforts were usually rewarded with some kind of an opportunity to do some task—usually something small—and build a relationship for the future.

The important point is to keep moving forward. If you don't reach out to prospects who don't hire you, it's highly unlikely these prospects will reach out to you if they become dissatisfied with the firm they chose in a competitive process or if another need comes up. Odds are, they feel badly about not having hired you in the first place, and may be embarrassed to request further assistance. An accounting client of mine once said something that I have often repeated in workshops: "It isn't that we lost. We just haven't won yet."

Close by Positioning for the Future

Every meeting has a close and, whether assuring client enthusiasm or following up on a lost opportunity, a Stage Six meeting is no exception. In this stage, the close or next step should position you for future business.

Positioning for another opportunity is easier with ongoing institutional clients that continually use the same service—for example, banks that need help with loan documentation or a manufacturing concern that requires regular audits. But you can usually find some sort of next step to leverage your client's enthusiasm for your services even when the client appears to be a "one time" buyer. With these clients, you might plan a next step such as the following:

- An introduction to another lead in the current client organization, such as another attorney on the in-house staff or the head of IT at another division

- An introduction to a lead in another company, such as someone in the same industry or geographic area

- An introduction to a potential referral source, such as a banker, attorney, or accountant who also serves the client

- The scheduling of some future contact with the same individual to follow up on his or her progress

- An invitation to a social or sporting event to cement the relationship

- Accompanying a client to his or her industry or trade association

If doing good work is the key to new business, you should make sure you use your enthusiastic clients to help build the practice of your dreams.

Closing to position for the future is equally important in situations in which Stage Five ended with a "no." If the client or prospect has chosen another vendor, then you should use Stage Six to explore the reasons behind this choice. As part of this discussion, you should close by establishing some future follow-up contact—for example, a call to see how the project in question is going, some form of social contact, etc. Even the slightest gesture might lead to a very positive result! I worked with an accounting firm that lost an audit proposal for a significant bank but still took several of the bankers to their private box to watch the local NBA team. Two weeks later, the competitor who had won the engagement announced some personnel changes, prompting the bank to call my client and award them the work. Representatives from the bank later confided that they were so impressed by the fact that the accounting firm had "courted" them even after the loss. Unfortunately, however, most professionals understandably want to forget the bad feelings associated with a loss as soon as possible and rarely follow up to keep the relationship alive. Resist this temptation!

Instead, close Stage Six to position for the future by doing the following:

- Ask to stay in touch to see how the project is going.

- Offer to be a sounding board for the decision-maker or user.

- Arrange a future time to talk to see what other problems or opportunities might arise.

- Send a personal invitation to one of your firm's seminars or events.

- Set up some sort of social contact, such as attending a sporting event.

Of course, these are only examples. As with any close, you will come up with the best ideas by collaborating with others in your firm.

Your next opportunity with a prospect might not come for years. But if it is a prospect worth pursuing, tracking the lead for the long term is always a good idea. I've seen many situations in which professionals have finally acquired substantial work from a prospect after one, two, or even three failed attempts over a period of years. On the other hand, if you fail to complete Stage Six—if you fail to establish a next step to keep positioning—odds are the lead will, like old generals, simply fade away. You will never learn of the next opportunity to play the SalesGame with this particular prospect.

Of course, you always need to prioritize your activities, regardless of what stage of the SalesGame you are playing. Stage Six is no exception. There will be some prospects that you decide not to pursue in Stage Six because you learn in Stage Three, Stage Four, or Stage Five that they will not help you build the practice of your dreams. As long as you make a conscious decision *not* to continue to position in Stage Six, you are playing the SalesGame effectively. However, positioning for desirable clients or prospects as part of Stage Six is an excellent way to improve long-term business-development performance.

Stage Six Recap

- Deliver services.

- Conduct client enthusiasm meetings to elicit client feedback on performance during and after the engagement.

- Ask for additional opportunities to be of service, such as repeat engagements, add-ons, introductions to others in the organization, etc.

- Elicit feedback on what we could have done better in the proposal/bid process.

- If the prospect could help you build the practice of your dreams, find a way to position for the future.

10

Chapter

The Importance of Preparation

Thus far, we have provided an overview of the six stages of the business-development process depicted in Figure 3.1. There is one remaining critical piece that has not been covered, however: planning the meeting. At the center of the image in Figure 3.1—and the key to being successful in business development—is *planning*. Planning, also called preparation, takes discipline. You must make it a priority to reach your potential. Every professional is capable of preparing at a very high level to improve their overall success rate.

The Will to Prepare

One of my favorite quotes is from legendary football coach Bear Bryant: "It's not the will to win that matters—everyone has that. It's the will to *prepare* to win that matters."

"It's the will to *prepare* to win that matters."

—Bear Bryant

Compare that approach with how most professionals operate. Planning for a business-development meeting is not a particularly strong suit for most professionals, primarily for two reasons. First, they're busy getting work out the door, so they tend to leave little or no time to plan. This is particularly troublesome because the best planning is done collaboratively, and it's difficult to find someone to use as a planning partner on short notice. Second, they don't have a system to facilitate the planning process, so they're usually inefficient and ineffective. For example, they plan for what they're going to say, not what they're going to ask.

I once worked with an attorney—a lateral hire who had been a U.S. district attorney—who illustrated this perfectly. After completing a workshop and small-group planning session, he reflected on what he had learned. He said that when he was a district attorney, he would never go into a deposition—much less a trial—without knowing every question he was going to ask, in what order, how he was going to ask them, and how he would handle various responses. He compared this with what happened when he joined the law firm. Given his experience in regulatory issues, his partners were thrilled to introduce him to their clients. Over the last few months, he had gone to meeting after meeting. But nothing ever came of them because there was no game plan—not even a follow-up discussion. As he put it, "I had no idea how many things there were to consider in meetings like these. We had purpose, but no next steps. We just went out and talked because it was just 'business development.'"

Best Practices in Planning

If accountants, attorneys, consultants, wealth managers, investment bankers —anyone who offers a professional service—want to be ready to perform at their highest level, they have to have the will to prepare, not just the will to win. The process of preparation is very much the same as with any game. Know the fundamentals, draw up a game plan, and practice—for example, rehearse the opening transition statement out loud or role play how to handle a particularly troublesome objection. This process is not something you can master by going through it once or twice!

Preparation should occur for *any* substantive business-development meeting. Imagine a professional football team that only prepared for the first game! The more important the meeting, the more time should be invested in preparing. One attorney I worked with for years was asked by his colleague why he spent so much time—sometimes hours—planning for a meeting. I loved his response: "Because the results I get are exponential." My colleagues and I routinely invest an hour or more preparing for a business-development call that will probably last no more than 30 minutes.

There are three best practices to guide you in your preparation efforts:

- **Have a system.** Using the same procedure each time is efficient, helps you to avoid missing important points, and facilitates teamwork. Using the SalesGame approach is, of course, the system we follow. It works well. But there are others out there, too. The important point is to avoid reinventing the wheel each time you plan.

- **Collaborate.** I cannot overstate the importance of preparing with someone else. Time and time again, I hear professionals in workshops generate great ideas for one another—for example, suggesting the right phrasing for a question or coming up with a creative close. Plus, collaborating makes the whole process more fun. Business development really is a team game.

- **Write it down.** Great ideas are ephemeral. I can't tell you how many times I've come up with the perfect question, only to forget it five minutes later. Writing down ideas also helps you to organize and refine them and will enhance your ability to remember them when you are making the play.

We have provided our version of a system for planning in Appendix B, "The Planning 'System.'" First is the Sales Planning Checklist, which includes the major points you should consider before going to a meeting. It is intended to serve as the catalyst for brainstorming and strategizing. Second is what we call a Play Diagram. It represents an attempt to put the most significant points on one page so you get a picture of the meeting rather than a script. It should follow the general order of the expected flow of the meeting. Used together, these tools will help you apply the skills (that is, the fundamentals) you learn in this book to execute a highly effective business-development meeting.

A colleague of mine often uses his football experience—he was a running back in college—to compare the SalesGame with how any good player prepares for a game. All players, regardless of the game, must work on the fundamentals. In the world of football, nothing could be more fundamental than blocking and tackling, but there are other intricacies of technique that go way beyond this—for example, how a receiver runs his routes or holds his hands, how a quarterback moves his feet and releases the ball, and how a guard fakes a block to set up a screen play. The same is true for basketball, baseball, soccer, and every other game, including solo sports and card games. There are always fundamentals to be learned.

The rest of this book explains the fundamentals of the SalesGame, such as how to set yourself up for success with leads and build the Scorecard. It also dives into some of the intricacies, such as the order in which questions should be asked and how to handle a rejected close. After you achieve an appropriate level of proficiency with these fundamentals, you're ready to start using them in a game. Let's start building the foundation of your game with a focus on the fundamentals.

Preparation Recap

- Prioritize planning time.
- Follow best practices.
- Follow a system.
- Collaborate.
- Write things down.
- Build your foundation by focusing on fundamentals.

Part Summary

The goal of the SalesGame is to convert qualified leads into enthusiastic clients who generate rewards commensurate with the value received. Until a contact recognizes a need and has the resources to satisfy that need, he or she cannot be considered a "qualified lead," and therefore should not be sold to. If a contact is a qualified lead, then any "selling" that occurs should involve listening to him or her to better understand what he or she wants to accomplish and how you can provide a value to him or her. By focusing on the value of your service to the client or prospect, you will generate more financial and personal rewards for themselves.

The relationship between the professional (you) and the players involved in the buying process is the most important factor in deciding who gets the work. These players can be divided into four categories:

- **The decision-maker:** This is the person (or people) who makes the final decision about a given service. The decision-maker controls the purse strings.

- **The user:** This is the person (or people) who will be working with you if and when a project begins.

- **The influencer:** This is someone who is not directly involved in the decision-making process—for example, a referral source—but whose support might help persuade the decision-maker to choose a particular firm or professional.

- **The coach:** This is anyone inside or outside the buying organization who offers suggestions, ideas, or counsel to assist a professional in obtaining work.

Professionals should identify and build relationships with as many of these players as possible to improve their business-development performance.

The SalesGame is divided into six stages:

- **Stage One:** This stage is all about building relationships with the client or prospect before the point of sale. This stage is not about selling. For younger professionals, it might take years for these relationships to grow to a point where they can be of help. For more senior professionals, this stage may be shorter. Stage One is the marketing part of the equation for successful business development. The more an individual, practice group, or firm can develop a vision of its ideal client base, the more effective and efficient marketing activities can be.

- **Stage Two:** In Stage Two, you express interest in working with a client or prospect, continue to build relationships, and position for an opportunity. This stage may be short, such as when a client calls with a new request. Or, it may take years—for example, if you are pursuing a major prospect. In this stage, your focus is on qualifying the lead—finding something the decision-maker wants to accomplish. This is not the time to start selling. When you have a qualified lead, you are ready to move to Stage Three.

- **Stage Three:** This stage begins when there is a recognized need and continues until you have a clear vision of what the client or prospect is trying to accomplish and how the service should be shaped—the Scorecard. This requires a dialogue between you and the client or prospect, which should not be hurried. While this stage includes relationship building with all those who have roles in the buying process, you should focus on learning the needs of decision-makers. The odds on being successful in the SalesGame are directly related to the amount of contact during Stage Three.

- **Stage Four:** Stage Four starts when you believe you have a shared vision of what clients or prospects want and their criteria for performance. It continues until there is a mutual, confirmed agreement on the Scorecard and your ability to deliver a corresponding service. Whether dealing with present clients or prospects, this stage should be a dialogue, not an event. You should use Stage Four to make sure you know exactly what is required to create an enthusiastic client. To be effective in Stage Four, you must do two things: Ask for the business and extend the stage to foster dialogue.

- **Stage Five:** This is decision-making time. You must be persistent and proactive to gain permission to start the work, or else discover that you will not acquire the assignment. This level of persistence is almost always in the best interests of the client or prospect as well as the professional. If stuck in a holding pattern, you must ask the right question: "What's standing between us and getting started?" This will either result in the project's launch or the identification of an obstacle that you and client or prospect can work together to overcome. One pitfall to avoid in Stage Five, especially when dealing with an "easy" sale, is starting the work without confirming the financial arrangement. While fees are almost always established earlier in the process, starting the work without confirming the financial arrangement can be a significant obstacle to achieving the goal of the SalesGame: creating an enthusiastic client.

- **Stage Six:** This stage starts when the client or prospect makes a go/no-go decision and continues until you express interest in working together again in the future. If you are successful in Stage Five, you can use Stage Six to make sure you have achieved the ultimate goal of the SalesGame: to convert a qualified lead into an enthusiastic client. Conducting client enthusiasm meetings during this stage is a must for all professionals who are serious about developing more business. You need not wait for the end of the engagement to conduct these meetings; interim meetings give you time to correct any shortcomings, particularly with long and complex engagements. If you were not successful in Stage Five, you should use Stage Six to explore ways to be more effective in the future and to begin positioning yourself for more opportunities with the same client or prospect. In some cases, following up in Stage Six may result in turning a "no" into a "yes." Either way, you should be ready with a "close" in Stage Six to proactively position yourself for future opportunities, assuming the client or prospect in question is one consistent with building your ideal practice.

Planning is a key discipline in effectively executing the six stages of the Sales-Game. To be successful, you must make time to plan for each business-development meeting. When it comes to planning, there are three best practices. First, have a system. Second, collaborate. And third, write it down. Having a system enables you to be more efficient and thorough in your preparation. Collaborating is important to generate strong ideas or test the ones you come up with. It also helps you to challenge your thinking on possible next steps. Writing down your preparation helps you visualize the meeting and promotes confidence in execution. All players, regardless of the game, must work on fundamentals. After players have achieved an appropriate level of proficiency with these fundamentals, they are ready to start using them in a game.

Play On

You've learned the goal of the SalesGame, the key players, how to advance through the various stages, and the importance of planning. The next part provides best practices, tools, and ideas to help you improve your performance. As with any game, the best way to get better at the SalesGame is to learn the fundamentals, and to practice, practice, practice! Don't sit on the sidelines. Start playing now. The more you play, the better you get!

Part 2

Best Practices for Setting Up the Game

The Sales Matrix: Four Types of Stage Two Leads

As any sports enthusiast will tell you, how you set up a game goes a long way toward determining its outcome. Back in the school-yard, choosing players for a pickup game, we all knew that our choices would play a large part in determining who won. As adults, we still set up the game, but in different ways. If you don't believe me, try standing around the first tee at a country club sometime. No doubt, you'll hear plenty of banter about various bets and how many strokes a player does or does not get.

Stage Two of the SalesGame is all about setting up the game. The best way to set up the SalesGame is to create relationships early and maintain them continuously throughout your career, whether that means staying in touch with alumni from your university days, networking with professionals from other fields who could become sources of referrals, or becoming involved in trade, professional, or community organizations. These relationships should be created before the point of sale.

> **Note**
>
> Appendix A, "Marketing and Lead-Generation Activities," provides many ideas for marketing activities you can use to create and maintain relationships. Unfortunately, they all take some time and effort, which is problematic for most busy professionals. Nevertheless, performing these activities is a necessary part of the game. Besides, you might enjoy them. Remember, the SalesGame is a game, after all! It's important to have some fun.

The main focus of this book is selling. That is, the goal of the SalesGame is to convert qualified leads to enthusiastic clients. The chapters in this part discuss how professionals can most effectively move from having a relationship with a contact to having a dialogue about business. That's what Stage Two of the SalesGame is all about.

Opportunities Are Often Won or Lost Early in the Game

Here's an example that might help demonstrate just how critical Stage Two can be. A few years ago, I was hired to do custom research for an international accounting firm that had just won a six-figure engagement to provide tax services for inpatriates and expatriates of a Fortune 500 company. All the Big Four firms had been invited to propose by way of an RFP. All the firms had outstanding technical capabilities in the field. One, however, had been doing audit work for the company. As an incumbent, it had some fairly strong relationships with the players. By comparison, my client was an outsider, with no previous contact before the RFP. This was not a good situation to be in, and certainly not in keeping with the best practices for playing the SalesGame—that is, building relationships and getting to know the players *before* the point of sale. Nevertheless, my client ended up winning the competitive proposal.

While very pleased with their victory, my client wanted a better understanding of what had actually put them over the top in the competition with their three competitors. (There's a novel idea—let's try to find out *why* we won so we can duplicate our success with some consistency!) I was asked to interview the members of the selection committee—an HR director, an assistant vice president of finance, and a tax director—to see what I could find out. I e-mailed each person an outline of what I wanted to talk about: how they selected potential vendors to send RFPs, what sort of contact they had with the various contenders, what they thought about the written proposal, and so on.

I was particularly amazed by their responses to the third question—what they thought about the written proposal. Each one offered roughly the same answer: "To be honest, I never really read the proposal." Keep in mind, my client invested hundreds of hours in its proposal. It was an inch thick and professionally done! Nonetheless, research I have conducted since this event indicates that fewer than 25% of prospects read the proposals they receive. When I asked the obvious follow-up question as to why this was the case, I received answers like, "Well, I shouldn't say I didn't read it. I did *skim* it."

[Translation: "I turned to the fee section after the letter of introduction and executive summary."] They typically went on to say, "But I pretty much had my mind made up from the first meeting."

> Research I have conducted... indicates that fewer than 25% of prospects read the proposals they receive.

What happened in that first meeting? How did my client win this significant opportunity? Simple. They set up the game. That is, they called in advance to find out what the prospect wanted to cover and who would attend the first meeting. Then they e-mailed some questions for the selection committee to look at in advance. In contrast, their competitors failed to set up the game. In addition, they made a wide array of mistakes while the game was in play. One competitor was unprepared. They did not even know the basics about the company, like a rough idea of how many employees were stationed in various countries. Another brought an out-of-town expert to the first meeting who would not be involved in servicing the account on an everyday basis—not at all what the prospect wanted. The incumbent committed a fairly common sin: They summarized all the wonderful things they had done for the client in the past but did not ask what the company wanted in the future.

Stage Two of the SalesGame is extremely important because it is the first time that professionals and clients or prospects discuss the possibility of working together. How well you handle this attempt to qualify the lead has a large impact on your eventual success. This initial discussion can take place in a number of ways. These can be divided into four major categories, as shown in Figure 11.1.

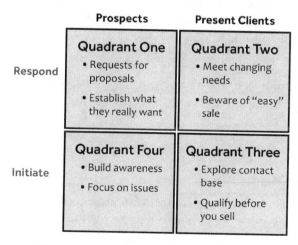

Figure 11.1   Types of Stage Two leads.

As you can see, this matrix is divided into four quadrants to highlight your actions and the best practices based on the type of lead (prospect or client) and the method of contact (respond or initiate). For more, read on!

Respond Mode

As shown in Figure 11.1, there are two quadrants in Respond mode: Quadrant One and Quadrant Two. Quadrant One, responding to prospects, is for the types of leads that most professionals associate with business development—namely, those that involve responding to an opportunity from a new prospect, whether in a formal or informal setting. Here are some examples:

■ An entity issues an RFP to several competing professional-service firms. This RFP is often accompanied by fairly formal rules of procedure and criteria for selection.

■ A social contact or friend expresses a need for assistance in dealing with a problem or opportunity either by a direct request or by mentioning the issue in some non-business setting—for example, at a party or walking off a tennis court.

■ A banker, attorney, or other referral source connects you with someone that he or she thinks needs your help.

■ A potential client contacts you as a result of finding you on the Internet —for example, on your firm's Web site.

I have found that most professionals do not even think of themselves as selling when handling leads in Quadrant Two, responding to present clients. These leads come from current clients. Here are some examples:

■ A current audit client calls an accountant to expand the scope of a present engagement or to request assistance in a new area, like tax.

■ An institutional or recurring client, like a bank loan officer or in-house counsel at an insurance company, calls an attorney with a new transaction or case.

Initiate Mode

Quadrant Three, initiating contact with present clients, one of two quadrants in Initiation mode, is most often referred to as *cross-selling*. It includes those leads where contact is initiated with current clients to explore needs, problems, or opportunities beyond the scope of the current engagement.

Here are some examples:

■ A consultant contacts a current client to discuss follow-up work to an engagement or to build awareness about other services that might be of use.

■ An accountant contacts clients to see if she can be of assistance in handling the reporting requirements created by new legislation.

■ An attorney meets with a current labor and employment client to see what other issues the company is facing, such as those dealing with intellectual property or taxes.

Quadrant Four, initiating contact with prospects, is the most unappealing to professionals because they associate it with cold-calling—that is, initiating contact with prospects to solicit work. However, cold-calling is only one type of qualification activity in this quadrant (and by far the most difficult). Here are some other examples:

■ An accountant or attorney takes a friend to lunch and expresses interest in working together if the right opportunity can be found.

■ A consultant follows up with someone he or she met at a trade or professional association meeting to see if there might be an opportunity to work together.

■ An attorney reaches out to an in-house counsel who used to be with a client but is now with a new organization.

While each quadrant is unique and has its own pitfalls, the difference between scenarios when professionals are responding versus initiating is by far the most significant.

If a Client or Prospect Starts the Process, It Is Probably a Qualified Lead

When a client or prospect initiates contact, you can assume that there is some problem or opportunity to be dealt with—that is, a *recognized need*. Otherwise, the contact would not have happened in the first place. But even if a client or prospect knows they need something, you should keep in mind that what they *say* they need may not actually be the best solution to their problem.

Here are some examples of scenarios in which clients *think* they know what they need, but actually don't:

■ A client tells an attorney that he wants to sue a family member to oust her from the family business, but the attorney knows that may be absolutely the worst way to resolve any differences.

■ A prospect contacts several accounting firms to obtain a new bid on her audit when what she *really* needs is a better means of raising capital than a traditional bank loan.

■ I'm contacted by a continuing client to see what dates I'm available for another workshop when what he is *really* seeking is to build a stronger business-development culture.

In my experience both personally and listening to other professionals, clients and prospects usually start the discussion by asking about your service—for example, audits, selling a company, workshop dates)—and cost. In these situations, your challenge is to convert the conversation about service and cost to one about goals and value. This is important even if the work is "pre-sold." In this way, you can achieve the ultimate goal of the SalesGame: an enthusiastic client. (More on this later in the book.)

Professionals are always more comfortable in this scenario because they are being asked for their assistance. They do not feel like they are selling; rather, they feel like they are serving. Of course, you still must qualify the lead—that is, convert service to value—even if it is an eager buyer calling. In most cases, the best approach is to slow the process down rather than be too anxious to get the work. As a managing partner I once worked with used to say, "Never let your clients hurry you into a relationship."

> "Never let your clients hurry you into a relationship."

When Initiating in Stage Two, Set Realistic Goals and Next Steps

If, on the other hand, *you* are the one initiating the process, you may have no idea whether the client or prospect needs anything. In this scenario, professionals tend to be much more uncomfortable. Almost all of them are high achievers. When they go to a sales meeting, they expect to sell something—or at least get an opportunity to write a proposal. That's what great rainmakers do, isn't it? But the truth is, this rarely happens when you initiate contact because the client or prospect rarely recognizes a need. Otherwise, they would already have taken some action to start the process.

This is undoubtedly the single biggest difference between responding to leads and initiating contact. Failure to understand this difference has caused tremendous frustration and disappointment for many professionals with whom I have worked. For this reason, when initiating contact in Quadrants Three and Four, professionals should set more realistic goals for the meeting. Here are some examples of reasonable goals:

■ Building a relationship

■ Understanding the client or prospect's business or company

■ Learning more about issues the client or prospect is facing

■ Understanding the buying process, including who the players are

■ Building awareness of firm resources that may be of use to the client

■ Obtaining advice on the best way to approach working together

Similarly, you should be ready to conclude Stage Two meetings with next steps that advance your cause rather than lead directly to work. Here are some examples of next steps:

■ Meeting someone else in the prospect or client's organization

■ Introducing someone from your firm to the prospect or client's organization

■ Introducing a third party who might be able to assist the contact in some way

■ Meeting at a firm seminar

■ Attending a trade association meeting together

■ Participating in a social or sports activity

The need to set realistic goals in Stage Two meetings is one reason I've advised many, many clients to go into an initial meeting with a prospect with no more than one or two other professionals. It's difficult to build chemistry with a large group—for example, a three-on-one or three-on-two meeting—and limits your options when it comes to establishing next steps. You're better off building some chemistry first and introducing, say, a functional expert to the prospect at a second meeting, when you're sure that the expert is in an area of interest.

Writing proposals for an unqualified lead—that is, someone who doesn't recognize a need—is a major pitfall that results from setting expectations too high when in Initiate mode. I've seen attorneys, accountants, insurance brokers, and investment bankers all fall prey to this trap, costing them time and effort—and usually reducing their chances of getting work in the long run. They want and expect something to happen when they initiate contact with a high-profile prospect and mistake a request for a proposal for sincere interest.

One of my favorite stories came in a workshop for a law firm. The former general counsel for a Fortune 100 company was in the session because he had joined my client in an of-counsel position. He was often asked by people in his company to meet with their friends or business colleagues. He told our group that he had developed a tried-and-true tactic to get rid of people he felt were selling to him—that is, people who were all about telling him why their firm was great as opposed to focusing on better understanding him, the way his department worked, and so on. He would simply ask them to write a proposal for him and the company about all the things they were promoting. They would leave the office with a smile on their face, thinking they really had an opportunity to work with the company. But the proposal they sent would almost never be opened. They forgot one of the most fundamental rules of the SalesGame: Jumping over Stages One, Two, and Three and heading straight to Four is rarely a formula for success. When initiating, establish next steps to keep the process moving, but don't try to go too far too fast. Otherwise, you'll find yourself writing meaningless proposals.

Why Initiate at All?

Given the greater comfort level when operating in Quadrants One and Two, many professionals could probably meet their chargeable hour goals without ever proactively going after clients. But while the comfort level and ease of responding to incoming leads is greater, there is a downside to building your practice only by responding to leads: If you operate exclusively in Quadrants One and Two, you allow your client or prospect to create your practice.

I have talked with many attorneys and accountants who did not enjoy life because they did not like the routine nature of the work they were doing. They were meeting or exceeding their chargeable hour goals. They were following the golden rule of business development: Do good work. But unfortunately, this got them more of the same kind of work they no longer enjoyed. They needed to do a little less actual work and invest more time in building the practice of their dreams! This is an even bigger problem for professionals who are kept busy by senior partners or directors in their firm.

They may stay busy, but they won't have the control and satisfaction that comes from building your own book of business. In this day and age, operating only in Respond mode is not enough if you want to build the practice of your dreams.

Nonetheless, professionals tend to handle many more opportunities in Respond mode than in Initiate mode. In my experience, prospect- or client-initiated calls make up 60 to 90% of opportunities. (This statistic would change dramatically if you looked at certain types of professionals. For example, some consultants probably initiate contact much closer to 60 to 70% of the time.) This makes sense if you remember how most professionals have traditionally marketed themselves—by staying in touch with clients, attending professional association meetings, giving speeches, networking, sending out e-bulletins, and so on. These activities are, of course, aimed at making the phone ring or getting an inbound e-mail request. Given the preponderance of leads that start with the client or prospect calling the professional, we'll start by looking at the best practices for handling Stage Two leads in Quadrant One.

> Operating only in Respond mode is not enough if you want to build the practice of your dreams.

Best Practices for Quadrant One: Responding to Prospects

The easiest way to discuss best practices for setting up the game in Quadrant One of the sales matrix is to consider one of the more difficult scenarios: the phone call or e-mail that comes in out of the blue. For example, suppose someone contacts you as a result of an Internet search. If you can handle this situation effectively, then responding to requests for assistance from friends, relatives, or other familiar individuals should be fairly easy. There are four best practices that will increase your effectiveness in these situations:

- Respond quickly.

- Get the right information.

- Go for a creative close.

- Build relationships first.

Of course, following these best practices will not guarantee that you'll win the game, but it will increase the chances of success and give you the satisfaction of knowing you've played the game well.

Respond Quickly

Although this best practice should be fairly obvious, many professionals botch it up. This is because they fail to understand what's *really* going on when a prospect calls. To clarify: When a prospect contacts you out of the blue, that person is trying to choose the right professional to assist him or her with a problem. If you respond quickly, it does not mean that everything will happen right away. But you should make that first contact as soon as possible, for two reasons:

- To determine whether this is an opportunity that is consistent with the services and solutions that you deliver

- To increase your chances of success in gaining an enthusiastic client

I once had a conversation with an attorney who had received an RFP from a $300 million company seeking a firm to coordinate its labor litigation on a national basis. Although the RFP had come in two weeks prior, no one had contacted the prospect to this point. When I asked why, he said that the due date for submitting the proposal was almost two weeks away, and he was "confident we'll be able to meet that deadline."

Let's think about this a moment. Suppose you are the lead in-house counsel at a $300 million company. You are looking for a firm to coordinate your labor litigation across the country, so you send out RFPs to two firms. One of the firms calls you right after receiving the RFP, thanks you for giving them the opportunity to submit a proposal, and asks a few questions about the situation. They even make an appointment to meet with you and others in your company to gather more information. In the end, you receive the proposal from this firm several days before the deadline after having reviewed a draft of it a few days before that. In contrast, the second firm calls two or three weeks later. If they want to meet with you, they have to squeeze it in the week before the proposal is due. They meet the deadline for the proposal, but just barely—the proposal is dropped off late in the afternoon on the appointed day. (Trust me...I've seen this happen many, many times!)

When deciding who will coordinate your company's labor litigation, you probably want a firm that is going to be responsive, stay on top of situations, and avoid creating headaches with last-minute emergencies. Given that, of the two firms I just described, who would you hire? Would you hire the firm that demonstrates that it is on top of things by the way it handles the proposal? Or would you choose the one that demonstrates it can meet deadlines...but just barely? (This is not a very hard question, is it?)

Whether responding to an e-mail, a Web site inquiry, a written RFP, or someone who's left a voicemail message on your phone, responding quickly works because:

■ It is common courtesy to say thank you for reaching out.

■ It makes a good first impression.

■ It gives you a head start on building a relationship with the prospect.

■ It gives you more time and therefore more flexibility to react to the opportunity—for example, contacting a referral source or meeting different players at the prospect's organization.

Tip

Young law firm associates and accounting firm managers have told me that they did not respond to a request received by a partner because the partner was away on business or holiday and couldn't be reached. I say, how about a little initiative here? Talk to another partner, take a chance and make the call yourself...do something! It's better that someone respond even if only to say thank you and to make the prospect aware of the partner's expected return date.

Get the Right Information

Again, let's assume you are responding to an e-mail, Web site inquiry, letter, or phone call that came out of the blue. That is, you don't know anyone at the organization making the inquiry—a situation I like to call a *blind request for services*. Table 12.1 summarizes the information you need to obtain on an initial call when responding to such an opportunity.

Table 12.1 Getting the Right Information		
What You Want to Learn	**Why It Is Important**	**Sample Script/Questions**
Who is calling?	Qualify the prospect by determining the size of the company, the number of employees, the number of of business locations, and so on.	"Tell me a little about your company."
		"What is your role in this process?"
	Qualify the person calling. Is he or she the decision-maker?	
		(continues...)

Table 12.1 Getting the Right Information (continued)		
What You Want to Learn	**Why It Is Important**	**Sample Script/Questions**
How did the prospect get you or your firm's name?	Establish how the prospect got to you—for example, was a referral source or some marketing effort on on your part involved?	"How did you get my name or the firm's name for this project?" "What led you to me/ the firm?"
What is the prospect trying to accomplish?	Find out the nature of the problem or opportunity— in other words, what led to the call.	"At the end of the day, what is it you would most like to accomplish with this project?"
What is the time frame?	Establish how quickly you need to set up a next step to follow first contact.	"What's your timing on this project?"
What is the next step?	Set up the rules of the game and establish what the prospect would like to accomplish as a result of the next step.	"When we get together or talk next, what would you like to get out of the discussion?" "What would you like to accomplish when we talk next?"

In the days before e-mails, voicemails, and caller ID, professionals had to jump into sales mode the second they answered the phone. These days, you will usually have a chance to prepare for a conversation before diving in. Even without the element of surprise, however, it would be advisable to keep Table 12.1 handy so you can refer to it before you pick up the phone to actually talk with a prospect. It will help you remember to get the basics before going further in the process—and thereby avoid that uncomfortable feeling when the call is over and you remember something you wish you would have asked. (Of course, some prospects may not need much prompting—that is, you'll be able to obtain the information you need without asking too many questions.)

Who Is Calling?

Simply said, you need to ask this question to qualify the importance of the prospect and determine how much time to invest in the opportunity.

Should you spend hours on research or simply call another professional who may be more suited to handle the needs of a particular prospect? You can use this information to make a go/no-go decision. Although it's important to bring in new business, sometimes the best course of action is to pass up an opportunity because it does not fit. Of course, we all know this—but it is still one of the hardest lessons to remember.

You should consider who is calling in terms of the person as well as the company. Is the caller the decision-maker or simply a functionary setting up a meeting? Of course, you can't just come out and ask someone whether he or she is the decision-maker. That would be pretty rude. A better way to get this information is to ask the person making the inquiry about his or her role in the process. The prospect will usually say enough in response for you to better understand how important his or her voice will be in the decision-making process. If the person making the contact is not the decision-maker, you must find a way to get to that player. This might require first meeting with the person making the initial contact, but at least that way, you will be able to plan the first contact with the player appropriately. That is, the next step should be clear.

How Did the Prospect Get Your or the Firm's Name?

In this competitive environment, most professionals spend a good deal of time on marketing efforts—giving speeches, networking, attending trade association meetings, or entertaining clients. Substantial sums of money are also spent on Web sites, direct mail, and social media campaigns.

> **Note**
>
> Many professionals say that giving speeches never seems to generate leads. But I've received incoming requests from prospects as a result of hearing me give a speech two, three, or even five years ago!

To generate more new leads, professionals should find out how current leads were generated. It's both informative and fun to see what's paying off—that is, what's generating inquiries. Playing the SalesGame without this kind of information clearly places you at a disadvantage. Establishing how the prospect found you—especially if it was through a referral source—is essential to setting up the game in a way that maximizes your chances for success.

Tip

If you are lucky enough to receive a referral from a contact, placing a follow-up call to that contact to say thank you and to learn more about the lead is key. You could spend hours researching a prospect and still not get the kind of qualitative information generated by a 10-minute phone call with the referral source.

What Is the Prospect Trying to Accomplish?

As mentioned, one of the most important challenges that professionals face in Respond mode is converting inquiries about service and cost into conversations about goals and value. This starts in the first dialogue with a prospect. Professionals need to find the Heart of the Matter—what's keeping the prospect up at night. The mistake most professionals make is they allow the prospect to focus on the service instead of the desired results.

Finding out what the prospect wants to accomplish is especially important in formal proposal situations that are often viewed as routine—for example, when a bank or government agency solicits bids. I have often been involved in opportunities like this and have routinely heard professionals guess at what the prospect is after. It is far easier to simply ask in the initial contact, "Why are you going through the proposal process in the first place?" You have to find out what the client wants to accomplish as a result of using a service at some point in the sales process. Why not ask on the front end of the opportunity? It could save a whole lot of time on both sides of the table.

> You have to find out what the client wants to accomplish as a result of using a service at some point in the sales process. Why not ask on the front end of the opportunity?

Of course, the prospect may not be able to give a precise answer to this question early in the process. This is because often, the prospect doesn't really know what they want. Finding out how clear the prospect is about their own goals is of value both to you and to the prospect. You can use this information to qualify the lead. In other words, do your services truly provide an opportunity or a solution to the prospect's problem? The prospect benefits from an early discussion of their goals so they focus on what they are actually trying to achieve and don't waste time pursuing options that will end up being dead ends. Starting this dialogue early in the process is truly a win-win.

I worked with a Big Four firm in China whose senior partner, Wong, was a born rainmaker. His firm received an RFP from a major Chinese bank to do a financial audit of five of their branches. Wong had a relationship with one of the members of the board of directors and asked him what value they were trying to get out of auditing such a small number of their hundreds of branches. After a dialogue, it became clear to both the senior partner and board member that the driving force behind the request was a desire to "westernize" the bank in view of the approach of membership in the world market. The firm changed its service to an operations review of bank headquarters—a project several times more expensive—and was rewarded with the engagement. I have often wondered how much time the other Big Four firms spent writing proposals for the wrong service.

Finding out what the client wants to accomplish is important in less formal situations as well. I knew an attorney who once spent an hour and half driving from downtown Los Angeles to Anaheim to talk about an "anti-trust" matter—his area of specialty—only to find out that the dispute was in fact between two family members over money that one had borrowed from another. Certainly this is an extreme example, and one that isn't as likely to happen today given our ability to google almost anything and learn about the company or person making the inquiry. But the point is clear: Time is valuable, so make sure you get the right information to make an intelligent decision about whether you want to pursue the opportunity.

> Time is valuable, so make sure you get the right information to make an intelligent decision about whether you want to pursue the opportunity.

What Is the Time Frame?

I often ask workshop participants to identify what they think is the "essential" information to obtain in their initial contact with a prospect. At least half of the time, no one in a group of 10 or 15 participants suggests finding out the time frame. One accountant even argued that he never asks this question. He explained that he likes to meet with the prospect as soon as possible, regardless of time frame, to demonstrate his interest.

Demonstrating your interest is admirable, but as we all know from dealing with high-pressure salesmen, someone who appears to be rushing you can push you in the opposite direction. When prospects are looking for someone to handle something like ownership transition, they may prefer to move slowly. In such a case, appearing to move too quickly can have a very negative effect. Besides, you need the answer to understand the prospect's time frame so you know where to place the next step on your priority list.

Establishing a time frame might also be the key to both getting the work and having a happy client. Anthony, a labor lawyer in Grand Rapids, told me about an opportunity that was "thrown" at him during a softball game one beautiful summer evening. As the game was winding down, one of his team members mentioned that he had a problem. The friend was an operations officer at a local company, and they were having some union problems. When Anthony asked about time frame, he found out that the National Labor Relations Board was visiting the company the next day for a preliminary investigation. Anthony invited the friend back to his home, where they spent the next several hours over a few beers preparing for the NLRB's visit. I don't know what kind of a softball player Anthony was, but he played the SalesGame very well. He ended up with a happy client who slept better that night—all because he knew how to get the right information in the initial contact.

What Is the Next Step?

Finding out what the prospect wants to do next presents a great opportunity for you to differentiate yourself. Most prospects are not experienced at buying professional services. A senior partner in a Salt Lake City accounting firm, Harvey, received a phone call from a small but fairly well-known high-tech company. Harvey told me the company was on the office target list, although no one had actually spoken to them. It is hard to win the game when you don't step up to the plate! The person calling was a controller type and said the company was growing and searching for a national audit firm to help them along their journey. A meeting time was set.

Armed with information about the controller with whom he had spoken and about the company as a whole, Harvey arrived at the appointed time. He was pleased that the receptionist seemed to know who he was and that he had an appointment. She told him that the people with whom he was to meet were expecting him but were currently in another meeting down the hall and asked him to have a seat in the lobby for a few minutes. He waited and, sure enough, people began to emerge from a door down the hall. To Harvey's surprise, the group included two partners from another firm.

When it was Harvey's turn to enter the room, he saw not just the controller who called him but three other executives, who turned out to be the principal owners of the company. Needless to say, the good feeling he'd had only a few minutes before quickly evaporated. If he had known there would be multiple executives attending the meeting, he would have researched their backgrounds as well as that of the controller. And he probably would have invited one of his colleagues along to balance the conversation. That way, one of them could listen while the other was asking questions.

How did this happen? Of course, I can't be sure. But I think Harvey's competitors did a better job of getting the right information—in other words, of setting up the game. One of two scenarios likely occurred. In the first scenario, during the initial contact, the competitors asked the prospect what they wanted to do at the first meeting—that is, they asked about the next step. The prospect probably said something like, "Why don't you come over with a couple of your partners and we'll have a meet and greet with the owners?" In this scenario, the competitors found out the rules by which the game was to be played. Based on my experience, however, I suspect that a second, different scenario occurred. When asked what they wanted to do at the first meeting, the controller likely said something like, "We didn't have a specific agenda in mind." The competitors then asked who would be involved in the process and suggested those players attend the meeting. Once the competitors knew the numbers on the prospect side of the table, they were better able to decide who to take from their own firm. Regardless of which scenario transpired (or whether it was a different one altogether), the competitors clearly gave themselves a competitive advantage over Harvey by getting the critical information in their first call with the prospect.

For the record, I would have recommended starting with a one-on-one meeting with the controller as a first step. This would have enabled the professional to get the lay of the land and to try to develop a coach before meeting the owners. But the issue here isn't whether the next step was ideal. Rather, the issue is whether you should use the initial contact to try to create a competitive advantage by finding out what's planned or suggesting a next step. At a minimum, you should use the initial call to avoid placing yourself at a competitive *dis*advantage, as happened to Harvey.

One last point: If at first you don't succeed in getting the right information from your contact, try and try again! I have taught workshops about this part of the sales process several times. Inevitably, participants begin thinking about meetings with prospects that they have arranged. The look in their eyes is unmistakable: Clearly, they are thinking about what they could or should have done differently. Often, participants will come up to me during a break and confess what they forgot to ask in the initial phone call. My advice is usually to give the prospect a call back to confirm the meeting and use the occasion to fill in any blanks that may not have been addressed in the first contact.

Casey, a managing partner of his firm's New York office, took this advice to heart. He called the lead in-house counsel of a bank with whom he had an appointment set up for the following week. The counsel was not in when Casey called, but Casey had a very productive conversation with the counsel's secretary. When Casey asked to confirm the meeting, she told him that it was on her boss's agenda for 10 a.m. the following Tuesday as planned. She then volunteered that the counsel had another meeting booked for 10:30. Casey asked who from the bank was going to be at his meeting with the counsel and learned that the counsel was going to meet with him alone because his assistant was on holiday.

Casey handled the phone call like a pro. You could see the look of relief in his eyes as he realized he had just avoided a major *faux pas*. He had been planning to bring three other attorneys from his firm to the meeting to impress the counsel with their depth. But you don't have to have played the SalesGame for long to know that a four-on-one meeting that lasts 30 minutes is not a good idea. The prospect would likely be overwhelmed, and the meeting would probably become more of a presentation than a discussion. That means that very little chemistry can be built. Casey's strategy and expectations for the meeting changed dramatically based on the short phone call with the secretary. He set up the game much better—and could do a much better job of preparing—when he called back and got the right information.

Go for a Creative Close

So much of what's been said in this part involves getting a head start on the competition—finding some way to be different. In the example from Salt Lake City, Harvey was put at a disadvantage by his competitors, who did a better job setting up the next step. It is amazing how many times the game is won because of the tone set in the early going. Professionals who play the SalesGame need to take advantage of every opportunity to differentiate themselves—to find a next step that is creative and does not just follow routine procedures.

By comparison, consider the moves made by Carter, a Denver lawyer whose firm received an RFP from a New York–based multinational consortium looking for legal assistance to build a dam in Wyoming. The RFP itself was almost half an inch thick. The firm had about six months to write the proposal, which was supposed to include an almost endless list of information regarding size, qualifications, and so on. The law firm had no insider contacts but was invited along with another large firm in Denver because of their location in the mountain states area. In addition, three other big-name New York firms appeared at the bottom of the RFP's transmittal letter as competitors.

Carter followed the first tip for setting up the game: He responded quickly to the RFP by calling the person whose name was on the transmittal letter. Unfortunately, according to the prospect's secretary, he was "out of town." Carter asked if he should leave a message or follow up later. The secretary volunteered that the prospect was in fact in Wyoming for a few days, getting a look at the dam site with several other executives from the consortium. Carter got creative in a hurry, the same way a great running back creates his own holes in the line. He asked the secretary if she knew the travel itinerary. He was informed that the prospect was planning to stay overnight in Denver the evening after next while *en route* from Wyoming to New York. Carter asked if the secretary could check to see whether the prospect might be willing to have dinner at the Brown Palace while in Denver. She did, and the dinner was arranged. During his conversations with the secretary, Carter also learned the names of the other two executives who would be in attendance and picked a colleague from his firm to join them at dinner.

Next, Carter called the firm's Wyoming office to get a rough map drawn up of the area, which he had printed in color. At an appropriate time during the dinner, Carter pulled out the map. Suddenly, his prospects became very animated, recalling their journey of the last couple days. They were particularly interested in an elk path that wandered through the area and actually started drawing it on the map. This was clearly an area of great concern in this age of wildlife conservation. The dinner ended with a time established for a conference call with the firm's resident expert on such matters. Within a few weeks, the engagement was secured, and the meter was running without a proposal ever being written. All I could think when I heard this story was that the other firms who received the RFP who were still grinding out the proposal, hour after grueling hour, page after grueling page, not even knowing they had already lost the game!

For those accountants who are saying, "Being a lawyer for a company building a dam is a lot different from doing an audit. How creative can you be when you're going after audit work?" The answer is that it does not take that much to be different. I worked with a large local firm that was asked to propose on an audit for a regional, multicounty transportation authority. As is the case with so many governmental proposal situations, the RFP limited the amount of contact that vendors could have with the prospect before writing the proposal. In fact, the only face-to-face contact was supposed to be at a bidders' conference—a setting with all the ambience and opportunity of a pool full of sharks. Nevertheless, Anita, who was assigned the task of handling the proposal, called the person who signed the transmittal letter and proceeded to get the right information. In the conversation, Anita learned the transportation authority was breaking away from a regional planning group and was setting up its own operations, including a new computer system that already had been purchased. In closing, Anita asked if she could meet with the person who was in charge of the new computer—a fairly low-level administrative type, as it turned out—before the bidders' conference because computers were obviously going to be part of any financial recordkeeping system. Her request was granted. Anita met with the computer jockey, who was feeling overwhelmed by his responsibilities and loved sharing his frustrations with Anita. She obtained lots of valuable information, including long-term plans of the authority and the politics of the board. Anita's firm won the engagement easily. Of course, Anita might not have been granted permission to meet with the computer jockey, in which case this story would not have had such a happy ending. But at least she tried to get a creative close. Even if she had failed, she would have had the peace of mind that comes from knowing she played the game as well as possible.

Build Relationships First

In the first edition of this book, the fourth best practice when handling an initial contact with a prospect was to keep that first contact short. This was much more important 10 or more years ago than it is now. That's because it was common for professionals to get telephone inquiries from unknown callers about their services. Because most professionals did not handle these calls very often as an experienced salesperson would, keeping the first contact short was important so they could get off the phone and plan their strategy moving forward. Today, however, technology has virtually eliminated phone inquiries from unknown callers. As a result, there is almost always time to plan a call in response to an e-mail, written request, Web site inquiry, or voicemail message. Here, the best practice is to take your time and use the first contact to set up the game, not to finish it.

> Use the first contact to set up the game, not to finish it!

Note

If you still take calls from unknown prospects, keeping the first contact short remains a good idea. It doesn't work in all situations, however. I have listened to many stories from attorneys and accountants describing situations when the entire "sale" happened in one call—for example, when an accounting prospect needed to meet a tax deadline or an out-of-state attorney needed specific representation for one of his clients.

Today, the bigger problem is remembering that, as discussed in Part 1, "An Overview of the SalesGame," you can't jump into the SalesGame at Stage Three. It's true that when someone contacts you about a service, it's fair to assume that there is a recognized need and probably a qualified lead. Nevertheless, you can't skip Stages One and Two and start getting into the details of the service. You need to build some chemistry with the person making the inquiry as part of the initial contact. If you can't, it's unlikely that the person calling will ever become the client of your dreams.

One of my own experiences provides a great illustration of how important this best practice can be. While I was on vacation in Hawaii, I received an e-mail from a prospect law firm from Chicago asking if I was interested in talking to them about business development. Even though there was a significant time difference and I wasn't crazy about working on my vacation, I followed the first best practice, respond quickly, and promptly replied to the e-mail to establish a time for a phone conversation.

I noticed in the initial e-mail that the prospect mentioned he had some "Michigan connections." When I did some quick research to prepare for the call—a Google search and a search on LinkedIn, I didn't see anything that linked the prospect to Michigan. So when we connected via phone, I made sure to start the conversation by asking about it. That was the start of a 30-minute conversation about him, his brothers, his wife (who was from Michigan, where he frequently visits), and so on. We both enjoyed the conversation, and I felt like we really made a connection before we got into the background leading to the request—a feeling that was validated by the fact that I obtained the engagement.

Later, at an informal lunch during the engagement, I was sitting with the managing partner and my contact at the firm. The managing partner was very complimentary and then asked my contact why he chose me. My contact thought about it a minute and then said, "Well, you know, I interviewed three other candidates for this project, but Larry was the only one who took the time to ask about me." Finding out about my contact's "Michigan connections" turned out to be not only enjoyable, but also a very effective way to differentiate myself. The bottom line is that prospects are people before they are clients. It's always a best practice to invest a little time building some chemistry.

> Prospects are people before they are clients.

Responding to Prospects You Already Know

The best practices in this chapter still apply when you respond to prospects you already know—for example, a business acquaintance or even an old friend. Common courtesy tells you to respond quickly. Setting up a creative close and keeping the first contact short is obviously not as important, although you should keep both points in mind. Your biggest pitfall is in gathering the right information, especially when it comes to finding out what your prospect wants to accomplish. Often, you will be so eager to provide assistance to someone you know and like, you may forget to slow down the process long enough to reach an agreement and manage expectations—that is, to convert your conversation about service and cost to one about goals and value.

One other word of advice should be given when it comes to handling opportunities with friends or social or civic contacts. The first contact with these individuals usually does not happen in a business setting. For example, a comment might be made on the golf course, at a party or dinner, or even walking out of church. You must remember that one of the best practices in Stage One is to avoid selling. Because of interruptions and distractions, selling at the country club or church simply does not work very well. In these situations, you should get the right information (remember Anthony, our softball player) and establish a next step that takes place in a business setting.

On a related note, going too far, too fast when a friend first mentions a problem can backfire. Dominic, who is an attorney, told me about a discussion he had when walking down the hall of a Holiday Inn one Sunday morning with the father of another member of his son's hockey team. This man was the CEO of a medium-sized manufacturing company. He mentioned a problem he was having with the Environmental Protection Agency, which was Dominic's specialty. Dominic began to talk about the regulation at issue and likely slid into legalese. One thing was certain: He got into more depth at the first contact than the CEO wanted, given the setting. How do we know this? Because after about a minute of talking about the regulation, Dominic looked up, only to see that the CEO had come to a complete stop several feet behind him, a look of confusion on his face. He wanted help, but he did not want a complex lecture at 9 a.m. on a Sunday while on his way to see his son play hockey. Dominic quit talking, apologized for getting too technical, and did what he should have done in the first place: He set up the game by asking to meet the following week. After that episode, the CEO couldn't be reached. Worse, their relationship was never the same because Dominic sensed the CEO was avoiding him. From then on, there was an air of tension between them.

Many professionals struggle with how much advice they should give in a social context. Using the initial contact to set up the game is a good way to differentiate between what is (free) advice from a friend and what is (valuable) professional advice from a well-trained expert. Something happens when the setting changes from a social environment to a business one. The prospect or friend seems to recognize that the professional is taking valuable time out of his or her day to discuss a particular problem. The professional also tends to take the discussion more seriously and usually will do some preparation for the meeting. If the friend is unwilling to meet outside the social context to discuss the problem, the professional should take this as a clue that the problem is not serious enough to warrant his or her assistance.

Does this mean that you should not give free advice to friends? Of course not. But you should recognize that free advice is usually viewed as having a similar value. The major point to remember is that when an opportunity presents itself in the form of a friend or social contact asking for advice or assistance, it is a form of initial contact just like receiving an RFP. Your job is to use this contact to set up the game as well as possible. Get the right information and go for a next step—a close, as we have been using the term—that meets everyone's needs and time frame. If the next step changes the setting from social to business, your chances of winning the game and ending up with an enthusiastic client who actually pays fees should increase substantially.

Best Practices for Quadrant Two:
Responding to Clients

Chapter 12, "Best Practices for Quadrant One: Responding to Prospects," summarizes the most effective way to set up the game with a lead that comes from a prospect. It is easier to set up the game when a current or past client calls you with a request for additional assistance. For the most part, two of the same four points discussed in the previous chapter are the most important in this scenario:

- Respond quickly.

- Get the right information.

The biggest difference is that the "build relationships first" rule does not apply. That's because you already know the person making the request. There are, of course, some exceptions to this, such as when there is a new decision-maker at a client organization. In this case, the best practice of getting to know the new person—even if the client itself is well-known—is every bit as important as when a prospect calls out of the blue. An even better practice would be to initiate contact with a new player in a client organization *before* a request for service is made. That way, you can build the relationship more comfortably, without the pressure of dealing with an immediate need. Reaching out to a new decision-maker to establish the relationship and his or her criteria for outstanding service in a sort of combined Stage Six/Stage Three meeting would be highly recommended. Of course, there will be cases when this might not be easy to do—for example, a litigation client who only contacts a law firm every couple of years and might have made some relevant changes in personnel in the interim.

Responding Quickly and Getting the Right Information

Responding quickly is always a good idea, regardless of whether the person requesting assistance is a client or a prospect. Being slow in any circumstance sends the wrong message—specifically, the message that the prospect or client is not important enough to warrant a quick response. If anything, the bar has been raised for responding quickly since the first edition of this book was published. Measuring response time in terms of hours, not days, has become the standard in the electronic age. As mentioned in the previous chapter, responding quickly doesn't mean you have to deliver a solution. You only need to acknowledge that the message has been received and establish a time to talk "live" so it can be explored.

> **Note**
>
> I've noticed many younger professionals using e-mail or texting as a substitute for a telephone or face-to-face discussion. Even when a client you know well requests a service, e-mail or texting is almost never an effective way to qualify the opportunity (Stage Two) or shape the service (Stage Three).

Getting the right information is less difficult when dealing with clients or friends because you already know the answer to two questions—who is calling and how they got your name. Plus, all of us are more comfortable talking to someone we already know. Of course, you must still learn what your client is trying to accomplish in order to provide sound advice. For example, I've had a number of situations over the years in which a client has contacted me to conduct a training program that wasn't really in my sweet spot. Learning this early in the process saves everyone time and gains the respect of the client. (I've also had multiple occasions when saying no to one opportunity was the primary reason I generated other, more appropriate and more profitable opportunities.)

Learning the client's time frame, desired deliverables, staffing, and cost should all be explored on a routine basis to make sure expectations are met and that you achieve your goal of ending up with an enthusiastic client when the work is done. This dialogue is clearly part of a Stage Three discussion. One of the most important best practices in Stage Three is to meet more and write less. This doesn't apply in a literal sense when a client requests an additional service, but it's still important to keep the concept in mind. In this quadrant, the best practice might be phrased as, "ask more and talk less." That is, the process may not require many meetings—in fact, it might happen in one conversation—but you want to slow down the process enough and ask the right questions to get the best information as early as possible.

Having a creative close isn't usually critical in Quadrant Two unless the opportunity involves a different kind of service than was previously delivered—for example, an IT project for what has traditionally been an accounting client or assistance in estate planning for what's historically been a wealth-management client. In these cases, your role is to gather the relevant information and then set up a meeting with an appropriate member of the firm.

Beware of the Easy Sale

Professionals usually do not associate Quadrant Two with business development. That is, they don't think of themselves as "selling." Rather, they see handling these requests as providing good client service. This often leads to them moving too quickly through the sales process. They assume—correctly, in most cases—that they are going to get the assignment and naturally want to seem responsive and helpful. They frequently accept the engagement, moving directly from Stage Two to Stage Five, without doing all they can to ensure they'll end up with an enthusiastic client.

As any good consultant will testify, you need to define the problem before you come up with a solution. Too many times, professionals assume they know what their clients want because they have worked with them before—for example, the attorney who does traditional lending work for a bank or the accountant who has done audits for the same client for several years. Often, these professionals will move directly to Stage Five—the final close—without bothering with Stages Two, Three, and Four to qualify the opportunity, shape the service, and make sure everyone is on the same page as to what's needed and how it is to be delivered.

It is an easy trap to fall into. In fact, I did just a few years ago while working with the New York City office of a regional law firm.

> Too many times, professionals assume they know what their clients want because they have worked with them before.

After consulting and conducting workshops for this firm for a number of years, the marketing director, Dave, and I had become good friends. So, when he called and said he wanted me to conduct a session for the Manhattan office, I was only too happy to oblige.

Dave was anxious to pick some dates. He had struggled for years trying to persuade this office to increase its marketing and sales efforts. Apparently, the office's managing partner had called Dave and wanted to "get something going right away." In the first contact, we focused on available dates instead of on what the true decision-maker—in this case, the office's managing partner—really wanted to accomplish. By the time I talked to the managing partner, long after the dates were in the calendar, he had already invited 35 participants to a session that should have had 15 at most. Worse, these 35 participants had backgrounds ranging from summer interns to senior litigators. I can still feel the sense of frustration as I tried to meet the needs of a group that was too large and diverse. Interaction between participants was minimal. Feedback after the session confirmed what I had suspected: My presentation seemed "wooden." Some participants felt we spent too much time on networking, while others said we did not spend enough time on that area. You get the picture. As I endured one of the most unpleasant sessions of my career, the words of the managing partner of a regional accounting firm I'd met at one of my other (more successful) workshops kept ringing in my ears: "Never let your client hurry you into a relationship!"

Fortunately, Dave and I remain friends, and I worked with the firm for several more years. But the fact remained that I did not play the SalesGame very well with this Stage Two/Quadrant Two lead. Because Dave was anxious to move ahead, I did not set the game up correctly in the first contact by arranging the right next step—in this case, a phone call with the decision-maker. I should have ended that first call with Dave by giving some tentative dates, to be confirmed after I had a chance to talk with the managing partner. I had temporarily forgotten that a professional does not win the SalesGame by getting the work. A professional wins by ending up with an enthusiastic client! Needless to say, I did not win in this situation because I failed to set the game up properly.

This doesn't mean there have to be multiple meetings to follow the business-development process when a client requests additional work. A lot of the time—if not the majority of the time—you can go from Stage Two to Stage Five in one conversation if there's a good working relationship already in place. Still, it's important that you not skip any steps along the way. The important point is to keep the six-stage process in mind as you speak with the client.

One of my favorite examples of jumping from Stage Two to Stage Five the *wrong* way—one that seems to resonate with workshop participants—is a story I mentioned in Chapter 7, "Stage Four: Trial Close," about a simple request I made to an accounting firm. I had received an unsolicited offer to sell a piece of real estate. The first call I made was to my accounting firm to ask what the tax ramifications of the sale might be. My contact at the accounting firm failed to ask the right questions, however. She simply said she could and would handle this matter for me. Two days passed, then three. The person who made the offer called me and said he was looking at other parcels and was anxious to hear my reaction to the offer. I called the accountant again, but only got her voicemail. Soon, I received a three-page letter, single spaced. It was full of accounting lingo, but it did not include an estimate of what I would owe the IRS if I sold the property.

> The important point is to keep the six-stage process in mind as you speak with the client.

All the accountant needed to do was ask a few questions to clarify the Heart of the Matter (in this case, how much I would need to pay the IRS if I decided to sell)—in other words, to qualify the need. Next, the accountant needed to shape the service (Stage Three) by asking about the expected time frame, cost, and, most importantly, deliverable (in this case, a simple phone call to convey the number). No lengthy and costly in-depth analysis was required! Then, the accountant should have extended the process by repeating back what she heard me say to make sure we were on the same page (Stage Four). Needless to say, I was not enthusiastic. In the end, the accountant did not achieve her goal, even though she did get the work.

Tip

Younger professionals can gain valuable experience long before they talk with prospects or even clients by using the six-stage process when fielding requests from a partner. For example, when a partner asks an associate to research a topic or a manager asks a staff member to analyze some data, the associate or staff person can use the six-stage process to make sure he or she ends up with an enthusiastic client (albeit an internal one). After all, who better to make enthusiastic users of your services than those who control your long-term destiny?

Best Practices for Quadrant Three: Initiating Contact with Clients

I f professionals operate only in Respond mode during Stage Two, they are less likely to generate the rewards they desire—money, personal satisfaction, leverage potential, etc. Although there may be some professionals whose inbox is always full of new requests for satisfying, profitable work, most of us need to at least occasionally initiate contact in Stage Two to build the practice of our dreams. For example, I love working in Europe because I enjoy the people and the culture, and because I always gain a different perspective. I've worked in one country or another every year since 1978, largely because I've continued to initiate contact with clients and related prospects. If I hadn't done that, I doubt I would have had many of the experiences that have enriched my practice and my life.

Clients: A Natural Starting Place to Initiate Contact

Successful professionals in any field almost always recognize the value of investing time with clients. The more face time you spend with a client, the more opportunities you will get to serve these clients. Initiating contact with clients is almost always easier than initiating contact with prospects for two reasons. First, you have many natural opportunities to initiate discussions about new work as you carry out current engagements with your clients. Second, you already have an established relationship with clients. This relationship is hopefully built on both trust and the knowledge that you can deliver valued services. That is, you have a track record. From a business-development perspective, these two factors are also two very important selling points—that is, positive Scorecard Factors (explained in Part 3, "The Scorecard: Add Value, Differentiate Your Service, and Build Strategy")—which is a major reason that a higher percentage of these opportunities come to fruition.

Cross-selling to clients—going after the "low-hanging fruit," as it's often called—has long been emphasized as a good starting point to build a good practice. In law firms, for example, a common avenue of growth is to respond to a lead from a prospect, do the work, assure enthusiasm (don't forget Stage Six!), and then initiate a discussion to explore other potential areas of need. In the last 10 years, however, I've come to prefer the term *cross-serving* to *cross-selling* because it better reflects the true value of initiating contact with clients from their perspective. Clients need and want to know how their professional advisors can help them with issues they may or may not be aware of or that might arise in the future. You should see initiating contact as a part of good service, not simply a way to generate more revenue.

Focus on Issues, Not Products

A common pitfall for most professionals is the tendency to talk about new services or products they want to sell instead of the issues on the mind of the client. One phrase that consultants use to describe this syndrome is to call a new product or service the "flavor of the month." Before 2000, the flavor of the month was Y2K assistance. After 2000, the Big Four firms in Europe pushed assisting with the conversion to the Euro. Most consultants who initiated contact with clients to discuss these "products" told them why they needed outside assistance but often failed to establish the dimension of the problem or what inside resources were available to address it. I interviewed many clients and prospects on the receiving end of this sort of sales pitch, and none were impressed. Whether they needed the service or not, they did not want to buy from someone who seemed to be telling them what they had to do. Today, some 15 years later, I see firms doing the same thing with issues like cybersecurity and wealth management.

Clients do not mind spending time talking with their accountants, lawyers, wealth managers, HR consultants, and IT consultants about the business and personal issues that are of interest to them. They benefit by receiving ideas, understanding trends, and being made aware of potential resources. By focusing on issues as opposed to products, you create value from the meeting itself. The vast majority of clients *want* you to invest time with them.

They get value out of discussing what's keeping them up at night with a trusted advisor. But they do not want to be sold any more than any of us do when our credit card company starts pushing travel insurance or hotel deals. If they feel this is happening, the value and communication goes away quickly. Hence the term *cross-serving*.

You should spend more time asking questions and less time talking about your products in Stage Two of the SalesGame. But of course, you need to provide useful information to balance the

> By focusing on issues as opposed to products, you create value from the meeting itself.

conversation. The odd thing is that many professionals operate under the assumption that the best way to prepare for a meeting to cross-sell is to increase product knowledge. For example, corporate attorneys think they need to be well versed in labor and employment services as a *prerequisite* for talking with a client about concerns related to human resources. Certainly, a minimal level of knowledge is required—for example, enough to set up a meeting with a labor and employment attorney. But they often fail to develop a list of questions to engage clients in a meaningful discussion of relevant business issues. Coincidentally, this belief that product knowledge is necessary when talking to clients about additional services is often a barrier to even having a discussion. Professionals fear setting up a meeting because they might be asked a question they won't be able to answer. That's too bad, since it's exactly those kinds of questions that open the door to setting up another meeting with someone who *does* know the answer.

Build Awareness of Resources

Of course, conversations with clients can't be a one-way street. Otherwise, you would never be able to inform clients of services that may address important needs. Most clients want to know what resources are out there to solve their problems. My favorite example is a very personal one. When I sold my research company several years ago, I was assisted by a long-time friend and accounting partner. Unfortunately, as he was helping me with the transaction, he failed to make me aware of his firm's investment management services. I ended up doing some pretty stupid things with the proceeds, like buying a radio station in Key West and some shaky aircraft funds. Fortunately, none of these bad decisions were catastrophic, and they were offset by other investments. But my wife and I did lose a lot of sleep wondering whether we were doing the right thing with our new-found wealth.

While I would not have wanted my friend to push me into using his firm's services, he could have initiated a discussion about my long-term goals and concerns. Somewhere in that discussion, he could have mentioned that his firm had a team of investment managers. In the lingo of the sales world, he might have made a *value statement* as part of his opening: "You know, Larry, we have a group of professionals in the firm who work with clients like you who've sold companies and made some money. They can save you a lot of time and worry!" Or, he might have asked some questions about my goals and concerns and then dropped some information about the service into the conversation. Remember, it is a game, and everyone plays it a little differently. For the record, I currently work with this investment management group and wish I would have known about them earlier.

Ironically, I recently worked with a firm whose core service is wealth management but also does tax-compliance work as well as estate planning. One of the partners told me about a client for whom he'd provided estate-planning services for years who asked if he could refer him to someone who could help him pull all his investments together into one comprehensive plan. Needless to say, the partner was amazed that his client wasn't aware of the core service his firm provided. The point is simple: Clients want to be aware of resources available to help them solve problems or take advantage of opportunities. You need some knowledge of the other services your firm offers. This can be a 30,000-foot understanding of what your colleagues do. However, it is at least equally as important to know the right questions to ask to engage clients in a discussion of the issues related to a service.

When you initiate contact with clients in Quadrant Three, they may not recognize a need for a particular service. That is, the client may not be a *qualified* lead but rather a *positioning* lead. In many cases, client awareness of resources turns into future business when a problem occurs or a need is recognized. Even when there is no need for a particular resource, by focusing on client issues and building awareness, you can create value for the client and may even get some creative ideas for new service areas. For example, a number of times over a period of years, my accounting friend *did* ask me questions about what my wife and I were doing to protect our wealth in case of death or illness. It wasn't until we were packing for a vacation in Hawaii and heard a story on CNN about a plane crash in which 300 tourists perished that I changed from a positioning lead to a qualified one. I called my accountant the next morning, before we left for Kona, to start the ball rolling on some estate planning. One of my colleagues calls this *facilitated self-discovery*—a very descriptive term that describes how the process of initiating contact with clients often works.

Best Practices for Quadrant Four: Initiating Contact with Prospects

In the minds of many professionals with whom I have worked, initiating contact with a prospect conjures up images of cold-calling, like the stockbrokers in the movie *Boiler Room*. But only a very small percentage (certainly less than 5%) of firms I have worked with do anything that could even remotely be considered to be cold-calling. Those that do usually use a special group of individuals who do this as a career, often called inside sales.

Recent studies have shown that even the impact of advertising has diminished because people are more and more skeptical of anyone pushing a product or a service. Consequently, more sophisticated approaches are being used to reach out to potential clients or customers—things like inbound marketing, discussed briefly later in this chapter. So there are still some things you can do to open the door with prospects you don't know. But more importantly, you can initiate contact with people you *do* know when considering this means of developing leads as well.

As a part of your overall lead generation, you need to incorporate both. What follows are some best practices to employ for leads who are unknown targets and leads who are known contacts.

Prospecting with Unknown Targets

Let's look at initiating contact with prospects, or *prospecting*, using the more difficult scenario first: initiating contact with a totally new prospect. When setting up the SalesGame with a prospect you don't already know, you'll want to keep these four points in mind:

- Choose the right situation.

- Sell the meeting, not the service.

- Be prepared for the first objection.

- Follow up, follow up, follow up!

Note

Prospecting has changed dramatically since the first publication of this book in 2004. Although only a little more than 10 years have passed, tools like e-mail, social media, and even texting—not to mention whatever's next—have become far more common ways to initiate a contact with a target company than phone calls or dropping by the office. Even voicemail has changed the game, as it's much, much harder to find someone who will answer their phone. I would like to make a disclaimer that I am not proficient at using these tools. I'm not on Facebook, and I use LinkedIn primarily to learn about those to whom I am talking, not to reach out to prospects. If you want to learn more about these tools, I suggest you consult with a specialist in that area.

Choose the Right Situation

Prospecting is something you should do only in unique situations, for three reasons:

- **Prospecting is expensive in terms of time.** Studies done in commercial banking found that setting up and making a single cold call can consume more than half a day.

- **The pay-off is relatively low.** This is particularly true in the short run. This is because you have no way of knowing beforehand whether the people you are calling on have any interest in buying.

- **If you engage in prospecting activities simply because you need more work, prospects often pick up a scent of desperation.** I have always found it is much easier to develop work when you're already busy.

So when *should* you engage in prospecting? Here are three of the most significant criteria:

■ The service is unique.

■ The prospect is part of a definable group that evaluates service providers on a routine basis.

■ You exhausted other avenues for initiating contact.

Scenario One: The Service Is Unique

My personal experience with prospecting stems mostly from the period during which my company (the Services Rating Organization) conducted syndicated market research primarily for accounting and law firms. My interviewers would talk to 500 or so people in one of 75 cities in the U.S. or Canada, asking about the 15 largest firms in their market area. After the data was analyzed, I would arrange meetings with the 15 firms to show them some of the results to qualify the leads—that is, to determine whether they were interested in purchasing the study. No one else had done syndicated research when I started the company in the early 1980s. My service was unique. As a result, I would routinely be able to arrange appointments with 12 or 13 of the 15 prospects and consummate sales with 70% of them.

On the other hand, I have used cold-calling techniques, such as dropping by a firm while in their city, to develop leads for my training services—something many people do even if they are not specialized in the professional service field. These efforts have never resulted in a paid engagement unless there was some form of relationship—for example, through a third party. Why the difference? Syndicated market research for professional service firms was unique in the 1980s, while sales training was not.

For an accountant to initiate contact with colleges or universities, using audit services as the entrée would probably not be a good use of time. On the other hand, I once worked with a Big Four firm that developed a package to assist colleges and universities in enhancing their ability to recoup more money from federal grant programs—something no one else was doing at the time. They were able to arrange meetings with almost all their significant prospects and ended up conducting engagements for many of them. Incidentally, after a few years, the Big Four firm was able to parlay several of these engagements to ongoing audit work.

Scenario Two: The Prospect Is Part of a Definable Group That Evaluates Service Providers on a Routine Basis

I once worked with a 30-person local firm that served a couple of small community banks. Tom, the young partner who handled these clients, loved working with them and saw a lot of potential in building this type of practice—not so much for audit services, but for the extra work the banks required in data processing, internal audit assistance, regulatory compliance, and so on. In fact, Tom's experience showed that the average community bank spent three times more on additional consulting services from its accounting firm than on the audit.

One year, Tom decided to start what he affectionately called the "Spring Road Trip." After the busy season, Tom and a manager drove around the state, calling on each community bank that fit certain size criteria. Tom found it was easy to identify these community banks and find who their officers were. The first year, they visited between 30 and 40 banks in a little over three weeks. The meetings were very easy to arrange because, according to Tom, "Bankers will talk to anyone!" The first year, the Spring Road Trip generated three qualified leads. Two of these three qualified leads were converted to clients.

The Spring Road Trip was so successful, Tom repeated it the next year and the year after that. This allowed Tom to develop relationships with many bankers over time. Due in no small part to these Spring Road Trips, Tom's bank now serves more community banks than anyone in the state. Tom doesn't make the Spring Road Trip anymore, however. He doesn't have to! Every bank knows his firm's name, and he works trade association meetings like a pro.

I have since seen two regional firms use this same approach with similar results. Initiating contact with municipalities, school districts, and even healthcare providers offers similar possibilities for professionals. I have also seen similar examples with attorneys. An attorney I know in the Northeast made a point of initiating contact with governmental entities that issued finance bonds. Insurance companies are another example of a definable group that routinely evaluates service providers. It is easy to determine which carriers or third-party insurance adjusters specialize in various kinds of cases. And their volume almost guarantees that they will occasionally have to try out new law firms because of capacity issues or conflicts of interest. Would this work as well with manufacturers or retailers? Probably not. These types of businesses are not in as limited or definable a group and do not evaluate service providers on a regular basis. That being said, certain companies may be good targets for prospecting for product liability work because they experience large volumes of cases—for example, a carpet or motorcycle manufacturer.

Scenario Three: You Have Exhausted Other Avenues for Initiating Contact

Initiating contact with prospects when no previous relationship exists is difficult and time consuming. Therefore, it should generally be used only as a last resort. First, you should try to initiate contact with clients or others they already know.

I work with many professionals who want to become more proactive at business development and think they should start prospecting. My first recommendation is that they go through their contact list and social media networks to see if any of their relationships already provide a more comfortable and productive way to initiate contact. In almost every case, following this advice generates an ample number of leads. If it doesn't work, professionals should see if colleagues might know someone from the organization they're targeting, ask their clients for advice, find appropriate trade groups or community activities, develop relationships with referral sources, and so on. Again, initiating contact with prospects where there is no previously existing relationship should be considered a last resort.

Sell the Meeting, Not the Service

One of the biggest problems professionals have when prospecting is that they see themselves as being too pushy or hard sell if they try to arrange a meeting with a prospect who has not requested assistance. I suggest you temper this perception by remembering these two points:

■ **You bring value to the table simply by meeting with prospects.** This is true even if you do not deliver a service. Benefits to the prospect include the formation of a relationship with someone who knows their function or industry; a sounding board or source of a second opinion for the present or future; ideas to run their lives or organization more effectively, profitably, with less worry, and so on; information about industry and competitor trends (limited by appropriate confidentiality); and knowledge of resources that might be useful in the long or short run. Whether sending an e-mail, making a phone call, or having a third party set up a meeting, you should communicate one or two of these benefits to the prospect. If these benefits are not enough to get you in the door, then it is probably not a lead worth chasing.

■ **Your goal is to establish a relationship with the prospect in a Stage Two meeting.** It is not to sell work. To do this, you'll spend a lot of time listening to the prospect, learning about him or her as a person first and as a business opportunity second. As one of the marketing directors for a major law firm put it, "Don't think of yourself as going out selling; think of yourself as going out listening!"

Any game is a lot more fun when you play it with realistic expectations. Similarly, you'll have more fun with the SalesGame if you understand that one measure of success (as any hard-core salesman

> "Don't think of yourself as going out selling; think of yourself as going out listening!"

could tell you) is simply getting an opportunity to talk with a prospect and build a relationship. You should keep score in Stage Two by the meetings you arrange and the relationships you build, not by the work that comes to you in the short run. I always say a professional had a very successful Stage Two meeting when initiating contact if he or she builds some chemistry and has any kind of next step—for example, if the professional agrees to check back in six months. Once a professional *does* arrange a Stage Two meeting, anything can happen. It's pretty hard to sell something if you can't get in the door!

If you believe the situation is right to initiate contact with prospects with whom you have had no previous relationship, the following sidebar offers suggestions as to the best way to proceed. As you review the sidebar, keep in mind the general caveat on which this book is based: These suggestions are what *tends* to work. You'll want to adjust your approach based on your own personal style and remember that there are no sure things.

Note

Professional athletes in golf, tennis, baseball, and football talk about being "in the zone." Card players probably say the same thing. When I was dialing for dollars, as I used to call it, I found there were days I could pick up the phone and get appointments with everyone I called. On other days, I could not even get through to an assistant. Don't force it. If you start making calls and cannot get through to anyone, don't let your confidence take a hit. Try again another day!

Tips for Approaching New Prospects

- Send a letter or e-mail of introduction. Make your letter or e-mail brief—a few sentences at most. Open with something about the prospect or the prospect's industry. Send the letter or e-mail as high in the organization as possible. If it gets passed down from a higher up, someone will always talk to you. Beware of sending too much information. Too often, prospects make their decision based on what you send and say no to a meeting. Finally, indicate that you will follow up in a specific period of time—usually a few days.

- Follow up with a contact in the specified period. Explain that the reason you are calling is to follow up on the e-mail or letter you sent earlier. It helps build trust. But avoid sending anything that's likely to be received on Monday morning or Friday afternoon, however. No one wants to add something to their agenda during these parts of the week!

- Work with the gatekeeper (usually an assistant) to build a relationship. For example, get his or her name and use it when contacting the prospect in the future.

- Don't try to get a prospect's attention on the phone if he or she is busy or not in a receptive mood. If it is not a good time, ask when you should contact the prospect again—and then do it. The prospect will usually talk to you if you keep reaching out when he or she tells you to. (In other words, guilt is a great motivator!) Ask permission to continue.

- State your desire for a face-to-face meeting. Stress the benefits of the meeting, not the service—for example, discussing a new industry or technical development, survey input or results, or what have you. Try to set a deadline for the meeting, such as a period of time you will be in the area. These kinds of discussions are usually not high on a prospect's priority list, so give the prospect a reason to meet you sooner rather than later. Otherwise, you will be calling forever.

Be Prepared for the First Objection

I will never forget the first prospecting call I made for my syndicated research company. My primary targets were national accounting firms. After considerable testing and development, I had finally completed the first study and was ready to see if I could find any actual buyers.

After sending a letter, I picked up the phone and called Kevin, the partner in charge of marketing for what was then Price Waterhouse. I had gotten Kevin's name from another client. After I gave my brief introduction, Kevin told me that all decisions for marketing research were made out of PW's executive offices in New York. It would have been easy to say that I would call New York or simply to go on to another prospect. Instead, motivated by fear of failure, I pushed a little. I agreed that the firm's headquarters would obviously need to be involved, but I told Kevin that I would show him the data on his firm in his market and so that he'd at least be familiar with the research. (This was another benefit of the meeting, not the service!) I asked to meet—even if only for breakfast or lunch—and to my delight, he agreed. We met for breakfast the following week. During our meeting, Kevin became intrigued by the data I showed him, and within a month I had sold his office the research package.

After calling several thousand additional research prospects, I know that this experience was very typical. Prospects are busy. (Aren't we all?) Their first reaction is always going to be to avoid adding something else to their agenda, especially if they aren't the ones asking for a meeting. Anyone who does prospecting is way too familiar with the phrase "I'm busy." When setting up the game, you must anticipate this first objection and be ready to respond. The most effective way to do this is to agree with the objection, stress another benefit that would result from the meeting, and then involve the prospect in choosing the best time to get together. For example, when I called Kevin, I agreed that headquarters would need to be involved, mentioned the type of data Kevin would see in the meeting even if he never bought the research, and asked him whether breakfast or lunch would be better for him.

When you attempt to set up the SalesGame with prospects, there are two common first objections:

- "I'm too busy."

- "We're happy with our current service provider."

When confronted with the first of these objections, it is fairly easy to agree that the prospect is busy. If you have worked with others in the industry and can say something that shows your experience, so much the better—

for example, "I know how crazy it gets this time of year at a college like yours with faculty contracts, fundraising activities, and so on."

If the second objection stems from the prospect's satisfaction with his or her current service provider, try complimenting the competition (but be honest) or agreeing that it's nice to have a good relationship with one's current provider. I suggest adding that your purpose in meeting is not to try to break up a good relationship but to give the prospect other options should the situation change. For example, you might say, "I know XYZ is a good firm. If you're happy with them, that's great. I certainly would not recommend changing firms for the sake of change!"

Regardless of the objection, your response should be followed by another benefit of the meeting and a second request to get together. If you are not successful on the second attempt, then let it go. Pushing more would probably become uncomfortable.

Of course, these examples assume two things:

- **That you can talk with the prospect, at least on the phone, to set up the meeting:** I'm often asked what professionals should do if they can't get a prospect to respond to e-mails or call them back. The answer is to be patiently persistent and reach out periodically. As one of my clients puts it, "We want to court them, not stalk them." Should you do this forever? Certainly not. But the world is full of examples of how persistence pays off.

- **That you truly believe in your heart that the service would really be of value to the prospect:** Prospects can easily recognize and almost always appreciate this kind of passion. In my case, I knew that the syndicated research package I was offering was an excellent value and could be used in a variety of ways by accounting and law firms. I'm certain that my passion for the service I was delivering was one of the reasons I had such a high rate of success getting in the door.

What sort of results should you expect from prospecting activities? That is, how many doors should open for you? Obviously, it depends on what you are selling. If you choose the right situations, you will usually be able to get a meeting with at least 50% of the prospects you call. But remember: Most prospects are well aware that professionals like attorneys and consultants sell time, and that it is an expensive commodity. When they can meet with one of these high-priced professionals at no charge, they'll usually take advantage of the opportunity if it is presented in the right way. The success rate in prospecting for realtors or insurance salespeople tends to be far less. If you do not get into at least 25 to 50% of the doors you are trying to open, you should take a step back and look at your service and how you are setting up the game. Maybe the service is not as unique as you originally thought. Perhaps your meetings are not giving prospects adequate benefits.

The bottom line? One of the easiest ways to increase your success rate in getting a meeting is to be ready for that first objection. We all know it is going to come. Try at least twice to set up a meeting using the approach I described here. Even if you are not successful, at least you will know you have given it your best shot.

> One of the easiest ways to increase your success rate in getting a meeting is to be ready for that first objection.

Follow Up, Follow Up, Follow Up

Almost everyone would agree with the importance of following up when prospecting—or for that matter, with almost every sales and marketing activity. But few know how difficult it can be. At a minimum, it requires organization, discipline, and persistence.

In my workshops, when prospecting is a topic of discussion, most professionals simply want to find out how to get in the door. They fail to understand that this part of the process is relatively easy. It's after a meeting happens that things get hard! That's when you have to keep positioning for the elusive window of opportunity, when the prospect wants some kind of assistance. The window could open in a matter of days or weeks, as it did so often with my research product because it was such a new idea. On the other hand, it could take years for the right set of circumstances to create an opening—for example, a decision-maker retires, a conflict of interest arises on a specific case, a service provider merges with another firm, someone retires, and so on. You need to be in contact with a prospect—usually two or three times a year is adequate—so you know when the window is open and you can take advantage of the opportunity.

I once worked with an office of an international accounting firm that was targeting the five largest financial institutions in the city, not counting the three they already served. We devoted most of a two-day workshop to approaching and meeting with these prospects. They had no difficulty getting in the door; they already had contacts inside most of them and the others were willing to meet simply based on the firm's strong reputation in banking. They were also able to set up the initial meetings, which, according to the participants, went very well. Where they had trouble was in the follow-up phase. Two years later, my company did our syndicated research study in the market, and I met with the managing partner of the office. His shock was evident when he learned that two of the smaller banks on their target list had switched accounting firms and his firm had not been invited to propose. Someone had failed to follow up to find out that the window of opportunity was open.

How could this happen? Simple. The first call was followed by a second, but then busy season hit. The prospect fell through the cracks and was never contacted again. Later, when I talked to the bank president at the request of the managing partner, he told me he had left the decision up to the CFO and financial staff. I then called the CFO, who said he did not invite the firm in question to propose because he was disappointed with the fact that they seemed so interested in his work and then, as he put it, "seemed to disappear." The firm would have been better off not initiating contact with the prospect in the first place than to create a bad image by not following up as promised.

Contrast this example with the earlier story of the local firm that called on banks on a Spring Road Trip each year. They used the same approach and ended up with a large and profitable practice in the area. They were successful because they were patiently persistent in their follow-up after they made contact. They positioned themselves with their prospects until the window of opportunity opened. Then they at least had a chance to propose on the work in question. Better yet, they knew the people and the institution when they finally got an opportunity to provide services. They established relationships before the point of sale. They even deposited some "coins in the trust bank" by following up when they said they would.

If you plan to do any prospecting, remember that you are starting a long-term process. Golfers quit after 11 or 12 holes. NBA teams don't quit at the end of the third quarter. Likewise, you should not set up the SalesGame if you are not committed to playing all the way!

One more point should be made about appropriate follow up. After a business dialogue has been initiated, a prospect can be in Stage Two for months or even years. You can't simply call and say, "Has anything changed since the last time we talked?" The best practice in Stage Two is to mix substance—that is, bringing some value to the prospect—with relationship-building activities. I've worked with clients who err on one side or the other of this equation. Better to mix substance, like attending a client seminar or sending a personal note highlighting an important point in an e-bulletin, with a round of golf or a ball game.

> You should not set up the SalesGame if you are not committed to playing all the way!

Prospecting with Known Contacts

When in Quadrant Four, it is much more comfortable to initiate contact with people you know as a means for developing leads. For example, you might initiate contact with the following:

- Firm alumni who hold positions of responsibility with prospect organizations
- Client alumni who have moved to a new organization (former client personnel are in fact the biggest source of new business apart from clients themselves)
- College classmates who are now with prospect organizations
- Contacts in trade or professional organizations
- Friends, neighbors, and relatives in relevant business positions

These examples are not really cold-calling, but they do represent another version of initiating contact with prospects. When participants in strategic selling workshops identify meetings they want to plan, there is generally no shortage of opportunities to initiate contact with people they already know. These meetings are certainly less difficult than a cold call, and rarely violate any state's ethics policy.

Note

You can hopefully see how easy prospecting is when you are dealing with contacts you already know. More importantly, you hopefully have an increased understanding of the importance of building your network and being involved in the right trade, community, and professional organizations!

Exploring Your Contact Base

Initiating contact with people you already know is the easiest way to build an inventory of leads in the short run. I constantly hear comments about how professionals would be able to develop business if they could just get in the door. What they do not realize is that they did the right things up to this point with the contacts they already have, they are in the door already.

As part of most workshops, I ask each participant to identify a potential meeting to plan during the session.

Here are some examples of meeting ideas that participants have come up with:

■ **A meeting with the CEO of a shipping line in Scandinavia:** In this case, the shipping line had just merged with another line. Each company was to be audited by a different Big Four accounting firm. No formal request for proposal had been issued. The workshop participant, Halvor, was a consultant with a Big Four firm. Before that, the CEO of the shipping line had been a mentor of sorts. Obviously, this is a lead and might have resulted in an opportunity, even if Halvor had done nothing. But by having the meeting and getting an early start, Halvor improved his firm's chances of winning the game by retaining and satisfying this important account.

■ **A meeting with the in-house counsel of a chain of car dealerships:** The in-house counsel had worked with an attorney in my workshop, Michael, at a previous employer. Although they had a good business relationship, Michael had not moved to Stage Two by expressing interest in working with the in-house counsel at his new place of employment. The meeting was the first step in a long-term positioning effort for the legal work because the family that owned the dealerships was close to another law firm. Nevertheless, within six months of the meeting, some smaller engagements did come Michael's way. His firm now has both a relationship and a track record with the dealerships.

■ **A meeting with a fellow participant in a client seminar:** A wealth manager, Nancy, who works with a major bank, met Jennifer at a seminar the bank held on developing and carrying out business plans. They talked for a while at the reception after the seminar and established a little chemistry. Jennifer was the daughter of a wealthy family and was just starting her own business. Nancy and Jennifer exchanged cards, and Nancy reached out to her using a LinkedIn invite later that week. Jennifer accepted the invitation with a note saying how much she enjoyed talking with Nancy. A week or two later, Nancy reached out again to suggest they get together to get to know each other better and talk more about Jennifer's business plans. A lunch was set up. While Jennifer's own wealth was relatively low compared to her parents, this was the start of a relationship that could lead to many opportunities for the bank, whether dealing with wealth-management issues, business banking, or estate planning.

■ **A meeting with a foreign national in charge of U.S. operations for his father's international retail business:** An attorney in my workshop, James, had met this prospect at a wedding. U.S. operations were just beginning to take off. This was a meeting James needed to have just to be sure that his friend or prospect knew he wanted an opportunity to work together if the right situation presented itself. Of course, it would be of value to this executive to be aware of the services that James's firm might be able to provide to help this growing company in this important phase of its U.S. expansion.

Note

The last example may leave you wondering, "Is this guy saying I'm supposed to sell to friends or hand out business cards at a wedding?" Let me be clear. There are times you play the game and times you do not. Personally, I have only talked about developing a professional relationship with a handful of friends and relatives. The father of one of my son's friends once mentioned that he was the partner coordinating his firm's business-development efforts, but I never pursued this obvious lead. I chose not to because I was already working with another firm in my city and did not want to create the perception of a conflict of interest. For the record, the professional I chose to represent me when I decided to sell my research business was a relative of my wife, Sue. I met him for the first time at—you guessed it—a wedding. He did a great job, too!

Most professionals would have an abundance of leads if they would simply express an interest to contacts they already have. As an attorney in my workshop said, quoting her father, "I've never met anyone who was offended because I said I would like to work with him." So why don't professionals set up the SalesGame with more people they already know? Two reasons stand out:

■ They are concerned about coming across as too pushy—that is, being seen as a "used car salesman," as I have often heard it phrased. I think this is largely due to not knowing how to approach the situation.

■ They fear being rejected.

There are generally two types of situations in which professionals initiate contact with leads with whom they already have some relationship. The majority of these opportunities stem from some form of business interaction, as was the case with the first two examples above. The third and fourth examples are based on exploring a social rather than a business contact, which presents some slightly different challenges. When exploring your contact base in either of these types of situations, the best practices are similar to those that apply when initiating contact with unknown prospects, albeit with some significant differences:

- Choose the right situation.

- Sell the meeting, not the service.

- Be prepared for the first objection.

- Follow up, follow up, follow up.

- Don't wait…initiate.

Choose the Right Situation

If you want to initiate a discussion about business with a former colleague or someone you've met in a Stage One activity like a not-for-profit board, trade group, meet and greet, or social setting, the most important point is to not sell while in this setting. Instead, use the opportunity to express interest in arranging another contact to explore a future business relationship.

If you've ever played a round of golf with a stockbroker who keeps trying to impress you with his investment prowess, you know why this tactic isn't very effective. Almost all professionals know they need to inform contacts of what they do if they don't already know—usually by asking what the contact does first. After this has been done, the best practice is to transition to a discussion about potentially collaborating by expressing interest in working with the contact in the short or long term, gauging the reaction, and going from there. You should *not* begin by asking who currently does their work, talking about how good your service is, or talking about what you could do for the contact. Assuming the contact's response is positive—and it almost always is—you should suggest getting together sometime to see if there's a way you might be able to help one another. That's it—mission accomplished!

One of my favorite illustrations of this approach was a partner at a law firm who had served for years on a prestigious not-for-profit board in New York City. After participating in a workshop, he approached me to confess that he was a little frustrated because he'd never developed any business from this activity, even though the board was populated with "movers and shakers." I shared with him the best practice I just described and he executed it perfectly. After the next the board meeting, he walked along Fifth Avenue with another member, Bill, who lived in the same direction. He was nervous but committed to crossing the bridge from Stage One to Two. "You know," he said, "you and I have worked together on this board for years. But we've never talked professionally. It might be fun to do that sometime!" Not surprisingly, Bill was delighted by the idea. It worked so well that the attorney used this same wording with a couple of other contacts. His suggestion always got a positive response.

Many professionals have shared a similar experience with me. They may be nervous the first time they express interest in working with a contact, and they're usually surprised by how receptive the contact is. Emboldened by this reaction, they are inevitably much more comfortable expressing interest the next time. It's a little like asking someone out on a date. Each time you do it, it gets easier.

With regard to choosing the right situation, there are two other best practices to consider:

- If you are nervous about making the transition to business, try rehearsing the conversation with a trusted colleague. If your colleague says you're not being too pushy, you're probably using the right words.

- If your contact is not a decision-maker, express your interest in listening to his or her advice, not in getting work. Assuming you have a good relationship, he or she will likely want to help you. But if your contact perceives that you're asking for something he or she can't deliver, it will just make everyone uncomfortable.

Sell the Meeting, Not the Service

As discussed, when prospecting with unknown targets, you need to set up the meeting by communicating the benefits that your prospect will gain from a Stage Two meeting rather than talking about the benefits of your service. The same goes when prospecting with people you know. To give you an idea of what I mean, let's revisit the examples of meeting targets from the beginning of this chapter. Table 15.1 outlines the ways in which a meeting would benefit each of the prospects.

One thing that makes the SalesGame fun is that each meeting is different. Consequently, the benefits gained by the prospect from taking the time to meet with you will also be somewhat different in each situation. When setting up the game, you will be well served to spend a few moments before going to a networking event or picking up the telephone to think of what your contact will get from your meeting even if no immediate opportunity to work together presents itself. You will probably feel more comfortable—and less like a car salesman—setting up the game by focusing on how your prospect will benefit from the meeting and not on the selling points of a particular service.

Table 15.1 Benefits of Meeting	
Prospect	**Benefits of Meeting**
The CEO of a shipping line in Scandinavia	Maintaining the mentor/counselor relationship with his former employee
	Becoming a more educated buyer when it comes to choosing accounting firms for the merged organization
	Getting ahead of the game when it comes to the decision he and his board will soon have to make
The in-house counsel for a chain of car dealerships	Maintaining the professional and/or personal relationship
	Providing a sounding board if questions arise as a result of his new position
	Ideas that might make him look good to his new employer
The fellow participant in a client seminar	Gaining a better understanding of how she can manage her assets to help grow her business
	Bouncing around ideas from the seminar
	Gaining more awareness of the resources that the bank has that might help her grow her business
The foreign national in charge of the U.S. operations for his father's international retail business	Gaining a better understanding of the nuances of doing business in the U.S.
	Having a sounding board to use as U.S. operations grow
	Obtaining introductions to relevant business contacts

Be Prepared for the First Objection

In my experience, these kinds of meetings are almost always easy to sell. The prospect already knows you and does not need a great deal of motivation to take the relationship to the next level. Many of these types of contacts are made in business setting anyway—for example, a meet and greet or a trade group event—so the very purpose of the activity is to develop business connections. If the contact is a former colleague or alumnus of your firm, there is almost never any resistance to moving to Stage Two. Nevertheless, if you are exploring relationships where there has been minimal previous contact—for example, with fellow seminar attendees—you should be ready for an objection such as "I'm really busy right now" and follow the same principles discussed earlier in this chapter.

Follow Up, Follow Up, Follow Up

Almost everyone appreciates follow-up—as long as it does not become annoying. When exploring business relationships, be sure to ask how and when the prospect would like to be contacted as part of follow-up. Simply beginning a dialogue about business is rarely enough. You need to continue to mix substance and fun so you're in the right position when the window of opportunity opens.

Don't Wait…Initiate

One of the best practices discussed earlier in this chapter was to choose the right time for prospecting with targets where there is no previous relationship. When you are mining for prospects in your contact base, the right time is generally sooner than later. Why wait to express interest in working with contacts?

You should approach these situations with a sense of urgency. Leads like these do not happen every day. Halvor, the consultant in the example with the CEO of the Scandinavian shipping line, may only find himself in such a situation once in his entire career. Any competitive advantage he has from his good fortune will eventually disappear if he waits too long.

As mentioned, leads that involve former client personnel are common. But for a given professional, situations like the one in the second example, with the in-house counsel at the chain of car dealerships, will happen once or twice a year at most. And, as we all know, the longer you wait to make contact with a friend who has moved, the more uncomfortable it becomes. In the third example, Nancy can take advantage of the goodwill created by the bank seminar, but this will last for only so long. Finally, James's opportunity to express his interest at the wedding in the fourth example is pretty clearly a one-time occurrence.

Prospecting: Dealing with Friends and Relatives

Setting up the SalesGame with friends, relatives, or acquaintances—that is, contacts not related to past or current business interactions—causes most professionals tremendous discomfort. Somehow, it seems wrong to the average accountant, lawyer, wealth manager, or other professional to use his or her interest in a church group or child's sporting league to make contacts with leads.

I often say in my workshops that getting business from a church group is a paradox. No one joins a church to generate business, but there are many examples of business developing from involvement with a church. I once conducted a workshop for a multi-office law firm on the East Coast. One participant was an individual named Tim, who had a great reputation as a rainmaker. (Later, Tim would go on to head up a very significant government organization during the savings and loan crisis.) When I made my paradox statement, one of Tim's partners raised his hand to disagree. "I don't know about that," he said. "Tim is in five different churches!" Of course, the room filled with laughter, and I learned my lesson: In the SalesGame, like any other, there are many styles of play.

Regardless of how aggressive you want to be, there are four best practices that will help you make the most out of these activities:

- **Be active in civic and social activities you truly like.** You will have much better results with these kinds of activities if you have a sincere interest in the activity itself. You will come across as more sincere, you will not feel like the activity is another extension of the workday, and you will have a common bond with other participants.

- **Be a leader in civic and social activities you truly like.** If you want to develop business from these activities, make sure those with whom you come into contact see the kind of person you really are. Clients and prospects love leaders and problem solvers. Almost by definition, leaders meet more people, too. Leaders are not just found in formal groups. The friend who put your last golf outing together probably scored as many goodwill points with you as the head of the PTA at your child's school.

- **Exchange background information.** It's hard for people to call on you for help if they do not know what you do. That's why you need an elevator speech that quickly covers both what you do and what your firm does. For example, when I give my elevator speech, I say "I do training programs in sales and marketing for professional service firms." I know a commercial litigator who says he "handles the problems that happen when deals go south." Remember, though, that the best way to get people interested in you is to be interested in them. Don't lead with your elevator speech. Instead, ask the people you meet what *they* do… but only after you've asked what I think is the best networking question ever: "What do you like to do when you're not working?"

■ **Express interest in working with contacts.** The most important point in the process. If a relationship has truly been established—and often, these relationships go back years—the biggest mistake you can make is to not let your friends and contacts know that you'd be interested in working with them. You need to set up the game here as well. Usually, a simple statement of interest is adequate—for example, "I'd love to have the chance to work with you if the right opportunity comes up." Then simply read the reaction, which will almost always be positive or affirming.

This last point needs more emphasis. I cannot fathom how many opportunities have been lost because a professional did not at least express interest in working with a friend when both parties would have been well served by such a relationship. I know of a Big Four firm that was not invited to propose on a Fortune 500's audit even though the firm's managing partner lived next door to a company board member. In the words of the managing partner, "I forgot to ask."

To make the same point in a more positive way, I will share a story about a workshop participant named Christopher. Christopher came up to me during a break and asked if I had any suggestions for approaching a friend with whom he had attended school and who now ran his family's company. I asked him if he had actually told his friend that he would like to have the opportunity to work with him. Christopher seemed somewhat surprised by this direct approach. But the next day, he said he was determined to tell his friend of his interest and that he would let me know the result by mail.

Several months later, the letter came. It included the following passage:

> By the end of the lunch I felt completely distracted and nervous because I knew I was being a coward about not telling my friend I'd like to work with him. I felt a lot like I did 10 years ago when I wanted to ask a young lady to a dance. I have no idea what I was afraid of. I picked up my coffee cup after we were done eating and the cup noticeably—at least to me—rattled on the saucer. I thought, "This is ridiculous!" and more or less blurted out, "I'd like to do your audit!" ' My friend laughed, told me he'd be delighted to work with me, and wondered why I had never asked before!

Which leads me to my "hanging onto the fantasy" theory—something I developed several years ago after extensive research. When my daughter Dana was 15, I began to notice that the circular driveway in front of my house had become a parking lot. Young men constantly showed up to talk to her, but they would "hang out" with us as well—playing basketball with my son and me, helping my wife move things. I asked my daughter to tell me more about these frequent visitors and she almost always described them as "just friends." I once was a young man myself, and I knew that most of the guys in the driveway were not there just to be friends. But they were afraid to ask for a date, just as I was at their age. It was safer to hang onto the distant fantasy of dating Dana than to actually ask her to go to dinner or a movie.

It brings to mind all the attorneys, accountants, and even consultants I know who have told me of their friends or business contacts whom they see as potential clients. They tell great stories with all kinds of analysis—plots and subplots about what could happen. They've done all the research and are ready to take the next step should the stars align. But when I ask them if they have actually expressed interest in working with their contact, I almost always get the same surprised look. It's as if these professionals are still hanging onto the fantasy of working with these leads the same way those young men in my driveway held on to their fantasy of dating my daughter. But if you remember that the purpose of a Stage Two meeting is to build a relationship and qualify the lead—to learn whether the client or prospect has a recognized need—and not to sell work, then it's unlikely you'll be rejected. Besides, if someone says no to simply discussing issues of concern to them and building a relationship, then it really is time for you to find a new fantasy!

Of course, you need to remember to ask in the right way—that is, by expressing interest in working with contacts or asking for advice rather than employing heavy-handed tactics. I'm often asked in workshops how to make this transition. I like to say it's a little like Paul Simon's song "Fifty Ways to Leave Your Lover." Each professional has his or her own style, and every friend or family member is different. Here are two of my favorite examples, although I'm sure I could come up with loads!

■ A wealth manager had been fishing buddies for many years with the owner of a chain of service stations. One day, when they were out on the water, the wealth manager said, "I must be a damn fool. Here I've known you all these years and I've never thought about working with you! That's crazy. We really ought to talk sometime to see if we could help one another." The fishing buddy laughed and replied, "I wondered why you never asked. Let's get together next week when we're not drinking these beers and we can talk more."

■ An accountant's college roommate was now an executive at a company on his firm's target list. They had dinner together with their families a couple of times a year. After some coaching, the accountant decided to express interest in working with his friend. When they were talking after dinner, he said, "I know your company has grown tremendously over the last few years. It occurred to me that I ought to at least let you know that I'd love to have the opportunity to work with you if there were ever something my firm or I could do that would really be of value!" Again, the suggestion was met with a positive response, and a follow-up lunch was arranged.

You will rarely be rejected if you express interest in working with someone you already know by using phrases like "I'd love to work with you if the opportunity ever presents itself." Of course, this does not mean you will get work. More than likely, the result will be an acknowledgement like a nod of the head, and the positioning game will begin. You can, however, take pride in the fact that you at least have started to set up the game. More importantly, expressing interest allows you to realistically evaluate the prospect "fantasy" and perhaps develop new ones. As you were no doubt told in your youth, there are plenty of fish in the sea!

So don't delay. Start setting up current and future games right away. As you'll see in the following parts, the SalesGame is too much fun to play for you to be sitting on the sidelines hanging on to old fantasies! If you don't have an inventory of leads, start prospecting with current and past business contacts or even those civic or social contacts you have spent a lifetime cultivating. With luck, you might end up with a qualified lead—someone for whom your skills and experience could make a difference—right away. More likely, you will build your inventory of positioning leads to create opportunities for the future. Either way, you can't lose. So set up the game and let's look at tools like the Scorecard and Ground Rule to help you play it well.

Part Summary

Stage Two plays a particularly important role in determining success or failure in the SalesGame because it is the beginning of a discussion about how you and your client or prospect might work together. This dialogue can be initiated in one of four ways:

- The professional responds to a request from a prospect (Quadrant One).

- The professional responds to a request from a client (Quadrant Two).

- The professional initiates contact with a client (Quadrant Three).

- The professional initiates contact with a prospect (Quadrant Four).

In Quadrants One and Two, you should be sure to convert requests for service and cost to conversations about goals and value. Even though the lead is probably qualified in Quadrants One and Two, you still have to slow down the process enough to be sure you have a qualified lead. You should have more limited expectations when operating in Quadrants Three and Four because the client or prospect may have no immediate needs. Agreeing to write proposals at this stage is usually unproductive at best and could be damaging in the long run. You should set realistic goals and next steps when operating in Quadrants Three and Four. Even though the results will be less stellar, you should spend at least part of your time initiating contact to build the practice you most desire and to create the peace of mind that comes from having your own book of business.

When dealing with Stage Two leads in Quadrant One, you should keep four basic points in mind:

- **Respond quickly.** Make some form of initial contact to thank the prospect for his or her inquiry and to demonstrate your interest in the opportunity.

- **Get the right information.** Find out the five critical pieces of information that will help you be more effective as the buying process moves forward. Specifically, you want to know how the prospect got your name, what the prospect is trying to accomplish, who the prospect is, what the next steps should be, and what the time frame is.

- **Go for a creative close.** End the initial contact in this stage with a next step, or close, that will differentiate you from the competition.

- **Build relationships first.** Don't skip Stages One and Two. Start the process by building some chemistry first.

Keeping the first contact short is not as important as it once was. Still, it's a good idea to keep phone interactions short, especially if the next step will be a face-to-face meeting. If someone with whom you have an established relationship inquires about your services in a semi-social or casual setting, the best practice is to get the necessary information and then set a meeting in a business environment to avoid selling in a Stage One activity.

When handling leads from current or past clients (Quadrant Two), you should still follow the four principles outlined previously (respond quickly, get the right information, go for a creative close, and build the relationship first). The latter two of these principles are somewhat less important when responding to clients but should still be considered to avoid problems during service delivery. The most important issue when responding to clients is to beware of the easy sale. In Quadrant Two, getting the work is easy. Professionals must remember that their true goal is to end up with an enthusiastic client, not to simply acquire another piece of business.

Few professionals can build the practice of their dreams by operating only in Respond mode—that is, in Quadrants One and Two of the sales matrix. Therefore, initiating contact with clients (Quadrant Three) is a natural place to start because professionals have both a relationship and a track record. The best way to approach these meetings is to focus on issues, not on products or services. You should prepare for such meetings by spending at least as much time developing questions to engage clients in a discussion of issues as you do building your own product knowledge. Clients welcome discussions with professional advisors that help them better understand the problems or opportunities they face—even if just as a sounding board—and the resources available to them. However, they do not want to be sold to by someone telling them about the latest new service or product they need to buy.

When operating in Quadrant Four, you have two options: initiating contact with prospects with whom you have no previous relationship and initiating contact with those you already know. The former is obviously the more difficult and time consuming, and is best used when one or more of three criteria are present: The service is new and unique, the prospect is in a definable group that regularly evaluates professional service options, and/or you have already explored your current contact base. You will be more successful initiating contact with new prospects if you remember the five best practices:

- When arranging the meeting, stress the benefits to the prospect of the meeting itself, not a particular service.

- Set realistic goals. Your goals should be to build a relationship and to learn about the prospect's situation, not to sell a service.

- Use a third party familiar with both you and the prospect to make the initial contact as "warm" as possible.

* Be ready for the first objection—for example, "I'm too busy" or "I'm happy with my current firm." That way, you can respond by agreeing, stressing another benefit of meeting, and asking again for a time to meet.

* Follow up. The window of opportunity to work with a particular prospect may open in a few days or in a few years. You need to keep following up to build trust and establish the relationship *before* the point of sale. Follow-up is best when it mixes substance—that is, providing some value to the prospect—with relationship-building activities.

Most professionals already know many people, such as business acquaintances, friends, and relatives. Initiating contact with these people offers a much more comfortable way to build your inventory of leads than prospects you have never met. The degree to which you want to initiate a business discussion with such contacts depends on your style and aggressiveness. When you do initiate a business discussion with these contacts, you should keep four best practices in mind. (Some of these are similar to the ones in the preceding list.)

* **Sell the meeting, not the service.** Communicate the benefits that your business acquaintance or friend will derive from the meeting.

* **Be prepared for the first objection.** This is especially true if you are setting up the SalesGame with someone you do not know well—for example, someone you met at a seminar or trade association meeting.

* **Follow up.** Rarely will these contacts result in immediate business. Also, without follow up, the interest you express may seem insincere, making your chances of acquiring the business in the long term very slim.

* **Don't wait...initiate.** You should initiate contact with these leads as soon as appropriate. There is little to be gained from waiting if there is a sincere belief that your services might be of value.

Expressing interest in working with contacts you meet through social, religious, or civic activities can seem like a paradox. Few professionals become involved in these activities to get business, but it is in fact what often results. To get the most out of these activities, you should at least follow the basic rule of exchanging background information and expressing interest in working together if the right opportunity arises.

Play On

Play On

Play On

Play On

Now that you are more confident in how to set up the game when developing leads, it's time to explore some of the key fundamentals that will contribute to your success as you play the game. Effectively using the Scorecard is a significant fundamental and the next part of the SalesGame. To win any game, you must know how to keep score—and that is exactly what you will do with the Scorecard!

Part 3

The Scorecard: Add Value, Differentiate Your Service, and Build Strategy

What Is the Scorecard?

I first mentioned the Scorecard in Part 1, "An Overview of the SalesGame." But what is the Scorecard in the context of the SalesGame? In short, the Scorecard is a shared vision of the best way to define and accomplish the client or prospect's desired objective. It is the primary tool that helps you summarize what will make the client enthusiastic—how the client will "keep score" and measure your success in achieving the true value he or she seeks. It is also the fundamental that helps you strategize to "win" the game. What form the Scorecard takes does not make much difference as long as it reflects the client or prospect's vision.

The Scorecard contains two basic elements:

- The objective that the client or prospect wants to achieve (the Heart of the Matter)

- The most critical factors that determine the best way to accomplish this objective (Scorecard Factors)

I like to convey these elements in the form of a simple T chart like the one shown in Figure 16.1. At the top of the T is a phrase that describes what the client or prospect wants to accomplish—that is, the Heart of the Matter, or the true source of value. In this example, the client wants to raise the level of both individual and company performance and quality by putting an emphasis on continuous learning—in other words, to "become a learning organization."

Becoming a Learning Organization

1. **Cost exceeds expectations**	—
2. **Provide training of internal personnel for the long term**	+
3. **Leading expert will participate on a weekly basis**	+

Figure 16.1 A simple T chart.

Below this phrase are three or four factors that the client must consider in accomplishing this goal—the Scorecard Factors. These generally describe how the client or prospect decides which professional to employ if the situation is competitive. If the opportunity is sole source, such as a current client calling to expand the scope of service, these factors will generally describe the parameters for successfully delivering the service. In some cases, the criteria may be a combination. In this example, the factor relating to cost ("cost exceeds expectations") is clearly something the client or prospect would consider in deciding whether to move ahead with the project. The other two factors ("provide training" and "leading expert will participate") are parameters that define the successful delivery of the service.

Following each Scorecard Factor is a rating that describes how it will affect the client or prospect's decision. I use plusses and minuses, but any rating system will work. The fact that cost exceeds expectations is usually an obstacle or barrier to using a particular professional service, so it is rated as a minus. If the client or prospect were to make a decision simply on this factor, the choice would probably be to pass on the service or to find someone else to perform the service who meets cost expectations. The fact that the firm is willing to train the client or prospect's own personnel to build internal resources for the long term is a plus—a good reason to proceed with the service. The fact that a leading expert will participate in delivering the service on a weekly basis is also a plus.

> **Note**
>
> This T chart is based on a competitive situation—that is, multiple professional firms proposing on the same work. But a T chart could also be used for many of the non-competitive situations that accountants, lawyers, wealth managers, consultants, and other professionals face every day. For example, you could use a T chart for a client who calls for assistance on a special project or to expand the scope of

service or a client trying to decide whether to use external assistance or internal personnel. Or, you could use a T chart for a prospect making a call based on a referral for a professional to handle a specific matter—for example, a piece of litigation, a due-diligence audit, an investment portfolio, a valuation, or a software evaluation.

Does this particular Scorecard, listing two plusses and only one minus, suggest that the client or prospect will buy the service? Not really. But what the Scorecard *does* do is make the decision more clear and tangible for both you and the client or prospect. In some cases, the fact that cost exceeds expectations might outweigh the positive factors of the service—in this example, the training of internal personnel and the participation of the expert. In other situations, these positive factors would be enough for the client or prospect to accept the fact he or she will be paying more than originally anticipated and hire you or your firm to help the client "become a learning organization."

As in any game, part of the fun comes from not really knowing how it is going to turn out. The relative weight of the criteria on this sample Scorecard will change depending on the situation, personality, and values of the client or prospect. Your job when playing the SalesGame is not to predict the future, but rather to focus on building the elements of the Scorecard itself and helping the client or prospect understand the ramifications of each element. Remember, one of the reasons business development is so much like a game is that you can't control the outcome. Regardless of whether the piece of business is acquired, you should be able to sleep better knowing you played the game as well as possible by seeing the Scorecard from the client or prospect's point of view.

Focus for the Future

In addition to conveying the objective that the client or prospect wants to achieve and the factors that determine the most critical way to achieve that objective, the Scorecard provides a road map for client enthusiasm and highlights the critical issues on which to focus should the client or prospect buy the professional service in question. This is just as true if the opportunity is sole source. Unfortunately, most professionals treat situations with no competition as an easy sell and forget to identify the criteria for successfully delivering the service. Remember: Beware of the easy sale!

> The Scorecard provides a road map for client enthusiasm and highlights the critical issues on which to focus.

In the example outlined earlier in this chapter, you must pay close attention to the first factor, the cost of delivery. Exceeding the expectation for the cost of service established by an estimate in the sales process would lead to a client that is less than enthusiastic. I can hear a chorus of professionals saying, "Cost is always important!" and that's true. But you no doubt realize that there are certain engagements for which we watch the total cost a whole lot more closely than others. According to the second factor, you should focus on training the client's internal personnel. When the engagement is over, these personnel should not only have new skills, but should feel as if they really learned something. (Hopefully, they will also communicate these feelings to their superiors!) Last but not least, according to the third factor, the leading expert must be visible on the job on a weekly basis if not more. The exact level of desired involvement should be clarified with the client before the engagement is sold to make sure you meet or exceed expectations and don't create an unrealistic commitment for the leading expert.

Compare the focus and clarity provided by the Scorecard in this example with a situation I encountered several years ago while conducting a workshop for a dozen professionals from a regional accounting firm. Three of the participants had recently been involved in a very important proposal that ended unsuccessfully. A manufacturing facility had just been spun off from a Fortune 500 company in a leveraged buyout by local management. The firm I was working with was one of four organizations invited to propose on being the audit firm for the newly created entity. The firm had written a proposal and made a presentation to the key members of management the week before the workshop. On a whim, I asked each of the three accountants who had been involved in the proposal and presentation to write down the three most important reasons the prospect should have chosen their firm without any discussion with their two teammates. I then asked them to share their reasons, which I wrote down on a flip chart. When we were finished, the flip chart contained not three or four reasons—not even five or six—but *eight* different reasons why the firm was the best choice. Only one reason was listed by two of the accountants who had participated in the presentation. Talk about a lack of focus!

Keep It Short

At first consideration, one might think that more content on the Scorecard is better, so the fact that eight reasons (that is, eight Scorecard Factors) were listed in the preceding example might be a good thing. Upon more careful reflection, however, most professionals would realize that few decisions are based on a long list of reasons. For clients or prospects, just remembering one firm's list of eight reasons after a day spent listening to three or four presentations is next to impossible. Your job is to make the client or prospect's decision more clear, not more confusing.

When confronted with a long list of reasons to hire a firm—especially in a presentation setting—most people are left feeling overwhelmed and over-sold. (As one prospect told me after he had listened to a presentation from one firm, "Nothing could be as good as they were telling me their service was!") The Scorecard provides focus and clarity both to you and to the client or prospect. The Heart of the Matter should be concise and the list of Scorecard Factors should be brief. The three accountants in the preceding example above were not in sync as to why their firm was the best choice. It is hard to imagine how the management committee on the client side could see the choice clearly! It is also easy to see how they could have chosen a firm with a more focused presentation.

Why Use the Scorecard?

One year, after the Los Angeles Lakers lost the NBA championship to their archrivals, the Boston Celtics, Wilt Chamberlain said he still thought that his Lakers were the better team. Celtics star Bill Russell's response said it all: "The only important statistic is the final score."

Every game needs a Scorecard. In the SalesGame, the Scorecard is even more important because it affects almost every stage in the business development process:

- **Stage One:** Generic Scorecard Factors can be used to send a clear and consistent message in networking or promotional events.

- **Stage Two:** The Scorecard is the key to qualifying the lead by determining whether there is real value for the client or prospect in using a professional service. That is, can the service help the client or prospect accomplish his or her objective?

- **Stage Three:** In this stage, the Scorecard can serve as a tool to help you and your client or prospect find the best way to accomplish his or her objective. It also serves as the foundation for developing a strategy for winning in competitive situations and for determining what will turn buyers into enthusiastic clients.

- **Stage Four:** The Scorecard tells you when it is time to make a trial close—that is, to determine whether you have the same vision as the client or prospect of what he or she wants to accomplish as well as the criteria for choosing a firm and/or measuring enthusiasm.

- **Stage Five:** The Scorecard makes sure you and the client or prospect agree on the service package to be delivered.

- **Stage Six:** The Scorecard provides a way to focus service delivery and a foundation for an assuring client enthusiasm (ACE) meeting.

Make It Fun

Using a Scorecard makes business development more fun. It enables you to focus on understanding needs, *not* on convincing the buyer to purchase a service. With a Scorecard, the process is more like playing a game than selling. (This is a big part of why I titled this book *SalesGame.*) In my experience, this shift in perspective takes a lot of the pressure out of the sales interview. Professionals often want to know how to convince the client. In Europe, participants often take it to another level, primarily because of semantics, and want to know the "arguments" they can use to persuade clients to buy. I've always said that as soon as you start to argue with a client or prospect, you've already lost. Convincing clients or prospects is not so much of an issue if you have listened carefully to what they want to accomplish and to their criteria for measuring performance.

> Convincing clients or prospects is not so much of an issue if you have listened carefully to what they want to accomplish and to their criteria for measuring performance.

More to the point, clients mention their dislike for the hard sell after they have been through the purchase of a professional service. The hard sell usually occurs when professionals view their mission as convincing clients or prospects that they are the best as opposed to listening to and interacting with clients or prospects to determine what is best from their point of view. This leads to one-sided presentations like the proverbial "dog and pony" shows, where a team of professionals overwhelms a prospect with all the reasons they should use a given firm's services before they take the time to define what the prospect wants. Even worse, when professionals attempt to convince clients or prospects, they often end up in an adversarial relationship. It is practically impossible to build a team approach when prospects or clients feel like the opponents. The pressure both parties feel in the sales process disappears when the focus is on building the Scorecard rather than convincing someone to buy a particular service.

Make It Tangible

Another advantage of focusing on building the Scorecard is that it makes your service more tangible. Of course, any service—whether conducting a computer review, developing litigation strategy, or providing investment advice—is by its very nature intangible. During the SalesGame, buyers are trying to understand exactly what they will receive when they purchase a service. Too often, professionals focus too much on why the prospect should buy the service and not enough on defining what the service is. One of the real assets professionals have when selling is the flexibility of creating a custom service to meet the specific needs and expectations of a given client or prospect. When the ticket agent for an airline sells an airline seat from point A to point B, he cannot change the departure time or reconfigure the plane. An accountant, lawyer, or consultant, however, can substantially modify a standard service or even create a new one to meet the needs of his or her clients. The problem is that creating a custom service also means that both you and the client or prospect must understand exactly what is going to be provided and, more importantly, how it will be evaluated. The more tangible form the Scorecard takes, the easier it is for you to provide a service that meets the specifications of the client or prospect—that is, to ensure you win the SalesGame by ending up with an enthusiastic client. Should there be any problems, the Scorecard also provides a tangible way for you and the client or prospect to communicate your differences. In other words, the Scorecard provides a road map for client enthusiasm.

Several years ago, I worked with a bank in Minneapolis to help develop the selling skills of commercial lenders. This was in conjunction with a program that the bank had already launched called *promise management*. I was not even using the term Scorecard yet—nor was the bank—but its promise-management program went a long way toward making services more tangible and providing a road map for client enthusiasm. In essence, bank representatives visited key clients on an annual basis to determine each customer's needs during the upcoming year and to reach an agreement about what the bank could deliver. This list of agreed-upon services—for example, lines of credit, interest rates, security, service personnel, amount of client contact—was put into a written list of promises that the bank made to the client. Bank personnel reviewed this list periodically during the year to focus their service efforts. More importantly, when bank and client personnel sat down at the end of the year to review the bank's performance, they had a tangible Scorecard to evaluate performance.

Compare that with a study done by Karen, a consultant from Key West, Florida. Karen had been hired as an outside consultant by a Fortune 500 company to determine why more than 50% of the projects undertaken by the company's own internal consultants had left their "customers" dissatisfied. With internal consultants, minimal selling needs to be done, and any costs are paper-only transactions between budget lines. How could so many customers end up unhappy? After spending many hours reviewing reports and interviewing both the users and providers of these consulting services, Karen came to a simple but not surprising conclusion: The consultants had not done a good job of gaining agreement on the desired outcome on the front end of the assignment.

The message is clear. Regardless of how easy it may be to acquire a given piece of business, you will have a difficult time winning the SalesGame—that is, ending up with an enthusiastic client—if you don't have a tangible Scorecard to guide the delivery of your service.

Start with the Heart of the Matter

Experts will tell anyone trying to learn a new game not to focus on the end result, but to play each facet of the game as well as possible. Gamblers know not to count their money until they leave the table. Football players know they must focus on the basics—blocking, tackling, execution—and not worry about the eventual outcome. Serious golfers know the importance of playing each shot one at a time rather than trying to shoot a particular score.

Similarly, when playing the SalesGame, you must first determine precisely what the client or prospect wants to accomplish as a result of using your service before any thought is given to winning or losing a particular engagement. In other words, qualify the lead before you sell. Finding out what the client or prospect wants to accomplish is the Heart of the Matter and the true source of value.

Over the last several years, almost every professional service firm has begun promoting the fact that they want to provide "added value" to their clients. These words can be seen in mission statements, advertising, proposals, and presentations.

> Qualify the lead
> before you sell.

So what is "added value"? Much like the old adage "Help is defined by the recipient," value is defined by the buyer. When playing the SalesGame, you must focus first on what the buyer defines as most valuable.

The best description of value I have ever heard came several years ago from a speaker in Brussels. Mr. Ian Percy, an expert in teambuilding and human resource development, was addressing 150 accountants from a Big Four firm. One of the participants asked Ian how those in the audience could carry his message of being in touch with their clients' deepest feelings. Ian responded, "Don't talk to your clients about how you're going to do their books, but about how you're going to change their lives!" It hit me like a lightning bolt between the eyes. Anyone can do your books. Doing the books is a commodity that is not of much value. And when dealing with a commodity service, price is usually much more significant. *Real* value comes from changing lives for the better. Changing lives for the better is not a commodity; thus, price is not anywhere near as important in the sales process. When professionals play the SalesGame, they should start by gaining a solid understanding of what the client wants to accomplish as a result of using a given service. Edward Bennett Williams said the same thing from a lawyer's perspective: "The ideal client is a rich man who is scared!"

"Don't talk to your clients about how you're going to do their books, but about how you're going to change their lives!"

—Ian Percy

"The ideal client is a rich man who is scared!"

—Edward Bennett Williams

Recognize the Difference Between Service and Value

During my research days, my staff interviewed more than 150,000 CEOs, CFOs, in-house counsels, etc. over an eight-year period and asked what they might need during the next 12 to 24 months from their service providers. Incredibly, fewer than 2% were able to answer this question. Why? I think it is a question of perspective. CEOs, CFOs, and in-house counsels seldom think in terms of services; they think in terms of what they want to accomplish.

For example, few people would say they want to use succession-planning services. But many people are probably grappling with the following questions:

■ How do I get my money out of the business but keep the operation?

■ What's the best way to sell this company?

■ How can I pass on the business to my eldest son in a way that's fair to my other children?

■ How can I preserve the legacy I've built with this business?

These questions describe the Heart of the Matter...and delivering answers (or at least options) is the way you can truly add value.

If you fail to recognize what the client or prospect wants to accomplish, then there is very little chance that you'll win the SalesGame. You won't wind up with an enthusiastic client who thinks you added value. The words used by the client or prospect are important, and they should be at the top of any Scorecard.

Table 18.1 provides examples from a variety of clients. In the left column is what the client or prospect wanted to accomplish—how a service provider could change the client or prospect's life and add value. In the right column is the service area that was being sold and would eventually help the client or prospect accomplish his or her objective. Although only two examples are given for each service type, many more could have been listed. This is because the Heart of the Matter will be different for almost every client or prospect. Finding these differences and shaping the service accordingly is the starting point for building the Scorecard.

A quick review of Table 18.1 makes clear the difference between what the client or prospect is *buying* (his or her source of value) and what you are *selling* (the service). When playing the SalesGame, you start by listening for phrases like the ones shown in the left column. When it comes to the Heart of the Matter, most clients or prospects will use these phrases three or four times in a single meeting. If you do not hear the client or prospect use this kind of phrasing, either you are not asking the right questions or the client or prospect does not know the answer. In either case, you have not found the Heart of the Matter and would not be able to provide true value. Without true value, any professional service can be viewed as a commodity, with the major differentiating characteristic being price.

Table 18.1 Value Versus Service Area	
What Clients Want to Accomplish (The Heart of the Matter)	**Service Area (What We Do)**
Help us into the future	Audit
Help us find a better means of raising capital	Audit
Create a legacy so we'll be remembered	Wealth management
Make sure my grandchildren can afford college	Wealth management
Keep this from ruining our image	Litigation
Make this a warning for others	Litigation
Ensure a good marriage	Due diligence
Make sure I don't lose my job	Due diligence
Provide horsepower to deal with buyer	Investment banking
Simplify the whole process	Investment banking
Bring us into the 21st century	EDP services
Help us make our customers happy	EDP services
Keep the authorities off our backs	Tax
Make this department shine	Tax
Get rid of internal bickering	OD consulting
Make us one company	OD consulting
Save our business from imports	Legislative assistance
Make our voice heard	Legislative assistance
Provide shelter for our investments	Intellectual property
Hammer the competition	Intellectual property
Help us better manage our growth	Billing outsourcing
Improve our revenue stream	Billing outsourcing

Getting to the Heart of the Matter When the Client or Prospect Calls

As discussed in Part 2, "Best Practices for Setting Up the Game," the sales process can begin in one of two ways: Either the client or prospect initiates contact, or you do. Each scenario creates a very different challenge when it comes to getting to the Heart of the Matter. When clients or prospects call you, the vast majority tend to ask about services and cost—that is, "Do you do X? What do you charge?" You need to convert this conversation about service and cost to one about desired results and value. The good thing is, you can usually assume you are dealing with a qualified lead when someone calls you in this manner, although this is not always the case. The caller may misunderstand the service in question or have unrealistic expectations. Remember, a qualified lead is someone who currently has something he or she wants to accomplish as a result of using your service.

If you initiate the contact, you are pursuing an unqualified lead. That is, you have no idea if the client or prospect wants to accomplish anything using professional services. This is true even if a client or prospect is currently using the service in question from another provider. For example, I have worked with many labor and employment attorneys who believe that everyone who has employees needs their services, even though they are happy with their current law firm.

The majority of opportunities will begin with the client or prospect calling you, so let's look at that scenario first.

Establishing What They Really Want: It's a Dialogue

When the client or prospect calls you, the first thing you need to do is test the assumption that you are dealing with a qualified lead. You begin such testing during the initial contact by asking questions outlined in Part 2— for example, "At the end of the day, what is it you would most like to accomplish with this project?" Most clients and prospects are more than willing to answer this question. Even if the client or prospect answers this question during Stage Two, you must continue to define true value from the client or prospect's point of view in the early part of Stage Three and possibly in Stage Four. Clients and prospects often change their minds and often use the sales process to better define their objective. You need to clearly identify what belongs at the top of the Scorecard before determining the factors the client or prospect will use to choose a professional advisor.

One of my favorite examples of how critical it is to determine what clients and prospects really want comes from an engagement in China. One of the largest banks in that country sent out RFPs to each of the Big Four international accounting firms to perform an international accounting standards (IAS) audit on 10 of the bank's branches. One accounting firm's senior partner, Wong, was naturally curious as to why the request was limited to auditing only 10 of the bank's hundreds of branches. When he engaged the bank's president in a dialogue on this subject, the true Heart of the Matter eventually became clear. The bank wanted to prepare itself for China's upcoming entrance into the World Trade Organization. In the words of the president, "We must westernize ourselves." Wong suggested that performing IAS audits at 10 branches would not really accomplish this objective. An operations review of headquarters would be a more effective way to achieve this goal. His firm was the only one to develop a proposal to respond to the Heart of the Matter—to westernize the bank—and won the engagement, even though the cost involved was significantly higher.

The challenge facing you when you respond to client or prospect requests is to slow down the process enough to make sure the lead is qualified—that is, that you know what the prospect wants to accomplish and that your services can achieve this objective. Failure to fill out the top of the Scorecard first can result in wasting time and pursuing an opportunity that you cannot win. Remember, Wong's competitors all wrote proposals, too. Even worse, if they had won, they would have ended up with a piece of business that they would not have been able to handle in a way that would make the client enthusiastic.

This was made even more clear to me when a law firm client in the Southeast was trying to acquire ongoing product liability litigation work for a large carpet manufacturer. The carpet manufacturer had sent out an RFP for a firm to serve as national coordinating counsel. The request detailed the number of cases they encountered and requested experience, capacity, and rate information. When I first talked with my client, several partners and associates at the firm were crunching the numbers to see how economically they could handle the caseload. But when I asked the group, "What led this company to send out for proposals in the first place?" their reaction was blank stares. After a few moments, one of the attorneys said that he thought the carpet manufacturer was trying to lower legal fees because the incumbent law firm was known for its high rates. A second attorney said she had heard the incumbent firm had mishandled a case. A third said that he'd heard a large verdict had been levied against the carpet manufacturer. Still another attorney thought the RFP was a political move because the relationship between the incumbent firm and the carpet manufacturer stemmed from a contact on the board of directors who had left the organization.

All their answers were based on conjecture. No one really knew the Heart of the Matter. They quickly realized the folly of investing time in the opportunity without anyone really knowing what the carpet manufacturer wanted to achieve by going through the proposal process. They then chose a delegate to talk with the carpet manufacturer's in-house attorney to determine what was behind the decision to issue the RFP. As it turned out, the real issue was making sure that the law firm that represented this carpet manufacturer understood that the mission in litigation was not to win the case as much as to "protect our image in the marketplace"—something the incumbent had failed to realize. They had won a favorable decision on the West Coast but also created a lot of bad publicity.

This example illustrates one other point about the role of cost when getting to the Heart of the Matter, especially in proposal situations. An overwhelming number of professionals assume that the reason a prospect is requesting proposals is to reduce the cost of service. But that's not always the case. Several years ago, on a transatlantic flight, I sat next to a member of a bank's audit committee. He divulged that his bank had gone through the proposal process earlier that year. He began to talk in a very animated manner about his experiences. One of his comments was particularly telling. In fact, he repeated it three or four times during the conversation. He said he felt "insulted" that the accounting firms who had submitted proposals thought the bank was seeking a small reduction in audit fees. As he put it, "They must be crazy to think we'd go through all that effort—interviews, reading proposals, sitting through presentations, changing relationships—just to cut a few percentage points off our audit fee!"

This audit committee member's comments reinforced a key finding that many interviews done over the years have uncovered. Although professionals often jump to the conclusion that sending out for proposals is a cost-cutting technique, clients and prospects are often after something more complex and personal. They may not even know what it is at the start of the process—they just know they want something they are not getting. Cost becomes a factor when you are not getting what you want because whatever you *are* getting will almost always seem too expensive. Cost may be a factor in the decision-making process, but it rarely, if ever, is the Heart of the Matter. If it is, you should think twice about pursuing the opportunity. At best, you will be acquiring a client who will view your services as a commodity that can be bought somewhere else for still less.

Does the challenge of finding the Heart of the Matter—that is, what is of true value—change if a current client rather than a prospect calls for assistance? Not really. In

> Cost may be a factor in the decision-making process, but it rarely, if ever, is the Heart of the Matter.

fact, the danger of saying yes to a sole-source opportunity coming from a client without first getting to the Heart of the Matter is even greater than when dealing with prospects. First, it's greater because it is so easy to simply say yes to clients without taking the time to find out what's at the top of their Scorecard. (Beware of the easy sale!) Second, if you take on a project with a client without knowing what the decision-maker truly wants to accomplish, you may end up losing revenues generated by other services. Any multi-disciplinary firm is full of stories about annuities being lost because of a single service gone awry.

Ask and Ask Again

Regardless of whether it is a client or prospect calling for assistance, you need to ask questions like the following early and often in both Stage Two and Stage Three to get the Heart of the Matter. You should take the advice to "ask and ask again" quite literally. Ask the question in different ways. If more than one professional is participating in the meeting, each can ask in his or her own style. Listen to the nuances in the client or prospect's responses. Not only will you have a better understanding of the Heart of the Matter, but clients and prospects will clarify in their own minds what it is they really want to accomplish.

- What's the main reason you asked for this proposal?
- What's the most important thing you want to achieve by using our service?
- What's the one thing we could do in this project that would really make a difference in your life? In the organization?
- If you could change anything about the service you are now getting, what would it be?
- If you could change one thing about your current situation as a result of working with us on this project, what would it be?
- What's the biggest problem you want to fix with our assistance?
- When this project is completed, what do you want to be different about your current situation?
- What do you see as the most desirable outcome of what we do?

These questions should generate responses like those shown in Table 18.1 in the "What Clients Want to Accomplish" column. If not, you should be very wary, because you are dealing with a client or prospect who does not have a clear project goal. Without a clear goal—the Heart of the Matter—it will be next to impossible to truly win the SalesGame by ending up with an enthusiastic client.

Getting to the Heart of the Matter When You Initiate Contact

One of the lessons I learned when selling research is that people do not buy a service or product, regardless of price, if they don't recognize the value being offered. I remember trying to sell a syndicated research package to the managing partner of a prestigious West Coast law firm. I had flown from Detroit to Los Angeles solely to meet with this managing partner— something I rarely did— because I wanted the firm as a client to add credibil-

> People do not buy a service or product, regardless of price, if they don't recognize the value being offered.

ity to my company. I sincerely believed the syndicated research package I was offering was of such value, at such an attractive price, that it would be virtually impossible for this potential buyer to say no. (My study cost $6,000, while a similar custom study would have cost at least $40,000.)

We sat in an impressive conference room high above Los Angeles, sipping coffee from imported English tea cups. As we paged through the report, I asked questions about his firm's marketing efforts, trying to find a good fit between my service and his situation. The voice in the back of my head kept saying, "There's *no way* he's not going to buy this package! The price is a drop in the bucket for this firm, and the information is outstanding." Well, the voice was wrong. After 30 minutes or so, the managing partner closed the report, pushed it over to me, and said, "There's really nothing here that's of any interest to me. We're growing fast enough already." His complacency with his present situation was obvious. There was nothing he wanted to accomplish from a business-development perspective, so my research package had no value at any price. My heart was broken (temporarily). It was a long flight back to Detroit. The lesson was a costly one, but valuable as well: Prospects do not buy

> Prospects do not buy what you are selling because of how valuable *you* think the service is. They buy because *they* see value in the service.

what you are selling because of how valuable *you* think the service is. They buy because *they* see value in the service.

The challenge facing you when you initiate contact is simple: You have no idea whether there is anything your client or prospect actually wants to accomplish. You have a lead, but not a qualified lead. Complacency, lack of interest or time, and/or politics may all prevent a client or prospect from seeing value in a service you offer. There are countless examples of what appeared to be an easy sale because the dollar savings were so significant, but in the end, dollars had nothing to do with value. Here are just a few:

■ A CFO of a $100-million company turned down a study to review his state and local taxes. The fee would have been calculated as a percentage of savings (estimated to be at least $1 million) with no up-front cost. Perhaps the CFO feared that any findings might reflect poorly on his past performance. In short, it may have been that the CFO derived more personal value from *not* buying the study. In any case, there was no sale.

■ The lead litigation attorney for an insurance organization was not willing to pay a higher hourly rate, even though the company was getting killed by settlement costs because he was working with a less than effective outside law firm. Why? Because the hourly rates were his responsibility and the settlement costs were chalked up to someone else's bottom line.

■ The owner of a small business had a $40,000 mistake on his tax return but did not want to switch to the accountant who pointed this out because of his loyalty to his current accountant, who was also a friend.

Ironic, is it not? We spend most of our lives measuring value in terms of money, but when we play the SalesGame, dollars (or euros or yen) have little to do with value.

So what's a professional to do? How do you get to the Heart of the Matter when initiating contact? The first thing you need to do is to recognize that there may be nothing that the client or prospect wants to accomplish. There may be no Heart of the Matter—and that's just fine. Based on my research, less than one out of 20 businesses are unhappy with their accounting firm at any given point in time. This gives some indication of how rarely professionals uncover a qualified lead when they initiate contact.

Once again, do not sell to an unqualified lead. There is no point in using a hard sell by expounding the virtues of a service until the client or prospect recognizes some connection between the service and something he or she wants to accomplish. Even so, building positive relationships with leads that turn out not to be qualified at the time of contact is a very beneficial activity. These relationships create an inventory of leads for the future. If you position with these leads, you will usually get a call when the right opportunity to be of assistance comes up. Play the SalesGame for the long run and good things will happen.

> Play the sales game for the long run and good things will happen.

Start Broad

One thing you can do to see if there is in fact a Heart of the Matter is to focus on broad-based questions that might help you to understand what the client or prospect wants to accomplish (if anything). One mistake that all professionals make—including me—is to ask questions about a particular service. For example, a wealth manager may be focused on portfolio management and ask questions related to that service area, but miss uncovering a need for loan restructuring or estate planning. You should tailor broad-based questions to the particular situation as well as to your own style. For example, most accountants would not feel comfortable asking someone in a first meeting to describe his or her hopes and dreams. On the other hand, many accountants *would* feel comfortable asking this question of a client with whom they have worked with for years and are meeting to discuss estate or succession planning services.

Here are some broad-based questions to consider:

- What are your goals for the coming year (or any time period)?

- What do you see as the biggest obstacles to achieving these goals?

- What's the toughest problem on your desk today?

- How would you describe the plusses and minuses of your current situation?

- If you could wave a magic wand and change one thing about the service you are now receiving, what would it be?

- What keeps you up at night?

- What are your hopes and dreams for your company, family, etc.?

- How could we be of greatest value to you personally?

- What's the one thing we might be able to do that would really make a difference for you, your company, your family, etc.?

- What are your biggest concerns about your state and local tax situation/product liability litigation/computer function/etc.?

Many of these questions would not be used in the early part of a Stage Two interview. Depending on the situation, they might not be used for several meetings. You must build genuine rapport before such questions would flow naturally in the conversation. But if you have one or two of these broad-based queries ready as the meetings progress, you stand a much better chance of getting to the Heart of the Matter (if there is one) and successfully playing the SalesGame.

Know How Your Service Might Benefit the Client or Prospect

If you are trying to determine whether a client or prospect might be a candidate for only a particular service, you'll want to get to the Heart of the Matter (again, if there is one) by focusing on the things the client or prospect might want to accomplish as a result of using various services.

Admittedly, this is guesswork, but it does provide some additional areas to explore in the sales meeting. For example, the primary ways my clients used my company's research packages were to build awareness of business development, improve planning efforts, and measure performance. So at almost every sales meeting, I asked questions like the following:

- What's the overall attitude of the staff toward business development?

- What have you done to plan and structure your business-development efforts?

- How do you measure the intangible part of your marketing efforts like, your image in the community?

If you are feeling a bit more aggressive or the client or prospect is generally unresponsive, then these questions could easily be turned into suggestions to get a better reaction. For example:

- One of the things our research package does very well is increase everyone's awareness of the need to do business development. The presentation gives them some ideas as to how to turn this awareness into action. How would that fit the situation in your office?

- Most of the firms using this research found it gave more direction and focus to their planning efforts. And it can reduce some of the endless guessing about who knows what about your firm. What kind of experiences have you had planning your marketing and sales efforts?

- Between seminars and advertising, membership and entertainment budgets, firms spend a lot more money in business development without really knowing the return on investment. One thing this tool does is give you a way to measure the intangibles—the image you are creating—not just the bottom line. How big an issue is this for you?

Of course, this type of preamble/question would not come early in the meeting. The first part of the conversation was more informal. Hopefully, my contacts would share what they were trying to accomplish—the Heart of the Matter—on their own. However, I was sure to explore each of these areas somewhere in the discussion if no other need was revealed. Inevitably, one of three things would result from this approach. First, my inquiries might uncover a connection between my research package and the goals of my contacts. Second, it might start my contacts thinking about an area of need they had not contemplated previously, which might lead to a future sale. Third, I might strike out altogether. But by remembering to cover these areas, I at least felt like I was playing the game to the best of my ability.

During a pre-workshop interview, a partner with a large CPA firm in the South related a story about a similar approach he used while calling on community banks. He knew that at the time the three issues most commonly on the minds of bank presidents were mergers and acquisitions, changing technology, and outsourcing such functions as internal audit and loan review. As he put it, "I'd just go in and talk with the bank president. Usually the CFO would sit in, too. You know bankers will talk to anybody. I'd ask about the local economy, employment—just make small talk. Eventually, though, I'd get around to asking about how they were using computers, what problems they were having with internal audit, and whether they thought about being an acquisition candidate—not in any particular order and not all at once. I just made sure to ask something about each area." He continued, "Sometimes, nothing came up. Other times, I'd hit a hot button. I just tried to relax and listen to what was on their minds." The best way to find the Heart of the Matter is contained in the man's last sentence: Relax and listen.

> Relax and listen.

A successful rainmaker I know in the United Kingdom coached his partners who were less comfortable selling with much the same words. His advice was to "smile, listen, and relax." Most people would agree that some tension is a good thing in any game. It makes the adrenaline flow. Too much tension, though, and it's hard to perform, as many golfers who play in the Ryder Cup will tell you. So relaxing is a good thing. Listening is an even better thing. Anyone who plays the SalesGame knows that. What are you listening for? Remember the words of Ian Percy. Listen for how to change the client or prospect's life.

Great opportunities come from listening to clients as well as prospects. A perfect example is Newton, who was the head of an accounting firm in Ohio. Years ago, he listened to one of his clients, a financial officer, who was worried about how to determine the real cost of a fire that severely damaged one of the company's factories. He had a good sense of the property damage but was not sure how to tackle the financial impact that would result from the temporary shutdown of operations during restoration. Newton volunteered his services to help the client accomplish his objective —to determine the true impact of the fire. Not only was Newton successful in helping the client, his efforts were admired by the insurance adjuster assigned to the case, who referred him to other businesses in the same situation. The firm now is recognized for this specialty throughout the Midwest and half of their business comes from helping clients reach settlements on business-interruption claims.

You want to hear your clients or prospects use phrases like the following:

- Help us find a fair settlement or this business might go under.

- Provide some peace of mind.

- Make us one company.

- Keep the authorities off our backs.

- Make this department shine.

- Help us into the future.

Then you know you are getting at the Heart of the Matter and have a qualified prospect. When you know you have a qualified prospect, it is time to build the next part of the Scorecard—the factors the client or prospect will use to decide how to accomplish the objective and/or to evaluate the service that is eventually chosen.

Shaping the Service: Features, Benefits, and Conditions of Satisfaction

The factors following the Heart of the Matter on the Scorecard are the key to differentiation and strategy. Throughout the process, they are simply referred to as Scorecard Factors. Scorecard Factors go a long way toward determining whether you win the SalesGame by ending up with an enthusiastic client. Finding and defining these factors is a source of challenge, fun, and satisfaction. As mentioned, the factors themselves can be any number of things, but can generally be divided into three categories:

- **Features:** These are characteristics that are an inherent part of the service and/or the professional(s) delivering the service.

- **Benefits:** These are the things a client or prospect receives from using the service.

- **Conditions of satisfaction:** These are the parameters the client uses to evaluate how well the service was performed.

Table 19.1 on the following pages gives examples of each of these.

Table 19.1 Examples of Scorecard Factors

Category	Examples
Features	Size of organization
	Experience with a particular project
	Experience dealing with a person (for example, any type of advisor)
	Reputation
	Structure of service team
	Commitment
	Track record with client
	Partner-to-staff ratio
	Client's importance to professional
	Experience with a particular industry
	Location of office (s)
	Depth of service team
	Contacts (political, business, etc.)
	Good chemistry
	Familiarity with client or personnel
	Leading-edge technology
Benefits	More ideas
	Improved profits
	Less worry
	Protection of assets
	Improved communication
	Increased security
	Enjoyable/easy to work with
	Access to top partners
	Fresh set of eyes
	Reduced costs
	More time
	More confidence
	Protection of reputation
	Enhanced reputation
	Access to third parties
	Peace of mind

Table 19.1 Examples of Scorecard Factors (continued)

Category	Examples
Conditions of satisfaction	Project completion dates
	Required amount of client involvement
	Channels of communication
	Staffing
	Size, shape, and form of deliverables
	Scope of work
	No surprises
	Independence
	Amount of professional involvement
	Timing of reports
	Frequency of communication
	Pricing
	Entertainment/social requirements
	Reciprocity
	No government intervention
	Billing approach/policy

Some of these factors are *hard*. They are factual, tangible, and cannot be contested. These include credentials and office location. Some of the factors are *soft* because they are more of an attitude, are intangible, and must be proven, such as commitment or chemistry. But all might be important in any given situation. There is almost an infinite number of factors. They vary by professional and service. Subtle differences can exist in both concept and wording for almost every client or prospect situation. I have played hundreds of rounds of golf and can't remember ever playing exactly the same shot twice. The same thing could be said, I imagine, for poker or bridge. Likewise, the factors on the Scorecard are always different, which makes playing the SalesGame a lot more fun than reviewing tax returns or writing reports.

Although the terms *features* and *benefits* have been used for years in the SalesGame, *conditions of satisfaction* requires some additional explanation. I first thought of the term outside my normal business environment. I was in Amsterdam on a Friday night at an Italian restaurant near the

Rembrandtplien. The restaurant had both inside and outside seating, the latter of which was very full given it was a beautiful summer evening. I thought I would try my luck and asked for a table outside in spite of the crowd. The *maître d'* advised me to take a table inside, have a glass of wine, and place my order. He would then move me to a table outside as soon as one became available. The inside of the restaurant seemed stuffy and dark, but I wanted to finish my meal in time to watch the Dutch team play in the FIFA World Cup on TV that night, so inside I went.

The interior was almost empty except for one man sitting a few feet away. He kept looking through the window at the tables outside as he, too, drank a glass of wine after placing his order. After a few minutes, the waiter delivered a salad and, a little later, his entrée. The man suddenly went ballistic. In very loud, broken English, he claimed that the waiter had "thrown" the food at him and that this was the worst service he had ever received at a restaurant. The commotion drew everyone's attention, including the *maître d'*s, who came over to calm the man down. It was a lost cause. A long and confusing debate ensued over how food should be served, which was irrelevant as the waiter had done nothing wrong. From the conversation, it became apparent that the *maître d'* had told the man the same story I had heard: Sit inside to order, and I will move you outside for your meal. Eating outside was this patron's condition of satisfaction. When that condition was not met, there was nothing the restaurant was going to be able to do that the patron would consider "right." If the problem had not been the presentation of the entrée, then it would have been the quality of the food, the size of the portion served, or the size of the bill. I realized that the *maître d'* would have been far better off telling the man that no tables would be available outside, apologizing for this inconvenience, and asking him to come back another night.

Do professionals make this same mistake? You bet! Consider a city that hired a regional law firm to handle a politically dangerous condemnation case because they wanted to use a female partner who had a reputation for handling high-profile cases. The partner was already overcommitted with other clients and was not very visible as the case progressed. Halfway through the matter, the city switched law firms, claiming they were not getting the results they wanted even though the case was nowhere near resolution. Or there's the example of a consultant, Neil, who was hired to do a risk analysis for a division of a company. The division president wanted Neil to submit a draft to him two weeks before the final report was issued so he could review the recommendations and begin to make any necessary changes before a visit from the parent company. The draft was delivered only a few days before the final report was submitted, and Neil was criticized for being "unresponsive." He was never hired again by either the division or the parent, in spite of his impeccable credentials and a thorough job performing the risk analysis.

When playing the SalesGame, you must focus on finding the conditions of satisfaction on the Scorecard—even when dealing with sole-source opportunities from existing contacts—or you will find it almost impossible to end up with an enthusiastic client.

When you shape a service for a particular client or prospect, you either consciously or unconsciously use some combination of features, benefits, and conditions of satisfaction to tailor the service being delivered. For example:

■ Should the attorney assigned have substantial experience with a high hourly rate or be less experienced with a lower hourly rate?

■ Should the wealth manager involve the next generation in estate planning or limit conversations to the matriarch or patriarch?

■ Should the consultant use client personnel so training becomes an ancillary benefit or should only external personnel be used to ensure objectivity?

■ Should the accountant write a detailed management letter as part of the audit or summarize findings in an oral presentation to the board?

Successful professionals have always tailored their services, but few considered it "selling." Building this combination of Scorecard Factors was just something they did to better serve their clients. Unfortunately, when some of these same professionals think they are supposed to be selling, they end up telling the client or prospect about how good their services are instead of asking the client or prospect what "good" means to them.

Selling through telling—for example, presentations, one-sided sales pitches, and lengthy proposals—does not work very well in the service arena for two reasons. First, one-sided communication limits your ability to tailor your services and create new ones. Consultants, lawyers, attorneys, wealth managers, and investment bankers almost always change what they do, even when performing services thought to be commodities—for example, audits or patent prosecution. The change might be something as simple as the amount of assistance the client's staff provides on the audit or how portfolio performance is shared with the client. Collaboration and dialogue lead to creativity, agreement, and better service for clients. Second, and more importantly, when selling through telling, you have very little information to use to ensure client enthusiasm. You must know the criteria on the client's Scorecard if you are going to win the SalesGame —that is, end up with an enthusiastic client—even when you are not competing with anyone else for the work.

> You must know the criteria on the client's Scorecard if you are going to win the SalesGame.

Find the Right Scorecard Factors

So where and how do you find the right Scorecard Factors? The where is easy—from a dialogue about the client or prospect's requirements and your own experience. The how is a bit more difficult, much as it is with other games. Everyone knows you have to put the football in the end zone (or the goal, for you European readers) to score. Actually *getting* it there is another matter.

Although there are no rules, the best way to start the process of finding the right factors is to ask the client or prospect what he or she thinks will be of greatest importance in choosing a professional or evaluating a service. The following questions generally work well when dealing with competitive situations. (You can modify them to fit your own style of communication.)

- What are some of the criteria you think you'll use when choosing between firms?

- How will you choose between service alternatives?

- What do you think will be the most important issues when you (or your company, your institution, or your organization) are deciding between the service professionals you're considering for this project?

- The request for proposal listed areas that would be considered. How important do you think each of them is in this process?

- What do you think is really going to make the difference when it comes time to choose between service professionals?

- What do you think it will take to get this work/win this proposal?

Several years ago, a law firm partner in a Washington D.C. workshop was in the middle of responding to a major RFP. When we were discussing questions like the ones in the preceding list, he asked me if I really thought he should be so bold as to ask his prospect what it would take to win the proposal. Wouldn't that seem overly aggressive? Everybody has to play the game in a way that matches their own personal style, of course, but I asked the attorney to think about how much time the prospect was requiring of him and his firm to go through the proposal process. Doesn't it seem fair that if professionals are going to make this kind of investment, they ought to know how the prospect is going to choose between alternatives? It is hard to play any game if you do not know how to keep score!

Don't Believe the RFP

I need to make one other point about getting to the right Scorecard Factors in a competitive situation: Don't believe the criteria given for how the organization intends to choose between competitors—that is, what's in the RFP. Time after time, I have seen businesses choose professionals based on criteria other than those they listed in the RFP. I once worked with a law firm in the Midwest that was proposing to handle litigation for a municipality. The municipality had created a real scorecard, assigning points to competing firms based on their rating of a dozen or more factors. The firm with the highest number of points was supposed to win. However, a firm with a lower number of points won. Why? Because it used inside connections during the sales process to uncover some important factors that weren't even mentioned in the RFP, like involvement of a senior partner. More recently, I worked with a firm in Norway proposing on a bank audit. The bank emphasized in the RFP that it did not want information about consulting services in the proposal; it was interested only in a basic audit. During the pre-proposal research, however, my client found many operational problems that had little to do with the audit. The partner in charge of developing the proposal asked for a 15-minute closed-door meeting with the bank president. He opened the discussion by saying, "I know you want us to propose on the audit only and we will. But I wouldn't be doing my job very well if I didn't take the time to share some of the problems that we came across in our research. Regardless of who you eventually choose for the audit, you need to look at some of these issues." Two hours later, the door reopened—and my client won the audit based on his ability to assist the bank in a wide range of other areas. These stories are hardly unique. A client or prospect that actually *did* make a decision using the criteria defined in an RFP would be far more unusual.

How could sophisticated businesses seem so fickle, as in these two examples? At times, it may be a function of not really knowing what factors to use. This might be because the buyer does not have much experience hiring professionals. In some cases, the buyer may never have hired a wealth manager, attorney, investment banker, or even an accountant before. Sometimes an RFP is developed by a committee and everyone throws in their ideas. Sometimes clients and prospects use a template from another organization's RFP. Probably the biggest reason for misleading information in RFPs is that decision-makers are busy people and simply don't take the time on the front end to really clarify what they're looking for. This is often true even for sophisticated buyers.

When you start a competitive process to acquire work, you should not assume the criteria the client or prospect initially outlines will be the factors used in the final analysis. In fact, in most instances you should assume the reverse: The initial criteria will *not* be the final factors on the Scorecard. This creates an opportunity for you to educate your client or prospect so he or she can make a more informed decision—another way you can bring value, even in the sales process.

Shape the Service, Even If the Work Is Sold

Learning what factors are on the Scorecard is important even when you are dealing with a sole-source opportunity—for example, a former client calling with a new case or a current client trying to decide whether to use internal or external assistance for a particular project. Getting the right factors on the Scorecard is probably easier in this kind of situation because you and the client already have a working relationship. This can be a two-edged sword, however. Familiarity makes it easy to forget to focus on the Scorecard before taking on the work. Once again, beware of the easy sale. The following questions should work well in a sole-source situation:

- What yardsticks are you going to use to measure performance on this matter?

- What are you looking for on this matter that's different from the others we've handled for you?

- When all is said and done, what's going to make you pleased with our efforts on this matter?

- How exactly does the company currently evaluate the performance of its outside advisors?

Once again, you will want to modify these questions based on your own style and relationship with the client. An attorney in Texas phrased the last question to a former client with whom he hadn't worked in a year or two like so: "OK Bob, so what does ABC think they want from their hired guns this year?" Smart question if you know how quickly the winds can change in any corporate environment!

Tip

A sole-source opportunity that is "sold" is not too dissimilar from a partner asking a younger professional to take on a new assignment or project. In this situation, I often recommend that the young professionals start using the Scorecard to make sure they end up with enthusiastic clients—in their case, the partners who have given them an assignment.

Know Your Selling Points

If Scorecard Factors came only from asking clients or prospects what they wanted, the SalesGame would not be anywhere near as much fun—nor would you be anywhere near as effective at tailoring the services you perform. Accountants, lawyers, engineers, financial advisors, consultants, etc. all spend years learning their professions and specialties. This knowledge defines a professional service. It should certainly be used to help clients or prospects make more intelligent decisions about how to accomplish their objectives, choose the right professional for a given task, and/or evaluate the service that is delivered. This seems like common sense, but I have been amazed over the years by how rarely professionals take the time to identify all the features, benefits, and conditions of satisfaction they have to offer.

Several years ago, in a workshop with a group of accountants, a partner wanted to discuss an RFP he had received from a current client. The partner, Matt, was concerned (if not depressed) because he felt sure he was going to lose his largest client, a bank, because of a change in political leadership. I asked the group to brainstorm all the factors they thought the bank could use to make a decision to retain its current firm or hire a new one. We filled one flip chart and most of another with ideas. The vast majority of these factors clearly favored the incumbent accounting firm. During this process, the expression on Matt's face changed from disconsolate to excited and enthusiastic. Matt saw what he brought to the table and felt confident he had more to offer the bank than any competitor—and he did.

If you play almost any game from poker to polo, you know how important it is to believe in yourself—to be confident you can win. In short, before you start selling, you should invest a few minutes thinking about what you have to sell—that is, the features, benefits, and conditions of satisfaction they can offer a client or prospect. If at all possible, this process should include input from others. I have never seen one professional be as effective as a team when it came to listing items that could be on the Scorecard. The team, by the way, does not have to come from the same discipline as you, nor do team members need to be particularly experienced. Strangely enough, the most important factor or differentiator is often the last one the group will mention in a workshop setting. You just need to take the time to collaborate.

This exercise—even if done alone—provides you with additional factors you can bring up in sales meetings either through questions or suggestions. In a perfect world, at least some of these factors will be used by the client or prospect to make a better decision about who will be hired or how your service will be evaluated. Sometimes, clients or prospects will not want to use any of them because they are not perceived to be important. Still, you would not be playing the SalesGame very well if you did not at least explore the client or prospect's reaction to potential Scorecard Factors.

Find Your Style

Each professional will develop his or her own style for introducing potential Scorecard Factors based on personal experience rather than the client or prospect's perspective. As an example, consider a consultant who feels that his experience on a similar project is something that should be a factor on the prospect's Scorecard. The prospect has not brought it up in response to any of the broad-based questions asked earlier in the interview, however. In that case, the consultant might say something like, "I've used ABC software with several suppliers with good results. You didn't mention previous experience as a factor you're considering, but I know several of my clients put it at the top of the list. How important is it to you?" Or the consultant might be more aggressive, and make a suggestion like so: "One thing you haven't mentioned is previous experience with ABC software. I've worked on these projects for a number of suppliers and understand the pitfalls. That kind of experience is invaluable on a project like this. Regardless of who you end up hiring, you really should find someone who's been down this road before."

Most professionals favor the first approach—asking a question—because it is less pushy. But again, this is a matter of personal style. In either case, the consultant should make sure to at least bring up an important Scorecard Factor for the prospect's consideration. If the prospect agrees with it, then the consultant has something that works in his favor. If not, then previous experience with ABC software simply is not on the Scorecard of this particular prospect, and the consultant needs to look for other factors that might be. In either case, you can be confident you have played the SalesGame well by making sure to introduce a factor that should be on the prospect's Scorecard.

Few Are Better Than Many

When building the Scorecard, you will be most effective if you focus on a few factors rather than many. Sometimes, finding even a single feature, benefit, or condition of satisfaction will help you differentiate your service from internal or external competition. For years I have watched accountants, consultants, and more recently lawyers write lengthy proposals full of reasons why the client or prospect should use them. I think the theory is that if enough good reasons are included in a proposal, the prospect would find something to like. As mentioned, the problem is that hardly anyone bothers to read the proposals in the first place.

The importance of quality over quantity really hit me when my wife Sue and I were looking for a new car in the early 1990s. We are from Detroit, and one of our factors was that the car be manufactured by an American company. Given that we had two children at the time (and an irrational dislike of minivans), we also wanted a big car. Eventually, we narrowed our choices down to a Cadillac and a Lincoln Town Car. Price, location of dealership, length of warranty, etc. were all similar. How would we choose? Then, the salesman tapped the dashboard of the Town Car and said, "You know, this is the only car built in the world today that has a cavity so you can add a passenger-side airbag." (Of course, these days, every car has passenger-side and even side-door airbags.) It was like a bright light turned on in my wife's head. Whenever the family went somewhere, she rode in the passenger seat, and the thought of having an airbag there made all the difference in the world to her. That single feature—a passenger-side airbag—overrode any other factor. It was a deal-maker for the Town Car. For the Cadillac, it was a deal-breaker. From my research experience, choosing a professional is very similar. There are often deal-makers and deal-breakers. The challenge for you is to find the "airbag" or deal-maker for each client or prospect—the factor that most clearly differentiates your service. Take for example the attorney with a law firm in Atlanta who acquired a major piece of litigation because she had tried several cases before the judge that was scheduled to handle the matter in question. Her rates were higher than the competition and she had not worked with the prospect—both factors that worked against her on the Scorecard. But the fact that she was familiar with the judge and had a good track record with him got her the work.

Even if there is not an "airbag" or deal-maker in a given business-development situation, clients and prospects very rarely consider a long list of factors when making their decision about who to use. When doing research through my research company, we asked thousands of people why they chose their accountant, lawyer, or consultant. Most would name one or two factors that were critical to them. Some named three. I honestly can't remember a single respondent who could recall more than three factors. Even if a formal RFP lists 15 or 20 factors that will be considered, the final decision always comes down to one, two, or three critical factors. As mentioned, the irony is that the *real* factors—the ones the client or prospect ends up using to make the decision—probably are not in the RFP!

If you doubt the power of finding and focusing on a few—three or fewer—Scorecard Factors when playing the SalesGame, ask friends or relatives why

> The final decision always comes down to one, two, or three critical factors.

they chose the city they live in or selected a particular school for their child. You will hear one, two, or three reasons—no more. Many other factors may have been considered before the final decision was made—just like you may see a list of 10 or 20 factors included in an RFP. The game is to whittle many factors down to a few that most clearly differentiate your service. This approach should hopefully be a collaborative dialogue that helps both you and the client or prospect to focus on what is really important in the selection process and, more importantly, in the delivery of the service.

Chapter

Differentiating Your Service and Developing a Strategy

After years of running workshops called "Strategic Selling," I decided I'd better not take my definition of the word *strategy* for granted, so I checked Webster's Dictionary. The definition was straightforward: "Strategy is the artful or ingenious use of resources and sometimes of deceit." While I would never recommend deceit as part of your strategy, most of the factors on any Scorecard could be looked at as resources—for example, office location, depth or breadth of staff, knowledge, ability to increase revenues or decrease costs, etc. So when we talk about *strategic selling*, we are talking about the creative or ingenious use of your and your firm's resources to shape services. In the SalesGame, that means establishing Scorecard Factors. These factors may be used to make sure a sole-source opportunity ends up as an enthusiastic client or to put forth the most convincing case as to why a certain professional should be chosen in a competitive situation.

> When we talk about *strategic selling*, we are talking about the creative or ingenious use of your and your firm's resources to shape services.

An accounting firm I worked with in Norway in the pre–Sarbanes-Oxley era provides an interesting example of how to ingeniously use resources to both create a strategy and differentiate a firm. The CFO from one of its banking clients was under pressure to reduce operating expenses.

To that end, he was looking for a way to reduce the overall cost of the audit function—both external and internal. Thankfully, the CFO was sophisticated enough to know he was already getting a fair price from my accounting firm client for the external audit. His focus was primarily cutting payroll costs by outsourcing the internal audit function. The client partner, Arne, came up with some creative ways to use resources—that is, to use Scorecard Factors—to shape the service and win the engagement. First, Arne stressed the synergy that only the incumbent external auditor could offer to save hours and costs. I'm sure the competition chose to emphasize different Scorecard Factors—for example, the benefit of a fresh set of eyes, greater objectivity, or maybe a stronger perception of independence. Second, Arne saw this as the beginning of a trend in a world of rapidly rising payroll and fringe benefit costs. His firm was the only one with sufficient banking work to justify hiring some of the client's experienced internal auditors to create a specialized—and profitable—practice in outsourcing. So Arne proposed that his firm hire the majority of the bank's internal audit team if, in return, the bank would award his firm a three-year contract to serve as the "outside" internal audit function. Talk about a win-win situation. The CFO got to sleep better knowing he was cutting costs without leaving employees out to fend for themselves—a major issue in the Norwegian culture. From Arne's point of view, this new staff could be a useful resource to stress in future opportunities. No other firm would be able to offer such an experienced body of internal auditors that a bank could use to outsource this pesky task. Arne got the work, of course.

Start Developing a Strategy Early

As discussed, collaborating to come up with the factors that might be on a client or prospect's Scorecard is an extremely important part of the SalesGame. To improve your performance, you should start thinking about Scorecard Factors early in the process. You want to come up with your strongest selling points—resources that can be used to differentiate yourself or your firm. Then you can start building a strategy by creatively using these resources as soon as possible, beginning with the next step after the initial contact. Here are examples:

■ An investment advisor from Atlanta had a referral from a lawyer to provide assistance to a large family-owned business located in a small town in Tennessee. The family needed help because its business was about to be sold to a New York Stock Exchange company. After talking at length with the referral source, the investment advisor decided to use his ability to deliver close, personal service as a key resource to differentiate himself and his firm. The competing investment advisory firm was larger and had a more impressive name. But, based on what his referral source told him, he felt this close-knit family would be more impressed by down-home Southern courtesy than big-city polish. He called the family and offered to meet them as soon as they'd like. By 11 a.m. the next morning, after driving 200 miles, he was sitting in the family kitchen, having a casual conversation with Grandpa, Grandma, and the children. The competition never had a chance.

■ Richard, an accountant from Detroit, had a personal friend, Michael, who was becoming more and more successful building upscale, high-priced residential developments. One day, Michael called Richard to ask where he should go in the long run for accounting advice. Michael was working with a sole practitioner but was not impressed with his big-picture advice, particularly when it came to understanding the construction/real estate industry. He did not think he was going to replace this incumbent but wanted to see what options were out there. Richard told Michael that although he did not know the residential real estate business that well, he had a partner who did, and recommended that all three of them meet. After one lunch, Michael was sold by how useful this specialized resource could be in developing a vision for his future.

■ A law firm in Denver received an invitation to propose on a major piece of litigation for a high-tech company located in Boulder. Nick, the partner handling the opportunity, did his homework and heard from several contacts that the case would probably go to trial because of its significance in the mind of the company's founder. One of the resources that this law firm was proud of was its state-of-the art, high-tech video mock trial room. Nick thought about driving out to visit the prospect but, when considering his resources and what might be on the prospect's Scorecard, instead suggested they come to Denver to hold their initial meeting. The company founder, president, and in-house attorney made the hour drive and were, of course, given a tour of the facilities during their visit. The founder was particularly impressed by the mock trial room and started asking how everything worked. The firm's high-tech resource turned out to be a big hit, and the strategy worked.

Note

Of course, in this last example, things could have turned out differently. Maybe the prospect would have felt the drive was too far, making the firm seem inaccessible. The element of uncertainty is what makes any game fun. If you could always control the outcome, most games would be pretty boring.

Use the Power of Three

When it comes to reasons, we have already seen the power of three. That's why I always suggest to my clients that they choose their three favorite Scorecard Factors when they prepare for a meeting and start to build an appropriate strategy. Of course, these factors might very well change—and probably should—based on client or prospect input during the sales process. Nevertheless, picking three favorites provides focus and helps you ensure you are ready for the common question that often comes up early in the SalesGame: "Why should I choose you (or your firm)?" This question is not meant to be mean; it's more of a way of saying, "Sell me!" In many cases, the client or prospect simply wants ammunition for when they are talking about your service with others in the decision-making process. If you have selected your three most important factors, you can be much more focused in your response. You might choose these factors because they differentiate you or your firm, they respond to an assumed client or prospect hot button, or they are relevant based on your past experience.

Suppose a consultant is talking with a client or prospect about whether the consultant or internal personnel should be used to develop appropriate security for the company's growing e-business. If the client were to ask the consultant why he would be a better choice than using the company's own people, providing a little information—like three important Scorecard Factors—will generally be more effective than going straight to the question, "What's important to you?" For example, the consultant might say:

> Well, I'm biased of course, but I've thought about your situation quite a bit and it seems to me there are three reasons why we're the best option for this project. First, we've worked with a lot of other businesses in similar situations, so we know what's out there without doing a lot of additional research. Second, you know how difficult it is to control the time schedules of internal people working outside their normal responsibilities.

I know my people can get this done by early fall, so you'll be ready for your busiest time of the year. Third, with our reputation in e-commerce, you and your customers can feel comfortable that we'll get it done right. Experience, commitment to getting the project done in time for your busy season, and our reputation are the three reasons that come to mind for me. But you're the buyer. What's important to you?

In my experience, four times out of five, the client or prospect will repeat back two of the reasons you just presented. Remember the power of three. It can provide focus and make you sound very convincing!

Implement a Strategy by Making Scorecard Factors Real

Strategy is not something you think about just during the first meeting. It should be the focus throughout the SalesGame. Most professionals I work with have very strong personal and/or firm resources available to accomplish their client or prospect's objectives. Unfortunately, they do not make these resources real and tangible to the client or prospect when they are selling.

During my 20-plus years in business, I can't tell you how many proposals I have seen from the Big Eight (Seven…Six…Five…Four) firms that contain a map showing the location of the prospect's operations relative to the office locations of the accounting firm. In some cases, clear plastic overlays and color-coded dots add glitz to this inspiring presentation. Compare this with an approach used by Ole, a Danish partner with one of my clients in Europe. In his first meeting with a prospect, Ole learned that the company was seeking more sophisticated financial advice because it was opening its first production and sales operation outside Denmark—predictably enough in Minnesota. Ole also learned that his firm would be competing with all three other members of the Big Four. Before the next meeting, Ole telephoned one of his partners in Minneapolis who worked in the prospect's industry and spent 10 minutes getting some background on the situation. During the second meeting with the prospect, Ole asked a few questions about the company's imminent foray into the U.S. marketplace. As might be expected, several questions arose about various legal issues related to operating in the U.S. and, more specifically, in Minnesota. Ole suggested that regardless of which firm the prospect eventually chose, answers to most of the questions were only a telephone call away thanks to his Minneapolis colleague. The next conversation was a three-way conference call that went extremely well. As one of my clients used to put it, "Don't talk about how you'll give the prospect advice. Give them advice!"

That is exactly what Ole did. He and his Minneapolis partner gave the prospect advice and made a Scorecard Factor real and tangible in the process. It is important to note that any of Ole's three competitors could have done the same thing but did not. In the SalesGame, sometimes it is not about being different as much as it is about finding the right strategy—the artful or ingenious use of resources—to make Scorecard Factors real.

Building a Strategy for the Long Term

In most of the preceding examples, the strategy being used was implemented during a short sales cycle. But you do not want to miss out on possibilities for using Scorecard Factors to win the SalesGame over the long run. For example, I once worked with Bruce, an accountant, who had opened an office in Ann Arbor for a regional firm. After he got things up and running, he contacted a friend who was a business owner in the community to explore whether they might work together. The friend told Bruce he only wanted to work with a firm "of substance." Bruce was smart enough to ask some questions whose answers revealed that his friend defined "substance" as having a staff of 30 or 40 people. (Don't even try to guess why this number was given. In my experience, sales discussions are full of these kinds of arbitrary definitions.) Because Bruce had fewer than five employees at the time, even counting the part-time college student in the mail room, there was little point in pushing for his friend's business. Nevertheless, Bruce's office went on to be very successful. Four years later, it made a small acquisition, and had reached 35 personnel. He brought his friend on a tour of the firm's new offices and reminded him of his comment years earlier. With a laugh, his friend told him, "You've done a hell of a job here. Sign me up!"

Another example is the environmental department at a law firm in the Southeast. This firm had lost not one but two opportunities because the prospects wanted to work with a firm that had an alumnus of the Environmental Protection Agency on staff. Over the next two years, the firm searched for the right person to bring on board to fill this gap and develop the resource these prospects had put high on their Scorecard. They eventually found an attorney who had been with the EPA for almost a decade and was searching for a way out of the government sector. The firm had continued to position with the prospects and made sure they met the new addition to the department. Sure enough, less than a year later, the firm had acquired several major engagements and its environmental practice was growing at a rapid rate.

As one marketing director used to say when his firm was not successful on a particular new business effort, "We didn't lose. We just haven't won yet!" The same is true when it comes to developing a strategy and making Scorecard Factors real in the long run. If you remember Stage Six—listen to your client or prospect and keep positioning—you can usually develop the right resources and create a strategy to build the practice of your dreams.

> "We didn't lose. We just haven't won yet!"

Don't Forget Negative Factors on the Scorecard

When you generate a list of factors in preparation for a sales meeting, you can be sure there will be at least some negative factors—features, benefits, or conditions of satisfaction that do not favor using your services. If negative factors fail to surface, then you should rethink your list and seek additional input to avoid being surprised by the prospect. Almost every sales situation has something that might be a negative factor working against using a professional's service.

In addition, there are a number of criteria that could end up being perceived as either a positive or a negative factor on the client or prospect's Scorecard. Industry experience is an excellent example of this. This feature is generally a positive factor favoring the professional or firm that possesses it. However, industry experience can be a negative factor as well. Some clients or prospects may feel a firm works too closely with an industry—or certain key competitors—and may hold this against them. Factors can be positive on one client or prospect's Scorecard and negative on another. The hourly rate of any leading law firm in most Midwestern cities looks high when compared with rates charged by smaller, local competitors, but like a bargain compared to a firm in New York or Washington, D.C.

As with most games, there are many ways to handle negative factors depending on the situation and your personal style. When Arnold Palmer hit his golf ball into the woods, he had that swashbuckling style that demanded he go for the green, regardless of the trees that happened to be in the way. Most of his golfing contemporaries, however, would chip it onto the fairway to avoid further disaster. Regardless of style, though, identifying the negative factors during preparation will help you do a better job in the meeting itself.

Be Prepared: Negative Factors Lead to Objections

Most professionals would not raise negative factors in a sales meeting because they might be damaging to his or her cause. But identifying potential negative factors during preparation enables you to respond effectively if the client or prospect raises them. In fact, any negative factors that surface should be catalogued as potential objections. For example, the depth of the service team might be an important factor on a given client or prospect's Scorecard. If lack of depth is in fact a weakness for your firm and therefore a negative factor on the Scorecard, you should be ready for either an objection ("You obviously know what you're doing, but I'm concerned about who else we can rely on.") or a tough question ("What kind of backup do you have for a project like this?"). Either way, you need to prepare a response to deal with this negative factor. Most experienced professionals recognize that the manner in which they respond under pressure is often more important than the objection itself. In other words, never let them see you sweat!

Part 4, "The Ground Rule: Improve Communication, Handle Objections, and Define Scorecard Factors," discusses how to handle objections in more depth. But the response to this particular objection might sound like this: "Backup is always an issue to consider. I'd want to be comfortable with the team's depth if I were starting down the same road. What kind of backup are you looking for on a project like this?" Or, if the negative factor surfaces as a question, you might say, "Well, I've got Mr. Smith and Ms. Jones, who usually work with me on these kinds of projects. I'd like to put together the right team that works from your point of view. What kind of backup are you looking for?"

Of course, precise wording is a matter of style, but wording and style are not nearly as important as identifying the potential objection in advance and preparing for it so you feel confident and avoid any surprises.

Let Sleeping Dogs and Negative Scorecard Factors Lie

One question frequently asked in workshops is whether the professional should introduce a negative factor in a sales meeting before the client or prospect raises the issue. The theory behind such a preemptive strike is that it helps to show that you are honest. If you bring up a negative Scorecard Factor, you may provide offsetting benefits to minimize the damage.

While there is no one right way to handle negative Scorecard Factors, introducing them before the client or prospect does usually ends up being a bad idea for three reasons:

■ Clients and prospects often have not thought of a particular negative factor before you introduce it. Consider Truman, an environmental consultant, who was meeting with a safety director for a large corporation. Truman thought that the fact that he had never spent any time inside the Environmental Protection Agency might be perceived to be a weakness by the safety director. Early in the meeting, Truman brought this issue up and explained that it should not be an issue because the EPA would not be involved if the project was done correctly. "I hadn't thought about the EPA's role in all this," the safety director replied, with a look of concern on his face. "In fact, it might be very helpful to have someone with good inside contact if we run into problems down the road." Score one for the opposition!

■ When you bring up Scorecard Factors that could potentially be negative, the conversation often ends up focusing too much on the negative and not enough on the positives on the Scorecard. Either you explain why the negative factor is not an issue or the client or prospect starts asking questions about the negative and a debate ensues. Why use precious time discussing a negative if it is unnecessary?

■ Perhaps most importantly, it is not a good idea to bring up negatives because you should first attempt to identify Scorecard Factors by asking questions. Even positive factors on the Scorecard should generally be introduced only after asking questions to see if the client or prospect raises it first. If the client or prospect brings up a positive, it has more weight because he or she has ownership of it. If a negative does not come up as a result of asking questions, why should you bring it up? How important could it be if it hasn't surfaced as a result of asking a series of open-ended questions like those listed in the previous chapter? As will be discussed in Part 7 "Closing: Establish Next Steps and Advance Your Cause," you need not worry about a hidden objection. Any significant negative factor not brought up by the client or prospect can and should be surfaced when you ask for a next step.

There are few absolutes when playing the SalesGame. I am sure introducing a negative factor before the client or prospect does work in some situations. But the bottom line and best practice is for you to be aware of the negative so you are ready to respond if the client or prospect raises the issue. But if it does not come up, you should not ask for trouble by bringing it up yourself.

Sell Responsibly

Sometimes, when preparing for a meeting by listing the factors that could be on a client or prospect's Scorecard, or even in the sales meeting itself, it becomes fairly obvious that using your service is not the best way to accomplish the objective at hand. If this is the case, you will be well served by sharing this conclusion with your client or prospect and continuing to maintain contact until the right window of opportunity opens. This builds credibility for the future and reduces the pressure of pushing services on someone who really does not need them.

An intellectual property attorney, Julian, who had recently been a lateral hire at a diversified Manhattan law firm, took me aside during a break in a workgroup session. He expressed his concern over the mission the firm had given him and the pressure he was feeling. The firm had a number of clients the partners knew had substantial IP work—an area of expertise the firm was lacking—which was going to competitors. The partners hired Julian because they wanted him to lead the charge to capture some of this revenue. Julian had called on a number of these clients. "I listen to the decision-makers at these clients and what can I say?" Julian said. "For the most part, they have good relationships with the patent attorneys who've done their work for years. These attorneys

> Maintain contact until the right window of opportunity opens.

know the inventors in the company. They know the company's technology and even know the company's philosophy and history. I think they're right where they should be. Why should these clients switch to me?" He continued, "I tell them to stay put. If they have a problem or a conflict situation, I'll certainly be ready to help them. How much harder should I be pushing?" I could hear the frustration in his voice. Julian was worried his firm would not keep him for long because he was not developing enough business in the short run. But Julian saw the Scorecard for these prospects correctly (assuming he had asked the right questions in these meetings). First, there was nothing these clients or prospects wanted to accomplish, as their current IP attorneys were already helping them achieve their objectives. Julian was initiating contact, not responding, so this should not have been a surprise. Second, the factors Julian mentioned—good relationships, knowing the company's inventors, technology, and history—are significant to anyone choosing a provider of IP services. Pushing himself on clients or prospects who were satisfied in their current situation would be a waste of time at best, and at worst could damage his firm's overall relationship with the client or prospect. His honest message to these clients and prospects was responsible and right.

Unfortunately, I couldn't really help Julian with this problem except to assure him he was on the right track. He was building relationships for the future. He needed to recognize that these Stage Two meetings had given him positioning leads, not qualified leads—that is, there was no Heart of the Matter. I hope the firm that hired him had enough good sense to wait one, two, or even three years to judge his business-development performance.

Does this mean Julian should stop playing the SalesGame with these clients and prospects? Of course not. He has opened the door and his honesty will be a factor on a future Scorecard should the right window of opportunity open. As was discussed in Part 2, "Best Practices for Setting Up the Game," Julian must begin the process of positioning with these clients and prospects, contacting them two or three times a year to build his relationship with them. Based on many similar experiences and given his field of specialty, the window of opportunity will eventually open before too long, and he'll begin to see the results of his sales efforts.

Make the Scorecard Part of the Permanent File

You create the Scorecard for a prospect at the beginning of the sales process. During the sales process, it is continually refined, becoming the focal point in Stage Six when the prospect becomes a client. The Scorecard should become a part of the client's permanent file and should be reviewed with the client on a periodic basis—certainly each time a Stage Six (ACE) meeting is conducted with the client. A client's situation, goals, and needs will change over time, and the Scorecard should be revised to reflect these changes—for both the Heart of the Matter and the key Scorecard Factors. In most professional firms, clients are served at some point by someone who was not involved in the sales process. Keeping the Scorecard in the permanent file helps everyone on the team know what's important to the client and how the firm will be judged when the work is done.

Part Summary

The Scorecard is a shared vision of the best way to define and accomplish the client or prospect's desired objective. The Scorecard can take any form as long as it enables you to visualize and share with the prospect or client two important elements: the most important objective the client or prospect seeks to accomplish from the service in question (the Heart of the Matter) and the most important factors the client or prospect will use to decide whom to choose to achieve this objective, evaluate performance, or both (the Scorecard Factors). The list of factors should be short—rarely more than three or four items—and should help you focus on key issues when delivering the service and discussing client satisfaction.

The Scorecard is used throughout the six stages of the SalesGame. It's useful in Stage One to develop a consistent message for networking and promotional activities. In Stage Two, it allows you to qualify the lead. The Scorecard can be used to determine criteria for selection and enthusiasm and to build a strategy in Stage Three. It is useful for the trial close in Stage Four to make sure you and the client or prospect are on the same page. In Stage Five, it can be used to agree on the critical success factors for a project. Most importantly, the Scorecard can be used to guide service delivery and establish a benchmark to discuss performance as part of Stage Six. The Scorecard focuses on meeting the needs of the client or prospect rather than on selling a service, thus relieving some of the stress inherent in selling situations. Finally, the Scorecard makes the service more tangible so you and your clients can manage expectations.

When building the Scorecard for a prospect or client, you must first find the true source of value—the Heart of the Matter—that is generated by your service. This should happen early in the sales process. True value is defined by what a service helps the client or prospect accomplish. It has little to do with price or other selling points. If a client or prospect can use your service to achieve his or her objective—that is, change his or her life for the better—then they have a qualified lead. When responding to client or prospect requests, you can generally assume you have a qualified lead. However, you must still engage the client or prospect in a dialogue to make sure you both agree on the desired outcome of using a service. This is especially true in competitive RFP situations, when professionals often focus on credentials or other selling points instead of first determining what the client or prospect wants to accomplish as a result of using the service.

When you initiate contact, you must remember that there may be nothing the client or prospect wants to accomplish. This is an acceptable conclusion in a business-development interview. In this situation, you have the opportunity to build a relationship and create a positioning lead for the future, not a qualified lead for the present. Best practices for finding the Heart of the Matter when initiating contact include starting with broad-based questions about the client or prospect's goals and ambitions and being prepared to introduce the benefits of the services being offered. Most importantly, you will be effective at finding the Heart of the Matter if you create a comfortable relationship, relax, and listen to your client or prospect.

Scorecard Factors include features (characteristics inherent in the service), benefits (what the client receives from the service), and conditions of satisfaction (parameters the client uses to evaluate how well the service was performed). You identify and define these factors by engaging the client or prospect in a dialogue and asking questions. Using a presentation or pitch to tell the client or prospect why you or your firm is better is rarely an effective way to build a Scorecard. In competitive situations, you should not believe the criteria for selection listed in the RFP. They are rarely the factors used to make the final decision. In sole-source situations, you should determine the Scorecard Factors even though the work may have already been sold. Failing to do so can result in an unhappy client when the work is done. One of the best ways to prepare for sales meetings is to develop a list of features, benefits, and conditions of satisfaction that, based on your experience, should be on the client or prospect's Scorecard. You can introduce these factors in a variety of ways, such as by asking questions or making suggestions, depending on your personal style. Introducing factors helps ensure that you communicate key selling points and helps the client or prospect make the best decision. When building Scorecard Factors, remember that few are better than many. In some cases, even a single factor can become a deal-maker.

Strategy is defined in Webster's dictionary as the "artful or ingenious use of resources." The Scorecard is a powerful tool for building a short- or long-term business development strategy and differentiating a firm. The resources that you can bring to your clients to help them accomplish their objective are positive factors on the Scorecard. You will be more effective if you develop a list of all the factors that might be on a client or prospect's Scorecard very early in the sales process. If possible you should develop this list with the help of a team, choosing the three strongest plus factors on the Scorecard. You can use these strong points to begin to implement a strategy to differentiate yourself as early as Stage Two. Knowing your strongest factors on the Scorecard also enables you to respond more effectively to the question, "Why should I choose your firm?" You can differentiate yourself not only by the unique nature of the resources you offer, but also by making Scorecard Factors real and tangible during the sales process. You can use Scorecard Factors to develop a long-term strategy by identifying and building resources that will help in future business-development opportunities.

You should also identify negative Scorecard Factors—issues that may work against you in the sales process—during meeting preparation. Some factors such as industry experience can be a positive in some situations and a negative in others.

Identifying negatives in advance enables you to respond to objections or tough questions more effectively. In most cases, you should not discuss any of these negative factors unless the client or prospect raises them. Most importantly, you should understand that Scorecards do not always favor your services as the best way to accomplish the client or prospect's objectives. In these situations, you should sell responsibly by communicating honestly with the client or prospect and building credibility for the future. You should maintain the Scorecard as part of the client's permanent file and update it periodically to ensure the entire service team understands the client's criteria for enthusiasm.

Play On

The best way to really get a feel for the Scorecard is to start using the concept right away. As you plan for any business-development meeting, think about what the Scorecard could be based on where you are in the process. The Ground Rule is a significant fundamental that you can use to help you build the Scorecard. This universal communications tool can be employed to promote dialogue, probe for deeper understanding of the Heart of the Matter and Scorecard Factors, and respond to objections. To add this tool to your business-development toolkit, read on!

The Ground Rule: Improve Communication, Handle Objections, and Define Scorecard Factors

Understanding the Ground Rule

Every game has certain elements—techniques, skills, tips, and the like—that are so fundamental to playing well that everyone from novice to expert knows them and tries to follow them. Some examples we all know from games (even if we do not play) include the following:

- Keep your eye on the ball.

- Lead from strength.

- Keep your head down.

- Play it one shot at a time.

The Ground Rule is a communication technique as fundamental to playing the SalesGame as any of the techniques listed are to their respective games. In fact, it is even a good communication technique for the Client Relations Game, the Internal Politics Game, and the Family Game. One of the most satisfying feedback comments I ever received came from a Dutch participant, who e-mailed me to say that while he hadn't sold any additional business as a result of the workshop, his wife and son told him he was easier to live with since he started using that "silly little white card" I had given to workshop participants to help them remember the Ground Rule. The best part is that we all know to use this technique, even if we have never thought of it as such. We just need to make the Ground Rule a conscious part of the way we communicate and continue to practice the technique. After all, that is the way you get better at any game!

Ironically, I started using the term *Ground Rule* 25 years ago, before the analogy of playing games for selling professional services ever occurred to me. I was facilitating a weekend business-development retreat for 15 partners of an international accounting firm. Two of the participants spent most of the first day arguing with each other: "Yes, but..." followed "Yes, but..." in rapid fashion. That night, as I sat in my hotel room, I realized I had to set some guidelines for the next day. Everyone was tired of the routine; it wasn't productive. The next morning, I requested that all participants listen to find something to agree with in the previous speaker's comments, and to start their own comments by first summarizing this area of agreement. In describing what I wanted, I used the term *Ground Rule*, and that's how we referred to the practice from then on. Everyone played along—and when someone did not, one of that person's partners would call him or her on it. We experienced a pleasant and productive session, and I knew I had discovered a simple and useful communication tool.

While it was a good tool to keep workshops running smoothly, I did not realize just how useful the Ground Rule was until a few years later. I was hired by another substantial accounting firm and the consulting arm of an international insurance brokerage to study their rainmakers. Most of these successful business developers intuitively used a style of communication that was very similar to the Ground Rule. Later, when I was the primary salesman for my research company making approximately 50 sales calls a month, I realized that this tool was one on which I could always rely.

Achieving Win-Win Communication with the Ground Rule

The basic principle underlying the Ground Rule is that you are responsible for making sure everyone involved in the communication gets a win, which is why it was so successful in the business-development retreat and for the rainmakers. What is a win? For the purposes of this book, a win is getting a sense of value from any communication exchange, be it a couple of sentences or a lengthy conversation.

For several years, I have worked alongside an industrial psychologist named Gary. Gary often teaches the first day of a three-day workshop, focusing on listening skills. He has repeatedly said that one of the most fundamental human needs we all have is to be heard and understood. We get value—that is, we satisfy a need—if we are heard and understood.

It occurred to me that if you follow the Ground Rule, paraphrasing what you heard the client or prospect say, you will provide the client or prospect with value simply by letting that person know that you heard and understood him or her. What an easy way to make sure clients and prospects get a win!

> We get value—that is, we satisfy a need—if we are heard and understood.

On the other side of the equation, you get value from listening, whether you are learning something you didn't know before (another family member will be involved in a decision-making process), finding out how the client or prospect feels (worried, concerned, excited), or simply finding something on which you can both agree (experience is helpful). Even if the information you obtain is negative, having it is of value. For example, one time, I attempted to sell my research package to an accounting firm in Halifax, Nova Scotia. The office managing partner started our discussion by saying, "I've decided not to buy this service." I was not pleased with his statement, but the information he was communicating was useful and, therefore, of value to me. It told me where I stood and how to handle the conversation.

In sales meetings, I always found it easier to deal with a negative client or prospect who told me where he or she stood. The more difficult meetings involved individuals who were negative but never disclosed their feelings. The term *passive-aggressive* comes to mind. Clients may not like it when their attorney tells them they cannot win a particular piece of litigation. However, knowing the probable outcome is undoubtedly of great value and extremely useful to deciding how to approach a case. The same can be said for an accountant who tells a client that some of his deductions will not fly with the IRS. The good news is that as long as they feel they are heard and understood, clients and prospects will get value out of the conversation. Getting a win is not about feeling happy; it's about getting value.

The Basic Elements of the Ground Rule

After I sold my research company and got bored with playing golf, I started looking for opportunities to run workshops again. Prospective clients were sending me examples of what they were using in current sales-training efforts. I knew then that the simplicity of the Ground Rule was what made it work. The materials were way too mechanical and complex. One example should make this fairly clear.

The following steps were on page 71 of a 150-page booklet that participants were supposed to read before attending one firm's training session:

1. Do I have enough background information about the client to know which opportunities to probe?

   Yes: Probe to determine if opportunity actually exists.

   No: Probe for background information.

2. Does the opportunity exist?

   Yes: Go to Question 3.

   No: Go back to Question 1.

3. Do I have a clear understanding of the opportunity?

   Yes: Go to Question 4.

   No: Probe to gain clear understanding.

4. Has the client or prospect expressed the opportunity as a need?

   Yes: Go to Question 5.

   No: Probe to confirm the need. Then go to Question 5.

5. Have I confirmed the need?

   Yes: Support the need.

   No: Go back to Question 1.

I have shown this page to workshop participants and watched them feverishly write down these pearls of wisdom. Someone in the room invariably starts to laugh when they read Question 5. "What is this?" they say. "It sounds more like the rules of *Monopoly*—'Go back to Question 1…don't stop at Park Place!'" The problem is that no one—not even a person who sells every day of his life—could possibly remember all this when he or she is face to face with a client or prospect. If you were to try to follow this discipline, you would be so overwhelmed with the formula that listening to the client or prospect would be out of the question. The phrase *Keep It Simple Stupid* (*KISS*) comes to mind. This kind of approach is way too left brain (logical, analytical, etc.), while selling tends to be very right brain (creative, intuitive, etc.).

Although the Ground Rule is very simple, execution under pressure is another matter. Fortunately, like any right-brain skill, such as kicking or throwing a football, swinging a golf club, or hitting a baseball, it improves with practice and repetition.

So here is the Ground Rule—the basic communication tool for playing the SalesGame—that will help you build the Scorecard in meetings with clients and prospects:

1. **Listen for value:** You're looking for new information, ideas, and feelings.

2. **Feed back value and agreement first:** The idea here is to let the client or prospect know you are listening and to confirm understanding. To achieve this, use the same words as the client or prospect as you paraphrase what he or she has communicated to you.

3. **Provide information, if necessary, and end with a question:** Now's the time to communicate your perspective. However, you want to avoid the danger zone (that is, providing too much information). Your goal is to maintain a conversational balance— a dialogue, not a one-sided interrogation. To keep control of the conversation, end with a question.

You can use this skill throughout the SalesGame:

■ **Stage One:** Use it to connect with new contacts and build relationships by having a balanced conversation.

■ **Stage Two:** Use it to gain a better understanding of what the client or prospect wants to achieve from using a professional service.

■ **Stage Three:** Use it to clarify the Heart of the Matter, handle objections, and define exactly what the client or prospect wants when the service is delivered, whether it is a feature, benefit, or condition of satisfaction (that is, the Scorecard Factors).

■ **Stage Four:** Use it to handle a rejected close, surface hidden objections, and deal with fee issues.

■ **Stage Five:** Use it to determine what's holding up a sale.

■ **Stage Six:** Use it to ensure enthusiasm and find out what could have been done differently if an opportunity did not result in a sale.

The remainder of this part looks at each of the elements of the Ground Rule and applies the communication technique to the most common situations faced by professionals in the SalesGame.

Ground Rule Step 1: Listen for Value

Everyone who sells—or who is involved in counseling, training, parenting, or any other occupation that involves connecting with people—should know the importance of listening. As a skill, listening is the cornerstone of the Ground Rule. So what are you listening for? In simplest terms, you are listening for something of value to you because that is how you get a win. Of course, you can find value in many different things, including the following:

- **New information:** This might be company background or statistics, industry trends, events that led up to the current situation, organization structure, responsibilities, etc.

- **Ideas:** These include ways to approach a given project, concepts that might be useful in other settings, suggestions for future action, approaches that have been taken previously, etc.

- **Feelings:** These include opinions, concerns, fears, hopes, and other emotions associated with the problem, service, or you.

- **Misc:** This includes anything that might be useful to you as you try to learn more about the client or prospect's goals and buying criteria.

When you find value in the words of a client or prospect, you have fulfilled half of the win-win equation. In other words, you have a win from the communication because you have found something useful to you for playing the SalesGame. Conveniently, when you paraphrase what you heard the client or prospect say, you usually also fulfill the *other* half of the equation. Everyone gets a sense of value when they know they are heard and understood.

Focus on Agreement

One way for you to find value in the words of a client or prospect is to listen for something on which you can agree, whether it is factual, such as industry trends, or emotional, such as fear of change. When you hear something that aligns with your own point of view, you get a sense of confirmation or validation. We all know the value of not feeling alone in the world. When you find an area of agreement—whether factual or emotional—you have a bridge for learning more about the client or prospect's point of view. I like to think of it as a starting point or beachhead from which you can explore the client or prospect's point of view about his or her hopes and dreams, goals, criteria for success, conditions of satisfaction, etc. The bottom line when playing the SalesGame is to find something with which you can agree when you listen to a client or prospect.

Feelings Are the Most Important Source of Value

Although information and ideas are excellent sources of value, feelings offer you a unique opportunity to find value when communicating with a client or prospect for two reasons. First, listening to someone's feelings and then validating them as part of the Ground Rule is a great way to build a relationship. Of course, this is true outside the world of business as well. Research done by my company (as well as others) makes it clear that having a good relationship is the main reason clients choose a particular professional or firm. But sophisticated research is not necessary to verify the importance of listening to and validating someone's feelings. Most salespeople intuitively know that people are far more likely to buy for emotional rather than factual reasons. Second, it is easier to agree with the emotional content of what someone says than the factual content, particularly when negatives are being discussed.

Take the office managing partner from Halifax, who announced he did not intend to buy my research package at the start of our discussion. I could understand and even agree with his feeling that he did not want to purchase the research package. Four or five potential buyers in every market did not buy the service, and, like the office managing partner, many more did not wish to buy it when our meetings started. The next step in the Ground Rule made it easy for me to agree with his feelings and say with a smile on my face, "I understand you don't feel this would be a good investment for your office right now and I appreciate you letting me know where you stand. While I wish it weren't the case, not everyone wants to buy our research package when I walk in the door!" I did not want to agree with the factual content of his comment—that he was not going to buy my research package—because we had barely started to play the game yet. More importantly, I found an area of agreement with him so I could explore his point of view about my research package. In short, I conveyed that it was OK for him to feel like he did not want to buy the package— after all, other intelligent people in his position had come to the same conclusion. I also avoided a confrontation about whether he should or shouldn't buy before I had any idea of what was on his Scorecard.

One of the best examples of listening for value comes from Frank, an attorney who headed up his firm's substantial litigation practice. He was an ex-Marine who had a reputation for being extremely tough whether dealing with people inside his firm or adversaries in the courtroom. In a workshop with about 20 of his partners, the discussion centered on the pressure they were all feeling from client in-house counsels trying to reduce hourly rates. Almost everyone was complaining about the lack of understanding shown by these in-house attorneys about the cost of hiring top-notch litigators who could achieve the desired results. After sitting quietly for 15 minutes, Frank spoke: "I don't think you're listening to what these guys are really saying. You've got to read between the lines and listen to how they're feeling. They're getting beat up inside their own companies by CEOs who can't understand why legal costs are out of control. They're in a lot of pain and we're arguing with them about hourly rates!" Frank continued, "We have to understand their point of view, show some empathy for their feelings, and find different ways to work with them so we can all get what we want."

Frank may have had a reputation for being tough, but he was also extremely sensitive to the feelings of clients and prospects, and it was easy to see why he was also a very effective rainmaker. I could almost hear him telling some in-house counsel who was complaining about fees, "I feel your pain!" He took the time to listen to their feelings. It was easier to agree with the emotional rather than the factual content of what was being said. He connected with in-house counsels by agreeing with their frustrations, but not their requests to lower hourly rates.

Ground Rule Step 2: Feed Back Value and Agreement First

After you have found value in the words of your client or prospect, the next step is to let him or her know that this input was useful and that his or her comments were heard and understood. This should occur *before* you provide any information or express disagreement. My field of endeavor has made me a constant observer of the way people talk with each other. Whether selling, talking with colleagues, or chatting with the family at home, it is amazing how first expressing the value received creates more productive communication. If you start by paraphrasing what you heard and building agreement, the other person will feel like you are listening and that he or she is being heard and understood. In turn, the other person will be more willing to listen and provide additional information.

Conversely, we are all too familiar with communication that starts with "yes, but…." We know that whatever follows the "but" will be negative and will disagree with our point of view. I

> Expressing the value received creates more productive communication.

have found that people in Shanghai and Chicago are equally familiar with this pattern of negative communication. (Of course, we know we should start by agreeing before we dive into the negative. That's why we insert the "yes" before the "but!") When someone starts by disagreeing with our point of view, we usually react by listening for things we can use in our rebuttal. That is, we are listening for disagreement, which leads to confrontation. Worse yet, we often do not listen at all. Rather, we *pretend* to listen while our minds are busy coming up with additional ammunition to defend our own point of view. "Yes, but…" follows "yes, but…," and constructive communication goes downhill fast. Professionals involved in business development need to avoid this destructive pattern at all costs.

I often insist that workshop participants follow the Ground Rule. As a result, the entire session becomes a laboratory for studying how we communicate. We assign one participant the task of listening for "yes, buts…." When he or she notices this pattern developing, the conversation is stopped so we can all discuss the effects of not following the Ground Rule. Similar observations emerge in almost every workshop. First, when accountants, lawyers, and consultants start communication with "yes, but…," most of them are not even aware they are doing it. They become aware of it only when it is brought to their attention after they've repeated the phrase three or four times. Second, when participants say "yes, but…" (or simply start with a "no"), it almost always leads to others in the session expressing disagreement with their point of view. It does not take long—literally less than a minute—for a conversation to start sounding like an argument. As soon as what appears to be an argument starts to occur, the business developer has almost always already lost. Third, when these arguments do arise, they are rarely based on real disagreement. Rather, they are based on *perceived* disagreement. Participants observing the argument often feel that both parties were saying the same thing in different ways.

The Ground Rule is such an effective tool for playing the SalesGame because it focuses on building agreement between you and your client or prospect. To achieve the goal of the game, agreement must be reached on the Scorecard. If you—or anyone—build on agreement, disagreement seems to disappear. Conversely, if you build on disagreement, then agreement tends to disappear.

> If you—or anyone—build on agreement, disagreement seems to disappear.

Most of us intuitively know the importance of building on agreement to develop a good relationship, even if we don't often do it. Patterns of communication developed since childhood determine how effective—or ineffective—we are at using our natural abilities to do what we know is productive. Each person has his or her own tendency to start with a "yes, but…" or, conversely, to start by expressing agreement. This tendency can be affected by the situation. For example, people rarely build on disagreement when they are on a first date or, say, attending a wedding. The last thing they want is to start an argument.

I have even found some regional differences in style. For example, my researchers and I found that people in Canada do not say "yes, but..." nearly as much as people in New York City. Also, people are more likely to build on the negative when discussing a subject they think they know well and feel passionately about.

You can make a conscious effort to build on agreement regardless of your personal tendencies. Focusing on the Ground Rule during sales meetings —and practicing it during day-to-day communication in the office and at home—is an excellent way to develop this skill to create more effective communication.

How to Connect with Clients and Prospects

In my pre-workshop interviews, professionals like lawyers, wealth managers, and accountants often talk about making a connection with a client or prospect and how it helped them acquire a piece of business. The Ground Rule provides professionals with a tool for making this connection. Imagine the two circles shown in Figure 23.1 represent the points of view of a prospect and a professional who have never met. Each circle represents the accumulation of the person's entire life experience—everything from early childhood (raised by one parent or two, in the U.S. or Australia, with siblings or without) to education (formal and informal, Ivy League or state university, small town or big city) to employment history (first job or late in a career, expert in a field or novice, on the way up or on the way down)—that affects the way the individual perceives the world. Hence, we use the term *point of view* to describe the unique way each of us sees the world. We filter what we hear through this point of view.

Figure 23.1   Building a common ground of agreement.

When you deal with a prospect for the first time, at the beginning of the conversation, these two points of view are totally separate. Neither party knows the other's background, feelings, biases, preferences, history, education, etc. However, as soon as one individual in the conversation hears something with which he or she can agree and feeds it back, the two points of view are no longer totally separate. They at least share one common area of understanding. This connection facilitates the exploration of each other's point of view. You can learn what's on the client or prospect's Scorecard. The client or prospect can learn how you might be able to provide assistance. More importantly, you and the client or prospect begin to view the world from an increasingly similar point of view. Of course, if a relationship already exists before a business-development interview, the two circles will already overlap to some degree, providing a common ground for the discussion. This is why one of the keys to winning the SalesGame is to build relationships before the point of sale.

Use Client or Prospect Words

When you first express agreement and value, you should repeat some of the actual words used by the client or prospect for two reasons. First, clients and prospects—and everyone else—will feel that you are listening when they hear some of their own words coming back at them. It is as if you have placed value on the client or prospect's words because you listened well enough to repeat them. When people think their input is valuable, they are likely to provide even more information. I have watched accountants, lawyers, and consultants in countless role plays as well as in real sales meetings ask a good open-ended question at the start of an interview, like, "How is your organization structured?" Clients and prospects respond well to this question because it is non-threatening and easy to answer. Unfortunately, however, they are too often rewarded for their efforts with a simple "OK"—a single-word response that hardly communicates the value received. Just once I would like to see the client or prospect jump up and say, "Excuse me! I just spent several minutes explaining how we're organized and I don't think you paid attention to a word I said!" That is usually what they are thinking, even if they don't say it.

Note

Most of us have a tendency to use one-word or short-phrase acknowledgements, like "OK," "I understand," "I follow you," or simply "Yes," just like the professionals I just described. Unfortunately, most of us are also conditioned to know that when we hear these phrases, the person with whom we are talking may be in another zone entirely, only pretending to listen. Wives and husbands have mastered this skill. While these words are forms of acknowledgement, they fail to demonstrate real listening or communicate value received. Nor do they provide a common ground of agreement. All business developers have been in conversations where they consistently hear "Yes!" and "OK!"...until they ask for a next step and are confronted with a resounding "No."

The second reason for repeating back your client or prospect's words is to provide a level of understanding that can be achieved only when you convey your perception of what was said and have it confirmed by either verbal or non-verbal agreement. As ridiculous as this may seem, I was once in a meeting when a client said he would pay up to $100,000 for a particular service. The consultant heard him say $10,000, and fed that number back—only to have the client correct him with a smile. If you can make a mistake of that dimension dealing with numbers, think of how difficult it is to understand the feelings expressed by a client or prospect. And feelings are almost always the Heart of the Matter!

Of course, this does not mean you should repeat *all* of the client or prospect's words and not interject your own interpretation of what was said. No one enjoys talking with somebody who constantly sounds like a parrot. A conversation is a two-way street. You can paraphrase and add your own words into the mix in Step 2 of the Ground Rule. The point is to understand and reach agreement on what's being said, not to mimic it. Nevertheless, the Ground Rule works better as a tool to demonstrate listening and build understanding if at least some of the client or prospect's words make it into your feedback.

> The point is to understand and reach agreement on what's being said, not to mimic it.

Smile

One other tip my workshop participants have found useful is to remember to smile when providing feedback or paraphrasing. This is especially true when dealing with objections. A smile tends to suggest you're not threatened or worried. The old phrase "Never let them see you sweat" comes to mind. Of course, smiling won't be appropriate in every situation, but it goes a long way toward sending the message that you're relaxed and that you don't feel pressured to sell work. Rather, you are more interested in developing a relationship and being a trusted advisor. I know from interviewing clients and prospects that they often raise objections or ask tough questions of attorneys, consultants, or other professionals. This is more to see how they will react than because the issue being raised is truly a concern. They want to know how you'll handle yourself in the heat of battle.

Ground Rule Step 3: Provide Information and End with a Question

S tep 3 of the Ground Rule offers the most opportunity for creativity and individual style. It is similar to the talent necessary to be a great running back or soccer player. How many times have you heard an announcer describe a run by Barry Sanders or a move by Pelé by saying, "You can't teach that!" Similarly, some professionals can handle this part of the Ground Rule with an intuitive grace that defies description. As with any right-brain skill, executing Step 3 of the Ground Rule is a function of practice, talent, and knowledge of the basics. Talent is a gift that can be greatly enhanced by knowing the basics and continuing to practice.

Communication Is a Two-Way Street

One question I am often asked is, "When do I stop asking questions and start talking about my service?" This is an understandable question. The client or prospect needs to learn about your service. None of us relishes a conversation in which one person asks all the questions but never shares his or her point of view. Step 3 of the Ground Rule provides you the opportunity to exchange information.

Professionals who are effective at using the Ground Rule have mastered the art of balancing the discussion. They seem to give and take in equal portions. When using the Ground Rule, you should try to balance the amount of feedback (Step 2) with the amount of information you provide from your own point of view (Step 3). Many workshop participants find that using a visual image of a scale, like the one held by Lady Justice, is a good way to think about this balance. On one side of the scale is feedback and on the other is information from your point of view. If the scale tips too heavily in either direction during the course of the discussion, the conversation is not as effective as it could be.

Of course, as in any game, there are always occasions when what should work does not. Consider a Denver attorney who attended my workshop. A prospect had come to him from a large San Francisco–based company to choose a firm to represent his company in a highly-specialized area of litigation. The attorney called me a few days after the meeting to report that he did just fine at the start of the interview. He provided good feedback, balanced the information flow, and ended with questions. He felt like he was in a groove using the Ground Rule…until the prospect rudely stopped him mid-sentence and said, "Why are you asking me these questions? I came here to interview you!" The Denver attorney had the good sense to agree with the prospect's apparent frustration and turn control of the interview over to him by asking what he wanted to cover. If you see that this is another use of the Ground Rule, you are getting the idea. This tool works in almost every situation!

Provide "Stage-Appropriate" Information

The information you provide can take a number of forms, depending on the situation and stage of the SalesGame. In Stage One and Stage Two, the information you share should help you build the relationship with the client or prospect. For example, you might tell a personal story that lets the client or prospect know you have both shared a similar experience. Sharing your own experiences fosters a connection and builds empathy. In Stages Three, Four, and Five, you are more likely to provide information about a service that responds to the needs of the client or prospect.

When handling objections, regardless of stage, you should generally provide very little information to avoid sounding defensive. In each of the following examples, notice all three steps of the Ground Rule—the professional listens for value, feeds back agreement, provides information from his or her own point of view, and ends with a question.

- **Example 1:** Using past experience to illustrate how the service responds to a recognized need (Stage Two)

  Client or prospect: Using an outside firm to develop these personnel policies seems like a good idea because we're not making much progress ourselves.

Professional: I wouldn't feel too bad about it. You're not alone. Getting long-term projects done, like writing these policies, always seems to take forever and can get pretty frustrating when you're balancing them with the rest of your responsibilities. We've had very good luck developing similar policies for ABC and XYZ companies in less than three months. Tell me, what's driving the development of these new policies?

■ **Example 2:** Using a story based on personal experience that supports, confirms, and agrees with the emotional or factual information provided by the client or prospect (early in Stage Three)

Client or prospect: We need to implement this system to boost productivity or we won't be able to keep up with the competition. But you know, I'm afraid of what's going to happen with overall operations when they install our new computer system.

Professional: No question new systems can change the lay of the land, so your concern is justified. I remember what happened when I was working at my former company and we had a new system installed. Everything was in turmoil for weeks. What are your biggest concerns with the new system being implemented here?

■ **Example 3:** Using benefits to position your service (Stage Three)

Client or prospect: I think this sounds like a good approach to the reorganization for tax reasons, but I'm not sure how it will fit with our strategic plan.

Professional: It is a good approach because it's going to save the company significant tax dollars. We'll be able to take the gains from your old cash cow and offset them with losses from the new division. You should save somewhere around $250,000. Tell me more about your strategic plan and let's see if we can find a way to make this thing work.

Achieving this balance is not as simple as it sounds. Each person has his or her own communication pattern that may interfere with this balance. The best way to improve use of the Ground Rule is to be conscious of personal tendencies and to work toward improving any weaknesses. The two most common mistakes are described next.

Watch Out for the Danger Zone

The most common mistake is to provide too much information. This tendency is understandable because we are more comfortable talking about our own point of view. When critiquing videotaped role plays in workshops, I often have participants use a stopwatch to measure the time spent on feedback versus the time spent on providing information. We measure how far the scale is tipping in one direction or the other. When they start talking about their service or credentials, it's as if many professionals become mesmerized listening to their own voices. It is not uncommon to hear one-word feedback ("OK," "Right," etc.) followed by several minutes of information coming from the professional's point of view.

> It's as if many professionals become mesmerized listening to their own voices.

So how long do you have before you enter what I call the *danger zone*? As a general guideline, more than two or three sentences pushes the envelope. Everyone watching these videos in a workshop seems to know exactly where the danger zone is. Sometimes, I ask them to hold up signs with the universal red circle with a line drawn through it when they feel the role player has provided too much information. When the signs go up, the professional shown in the video usually laughs because he or she has a voice in the back of his or her mind that says the same thing! I refer to this voice as an *internal coach*. It is a great asset for all of us. When it tells us we are talking too much, we know it is time to ask a question!

I call this the *danger zone* for two reasons. First, the more you talk, the greater the danger you will say something inconsistent with the client or prospect's Scorecard. Second—and this danger is far more likely to occur—the client or prospect will get bored in a hurry listening to you drone on about your service or credentials. Even professionals who are energetic and articulate can bore clients and prospects when they talk too much. When people are bored, they do not listen well, and are unlikely to be excited about any information that does penetrate their consciousness. It is like reading a 100-page proposal—the *real* reasons to hire a firm get lost in the boilerplate. To escape the danger zone, listen for that little voice in the back of your head and ask a question. A tool that I often recommend for these situations is a *checking question*. Just stop talking and ask, "Does this make sense?" or, "How does that sound?" These are not the most clever questions, but they are at least a means for you to reengage the client or prospect in the conversation.

Don't Interrogate Your Client or Prospect

This mistake is less common but can be very annoying to clients and prospects. Some professionals fail to provide enough—or any—information before ending with a question. If you do a commendable job providing feedback (Step 2 of the Ground Rule), yet repeatedly fail to provide information from your own point of view, most clients and prospects will get the feeling the conversation is too one-sided. As will be discussed later, not providing any information other than feedback can be effective when using the Ground Rule to handle an objection. But when an interview consists of question after question, with all the information coming from the client or prospect, the meeting seems more like an interrogation than a discussion—particularly if you don't take the time to build on agreement and paraphrase as part of Step 2 of the Ground Rule. As you might expect, attorneys are more likely to have this tendency, but certainly other professionals can fall into this trap as well.

End with a Question to Keep Control

The most important part of Step 3 of the Ground Rule is to end with a question to keep control of the interview. The most common problem that results from failing to end with a question is a role reversal. That is, the client or prospect starts interviewing you, and often ends up asking question after question. Instead of learning what's on the client or prospect's Scorecard, you must provide information about yourself and your services without having a framework to position your answers. This is at best a high-risk proposition. In some cases, the information you provide will directly conflict with the client or prospect's point of view.

A Los Angeles attorney relayed a story to me about a sales meeting in which he allowed the prospect to become the interviewer. His firm ultimately lost its bid for what was a major engagement because he provided too much information about how the project would be staffed (skewed toward associates to keep costs down) before he knew what the prospect wanted (partners only, and damn the cost). It's not that the attorney couldn't have staffed the engagement with partners; he just assumed the prospect would consider cost a significant issue. The prospect was a municipality, and the attorney had dealt with several similar organizations that *were* fee sensitive, so his point of view is understandable. The attorney explained to the prospect that he could modify the approach, but everyone knows how difficult it is to change a first impression.

The irony is that after the question on staffing was asked, the Ground Rule would have given him a tool to handle the situation even after he became the interviewee. Imagine if the discussion had gone like this:

Client: Tell me what your thoughts are on how you'd staff this project.

Attorney: [LISTEN FOR VALUE] I've thought a lot about that issue and, from your question, I realize it's on your mind as well. I'm glad you brought it up. It's one of the issues we need to discuss. [PROVIDE INFORMATION] There are a couple of ways to go about staffing, depending on your priorities. A lot of the municipalities I've worked with like to use our associates to keep costs down. On the other hand, this is a very important case. [END WITH A QUESTION] What are your initial thoughts on the matter?

As you can see, in this example, the attorney listened for the value in question, provided information from his point of view, and ended with a question—all from an interviewee's stance. Of course, conducting this kind of analysis is a bit like being the proverbial Monday-morning quarterback, but it does provide some indication of how powerful the Ground Rule can be in sales meetings.

In other situations, failing to end with a question and allowing the client or prospect to control the interview could lead to you giving away far too much intellectual capital without getting anything in return. I once worked with an international accounting firm that offered a package to analyze complex tax issues. They offered contingent pricing—20% of the savings realized from recommendations generated by the analysis. Two or three key service providers—gurus in this narrow and complex tax field—supervised most of the work from the national office. These gurus were usually brought in on the initial sales meeting set up by a local partner, which was generally attended by what seemed like a cast of thousands. (This was already a violation of one of the keys to winning in the SalesGame: In selling, bigger isn't better. Start small! Chemistry is key to selling, and you can't build chemistry in a large group setting.)

I was asked to observe a few of these meetings to determine why the package was getting a lot of interest but few signatures on the dotted line. After watching two or three, I had a pretty good idea what was causing the problem. The experts spent all their time providing detailed information about how the prospect could save tax dollars—but little time learning what was on the prospect's Scorecard. The professionals doing the selling were so busy providing information, they failed to make a connection with the prospect's hopes, dreams, goals, and ambitions. Worse, they would end their monologues without a question. That left the door open for the prospect representatives in attendance—all of whom were busy taking copious notes—to ask more yet more questions. At the close of the meeting, the prospect representatives had written down enough rules, regulations, and ideas to do most of the work in house or pass it on to their current tax advisor. In most instances, the prospect would not be as successful cutting tax dollars as they would have been had they hired my client. But they *thought* they would be. Unfortunately, this perception was enough to prevent the prospect from moving ahead in the sales process.

Even if you do not follow the Ground Rule in its entirety, you can still avoid the pattern of giving too much information by listening to that internal coach I mentioned earlier and asking a checking question like, "So how does that sound?" or, "What are your thoughts?" Even these simplistic questions usually help get the client or prospect talking.

Focus on Using Open-Ended Questions

Using an open-ended question (What…? Why…? How…?) when completing the Ground Rule is usually better than using a closed-ended question (Can you…? Are you…? Did you…?). By definition, open-ended questions cannot be answered with a yes or no. The client or prospect has to say *something* in response. If you listen well, you will find some emotion, information, or idea that is of value to you. Conversely, closed-ended questions are usually answered with a yes or no. It is hard to give feedback to a yes or no. In short, open-ended questions tend to sustain the pattern of win-win communication, while closed-ended questions tend to break it.

Practice Even When You Are Not Selling

We all understand the importance of practice to build skills and confidence. PGA golfers spend hours on the practice tee before and after they play a round. When NBA or NFL players come back after an injury (or a contract dispute), they are usually in great shape physically. However, it takes several games before their sense of timing returns. It is no different for professionals playing the SalesGame. You can't expect to ace an important meeting without spending some time preparing and practicing your skills in similar discussions with other clients or prospects.

This is a real problem for professionals. Many of them sell so infrequently that it is difficult to get in the groove each time—similar to playing golf a couple times a year. One way to get better at this technique is to practice even when you are not selling. Participants often practice using the Ground Rule even in my workshops. I have noticed that they also use it—and catch each other when they are not—when they are conversing during the cocktail hour or over meals. You should make a point of using the Ground Rule in discussions in the office, in routine conversations with clients, and even at home with family and friends. No matter what your talent level, you will improve your ability to provide just the right amount of information and end with a question.

You have looked at the steps of the Ground Rule: listening for value, feeding back value and agreement first, then providing information and ending with a question. The following chapters in this part of the book apply this technique to the two primary ways you can use the Ground Rule in business-development interviews:

- To define exactly what the client or prospect wants (that is, refine the Heart of the Matter and Scorecard Factors)

- To explore objections and determine any relevant offsetting benefits

Refine the Heart of the Matter and Scorecard Factors

Part 3, "The Scorecard: Add Value, Differentiate Your Service, and Build Strategy," addressed how to uncover the Heart of the Matter and the Scorecard Factors. However, as stated at the outset of this part, one of the most significant uses of the Ground Rule is to better understand and even refine the client or prospect's Scorecard. During this dialogue, clients and prospects often generalize or use words that can be interpreted in multiple ways. Worse, they presume the professional knows what the problem is. And guess what? As professionals, we fall right into that trap. It takes us only a few seconds to develop a theory on what the issue is. Often, that means we accept the client or prospect's immediate or first answer to our questions. The Ground Rule is our antidote to that trap.

Getting to the "Real" Heart of the Matter

Part 3 explored how to move from service to value in a conversation and how to use questions to effectively do so. Using the Ground Rule to provide acknowledgment and validation to the prospect or client's point of view can help you pave the way for those questions to yield more substantive answers. Consider this example from a wealth-management scenario:

> **Professional:** What is the one thing we might be able to do that would really make a difference for you and your family?

Prospect: It is really important for us to have strong performance in our investment portfolio. To me, that would probably make a big difference because to this point, we've pretty much done that on our own. We've done OK, but it's probably time to have someone with more expertise take care of it.

Professional: It is certainly understandable and natural that strong performance would be on your mind when you are thinking about your investments. Those words come up often, and it is definitely something I think about in terms of my own investments. I'd like to dig a little deeper on that, though. When you think about performance, what, ideally, would you like that strong performance to achieve for you?

In this case, the wealth-management professional followed one of the best practices from Part 3 in asking and then asking again, but she did so by employing the Ground Rule to lead into the follow-up question. By using Step 2 of the Ground Rule and building the common ground of agreement, you also build more trust, which allows for more open sharing. In this case, the use of the Ground Rule yielded the following:

Prospect: As I said, we've always done this on our own, and I've felt pretty good about the performance. But with my upcoming retirement, we won't have any regular income as we have for the past 30 years. So to me, having strong performance means being able to maintain our lifestyle in this next phase—something that, quite frankly, I've been worrying about a lot.

The professional could have easily made an assumption about why performance was important. (It is always important!) However, by using the Ground Rule, she got much closer to the true source of value—the real Heart of the Matter—and was able to uncover a significant aspect of what it would take to turn this prospect into an enthusiastic client.

Responding to Positive Scorecard Factors

Most professionals recognize the importance of handling objections in an effective manner. However, it is just as important to be effective when responding to positive comments by the client or prospect. In many interviews, for example, a prospect or client might stress his or her desire to work with professionals who are responsive. Upon hearing this comment, most professionals assure the client or prospect that they and their firms are responsive and promise to serve them accordingly. Few professionals take the time to really explore the meaning of *responsive*, however. They fail to determine what that particular client or prospect means by the word and how they will be judged using this standard of performance.

I think of this as being like a football team running out of energy in the fourth quarter or a baseball team without a closer to finish off the game. As we have all heard, being close only counts in horseshoes. You need to use the Ground Rule to really finish off a conversation about what the client wants. Consider the wealth-management firm in Chicago that obtained an engagement partly on its pledge to be responsive. They returned phone calls on time, etc. However, the client ended up being less than enthusiastic because his definition of *responsive* had a unique twist. He wanted his professional service firms to hold periodic meetings to evaluate performance. This illustrates the danger in failing to really define a desired feature, benefit, or condition of satisfaction.

When dealing with positive factors on the Scorecard, you should use the Ground Rule to do the following:

- Clarify the desired feature, benefit, or conditions of satisfaction.

- Establish exactly what the client or prospect wants so you can ensure their enthusiasm from the service.

One common pitfall is to move too quickly when you hear a comment from a client or prospect that relates favorably to the characteristics of your service. Using the Ground Rule to follow the two preceding steps slows down the discussion, helping you focus on establishing what the prospect or client really wants rather than on simply making a sale. This is particularly true when you are the sole source being considered. As has been said many times, beware of the easy sale.

Slow Down and Peel Back the Onion

I think of this process as being like peeling back an onion. Each layer of skin on the onion looks a little different from the one you just removed. Sticking with the *responsive* theme, think of the outer layer of the onion as being responsive. The next layer is to return phone calls. The next is to return phone calls within 24 hours. Maybe the next layer is to give the client a personal cell phone number, etc.

Imagine a conversation between an attorney and in-house counsel considering whom to use to defend the company in a suit charging wrongful dismissal.

Attorney: Tell me a little about how you like to work with outside counsel on cases like this. Obviously, I know you want to win this case, but what other criteria are you looking at to determine whether or not we're doing the right kind of job?

Prospect: Number one is to win this case. We must make a point that discourages anyone else from doing the same thing. After that, I'd say that I want outside counsel to be responsive, to pay attention to what's going on. It drives me crazy when an attorney doesn't stay on top of things and I have to make sure they're doing the job.

At this point, the outside attorney has begun to establish the Heart of the Matter (make others less willing to initiate the same kind of suit). And she has heard at least one condition of satisfaction (be responsive). The attorney's job is now to explore the prospect's point of view to discover exactly what he means by *responsive* to try the case in a way that creates an enthusiastic client. The Ground Rule is effective for this purpose. The conversation might proceed like this:

Attorney: [FEEDBACK] Certainly, if this case is handled right, the outcome would discourage others from making the same claims. That's clearly our primary objective. I can understand your concerns about being responsive. You want someone who's on top of things. [INFORMATION] I'd like to think that's how I work with my clients. I worked with one company last year where we had phone calls set up every other day to make sure he knew what was going on. Every client is different, though, and I've heard that word *responsive* used in a lot of different ways. [QUESTION] How are you defining the word? What sorts of things tell you that your lawyer is being responsive?

Prospect: I like the idea of regular phone calls to get updates. That's the kind of thing I'm talking about. Although, I don't know if I'd want to do it every other day. I'm more interested in knowing your strategy, developments on the case, that sort of thing. I trust your judgment but I want to be apprised of your decision-making so I can have input if I need to.

The attorney used the Ground Rule to further explore the prospect's point of view about responsiveness. She peeled back the onion one layer and found that for the prospect, *responsive* means periodic phone calls to help the prospect stay abreast of strategy and developments.

Provide Information to Position Your Service When Dealing with Positive Factors

Notice how the attorney provided information as part of Step 3 of the Ground Rule. Providing information from your point of view is generally a good idea when dealing with positive factors on the Scorecard. This information positions your service by providing evidence that it can in fact do what the client or prospect wants. It can also generate some ideas for the client or prospect as to what might be meant by the word *responsive*, as in the example. The only pitfall for you is to avoid the danger zone—that is, avoid providing too much information. Otherwise, you run the risk of saying things the client or prospect does not want to hear or losing his or her attention altogether.

At times, the attorney may need to go still further—peel another layer off the onion—to know exactly how to shape the service to deliver what the prospect wants. She knows more about what the prospect means by the word *responsive* but she does not yet know exactly what she needs to do to make sure the prospect will see her as responsive throughout the engagement. The conversation might continue something like this:

> **Attorney:** [FEEDBACK] I welcome that kind of input. Two heads are better than one, as trite as that sounds. We can talk periodically to make sure you're up to speed on what we're doing, certainly when it comes to major developments or strategy. [INFORMATION] The example I gave you of checking in every other day was a bit on the extreme side. I know this is just one of many situations you're dealing with right now. [QUESTION] How would you like to set this up so we get your involvement but don't monopolize your time?

> **Prospect:** Let's say we set up a regular time to talk. Toward the end of the week, Friday is usually good for me. Say an 8 a.m. conference call. We can review what's going on and talk about developments you expect in the coming week. If things change for any reason, we can adjust. This kind of a setup would be useful to start.

> **Attorney:** [FEEDBACK] Sounds good to me. I'll put it in my calendar right now. Let's plan on talking at least once a week on Friday at 8 a.m., I'll call you. Obviously, we might need to adjust a little as you say, but I'm comfortable with this arrangement for now. [INFORMATION] There are some other areas I suspect we might need to talk about. For example, staffing from both your end as well as our own. I'm sure you've got some other issues you want to look at as well. [QUESTION] What other areas are most important to you to make sure we're doing the right job for ABC?

By using the Ground Rule, the attorney has identified what the prospect means by *responsive* and established what must be done during the handling of the case. The prospect will perceive the attorney as delivering on this standard of performance. As with any game, there are no guarantees, but the attorney has played well enough to feel confident that this prospect will be enthusiastic when the service is delivered. At a minimum, the attorney has defined one of the criteria he can use to debrief the prospect when the case is over (assuming she is hired).

We have applied the Ground Rule to one positive factor that could come up in a business-development interview—that is, responsiveness. But the same approach could (and should) be used for all issues that lead a client or prospect to choose a particular firm or professional. These include words and phrases like the following:

- Personal service

- Industry experience

- Timeliness

- Depth of the team

- Close cooperation

- Understand our business

These phrases are too vague to shape the service in a way that the client or prospect will be enthusiastic after it has been delivered. You must peel back the onion with each example.

The good part about this process is that it can be fun. Once professionals catch on to this approach, they usually find it interesting. They are focusing on understanding the client, not just trying to make a sale.

One participant shared a story with me after a workshop that I think illustrates how important it is to slow down the selling process. It demonstrates that we rarely know what a client or prospect means when he or she uses these generic terms. The participant, Jesse, was a partner in a large accounting firm talking to a CFO prospect who felt his previous firm failed to give him "personal service." Of course, this is something any professional in an interview with a prospect loves to hear because it provides an idea of what the client or prospect wants—that is, it is a positive factor on the Scorecard—which can guide service delivery.

As the conversation unfolded, Jesse used the Ground Rule to peel back the personal service onion and found several layers. First, *personal service* was defined as contact beyond just doing the audit. The next layer revealed the CFO's desire to be entertained. Eventually, Jesse learned that this CFO was a huge hockey fan and wanted to be taken to a Detroit Red Wings hockey game during the year. Apparently, the previous firm had a private box in Joe Louis Arena, the home of the Red Wings. They had entertained the owner and previous CFO at least once a year, but had never invited the current CFO. Like most other organizations in Detroit, Jesse's firm had season tickets to the Red Wings, so it was easy to fulfill this condition of satisfaction—and certainly a lot more fun than returning phone calls in 24 hours. This was not necessarily a rational condition of satisfaction, but rationality is rarely the key to successfully playing the SalesGame.

> Rationality is rarely the key to successfully playing the SalesGame.

How to Handle Objections

The Ground Rule is particularly useful for handling objections or negative factors on the Scorecard. When confronting objections, you should use the Ground Rule to do the following:

- Explore the negative to determine exactly what the issue is from the point of view of the client or prospect.

- Determine what factors might offset the negative.

As any professional who plays the SalesGame knows, the objection that is raised first may have nothing to do with what is actually bothering the client or prospect. For example, most professionals have heard objections regarding a firm's size—for example, it's too big or too small. These factors are usually a reflection of very different concerns of the client or prospect—for example, cost or experience. So your first task is to peel back the onion to learn the true source of the objection.

> The objection that is raised first may have nothing to do with what is actually bothering the client or prospect.

When handling objections, it's most effective to use the first two steps of the Ground Rule—listen and provide feedback—and then ask a question without providing much information, if any, from your point of view. That's because the more information you provide, the greater the likelihood you will sound defensive. It is an easy trap to fall into, particularly when discussing issues you feel strongly about—for example, fees.

Providing too much information before the objection has really been explored often creates an even bigger problem. For example, consider the financial services partner, Sean, who heard an objection while he was calling on a credit union. The CEO expressed concern about Sean's lack of experience in the CEO's industry. Sean responded by detailing his experience with banks in general. Instead of easing the CEO's concerns, Sean alienated himself further by talking about his experience serving a primary source of competition.

Don't Handle the Wrong Objection

Even if providing too much information does not get you into trouble, why waste time dealing with an issue that has no substance? You should avoid expressing too much of your point of view until you have clearly identified the objection that is worrying the client or prospect. You can provide a small amount of information, especially if the client or prospect raised an objection that is more of a factual misunderstanding than a perceptual difference. For example, suppose you are in in a Stage Two interview and the conversation goes something like this:

> **Prospect:** Your firm works with such large clients, but my business is much smaller. It's true we're growing, but we're not trying to be the next Microsoft. I don't know that this would be a good fit.

> **Professional:** [FEEDBACK] Believe me, I've heard that comment before. I've talked with a lot of people who tend to identify us with some of our larger, better-known clients and feel that we might not be a good fit. Those big clients are a curse and a blessing. We love working with them, but it's frustrating when we're perceived as being a firm that only serves big clients. [INFORMATION] Actually, we work much more with clients that are your size or smaller. [QUESTION] What are your concerns about the fact that we work with these larger clients?

The question at the end of the Ground Rule is the key to handling the objection because it enables you to explore the real meaning behind the prospect's comment.

Tip

As mentioned, it's a good idea for you to have a smile on your face when making this comment to look more confident and relaxed.

When I use this example in my workshops, I ask participants to tell me what they think might be the real problem. That is, why is working with big clients perceived as a negative? Inevitably, I get answers like these:

- **Lack of attention:** The prospect is worried that the big clients' needs will come first.

- **Big clients mean big fees:** The prospect is worried that he or she will have to pay those big fees, too.

- **Limited understanding of the needs of the small businessman:** The prospect is thinking, "We don't even have an internal accounting staff!"

- **Turnover:** The prospect is worried you will send the inexperienced staff to him or her.

Each of these problems obviously requires a different response. You might deal with the prospect's concern about a lack of attention by using references. You might deal with the fee issue by setting a "not to exceed" estimate. You could handle lack of understanding by follow-up meetings to demonstrate your ability to assist smaller clients. And you could handle turnover by offering a commitment—that is, a condition of satisfaction—not to change staff for a certain period.

You must use the Ground Rule repeatedly until you have explored the objection and understand exactly what is of concern to your client or prospect. The point of view diagrams used in Figure 23.1 to illustrate how the Ground Rule helps you make a connection can also be used to illustrate this process. Using the same example, when the prospect expresses a concern that the firm works with big clients, that person is sharing some of his or her point of view. To address this objection, you need to get behind it—peel back the onion—to understand why the comment was made. The question that concludes the Ground Rule in the sample dialogue works well for this reason. Once again, it's like peeling back the onion to reveal deeper and deeper layers.

Prospect: I guess what bothers me is that your big clients are going to get more attention, for reasons I can understand. If they say "Jump," you're going to say "How high?" You can't do that for everyone. Some of the smaller clients just aren't going to get that same kind of attention.

Professional: [FEEDBACK] It would be foolish of me to argue that big clients aren't important. And you're right—we want to be responsive when we're working with them. If I'm following you, your concern is that you're not going to get the type of attention or service from us that you deserve. [INFORMATION] I can understand that. In fact, smaller clients require more attention in some ways than the big clients. You've worked with other professionals. Tell me, [QUESTION] what sorts of things do they do that make you feel like they're paying attention, giving you the service you want?

Prospect: Well, I can give you an example. The accountant that I had been working with until now used to stop by every couple of months and just talk. I always felt he had time for me and, I guess more importantly, I always felt a little more on top of it when he left. Somehow talking about what was on my mind helped me focus. That ought to give you some idea of what I'm talking about.

Professional: [FEEDBACK] Thanks. That example tells me a lot. A little informal conversation over a cup of coffee to discuss what's going on can help focus your thoughts. It's amazing how that can make a person feel more on top of it, as you say. It helps me to talk through whatever's going with a colleague every now and then. [INFORMATION] I've been down that road with some of my clients, too. Those informal conversations can be valuable for everyone. [QUESTION] When you said you'd just talk, what were some of the topics discussed?

Prospect: Everything, I guess…from sports to movies to family. But I suppose we spent most of our time on business—you know, whether the company was performing well, what employees were driving me crazy, my latest, greatest plans for expansion. That was always valuable. I needed someone objective to bounce my crazy ideas off of!

The accountant in this example used the Ground Rule three times to explore the prospect's point of view. Each time was like peeling off another layer of the onion to reveal a better understanding of what the prospect wanted.

This example is typical of many situations I have observed in sales meetings when the Ground Rule is used effectively to handle a negative. What's remarkable is how often an obstacle to working with a firm turns out to be a road map for establishing what's really on the client or prospect's Scorecard. In this example, the prospect wants an accountant who will stop by for informal visits three or four times a year so he can have someone with whom to share his ideas—clearly a condition of satisfaction.

According to the workshop participant who told this story, he acquired the engagement in part because he made sure he included routine, informal visits as part of the proposal letter. As an aside, the total annual fees on this supposedly "small" client were more than $100,000—and that was several years ago!

Explore Offsetting Benefits

Sometimes, when using the Ground Rule to explore the negative, you may uncover a gap between what the client or prospect wants and what you can deliver. This gap may be factual or perceptual. For example, suppose an attorney has a billing rate of $350 per hour. He meets with the in-house counsel at an insurance company that has a policy of paying a maximum of $175 per hour. This is clearly a factual gap. Once this gap has been identified, the attorney can explore offsetting benefits, using the Ground Rule to identify other factors that might be on the in-house counsel's Scorecard. The conversation might sound something like this:

> **In-house counsel:** It's really a matter of company policy. We only retain outside counsel that have a billing rate of $175 per hour or less. Unfortunately, your rate is way beyond our maximum.

> **Attorney:** [FEEDBACK] We've run into that before. Certain organizations have set a cap on the rates they pay to outside counsel. I appreciate you being straightforward on the issue. It's a constraint we'll have to deal with. [QUESTION] I'm sure you look at other factors besides hourly rates, though. What else does the company consider when choosing outside counsel?

By ending with this open-ended question, the attorney can learn what other issues might be on this in-house counsel's Scorecard. In some cases, outstanding performance on these other factors may outweigh the negative related to hourly rate. In other cases, this is useful information should they come to some compromise on the fee issue on some future matter.

Perceptual gaps can remain even after repeated use of the Ground Rule to explore the client or prospect's point of view. Again, you can use this versatile tool to find out what else is on the Scorecard. Consider the earlier conversation between the accountant and the prospect who felt they were not a good fit because of his perception that the accountant's firm worked with large clients. Sometimes, no amount of questioning can sway the prospect from his vague fear or concern:

Prospect: Your firm works with such large clients, but my business is much smaller. It's true we're growing, but we're not trying to be the next Microsoft. I don't know that this would be a good fit.

Professional: [FEEDBACK] Believe me, I've heard that comment before. I've talked with a lot of people who tend to identify us with some of our larger, better-known clients and feel that we might not be a good fit. Those big clients are a curse and a blessing. We love working with them, but it's frustrating when we're perceived as being a firm that only serves big clients. [INFORMATION] Actually, we work much more with clients that are your size or smaller. [QUESTION] What are your concerns about the fact that we work with these larger clients?

Prospect: There's nothing specific, really. I just think that working with a firm like yours could be a problem. We're a small company and you're better known for working with big organizations like ABC and XYZ.

Professional: [FEEDBACK] As I said, having some big-name clients on our list can work against us. It's unfortunate, and I have heard others express that same concern. [QUESTION] You mentioned that it could be a problem for you. Can you give me a better idea of what you mean, or how that might happen?

Prospect: Not really. It's not so much a specific concern. It's more like a sense of comfort. We work with a smaller bank, too, and a smaller law firm. Don't get me wrong. I like you and respect your firm, and I appreciate you taking the time to talk with me. It's just that I don't think the comfort level would be there.

Professional: [FEEDBACK] I appreciate your honesty, and I'm glad that you have respect for the firm and that our chemistry is good. And believe me, for us to work together, I'd want you to feel truly comfortable with the relationship. [INFORMATION] Certainly, I'm a bit frustrated because I'd love an opportunity to build a relationship with you and your organization. [QUESTION] Besides the size of the firm and its clients, what are some of the other things you consider when you're evaluating any advisor?

Again, this last open-ended question should help you learn what else is on the prospect's Scorecard. If it does not, at least you have the comfort of knowing you are playing the game well. It's like when a golfer who is stymied by a tree tries to hook or slice the ball around the obstacle. It might not work, but it is the best alternative given the situation.

Don't Be Stopped by Any Negative Factor or Objection

The key point to remember when using the Ground Rule to handle objections is that the negative you are dealing with is only one factor on the Scorecard. I worked with a consulting firm that started in one city, grew very large, and then opened an office in a second location in another state. The consultants in the home city complained about how difficult it was to sell work because they were perceived as being too big. The consultants at the second location complained about how hard it was to sell work because they didn't have an established reputation in their market or were perceived as not being large enough to handle important projects. Both groups felt they had a difficult sell and used their respective negatives as an excuse. The fact of the matter was they were allowing this single factor related to size to discourage them. Their task was to first make sure that the size issue was explored, clarified, and understood. If size continued to be an issue, it was still only one factor on the Scorecard. Their challenge was then to find other factors—features, benefits, and conditions of satisfaction—that might outweigh the concerns about size.

These consultants were like many, if not the majority, of professionals with whom I work. The whole analogy of selling being like a game comes in part from this type of frustration. If you were on a basketball team and your tallest guy was just over 6 feet tall, you might give up before the game even got underway if your opponent's front line averaged 7 feet. Or if you were a golfer who could drive the ball 225 yards, you might give up before you take on the club champion, who hits it well over 300. But the beauty of any game is to garner the resources you *do* have to meet the challenge at hand. Remember, the definition of strategy is the artful or ingenious use of resources. In the basketball example, maybe a strategy that uses speed and quickness would work. In the golf example, we all know the phrase "Drive for show, putt for dough." In the SalesGame, you must address negatives and objections as challenges to be understood and overcome by other resources. Negative factors on the Scorecard should not be seen as obstacles that reduce confidence or halt progress. Sometimes you may be able to gain a happy and enthusiastic client in spite of the negatives and sometimes you won't. As in any game, sometimes you win and sometimes you lose.

Regardless of the outcome, using the Ground Rule to first explore and then offset a negative enables you to walk away with the satisfaction that you played as well as possible. After all, at the end of any game, that is all we can ask for.

In the SalesGame, you must address negatives and objections as challenges to be understood and overcome by other resources.

The next chapters examine more specifically how to apply the Ground Rule to the two objections mentioned most frequently in my workshops: objections relating to price and clients and prospects who are satisfied with their current provider. The final chapter in this section provides tips on how to handle other frequently encountered objections.

Chapter

Handling Price Objections

When practicing the Ground Rule in workshops, price is probably the objection or negative Scorecard Factor that participants most want to discuss. This is for three reasons. First, the vast majority of people are concerned about what they pay for what they buy, whether it is a car, a stereo, or a professional service. Second, price is easily measurable and can be used to differentiate firms. Third, most of my clients did not build a book of business by being the lowest-cost provider. Rather, they built their book of business by providing quality and value. This type of professional is going to face questions about price because the competition is usually willing to provide the service—whether investment advice, an audit, a legal filing, outsourcing, or a consulting project—for less.

There is no magic formula for making an objection based on price go away. Assuming everything else is equal, if one professional offers to do a tax return for half of what another professional offers, most buyers will have a hard time rationalizing using the higher-priced provider. This would be a tough sell for higher-priced providers regardless of how good they may be at using the skills discussed in this or any other book. However, the following suggestions using the Ground Rule should help you handle this objection as well as possible.

Do Not Discuss Price Until You Know What You're Selling

Suppose a prospect is in a meeting with a professional and price comes up early in the discussion. It might sound something like this:

> **Prospect:** This project sounds interesting enough. But what's it going to cost?

I was often confronted with this question when selling research. You may have a specific answer for this question, as I did, since the research package had a set price. However, I did not want to discuss price early in the discussion because I did not know whether or how my service was going to be of value to the prospect, nor did I know what was going to be required to generate an enthusiastic client. In other words, you should avoid discussing fee issues until you at least know what you're selling—usually late in Stage Three and often not until Stage Four or even Stage Five.

Unlike my situation selling research, most professionals will not know how to price their services early in meetings because they will not know what's on the client or prospect's Scorecard. For example, will a condition of satisfaction require using higher-paid staff? Meeting an accelerated timeline? Writing a detailed report and giving a presentation to the board? These are just examples, but the answer to each of them affects price. Whether you are an accountant, an attorney, a consultant, or another service professional, it is difficult to discuss price because the scope of the service has yet to be determined.

If price comes up early in the sales process, your best move is to use the Ground Rule to ask permission to delay any discussion of price until the needed service can be better defined. For example, you might say something like this:

> **Professional:** [FEEDBACK] Well, I'm excited about the project, too. If we can find the right fit, it should really make a difference for your company. I'm sure cost will be something that we'll take a look at as we discuss this idea. [INFORMATION] I'd probably be doing us both a disservice to talk about price now because I might be way off the mark. I'd like to learn more about your situation first. [QUESTION] Could we come back to price after we find out more about how the project might fit with your goals?

Notice the use of a closed-ended question at the end of this statement. While this is unusual, I have found it works well in handling a potential price objection. Most clients and prospects understand the importance of knowing what they are buying before they discuss price. As a result, few if any will answer "no" to this closed-ended question. And if they do, they probably are not the client of your dreams anyway.

Establish a Frame of Reference

Almost always, either you or your client or prospect will need to address price in the sales equation. This is a sort of a moment of truth. It might occur late in Stage Three (if price is discussed as a condition of satisfaction) or early in Stage Four or Stage Five when you try to close. Many professionals are in such fear of an objection when price is discussed that they fall subject to what I call the *Chicken Factor*. In short, professionals often understate the cost of a service because they fear the client or prospect will object. I saw this tendency in action in a workshop for a law firm in upstate New York. The head of the firm's environmental group was preparing for a meeting with a utility company client to discuss an environmental audit. In advance of a role play based on the situation, Dean, the partner, was asked how much he thought this audit would cost. He responded that the figure would be in the area of $100,000. When asked the same question during the actual role play, however, Dean's response was somewhere around $75,000. Even in a workshop setting, Dean cut $25,000 from the price of the project simply because he was worried the "client" would object.

Everyone knows that it is more difficult to increase price than to reduce it. In this case, suppose Dean quoted $75,000 to the *real* utility company executive. The executive would be disappointed to say the least if the cost turned out to be $100,000 or more, regardless of how the increase was justified. This problem is exacerbated by the fact that most professionals tend to underestimate the time—and therefore the cost—it will take to perform any service. In other words, had the firm been engaged, the *real* cost of the environmental audit would have probably been closer to $125,000 or $150,000! How enthusiastic would the utility company executive be looking at final numbers like these?

You can improve how you handle discussions about cost by being more confident in your ability to respond to price objections. Use the Ground Rule to explore the client or prospect's frame of reference leading to the objection. The frame of reference can be based on many factors, such as the following:

■ The amount charged by competitors

■ The amount charged by previous service providers in the same area

■ The need for a predictable budget

- The client or prospect's experience with professionals selling other types of services

- Unrealistically low expectations of cost based on lack of experience with a service

- The client or prospect's organization policy—for example, caps on hourly rates paid to outside professionals

- Budgetary or timing constraints

- Hourly rates versus total fee versus "not to exceed" estimates versus total cost of transaction—for example, in the case of litigation, including settlement costs as well as attorney fees

When you first encounter the phrase "it's too expensive" or a similar price objection, using the Ground Rule to determine the frame of reference can help you in one of three ways. One, you'll be able to shape your service to respond to the cost concern. Two, you'll identify other Scorecard factors to offset the price negative. Or three, you'll know this probably isn't a client you really want to work with anyway.

Don't Lose an Opportunity Because of a Small Price Difference

In the case of the environmental audit, suppose the sales process has reached Stage Three. Dean and his prospect have discussed how the service would be of value to the company, what would be entailed in the audit, etc. Eventually, the conversation would turn to pricing as a condition of satisfaction. Odds are, it would sound something like this:

Prospect: So what do you think something like this would cost?

Dean: It's hard to be precise because we haven't talked to your people or reviewed any records. But based on our experience in similar situations, I think we're probably talking about a fee in the area of $100,000.

Prospect: $100,000! That seems like a lot just to tell us where the problems are. I mean, we won't really haven't *fixed* anything—we'll just have found out where the skeletons are.

Dean: [FEEDBACK] $100,000 is a lot of money. It's upsetting to hear a number like that. And you're right, unfortunately. You could spend $100,000 and end up with a list of problems to fix, and that's going to cost more. [INFORMATION] Your reaction to these numbers isn't unusual and it's certainly understandable. [QUESTION] What kind of costs were you anticipating?

The prospect's response to this open-ended question will tell Dean a lot about the situation in which he finds himself. Sometimes the prospect will simply say that he or she did not have any numbers in mind. The person was merely surprised or frustrated, but understands how costly an environmental audit can be. In cases like this, the objection may very well disappear without the attorney having to justify the cost.

On other occasions, the prospect might mention a number that is not far off the $100,000 figure. Don't be surprised if the difference is minimal. If the difference is small enough, most professionals will accept a lower figure. They don't want price to be a deal-breaker and are willing to compromise.

Using the Ground Rule to explore the client or prospect's frame of reference will often uncover small differences in competitive proposal situations or when dealing with new prospects used to working with less expensive profes-

> If the difference is small enough, most professionals will accept a lower figure.

sionals. I worked with a law firm in the Midwest that lost a major engagement for a municipality in spite of the fact that it had far better credentials than the competition. It's blended rate was $1 per hour more than the firm that won. If you have worked in the municipal arena, you know how any quantifiable difference in cost—even $1 per hour—can affect the outcome in a competitive bid situation. The Midwest law firm should have found—or at least tried to find, as these situations are often more like bids than proposals—the prospect's frame of reference. I am sure it would have eaten the $1 per hour rather than have this insignificant amount be a deal-breaker!

Show Them You Really Can Be More Valuable

The client or prospect's frame of reference may come from past experience. So when clients or prospects say a service is too expensive, they may simply mean it is more than they are used to paying for the same or similar services. Most professionals who charge higher rates believe—and want their prospects to understand—that these differences are not as great as they seem because their experience and knowledge make them more efficient and valuable. Again, if you use the Ground Rule, you may find that the difference is relatively small, and can move forward by establishing a condition of satisfaction regarding price.

For example, a large law firm in Connecticut was successful in bringing in a number of middle-market businesses that were concerned with the higher billing rate of a larger firm. The firm knew that billing rates weren't as big an issue as total cost. It determined the kinds of services being used and the costs incurred. Then, assuming it thought it could perform the same services for a similar cost, the firm would make an offer to match the total fee paid for general legal services during the previous year for the coming 12 months. The firm tracked its actual costs over that period, built relationships, and demonstrated how it could be of value. In almost every case, the firm was able to convert these middle-market businesses to enthusiastic, long-term clients by proving that it was not the hourly rate that was important but the firm's ability to use its experience to get the job done efficiently and create real value.

Don't Let Their Budget Get in the Way of Working Together

Budgetary issues can also cause the client or prospect to say a service is too expensive. In the example of the environmental audit, the executive might have had a number in his budget that was less than $100,000 and been worried about how he was going to handle this problem internally. In that case, he might have responded to the attorney's open-ended question like so:

> **Prospect:** I knew we were going to have to do something like this based on what's been going on around the country. In fact, I've already asked for $50,000 in our budget for this year. I didn't think it was going to be twice that figure! I'm afraid you're going to be too expensive for us on this project.

> **Attorney:** [FEEDBACK] You were certainly right to start planning for this. We've been in touch with a number of utilities that are in various stages of an environmental audit as we speak. There's a lot of concern about the EPA's last couple of rulings in this area, so budgeting some funds was a good idea. [INFORMATION] When you're looking at a new service area, it's hard to estimate costs. I'm sure you've run into expenditures that were necessary but not in the budget. [QUESTION] How has ABC Utility handled situations like this in the past?

As is true for using the Ground Rule to handle any negative, this application would enable the attorney to peel back the onion and learn that the *real* objection is not the price of the environmental audit but the relationship of that price to a line item in the client's budget. Lots of options open up with this realization. All companies have ways to deal with unexpected but necessary expenditures. I have also seen firms adjust their billing schedule to spread cost out over a period of time or different phases of a project. Of course, you may not always be successful in getting around budgetary constraints. But the idea is to use the Ground Rule to establish exactly what the problem is when the client or prospect claims an estimate is too expensive.

Win or lose, you want to know you have played the game well.

The open-ended question used as part of the Ground Rule to establish a frame of reference for price objections will depend on the words used by the client or prospect. The following questions and others like them work in different situations:

■ What kind of range are you looking at?

■ How far off are we from the competition's number?

■ How does it compare with your previous experience?

■ How are you measuring cost? Are you using hourly rate, total cost of service, or something different?

■ When you say the cost is too high, what sort of comparison are you looking at?

As discussed, these questions will get a much better response—and will probably be heard much differently—if they are preceded by the first two parts of the Ground Rule. That way, they won't sound so aggressive.

Determine the Scope of Service

No professional service is truly a commodity. There are too many different options for deliverables, timing, work process, staffing, etc. If the difference between the client or prospect's frame of reference and your estimate is substantial, you need to use the Ground Rule to explore the scope of the service in question. This is especially true when you are confronted with competitive bids. In response to an accountant using the Ground Rule to establish the frame of reference, a prospect might respond with something like the following:

> Prospect: The difference is substantial. Both of your competitors are $25,000 under your estimate, and that's $25,000 we can use in a lot better ways.

> Accountant: [FEEDBACK] That is a substantial difference. And it's certainly in your best interest to go with the best deal assuming everything else is equal. [INFORMATION] I know I would.

> [QUESTION] Beyond an opinion on your financials, what else have you discussed about how they'll approach the engagement? How are they going to work with your staff, what will the timing be, those kinds of things?

It may be that the competition is willing to deliver exactly the same product as this accountant but that the competitor is low-balling the fee to buy the business for one reason or another—for example, to get the foot in the door before pursuing other more lucrative opportunities with the same client. In other cases, you might learn ways to repackage your service so you can match competitors' pricing. The Ground Rule is not a guarantee of success. It is merely a tool you can use to make sure you are playing the SalesGame as well as possible, not unlike a good poker player who has to use other skills, like bluffing, when he is not blessed with good cards.

Note

Of course, the prospect may not tell the accountant. If the prospect does not want to help you by giving you the necessary information, I believe you would not be successful anyway.

In situations where you are dealing with a substantially lower priced competitor, there are many questions that you can ask to clarify scope. These include the following:

- What kind of staffing will the competitor be using?

- What sort of commitments are they looking at as far as project completion is concerned?

- What kind of recommendations are they going to give you as part of the project?

- How much are they using your internal resources?

- How much face time will you have with their top experts?

Regardless of the question, you need to use the Ground Rule to continue to explore the client or prospect's point of view in enough depth to understand the scope of the project for which you are competing. Of course, there are many cases in which the client or prospect will not really understand the scope of the project. This line of questioning creates an opportunity for you to use your own experience to help the client or prospect better understand what he or she is buying.

While determining scope of service is commonly done when dealing with competitive situations, it can also be beneficial when dealing with a client or prospect who is using a service for the first time. In this case, the questions are aimed more at understanding how much the client knows about the service.

Establish Offsetting Benefits

Of course, every professional will confront situations when his or her price is higher than the competitor's or higher than the client's perception of what the cost should be. But remember: As with any negative factor on the Scorecard, the fact that your price is higher—and for many high-quality firms, this is frequently the case—is still only one issue in the decision-making process. In this case, your job is to find the other factors that might offset cost. For example, suppose that an investment banker and a prospect have been engaged in a discussion. The frame of reference and scope of service have already been explored. The Ground Rule might sound something like this:

> **Prospect:** It sounds to me like your approach to handling this acquisition is the same as the other firms, yet your pricing is substantially higher. I don't think it makes a lot of sense to use you on this deal.

> **Investment banker:** [FEEDBACK] If I'm sitting where you are, I can see why you might want to use another option. Cost is always an important factor. I've never met a client who wasn't interested in saving money. [QUESTION] But before we call it a day, tell me what other factors you're looking at besides price?

Or, if the investment banker wanted to be even more aggressive, he could end his use of the Ground Rule with a closed-end question like this one:

> **Investment banker:** [QUESTION] Before we call it a day, is price the only factor you're looking at?

Admittedly, the prospect might not provide useful information on ways to offset cost or may not answer at all. But it's a little like firing off three-pointers in a basketball game when you're down by 10 with 30 seconds left to play. To play the game well, you take your best option and see what happens!

28

Chapter

Handling Objections from a Satisfied Prospect or Client

Dealing with a client or prospect who is happy with his or her current provider is second on the list of objections most frequently faced by professionals. This is especially true for those professionals who are initiating contact with prospects with whom they have not worked before or with a client for whom they are trying to expand their service into an area they have not delivered in the past. In these scenarios, you must first establish a need (the Heart of the Matter) before you discuss your credentials or reasons why your firm is better. Of course, in most cases, when you initiate contact, prospects and clients often don't perceive they have a need.

Explore Gaps in Coverage

The same approach applies to handling this objection as for handling objections in general. In short, you need to first use the Ground Rule to explore the objection and get more information.

My insurance consulting clients introduced me to the phrase "gaps in coverage," which is usually the first area to explore. In other words, you need to determine what services the prospect is getting from his or her current vendor and whether there may be some areas of need that are not being addressed by these services. Suppose an investment advisor and a prospect are meeting for the first time because a mutual friend suggested they get together.

The conversation might sound something like this:

> **Prospect:** I certainly appreciate the fact you came by and I've enjoyed our discussion. I'm glad Bill suggested we get together. But I've got to tell you, we've worked with ABC firm for years and we've been happy with what they've done for us. We're not really interested in making any kind of switch right now.

> **Investment advisor:** [FEEDBACK] Nothing wrong with that. That's the kind of relationship you *should* have with your investment advisory firm. If you're getting what you need and you're satisfied with your current firm, you shouldn't make a switch. That's something you ought to do only when it makes good business sense. [QUESTION] What kinds of things has ABC traditionally handled for you and your company?

Or, the investment advisor might say something like this:

> **Investment advisor:** [FEEDBACK] That's understandable. ABC's a good firm and it sounds like they've done well by you. The last thing I want you to think as a result of our discussion today is that I'm out here trying to push you to make a switch. I just wanted to take advantage of this opportunity to get to know you and your company a little better. You only want to make a change as important as this when there are good business reasons to do so. [QUESTION] What kinds of things has ABC traditionally handled for you and your company?

Remember, early in the SalesGame, the primary objective should be to build a relationship, not to sell work. So there is no reason for the investment advisor in this discussion to feel defensive. The question used to end both examples should work well because it is built on agreement (that is, you should not switch if you are getting good service). It is also non-threatening and explores gaps in coverage. Of course, most professionals know they should never speak negatively about the competition, even if the prospect does. If you do not respect the competition or it is unknown to you, it is best to avoid making any remarks about it at all, as was done in the first example. If the competition *is* good—and it usually is—you should first acknowledge this fact during the feedback portion of the Ground Rule, as was done in the second example.

Depending on the interview, other non-threatening questions could be used to end the investment advisor's comments, such as the following:

- How long have you worked with your current firm?

- How did you first come to use your current firm?

- How did you choose your current firm?

If you do not know the answers to these questions before the conversation, you would generally ask them before inquiring about gaps in coverage. You should learn more about the situation before moving ahead. If prospect has a longstanding or special relationship with the current provider (for example, a relative or longtime friend), you will need to go even slower. Ensure you build plenty of agreement to avoid antagonizing the prospect. Focus on building the relationship for the long run.

> Focus on building the relationship for the long run.

Why focus on gaps in coverage? Many if not most prospects do not fully understand the variety of services that a professional firm can render. They usually think only of the services they have been getting from their current provider. Exploring gaps in coverage helps you determine what prospects are receiving as well as what they might *not* be receiving. You can then use the Ground Rule to explore other potential service areas—areas where you can truly be of value—to identify a Heart of the Matter, if one exists. For example, an accountant discussing audit work might inquire about issues related to estate or transition planning. Or, an attorney talking to a bank prospect who is satisfied with the firm it uses to handle real-estate transactions might ask about how the bank handles troubled loans. If an area is uncovered in which the prospect is not being served, then obviously you have a new area to explore. The objection of "We're happy with our current firm" is not a factor if you are no longer talking about the same service the current firm is providing.

Find Out What They Like—and Don't Like—About Their Current Firm

If no gaps in coverage are revealed by this line of questioning, then it is time to move on to the next best option: finding out what the prospect likes—and doesn't like—about his or her current firm. In other words, you need to ask questions about what makes the prospect satisfied.

After a discussion of gaps in coverage, the investment advisor in the previous example might say something like this:

> **Investment advisor:** [FEEDBACK] You mentioned that you're happy with ABC. That's the kind of respect we all want our clients to feel. I'm always curious as to what makes a client satisfied. [QUESTION] What is it that ABC does that you like as a buyer?

This area of exploration assists you in two ways. First, you might learn that "I'm happy with my current firm" is nothing more than a smokescreen. If nothing specific comes up in response to this line of questioning, odds are the prospect is simply using "I'm happy" as a way to avoid being pushed into a sales conversation. Second, if the prospect is genuinely pleased with the current firm, this question helps you identify what's on this prospect's Scorecard for the long run. For example, if the prospect says he or she likes the fact that the current service provider makes suggestions about how to improve the plan options, you should position with this prospect by sending suggestions or ideas that have a similar intent.

Of course, you need to use the Ground Rule to explore and really understand the prospect's responses. If a prospect says he likes his current firm because it is responsive, you need to find out the true meaning of the word *responsive* to this specific prospect. This is the same approach used to define positive factors on the Scorecard.

Eventually, this part of the conversation will wind down as the prospect runs out of positive attributes he likes about his current firm. Then it is time to switch and ask a question like one of the following:

- What about your current firm are you *not* satisfied with?

- What things would you like to change about the way your current firm works with you?

- What aspects of your current firm's service would you like to see improved?

Or, if you want to have more fun, ask your prospects what they might wish for if they could change anything about their current service:

> **Investment advisor:** [FEEDBACK] This has been an interesting discussion. Thanks! Most of my clients also want a provider who sends them new ideas and knows their industry. Let's go in a different direction. You're obviously a buyer who knows what she wants. [QUESTION] If you could wave a magic wand and change one thing about the service you're getting, what would it be?

Most prospects respond well to this question—especially if you ask it with a smile on your face—because it asks them to name just one thing they would change rather than to come up with a list of complaints. If they respond, then you have at least one item you can use to build a strategy as you position yourself with this prospect over the months and perhaps even years to come.

This line of questioning may or may not yield much input, but that is of course the nature of the SalesGame. A football team can have a great game plan, but that plan will go out of the window if the star player is injured in the opening quarter. Likewise, when you enter a business-development interview, you never really know what you are going to find. Your ability to adjust to the current situation is critically important to your long-term success.

If the prospect's current provider is doing a great job both in terms of the quality and breadth of services, there is not much hope of developing business in the short term. The best you can do in this situation is to avoid alienating the satisfied prospect by pushing too hard. Instead, build the relationship and hopefully get an idea or two to tailor your follow-up positioning to the needs and interests of the prospect.

Of course, sometimes the objection isn't about replacing a current provider but rather using a service for the first time. I've seen this happen in the investment banking world, when clients or prospects feel like the banker they're talking to is pushing to sell when they're not really sure they want to buy. You would be better served by not pushing at all, and instead becoming a trusted advisor. You might do this for years if the prospect could become the client of your dreams!

> You would be better served by not pushing at all, and instead becoming a trusted advisor.

Handling Objections Phrased Like Questions

Sometimes, objections can be couched in questions. For example, rather than saying "I'm concerned you don't have enough experience for a project like this," a prospect might say, "How much experience do you have on projects like this?" In either case, you will find that using the Ground Rule to respond works well. The primary difference is that you must make some attempt to answer the question when providing information before ending with a question. Clients and prospects generally do not like the age-old trick of simply answering a question with a question. Using the preceding example, a professional with relevant experience in his or her background might respond with something like this:

Professional: [FEEDBACK] It's an interesting project! I'm sure that working with someone who has experience will be useful to you in achieving your objectives. [INFORMATION] We've done projects similar to this several times before, working with ABC and XYZ companies. [QUESTION] What kind of experience do you think is most important on this project?

Note

If you want to mention that you've done a project with another company, be sure you get that company's permission first.

Responding to this question is obviously more difficult if you lack experience. If this is the case, you might respond in the following manner:

> **Professional:** [FEEDBACK] It's an interesting project! I'm sure that working with someone who has experience will be useful to you in achieving your objectives. [INFORMATION] I wish I could say I have done a project exactly like this, but to be honest, I haven't gone down this exact road before. I did do a project for ABC that was similar in that it [DESCRIBE SIMILARITY]. [QUESTION] What sort of experience do you feel is most important on this project?

In both examples, your ability to respond will depend on your having done some homework—for example, identifying and contacting clients whose names can be used as references and/or determining elements of experience to emphasize. Much like a professional golfer practices a particular golf shot for the course he's going to play, you need to be ready for the tough objection or question that is usually part of any business development interview. While the Ground Rule is a right-brain skill like swinging a golf club or shooting a jump shot, it also has a left-brain application. Using the Ground Rule to respond to an objection will work wonders for your confidence!

Always Be Prepared for "Why You?"

One tough question that you should be ready for whenever you are involved in a selling situation is "Why you?" In other words, why are you the best choice for a particular engagement? Some clients and prospects ask the question because it seems like a natural question for a buyer to ask. Others simply want to hear how well you respond, almost like a test. Many clients and prospects ask this question not to be difficult, but because they need ammunition to convince others within their organization.

You have to be careful when answering this question because it can easily lead you into the danger zone. The danger zone is particularly treacherous early in the sales process—for example, in a Stage Two or early Stage Three interview—because you are providing reasons to buy without much input from the client or prospect. To be effective, you need to be crisp, clear, and most of all, brief. And as is always the case when using the Ground Rule, you need to end with a question to keep the client or prospect involved in the conversation.

Use the Rule of Three

The key to success when responding to "Why you?" is to know the three best reasons to use your firm *before* the meeting starts. I call this the Rule of Three. You can usually identify these top three reasons as you develop the Scorecard as part of the normal preparation process, which was explored in Chapter 10, "The Importance of Preparation." If you are early in the sales process, these reasons are based more on guesswork and experience than on specific client or prospect input. Nevertheless, you still need to identify them to prepare your response.

> The key to success when responding to "Why you?"
> is to know the three best reasons to use your firm
> *before* the meeting starts.

Suppose a client or prospect asks "Why you?" in a Stage Three interview in response to an RFP:

> **Client or prospect:** Let's cut to the chase. When all is said and done, why do you feel we should use ABC firm on this project?

Using the Ground Rule and the Rule of Three, your response might sound like this:

> **Professional:** [FEEDBACK] Good question. I was thinking about that yesterday on my way home from work. I came up with three things. First, we've worked on similar projects. We know what needs to be done and what the pitfalls are. Second, our staff is available to start on the engagement right away, so you'll get what you want quickly. Third, we've had a long relationship working on various projects, so you know us. We're a proven commodity and we work well together. So we have experience, availability, and a track record working together. But I'm biased. I could talk about "why us" until the cows come home. I'm here to learn about what *you* think will be important. [QUESTION] What are the most critical factors you're looking at as you make this decision?

What's amazing about this approach is how often the client or prospect responds to the question that ends this application of the Ground Rule by restating one, two, or even all three of the points you just made. (Of course, there is nothing magical about the three reasons I mentioned here. They are only examples. Each professional must determine his or her top three when he or she starts thinking about the Scorecard and sales strategy in advance of the meeting.)

Personally, I love to hear this question for a couple of reasons. First, it usually indicates the client or prospect is approaching the purchase of professional services with an open mind. Second, it provides an opportunity to build the Scorecard by focusing on my strong points. A number of my workshop participants have also had good results with this technique. It is easy to use and almost guaranteed to put an item or two on the Scorecard that will favor choosing you or your firm.

Tip

Of course, as in any game, you'll be more effective if you practice—that is, say it out loud—before you go to the meeting. Better still if you can practice with someone else.

Tips for Handling Other Objections

This chapter contains tips for handling several other objections that you may confront. For each objection, I've listed possible issues that might be revealed by peeling back the onion as well as a suggested response. Regardless of the specific objection, the Ground Rule provides a model for responding. Obviously, every situation is different and the words you use will change accordingly. But these examples should provide some ideas of the best way to proceed.

Distance

Possible Issues

- Accessibility

- Travel costs

- Charging for travel time

- Loyalty to current service providers and/or to the community

- Lack of contacts in the local marketplace

- Lack of understanding of the local marketplace

Suggested Response

Client or prospect: Your background and experience are good, but we're in Iowa and you're located in Chicago.

Professional: [FEEDBACK] I know we're not right down the street. I could talk about e-mails, cell phones, video conferencing, and so on, but what's really important is how you *feel* about the distance. [QUESTION] What specifically concerns you about the fact that we're in Chicago and you're in Des Moines?

Depth

Possible Issues

- Reputation
- Ability to get the job done quickly
- Costs related to bringing others in for a project
- Backup of key players on the engagement
- Loyalty to another firm
- Age/experience of key players

Suggested Response

Client or prospect: I don't know if your Tokyo office really has the horsepower we need for a project of this dimension.

Professional: [FEEDBACK] No doubt this project is going to be a big undertaking. You're going to want to be comfortable that we have the horsepower you need to make sure things are done correctly. [INFORMATION] We do have substantial resources in Tokyo and can add to those as required. [QUESTION] When you say "horsepower," what specific issues are you concerned about?

Too Little Experience

Possible Issues

- Being a training ground

- Ability to get the job done right

- Risk to the decision-maker for choosing an inexperienced firm

- Fear of too many mistakes being made on the project

- Cost from inefficiencies

Suggested Response

> **Client or prospect:** I'm concerned about the fact that you haven't done a project like this before.
>
> **Professional:** [FEEDBACK] I understand your concern. This is an important project and you want to be sure it goes well. You've got a lot riding on it, and you're right. We haven't done something exactly like this before. [INFORMATION] We have done work that gives us good experience on important aspects of the project, like [INSERT EXAMPLES]. [QUESTION] What could we do that would make you more comfortable with our ability to get this project done right?

Too Much Experience

Possible Issues

- Sharing proprietary information

- Cost of service

- Not wanting to share a professional service firm with a specific competitor

- Loyalty to the current firm

Suggested Response

Client or prospect: You certainly know our industry. That's one of the things that concerns me. You work with too many of our competitors.

Professional: [FEEDBACK] Thanks. We've worked very hard to build that experience. No question, it helps us do a better job working with our clients in ABC industry. And it is a competitive industry to say the least. [INFORMATION] Unfortunately, it is kind of a two-edged sword. Clients sometimes worry about the fact that we work with their competitors. We've been able to handle this in a number of ways. For example, we've set up different service teams—sometimes even from different locations —to handle competitors. [QUESTION] What specifically concerns you about the number of clients we serve in your industry?

Resistance to Using a Firm in a New Area

Possible Issues

- Loyalty to another provider

- Doubt about ability in the new area

- Wanting to avoid using one firm too much

Suggested Response

Client or prospect: We've always thought of your law firm more for corporate deals. We've never really thought of using you on a labor matter like this.

Professional: [FEEDBACK] That's understandable. We've been doing your corporate work for years and we've never been great at making sure our clients know everything we do. [INFORMATION] We have a substantial labor and employment law practice, though, and I know we could do a great job on this case. [QUESTION] What issues are you looking at to choose a firm for this matter?

You Are All the Same

Possible Issues

- Loyalty to another provider

- Fee resistance

- Not the real decision-maker

Suggested Response

Client or prospect: Frankly, most accounting firms are pretty much the same when it comes to this kind of work. I mean an audit is an audit, right?

Professional: [FEEDBACK] That's a common perception. And there is some truth to it, since we're all delivering an opinion on financial statements. [INFORMATION] But there are some differences in the way various firms work with their clients. After all, clients are different and need different things from their accounting firm. [QUESTION] You've obviously had some experience working with professionals. At the end of the day, what tells you one firm did a good job and another didn't?

Part Summary

The Ground Rule is the fundamental communication tool for playing every stage of the SalesGame. Its effectiveness stems from its simplicity. It involves three steps: listening for value, feeding back value and agreement first, then providing information and ending with a question. Everyone uses this skill already. You only need to make it a more conscious behavior through practice and repetition.

The primary requirement of using the Ground Rule is communicating in such a way that everyone involved in the conversation gets a win. A win is defined as getting a sense of value. Clients and prospects can get value from useful information as well as knowing they are being heard and understood. You get value from learning more about your clients and prospects. Certain information may not be pleasant to hear, but is still useful and therefore of value.

Step 1 of the Ground Rule is to listen for value. You should listen to your client or prospect for anything that is useful for him or her. If you get useful information, you are getting a win from the communication, thus fulfilling the first half of the win-win equation. Useful input might be new information, ideas, or feelings. Listening for a client or prospect's feelings is especially important because it helps you develop your relationship and is usually an easier way to build agreement. Finding areas of agreement enables you to build a common base from which to further explore your client or prospect's point of view. Unfortunately, most people tend to focus on areas of disagreement when they listen, which often leads to confrontation.

Step 2 of the Ground Rule requires you to feed back value and agreement. By building on agreement, you create a much more positive, constructive conversation. Paraphrasing the value using at least some of the client or prospect's words makes the feedback more effective. If you build on disagreement by starting with phrases like "Yes, but," agreement disappears and discussions tend to become argumentative. When it comes to building on agreement or disagreement, everyone has their own tendencies. These are a result of communication patterns learned over years. You must work on these tendencies by being more aware of how you provide feedback and practicing this skill in and out of business-development situations. When you perform this second step of the Ground Rule, you connect with clients and prospects and build the relationship. If dealing with objections, you'll usually want to smile when providing feedback. In this way, you project an image of calm rather than appearing defensive or worried.

In Step 3 of the Ground Rule, you provide information, as necessary, and end with a question. As much as possible, you should balance the information you provide with the amount of feedback you give to clients or prospects. This information may be used to make an emotional connection with the client or prospect (perhaps by sharing a personal experience) or to position a service (by communicating important features, benefits, or conditions of satisfaction).

Two mistakes are common with Step 3 of the Ground Rule. First, professionals enter a danger zone by providing too much information. This can bore the client or prospect, cause the professional to sound defensive, or cause the professional to emphasize the wrong selling points. Second, they fail to provide enough information and only ask questions. This makes the business-development interview seem like an interrogation.

The most important point to remember is to end with a question. Open-ended questions are better than closed-ended questions because they elicit more substantive comments from the client or prospect. To be effective, professionals must find the right balance between providing information and asking questions. Regardless of talent level, all professionals can improve their use of this skill by practicing its use both in and out of business situations.

The Ground Rule can be used to refine the client or prospect's Scorecard or to better understand objections. On the Scorecard, the Ground Rule can help you get to the "real" Heart of the Matter and to respond more effectively to positive Scorecard Factors.

You should use the Ground Rule to respond to positive comments from clients and prospects, like their desire to work with firms that are responsive or that provide personal service. You should first clarify the desired feature, benefit, or condition of satisfaction and then establish exactly what the client or prospect wants to ensure enthusiasm. This process is like peeling the skin off an onion. When each layer is peeled off, it reveals a deeper layer. Responsiveness can become returning phone calls or providing periodic updates on how a project is going. The Ground Rule is also a good way to position your service by providing information such as evidence or ideas to improve the working relationship.

The Ground Rule is an excellent tool for handling objections. You should first use it to explore any negative factors on the Scorecard, like "Your firm is too big" or "You're too expensive." The real issue is frequently different from the first objection expressed. When dealing with objections, you should provide little if any information as part of Step 3 of the Ground Rule. Objections can often be turned into positive factors on a Scorecard. For example, "too big" can be converted to a condition of satisfaction related to personal service. If objections cannot be resolved, you should use the Ground Rule to explore offsetting features, benefits, and conditions of satisfaction. Remember, any negative is only one factor on the Scorecard.

Professionals who offer high-quality services frequently encounter price objections. When prospects raise this issue early in the sales process (Stage Two or at the beginning of Stage Three), you should use the Ground Rule to ask permission to delay the discussion of cost until the needs and service have been defined (late in Stage Three or Stage Four). If prospects still want to negotiate price before the service has been defined, you should recognize that this probably is not an opportunity that will generate rewards commensurate with value received.

When cost is raised as an objection after the needs and service have been defined, you should use the Ground Rule to explore the client or prospect's frame of reference. For example, is the client or prospect comparing your price with competitors' prices, with previous experience, or with a line item on a budget? You can then determine the gap between your price and what the client or prospect has in mind. If the difference is small, the best strategy might be to adjust your price to meet the client or prospect's condition of satisfaction. You might also establish a mutually agreeable "not to exceed" price strategy for short-term delivery of service to demonstrate value before continuing the relationship. If budgetary constraints are the issue, you can use the Ground Rule to explore other options, such as breaking the engagement into phases or finding other sources of funding. When the frame of reference has been established, you should use the Ground Rule to explore the scope of service to see if the client or prospect is making an apples-to-apples comparison. This is particularly true in competitive situations. Assuming the scope is the same and nothing can be done to reshape the service, you should use the Ground Rule to see if there are any Scorecard Factors that might offset this negative.

When initiating contact, you will frequently confront an objection that clients or prospects are "happy" or "satisfied" with their current service provider. In this case, you should use the Ground Rule to determine what services the prospect is receiving from his or her current provider to see if there are any potential areas of need that are not being addressed. In other words, you should explore gaps in coverage. Remember, most buyers think only in terms of the services they are currently getting, not in terms of new or different services that might help them accomplish other business or personal objectives. After you have explored gaps in coverage, use the Ground Rule to determine what prospects like about their current service provider. This information can be useful for long-term positioning. Finally, you should use the Ground Rule to identify any areas where the current service provider is not performing well. If weaknesses exist, you can use them to develop a strategy for short- and long-term positioning efforts. Throughout this process, you should not make any negative comments about the competition. If the prospect does not perceive a need, it's best to be seen as a trusted advisor than as someone pushing for a sale.

You can use the Ground Rule when they encounter objections disguised as tough questions. For example, you might be asked about your experience, which can be a hidden objection if this is a weak point on the Scorecard. You must provide some information in Step 3 of the Ground Rule when responding to tough questions to avoid answering a question with a question. One of the most common tough questions you will likely encounter is "Why should I choose you?" To avoid the danger zone when responding to this question, prepare for the meeting by choosing the three most important reasons the prospect should use you or your firm.

You can provide these three reasons in Step 3 of the Ground Rule. You should then end with a question to see how the client or prospect reacts. Generally, clients and prospects will accept one or two of these reasons, thus creating positive factors on the Scorecard.

There are many objections that could surface in meetings between you and your client or prospect. Some of the more common objections include those related to distance, depth, experience, using a firm in a new area, and the perception that all firms are the same. You need to use the Ground Rule to explore what is really behind any negative. The goal of the SalesGame is to end up with an enthusiastic client. This requires truly understanding the client or prospect's point of view, not using sales tricks to overcome an objection. When exploring objections, you may find the issue disappears because it was not really important. Or, you may find ways to reshape your service to turn a negative into a positive. If the objection still exists, you should use the Ground Rule to find features, benefits, or conditions of satisfaction to offset this negative on the Scorecard.

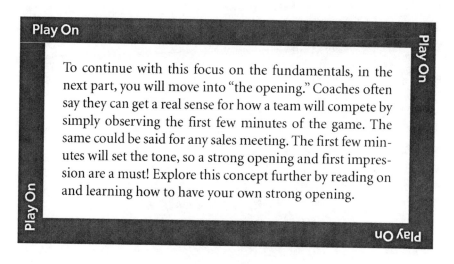

Play On

To continue with this focus on the fundamentals, in the next part, you will move into "the opening." Coaches often say they can get a real sense for how a team will compete by simply observing the first few minutes of the game. The same could be said for any sales meeting. The first few minutes will set the tone, so a strong opening and first impression are a must! Explore this concept further by reading on and learning how to have your own strong opening.

Part 5

The Opening: Start the Game

Creating a Favorable Impression

A nyone who plays a game knows how important it is to get off to a good start. If you're a golfer, nothing will put you in a worse mood than hitting your opening tee shot into the woods and ending up with a double bogey! Sure, you can recover from a bad beginning, but it makes winning a lot more difficult. The SalesGame works the same way. If you open badly, it is difficult to bounce back.

The good news is that opening is a simple skill, requiring only a few minutes of planning and some practice to execute well. The most important point is to have a plan that moves you and the client or prospect quickly through the anxiety that is a natural part of the beginning of the sales interview.

The opening of almost every face-to-face or telephone sales conversation consists of three parts:

- Creating a favorable impression

- Building rapport

- Making the transition to business

This chapter focuses on the first of these: creating a favorable impression in the first meeting between you and your client or prospect.

> ### Note
>
> Obviously, creating a favorable impression is more important early in the sales process. However, regardless of where you are in the business-development process, it's important to make a good impression at the start of any meeting. Even if you are speaking on the phone with out-of-town clients to ensure enthusiasm in Stage Six, you should work to create a favorable impression when the meeting starts. For example, you might make sure the conversation is taking place at a convenient time. In this case, setting up a time and agenda for the telephone meeting in advance and asking permission to continue once the client is on the phone is a common courtesy that should create the right impression at the start of the conversation.

There are four points you should remember to create the right impression:

- Dress for the game you are playing.
- Create an air of confidence.
- Be on time.
- Contact the client or prospect if you will be late.

Dress for the Game You Are Playing

Much has been written about how to dress for business. My intent is not to detail the same information here. When it comes to selling professional services, the bottom line is not how expensive your suit is but how you are perceived by the client or prospect.

Over the last few years, the business dress code has changed. Suits gave way to business casual and even blue jean Fridays. More recently, however, I've seen business casual morph back to suits—although with an open collar and no tie. No doubt the styles of acceptable dress will continue to evolve. The important point is to dress appropriately for the particular client or prospect you're meeting. Your appearance is a big part of making a good impression.

While your dress is more important in a first meeting, it matters to some degree in almost every contact with a client or prospect. I once showed up for a breakfast meeting in Honolulu with the managing partner of an accounting firm. I wore a Brooks Brothers pinstripe suit that had served me well in similar situations. In this case, however, the managing partner greeted me with a slight frown. "You can't wear that to the office!" he said.

He promptly sent me to the hotel gift store to purchase an aloha shirt—a standard and customary piece of apparel in Oahu. I got off to a bad start, but I was able to recover by making the right impression in later meetings with my new attire.

Even little details in dress can make a difference. I worked with an attorney in Buffalo who specialized in construction litigation. He made sure he had a hard hat in the trunk of his car at all times. He even had his two children play with the hard hat before he wore it the first time so it did not look too new! When he met a client or prospect on a job site, he removed his suit coat, rolled up his sleeves and put on his hard hat. He looked right at home. More recently, I worked with a consulting firm where the dress code was extremely casual—to the point that even wearing dress slacks and a sport coat would have made me look out of place. If you are not sure what attire is appropriate, check with a coach, the client or prospect, or even an administrative assistant who works at the organization.

Tip

Generally, it's best to err on the side of being more dressed up than your client or prospect. After all, you are being paid to give advice and counsel. You need to look more like a trusted advisor than one of the company employees.

By the way, don't forget about footwear. It's amazing how many of my clients, when asked how a service provider could improve its offering, replied "You could tell them to shine their shoes every now and then!" Once, on a flight from Key West to Chicago, I realized I had only the sandals I was wearing. I couldn't believe how many strange looks I got the next morning in the hotel lobby. Fortunately, I was able to find a shoe store before my scheduled meeting!

Tip

Before any face-to-face contact, check your appearance in a mirror, make sure your hands are dry, and use breath spray. Telephone meetings are easier, but you should make it a point to eliminate any background noise. If you're video conferencing, consider the background that the person at the other end will see. That can distract the client or prospect or diminish your credibility.

The point of these stories is fairly simple. You should not allow anything about your appearance to distract the client or prospect or damage your own credibility. In addition to the wrong outfit, a crooked tie, bad breath, sweaty hands, or lettuce between the teeth can do both.

Create an Air of Confidence

For wealth managers, accountants, lawyers, consultants, investment bankers, and other similar professionals, an aura of self-confidence is key. These professionals are supposed to know what they're doing and to look the part. You must make a conscious effort to project this image in the opening of the sales interview. Little things go a long way toward achieving this objective:

- Direct eye contact

- Smiling

- Good posture

- Firm handshake

These are all requirements for a good opening.

I suppose you could add "be well rested" to the list. I know one regional accounting firm that actually sets a curfew—although I don't think they conduct bed checks—for professionals making sales presentations on the following day. The message communicated by this firm is clear: If you are playing in an important SalesGame, you must make sure you do everything in your power to feel centered, in control, and confident. That is good advice for all of us.

Be on Time

Punctuality is critical to creating a favorable impression. I once walked into a managing partner's office 45 minutes late because I failed to check a map to estimate the driving time beforehand. His icy glare was enough to teach me to be better prepared the next time. Of course, no professional has complete control over timing—planes are late, traffic accidents block expressways, etc. Nonetheless, recovering from a bad beginning caused by a late arrival is similar to coming back from 20 points down in the first quarter of an NBA game. It's doable, but most professionals would rather not fight that sort of uphill battle!

Contact the Client or Prospect If You Will Be Late

This is advice that all professionals should follow when an unexpected delay occurs. Thank goodness for cell phones! A quick call, text, or e-mail to a client or prospect usually minimizes the damage if you are running late. On more than one occasion, I have heard of lawyers who have created a favorable impression by this simple act of courtesy. If you are qualifying a lead in Stage Two, I suggest talking to the administrative assistant to minimize the chance of a cancelled appointment. Of course, these days, it is getting harder and harder to actually get a live person on the phone, so e-mailing and texting are usually better ways to let the client or prospect know you'll be a few minutes late.

Chapter

Building Rapport

Regardless of your profession, developing good relationships is the foundation for building trust, developing business, and delivering service. For this reason, opening the sales meeting with a little semi-social banter is a requirement. This small talk also serves a purpose: It helps both you and the client or prospect get through the nervousness that is often part of a sales meeting.

The time it takes to build rapport will depend on many factors, such as the nature of the relationship, the geographic location, and the time available. Typically, longer periods are required earlier in the sales process. I've often seen very useful information come up during this type of small talk—for example, a client or prospect's connection with a person or place that is shared by you. On the other hand, you don't want to overdo the small talk. The following tips should help improve your ability to build rapport in the opening of the meeting.

> The time it takes to build rapport will depend on many factors, such as the nature of the relationship, the geographic location, and the time available.

Introduce the Players First

Whether on the phone or in person, clients and prospects will appreciate knowing who the players are early in the meeting. Obviously, this is not much of a problem if there are only one or two people present. And of course, it isn't necessary in meetings with clients you know. But when the group is larger—for example, a presentation setting— introductions can be a bit more complex and need to be thought out in advance. Handshakes should be coordinated, business cards passed out in an orderly fashion, and precautions taken to ensure everyone does not talk at the same time.

To make sure the introductions go as well as possible, remember the following points:

- Have a designated opener who speaks first, introduces everyone at the meeting, and makes the transition to business when the time comes.

- Move from one side to the other—usually right to left—to facilitate eye contact and handshakes.

- Speak slowly and give first and last names followed by a single sentence or two to describe why each person is at the meeting.

- On a telephone conference call, have each person speak after they are introduced, providing a single-sentence explanation of their role, so there will be a connection between their voice and name.

- When the client or prospect introduces the players from his or her team, write down the names on a notepad, ideally in the same arrangement as the seating.

- If offered a business card, look at it carefully before you put it away. Putting it in your wallet or briefcase too quickly might be seen as disrespectful. Some professionals like to leave the card(s) on the table in front of him or her to aid in remembering name(s).

Of course, these rules also apply for creating a favorable impression—for example, eye contact, a dry and firm handshake, etc.

Keep It Simple

I have heard many sales professionals—as opposed to professionals who sell—talk about how they use what they observe in the office as a way to start small talk. For example, they ask about photographs, trophies, or diplomas. This is not a bad technique, but there is always the risk that the item selected does not belong to the client or prospect or evokes the wrong emotion.

("Yes, that's my family. Well, those are my kids anyway. My wife and I divorced last year.") From my experience, you should also stay away from the standard question, "How's business?" This question can cause you to make the transition into business without first establishing the relationship. It can also lead the conversation into subjects you really do not want to discuss.

Obviously, building rapport is easier if the relationship exists before the point of sale. That is why it is so important to build relationships with people through community, social, or sports activities. When the relationship turns to business, a common ground such as last week's golf game or the upcoming fundraiser already exists.

If there is no pre-existing social relationship, the best approach is to keep the topic light and simple. I find that talking about the weather—a subject about which everyone has an opinion but not a very strong one—is an easy way to open with little risk. You can also talk about the view from an office window, a recent sporting or entertainment event, or some other non-business topic you discussed the last time you spoke with the client or prospect. Any of these subjects are safe and provide an opportunity to build rapport. Telephone meetings are much the same (view from the office window aside). Weather and cultural events are topics that evoke little stress and serve to break the ice.

Regardless of the topic chosen, you are well advised to have a topic in mind *before* you enter the client or prospect's office or make a telephone call. Fumbling for words to open the meeting hardly projects an air of confidence. Failing to choose a good topic for small talk can also cause you to make the transition to business too quickly—that is, before you or the client or prospect start to relax. Worse, if you open the meeting without a topic for small talk, you will likely feel unprepared and under pressure. It would be a little like walking up to the first tee while you are still tying your golf shoes. It can be done, but you probably won't hit your best shot!

Keep It Short

When building rapport, some professionals indulge in small talk longer than necessary, limiting the time available for the real purpose of the meeting: building the Scorecard. This can be true at any stage in the business-development process.

I was guilty of this error early in my sales career and I watched many others make the same mistake. The business lunch provides a classic example of this problem. Obviously, there will be occasions when you spend an entire lunch building rapport. After all, a cardinal rule of selling is to get to know prospects as people first—their personality, style, likes, and dislikes. However, accountants, lawyers, and consultants sometimes engage in small talk for 45 minutes even when they already have a good relationship with the client or prospect. As a result, time runs out before they are able to explore the client or prospect's objections or conditions of satisfaction.

I think professionals dwell on small talk because they feel that as long as the client or prospect is talking, things are going well. It is like a voice in the back of their head saying, "This is going to go well. This guy likes me!" What they forget is that a lot of clients and prospects engage in small talk because it is easier than discussing business. This is particularly true in a Stage Two meeting if you are initiating contact. Clients and prospects may not be favorably inclined to purchase whatever they perceive you to be selling. In short, the voice saying, "This is going to go well!" is probably sending you the wrong message. Based on my research, I do not think clients and prospects are intentionally trying to put you off. It is more of a general discomfort that many people feel in sales situations.

Another reason professionals tend to spend too much time building rapport is that they operate under the assumption that the client or prospect should make the transition to the business discussion. This assumption is based on a sense of courtesy and a desire to avoid making a pitch. However, most clients and prospects are waiting for the professional to make the first move. In many cases, they are squeezing the meeting or phone call between several other activities and have not given it much thought. Again, this is more typical when you are initiating contact than when you are responding.

So how much time should you spend building rapport? Unfortunately, there is no single answer. It depends on the culture in which you are operating. More small talk takes place in Columbia, South Carolina than in New York City and in Barcelona than in London, but there are no specific guidelines. The length of the small talk goes back to its purpose: developing a comfort zone between you and your prospect or client. As soon as you sense the anxiety has subsided on both sides of the table, you should make the transition to business. The professor teaching my public speaking class used to say, "The butterflies in your stomach won't go away, but you're ready to start once they're flying in formation."

> "The butterflies in your stomach won't go away, but you're ready to start once they're flying in formation."

Making the Transition to Business

As mentioned, two reasons professionals spend too much time on small talk are that it feels like small talk makes for an easy sale and that it's the client or prospect's responsibility to make the transition to business. But there's a third reason: Often, professionals don't know *how* to make the transition to business. The approach discussed in this chapter will help consultants, lawyers, and accountants get more comfortable with this transition.

Have a Plan

When I first started public speaking, I used to get so nervous that the hair on the back of my head would stand up and I'd start to shiver. To combat this, I made sure I had the first few sentences of my speech down cold. In the same way, Bill Walsh, former coach of the San Francisco 49ers, used to script the first 20 plays of a game to ensure that the nervousness that he felt at the beginning of each game did not interfere with his decision-making. That way, regardless of what happened during the first few minutes of the contest, his playbook was in place. Many coaches now replicate this approach.

The same thought process applies when it comes to making the transition to business in a meeting. Simply put, you need to have a plan. I have often seen professionals plan sales meetings on the car ride out or even in the elevator ride up to a client or prospect's office. This is not a good idea. It's far better to plan in advance and then rehearse the transition to business—yes, actually say it *out loud*—during the car ride out or elevator ride up. With a very small amount of rehearsal time, you will be much more confident, and you'll make a smooth transition from small talk to business.

Don't Make a Pitch

One of the biggest mistakes professionals make is that they start the transition to business by making a pitch—that is, telling the client or prospect about their services. This often ends up one-sided and too long. Although it is certainly permissible and even advisable to include a value proposition as part of the opening, these comments should be kept to a minimum—a sentence or two. (A *value proposition* is simply a short description of the benefits the client or prospect might receive from the service being discussed.) I have seen partners from various firms talk non-stop for 15 minutes before the client or prospect can get a word in edgewise. It's easy to understand why this happens. First, everyone talks more when they are nervous, and most professionals are nervous at the start of a sales meeting. Second, when professionals make a pitch, they are talking about their livelihood. They are in their comfort zone. When these two factors are combined, professionals get on a roll and fail to notice they are losing their audience.

A consultant once told me that he had read that a professional has only two minutes from the start of the transition to engage the client or prospect with a question before MEGO sets in. Of course, I had no idea what MEGO meant, so I asked. I loved the response: "my eyes glaze over." I certainly believe this guideline based on my own experience. Keep the transition brief—more like 30 seconds than two minutes—and to the point. This is another good reason to have a plan and rehearse aloud before the meeting. When coaching people for sales interviews, I have noticed that after even one rehearsal, their transition to business inevitably became shorter and crisper, and that the person sounds more confident and professional.

> Professionals get on a roll and fail to notice they are losing their audience.

Even if you are in Stage Four conducting an oral presentation, getting the client or prospect involved quickly should be the rule. In a more formal setting, like opening a presentation, you will talk more than a couple of minutes. However, talking for even 10 minutes without engaging the client or prospect is risky. Engaging the client or prospect may be as simple as previewing the agenda and asking a question like, "How does that sound for our agenda?" Regardless of how you do it, you should make some attempt to foster at least minimal two-way communication as soon as possible.

A Universal Meeting Tool: TEPE

After years of experience, I have developed a tried-and-true routine for transitioning to business. It's a universal communication tool for opening a meeting in any setting. It is called the transition statement or opening and has four parts:

- ■ **T:** Thank the client or prospect

- ■ **E:** Express interest

- ■ **P:** State the purpose of the meeting

- ■ **E:** End with an easy-to-answer, open-ended question

The acronym TEPE is a good way to remember this routine—both what to say or ask and in what order. As mentioned, you should write out your opening and practice it out loud whenever possible. The key phrase there is "whenever possible." Sometimes, it's not possible because there's no time. The beauty of TEPE is that it can help you develop your opening on the fly. Let's examine the four parts of TEPE.

T: Thank the Client or Prospect

I have sold professional services and watched others do the same in more than 30 countries on five different continents. Most experienced business developers start their transition to business with "Thanks for taking the time to meet with me today" or a similar phrase…and it always works. Even if you initiate small talk or introductions with a thank you, you can use the phrase again to begin the transition to business. You'll find that whether you're in the office or at a restaurant, the client or prospect will straighten up and make eye contact. "Thank you" seems to be a universal way of announcing that it's time to turn to business.

While a simple thank you is my favorite way to start the transition to business, there are other techniques—for example, starting with a series of questions that show your preparation. But I have always liked saying thank you because of its simplicity and high probability of success.

> "Thank you" seems to be a universal way of announcing that it's time to turn to business.

E: Express Interest

One question I am often asked in workshops is when you should ask for the business. Sales texts will tell you early and often. However, most participants do not recognize the difference between asking for the business and expressing interest. Asking for the business should not occur until Stage Four (trial close), while expressing interest should be part of the opening in Stage Two and Stage Three. When you express interest, you communicate that you would like to work with clients or prospects *if* a suitable fit can be found. I can't emphasize the *if* enough. When I am in a sales meeting, I often say it a bit more loudly than the words around. Clients and prospects need to know that *this* is your goal—not just to sell them something. As the opportunity becomes more defined—for example, later in Stage Three—the *if* can be dropped from the expression of interest.

An expression of interest is an important part of the opening transition statement. This recommendation emerges from both personal experience and interviews conducted by my research company. As mentioned, my interviewers always ask respondents why they chose the professional service firm with which they were currently working. The reason given at the top of the list was usually the relationship or chemistry the buyer had with the professional. The second most frequently mentioned reason for picking the professional was his or her reputation. The third reason was close behind. In fact, there was no statistical difference with the first and second reasons when the margin of error was considered. Clients chose the professional because that professional "wanted our business more."

This was driven home to me even more vividly when I sat in on a meeting with an attorney in Tampa who was calling on the head of a large construction company. After several minutes of conversation about his business and construction projects, the CEO—a tough-as-nails guy who also owned the company—looked at the attorney and said, "Quit beating around the bush! What are you out here for anyway? Don't you want to work with my company?"

It makes sense that clients and prospects want to work with professionals who want to work with them…so tell them! A sage old lawyer in Denver used to say, "I've never known anyone who was offended if I said I wanted to work with him!"

Expressions of interest might sound something like the following:

- "I'd love to have the opportunity to work with ABC Corp. if we can find the right fit." (This might be said to a prospect in a Stage Two meeting.)

- "ABC would be a great company for us to work with when the time is right. You're the kind of middle-market manufacturing client that we find it mutually beneficial to work with." (This might be said to a prospect in a Stage Two meeting.)

- "You know how much I like working with you and the bank, Bill. I'd be really interested in discussing these issues to see if we can be of assistance!" (This might be said to a client discussing additional services in a Stage Two meeting.)

- "We've really enjoyed working with you over the past several months and want to make sure you're an enthusiastic client so we can continue the relationship in whatever way makes the most sense." (This might be said to a client in a Stage Six meeting.)

Regardless of phrasing, expressing interest up front is honest, straightforward, and even complimentary—all of which a client or prospect will appreciate. Besides, as the CEO of the Tampa construction company made very clear, most buyers know what you are up to anyway. You might as well score points for being direct rather than risk being seen as aloof or coy!

P: State the Purpose of the Meeting

The third step in the transition statement is to summarize the agenda for the face-to-face or telephone discussion—that is, the purpose of the meeting. As you prepare for this part of the opening transition statement, keep two important points in mind:

- The purpose of the meeting is directly tied to the stage in the business-development process. For example, in Stage One and Stage Two, you are by definition building the relationship and qualifying the opportunity—that is, determining whether the client or prospect perceives a recognized need. In Stage Three, you are clarifying the desired results of the engagement and/or shaping the service. In Stage Four, you are making sure you share a vision of the Scorecard with your client or prospect. In Stage Six, you are ensuring your client or prospect's enthusiasm.

- You should be transparent when expressing the purpose of the meeting. If you feel you can't tell your client or prospect what you'd like to accomplish in the meeting, you probably have the wrong purpose. As always, rehearsing by stating your purpose to a colleague before the meeting is a good way to see if the purpose is too aggressive or inappropriate in some way. Building trust between you and the prospect or client is paramount both in selling and delivering the service, and being transparent at the front end of the discussion is critical to building trust. No one wants to feel like the person they're talking to has a hidden agenda!

Ideally, the purpose of the meeting will have been agreed on in advance via e-mail, a telephone conversation, or what have you. This part of the transition statement should simply confirm what has already been communicated. If it was not possible to establish this agreement in advance, then it's even more important for you to provide the client or prospect with a brief statement of purpose at the beginning of the meeting. Here are some examples of purpose statements for both scenarios:

- "As I mentioned in my e-mail, I thought we could get to know each other today and see what issues concern you the most about the upcoming litigation." (This statement could be used in Stage Two, when responding to a client or prospect request.)

- "In this call, I wanted to make sure I understand the work plan laid out in your proposal request and to learn more about what you want to accomplish from this project." (This statement could be used in Stage Two, when responding to a client or prospect request.)

- "I'd consider today's discussion productive if I could learn more about ABC Corp. and get your advice on the best way to position for an opportunity to work with the company in the short or long term." (This statement could be used in Stage Two, when initiating.)

- "As we discussed on the phone, today is about us having a chance to meet face-to-face and look at some options for how your organization can best handle the new legislation." (This statement could be used in Stage Two, when initiating.)

Notice that in each case, the professional mentioned only two agenda items. While there are no rules, mentioning more than this tends to cause some anxiety for clients and prospects. They start wondering, "How long is all this going to take, anyway?"

One technique some professionals use to set the agenda is to tell the client or prospect exactly where they are in the business-development process and where they intend to go in the current meeting. This straightforward approach might sound like this:

- "Let me make sure I understand where we are. We've agreed you really want some outside assistance implementing this project because you want to focus on your core business. Right? Today, I'd like to know more about what you're looking for in that outside assistance that would make you a happy client." (This statement would apply in a Stage Three meeting.)

■ "Based on our last two conversations, I think we've got a great understanding of your needs and how we can help. Today I'd like to see if we're on the same page as to exactly what you want us to do and what other issues we may need to consider to move ahead." (This statement would apply in a Stage Four meeting.)

This part of the transition statement also provides an excellent opportunity to talk a little about the service being offered—that is, to make a short pitch or value proposition—particularly if you initiated the discussion in a Stage Two meeting. The easiest way to talk about the service is to simply mention some of the ways it can help the client or prospect accomplish his or her goals. This is admittedly a more aggressive style. You might not feel comfortable using it, but it can work for the right person. Here are some examples:

■ "Today I wanted to introduce myself and our firm and describe how XYZ service has helped a number of our clients feel more confident that adequate security systems are in place to protect their customers' data."

■ "As I indicated in our phone call on Tuesday, in this meeting, I want to explain how we've helped a number of similar organizations save significant amounts of money on their state and local taxes and to learn more about your situation to see if there's a fit."

■ "What I wanted to do today is to better understand your situation and talk about how we've approached some similar transactions to save clients time and protect their investments."

■ "As we discussed, I want to take this time to explain how our approach can provide you with some peace of mind by reviewing your current employment policies and making sure your company is doing everything possible to avoid litigation."

Of course, each professional will find his or her own words to establish the agenda for the meeting. Regardless of style, clients and prospects appreciate knowing where they are headed at the start. Stating the purpose for the meeting is an important part of the transition statement, both as a courtesy and to provide focus for the meeting.

E: End with an Easy-to-Answer, Open-Ended Question

As you make the transition to business, the most important criterion for a successful opening is getting the client or prospect involved in the discussion as soon as possible.

To achieve this, try following the agenda with an easy-to-answer, open-ended question. In this way, you can:

- Avoid MEGO.

- Help both you and the client or prospect to relax by discussing a non-threatening topic.

- Minimize the risk of raising the wrong selling points and creating disagreement and/or objections.

- Get a read on the client or prospect's attitude about your service.

- Start a collaborative effort at building the Scorecard.

Failing to involve the client or prospect quickly is the most common mistake made during the opening.

You are already aware of the difference between open-ended questions (what, why, how, where, when, etc.) and closed-ended questions (did you, can you, will you, have you, etc.). The first question after the transition statement should be open-ended to get the client or prospect talking. It should also be easy to answer so no one feels any pressure. The main thing is to make the first question be one that does not put the client or prospect in a difficult position.

Few clients or prospects would like to start a sales conversation by telling you exactly what they want from their accounting, law, wealth-management, or consulting firm because they simply do not know what's available. According to my company's research, more than 90% of 150,000 respondents said they did not know what new services they needed from their professional service firm during the coming year. People think in terms of their problems and opportunities, not in terms of legal, accounting, or consulting services. Asking someone about their problems and opportunities before everyone's had a chance to relax is also uncomfortable, so forget opening the meeting with often-used and almost-always-ineffective questions like, "What do you want from a law firm?" or "What's keeping you up at night?"

So what does work? I've found that questions about the person, the history of the organization, or the organization's structure all work well because each one is generally easy for a client or prospect to answer. Asking the client or prospect about himself or herself is especially effective if you don't know each other well. If you take a few minutes beforehand to check out the person with whom you are meeting on LinkedIn or Google (or whatever new source of information becomes available on the Internet in the years to come), you can mention something about the person—for example, where he or she went to college—to show you did your homework.

Here are some examples of good questions to ask at the end of the transition statement:

- "You went to school on the East Coast. How did you wind up in the Midwest?"
- "How did you start this company?"
- "How did you end up working for ABC Corp.?"
- "Tell me a little more about the history of your group."
- "What are your responsibilities at ABC?"
- "What are some of the differences between what you're doing now and what you did in your previous position?"
- "How is ABC Corp. organized?"
- "How would you describe your competition?"
- "How have you been dealing with this difficult economy?"
- "How has the organization's performance been over the last few years?"
- "What led to your call last week?"

Of course, this list is only a set of general examples, which should be tailored to real situations. You need to determine the best question to open any given meeting and then rehearse it as part of the opening transition statement to make sure the discussion gets off to a good start.

Make TEPE Your Routine

Almost everyone who plays a game or sport on a professional basis has a routine they follow time after time. A professional golfer goes through the same routine—alignment, stance, grip—before hitting any golf shot. Before shooting a free throw, each NBA player bounces the ball a certain number of times, wipes his hands a certain way, or says his mantra. Serious card players pick up and organize their hands in precisely the same way on every deal. This repetitive routine helps calm the nerves and settle the mind. Likewise, professionals who play the SalesGame would also do well to follow the same routine for every meeting when making the transition to business.

The idea is to put the four parts of the transition statement into one routine. To illustrate, let's draw on the individual parts of the transition statement you've seen so far. If you are responding to an opportunity, the routine might sound something like this:

"Thanks for taking the time to meet with me today. I'd love to have the opportunity to work with ABC if we can find the right fit. As we discussed on the phone, today is about us having a chance to meet face-to-face and look at some options for how your organization can best handle the new legislation. Before we start, though, tell me how you went from Rutgers Law to becoming inside legal counsel at ABC Corp." (This transition statement would apply for a Stage Two meeting.)

If you initiated the meeting, the routine might sound like this:

"I appreciate you talking with me this afternoon. I'd love to have the opportunity to work with ABC if we can find the right fit. I'd consider today's discussion productive if I could learn more about ABC Corp. and get your advice on the best way to position for an opportunity to work with the company in the short or long term. I see you spent several years at IBM—what led you to making the leap and starting your own company?" (This transition statement would apply for a Stage Two meeting.)

Simple, Isn't It!

In most games, it can be difficult to control what happens at the start. If you're a golfer, you know how many times that first tee shot ends up in the woods or out of bounds. It's also hard to control an opposing point guard who drains his first couple of three pointers with a hand in his face or to bounce back when playing a team that shoots 70% in the first quarter. That being said, professionals playing the SalesGame can get off to a good start to any business-development meeting by doing the following:

- Taking a few minutes to plan their opening, including introductions and small talk

- Developing a simple transition statement (TEPE) that includes a thank you, an expression of interest, a statement of purpose, and an easy-to-answer open-ended question

- Practicing the transition to business to perform well in the face of the tension that is inherent at the start of any meeting

Once you are off to a good start, you can have fun in the SalesGame by focusing on the reason you are meeting with the client or prospect in the first place: building a Scorecard to shape the delivery of future services.

Part Summary

Creating a favorable impression is the first part of a good opening. While this is obviously most important when building new relationships, you should do so for every meeting. Appearances are critical to making a good impression. You should dress in a way that does not call attention to your appearance. That way, your client or prospect can better focus on what you say. Check with someone who is familiar with the client or prospect to determine appropriate attire. Err on the side of overdressing rather than underdressing. Direct eye contact, a smile, good posture, and a firm handshake all contribute to making you appear confident and capable. You should also be on time for all visits and phone calls to avoid creating an unfavorable impression.

Relationships are the foundation of selling. Every meeting should start with some small talk to build rapport. It helps ease both the buyer and the seller through the nervousness inherent in any sales meeting and sometimes yields important information. Before you begin the meeting, you should develop a plan for handling introductions and have ideas for small talk. The best topics for small talk are simple and a low risk—for example, the weather, a recent sporting event, etc. The most common error professionals make when building rapport is to wait too long for the transition to business. This is particularly true if they are initiating contact. The appropriate length of time to build rapport will depend on many factors such as the history of the relationship, the culture, and the type of meeting. The best practice is to initiate the transition to business as soon as you start to relax and sense that your client or prospect is doing the same.

One reason professionals spend too much time on small talk is that they do not have a clear plan for making the transition to business. There are many ways to make a transition statement. The one you choose is not nearly as important as preparing it ahead of time and rehearsing it to build your confidence. The most important pitfall to avoid is starting the meeting with a lengthy pitch about the service you offer. You have only a short amount of time—a minute or two at most—to make the transition from small talk to the substance of the meeting. One routine that works well is represented by the acronym TEPE. First, you thank (T) the client or prospect for taking the time to meet. This is a universal code for announcing the end of the small talk and the start of the business discussion. Second, you express (E) interest in working with the client or prospect if the right fit can be found. Expressing interest is different from asking for the business. Asking for the business should not take place until late in Stage Three or Stage Four. Third, you should state the purpose (P) of the meeting. In most cases, the purpose of the meeting should be established in advance and should include no more than two or three agenda items. You can use this part of the transition statement to briefly describe potential benefits that the client or prospect may receive from your service. Fourth, you should end (E) the transition statement with an easy-to-answer open-ended question. This question will likely be historical in nature and should focus on a subject that the client or prospect is comfortable discussing.

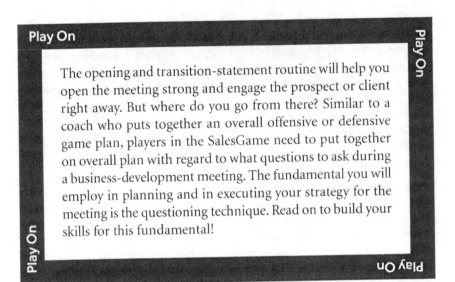

Play On

The opening and transition-statement routine will help you open the meeting strong and engage the prospect or client right away. But where do you go from there? Similar to a coach who puts together an overall offensive or defensive game plan, players in the SalesGame need to put together on overall plan with regard to what questions to ask during a business-development meeting. The fundamental you will employ in planning and in executing your strategy for the meeting is the questioning technique. Read on to build your skills for this fundamental!

Part 6

Questioning Technique

34
Chapter

Questions:
A Fundamental Tool in the SalesGame

As has been noted in each part of this book so far, questions are critical. In every business-development meeting, you should plan your overall question strategy as well as the types of questions you want to include. Think of it this way: Questions are as important to the SalesGame as golf clubs are to golf. In golf, depending on where you are on the course—on the fairway, in the rough, in a bunker, in the trees, or on the green—you carefully select your club to achieve the desired outcome. The same thing applies in the SalesGame. Questions are the tools that professionals use to get the best information from the client or prospect. The question they ask depends on where they are in the process and what they are trying to achieve.

The good news is that we all have been asking questions for our entire lives, so the skill is not new to anyone. The bad news is that most professionals have very little idea of how to use questions to maximize their chance of success when playing the SalesGame. Asking the right questions at the right time is a critical element in being successful in a business-development meeting. A golfer can have a very expensive set of clubs, but if she tries to use a wedge to drive the ball on a par five, she's probably not going to be very successful.

I've read a number of articles and books that discuss questioning techniques. Some of them amaze me with their complexity. Page after page discusses different classifications of questions—tactical, strategic, organizational, and orientation questions; questions that open the discussion;

questions that close the sale; and on and on. The purpose of this part of the book is *not* to go into great depth categorizing and classifying different types of questions. That's already been done several times. What's more important is to keep things simple. This part of the book focuses on best practices for asking questions. These best practices can be summarized into three main areas:

- Start broad and easy.

- Choose three to five areas of inquiry.

- Ask the must-ask question.

This chapter covers the first of these: start broad and easy.

Start Broad and Easy

Each meeting is different. That means the definition of "broad and easy" will differ depending on the situation. Generally, questions asked when someone is calling for help on a lawsuit will be more specific than questions asked by a professional who has initiated contact with a new prospect. In the first case, a broad question might be, "What led to the lawsuit being filed?" In contrast, when initiating contact with a new prospect, a broad question might be, "What led you to start this business?"

Both of these examples would also be relatively easy to answer because they are historical and personal—two of the criteria for questions discussed in Chapter 33, "Making the Transition to Business." Starting with more broad and easy questions helps both you and the client or prospect to feel more relaxed and comfortable. It's also the best way to develop a better understanding of what's really in the client or prospect's mind during a business-development meeting.

One phrase I use a lot in workshops is, "Go from broad and easy to narrow and hard." This is important whether you are building a relationship, qualifying an opportunity, defining the Heart of the Matter or Scorecard Factors, or gauging client enthusiasm. In other words, starting broad and easy helps you in all six stages of the business-development process to achieve the goal of the SalesGame: converting a qualified lead into an enthusiastic client that generates rewards commensurate with value received.

> Go from broad and easy to narrow and hard.

Emphasize Open-Ended Questions

The first element of going broad is emphasizing the use of open-ended questions throughout the business-development meeting. Here are some examples:

- "What led you to start this business?"
  (Ask this earlier in the conversation.)

- "What is your role in the organization?"
  (Ask this earlier in the conversation.)

- "How have you managed your investments in the past?"
  (Ask this earlier in the conversation.)

- "What do you want to accomplish as a result of this lawsuit?"
  (Ask this later in the conversation.)

- "How do you want things to be different if you implement this program?"
  (Ask this later in the conversation.)

- "What are some things you think we could have done even better?"
  (Ask this later in the conversation.)

Having watched hundreds of professionals in business-development meetings, I've found that most professionals use too many closed-ended questions. Here are some examples:

- "Were you tired of being part of such a big organization?"

- "Do you report to Bob?"

- "Have you managed your investments yourself in the past?"

- "Is getting even your primary objective?"

- "Do you expect to see an increase in revenues from this program?"

- "Did we get the final draft of the report to you in time for you to review it?"

Everyone knows the difference between open-ended and closed-ended questions, and that open-ended questions are generally preferable. Nevertheless, the overwhelming number of professionals I work with still use closed-ended questions. Emphasizing open-ended questions is a best practice for two reasons:

- Asking closed-ended questions involves risk.

- People like to talk.

The Risks of Asking a Closed-Ended Question

Certainly, you can occasionally ask a closed-ended question and wind up with the same result as you would if you asked an open-ended one. However, the risk factor is higher with closed-ended questions. For example, asking a closed-ended question might result in the following:

- You might plant a negative seed that was not there. For example, asking "Is the cost too high?" could cause the client or prospect to decide that it is. Better to ask "What are your concerns?"

- Some closed-ended questions could make you appear arrogant because in essence, you are telling a client or prospect what the problem is rather than listening to his or her opinion about it. For example, rather than asking "Don't you think that leadership is the key issue here?" go with "What do you see as the biggest problem?"

- You may limit the amount of information that is gathered in the meeting. For example, asking "Are you worried about offending your partner?" will yield less information than asking "What's troubling you about this contract?"

In most games, the sensible move is to go for the low-risk play (that is, asking open-ended questions) unless there are special circumstances. Asking a closed-ended question is a little like going for a first down on fourth and four deep in your own territory. It doesn't make a lot of sense unless it is late in the game and the clock is running down.

People Like to Talk

I know the fact that people like to talk isn't rocket science, but most professionals in sales meetings forget this simple fact. Open-ended questions give the client or prospect a lot more opportunity to talk. For my first several years running workshops, I'm sure I talked way too much. I felt the audience would value that because of the knowledge I had to share. Unfortunately, participants often went away without as much enthusiasm and passion for the material as I would have liked. For many years now, I build plenty of participant involvement into the agenda. (After all, to be a participant, one must participate!) As a result, my audience generally leaves a lot more excited and feeling they got great value. Sure, they value my knowledge but they value their own opportunity to express themselves even more. Of course there are always exceptions, like a prospect who seems to not want to say anything.

> Open-ended questions give the client or prospect a lot more opportunity to talk.

But in the vast majority of cases, asking open-ended questions will get you more information and will result in the client or prospect feeling like he or she had a good conversation. People like to talk!

Use Closed-Ended Questions to Confirm or Verify

All that being said, closed-ended questions do have their place. In particular, they are good for verifying what you have heard. For example, you might use closed-ended questions when providing feedback in step 2 of the Ground Rule or while you are in the sales process. Also, the closer you are to the end of a segment of a meeting, the more useful closed-ended questions become—for example, to verify the Heart of the Matter after a dialogue or to restate the conditions of satisfaction at the end of phone call. Here are a few examples:

■ "So if I follow you right, what you really want out of this project is to bring this organization into the 21st century when it comes to the company's technology. Are we on the same page?"

■ "Am I right that the two critical issues on this syndication are turning it around in 30 days and making sure we use John and Debbie on the deal?"

One of my competitors calls these "checking questions." That is, you use them to check with the client or prospect to make sure you really understand each other. I find this term very useful to keep in the back of my mind when conducting meetings. While you use open-ended questions to find out what you don't know, you use checking questions to verify what you think you *do* know.

Checking questions are also useful if you feel like you're talking too much or you're in a situation that doesn't lend itself to two-way communication, such as a presentation. We've all heard that little voice in the back of our heads saying "Shut up! You're talking too much!" When you hear that voice, ask a checking question. Try something like, "Does this make sense?" or, "Are we on the same page?" It may feel silly, but you'll at least get some head nods or eye contact, which will let you know whether your client or prospect is listening. And, more often than not, someone will jump into the discussion with a comment or two, which will give you time to reboot. Does that make sense?

> While you use open-ended questions to find out what you don't know, you use checking questions to verify what you think you *do* know.

Note

A closed-ended question for a professional playing the SalesGame is similar to a putter for a golfer. You have to use it at the right time and for the right reasons. Using the putter doesn't make much sense when you are on the tee or 150 yards out because the club is not designed to help you get loft on the ball or hit the ball a significant distance. However, when you are on the green or even on the fringe, it's time to pull the putter out of the bag because it is designed for a smooth, more refined shot. In short, it's the right club to use to finish the hole.

Ask BIG Questions First

As a general rule, I encourage my workshop participants to start with broad information gathering (BIG) questions. Going back to the previous example, the litigation partner should have started with a question like one of the following:

- "How has the company been doing over the past year?"

- "What are some of the company's goals for the coming year?"

- "How is the legal function organized?"

- "What kinds of legal issues is the company dealing with these days?"

- "What are the toughest problems facing the in-house counsel?"

By starting with questions like these, the litigation partner in the preceding example might have learned much more about what the in-house counsel and/or the company was trying to accomplish as well as what they might need from a law firm. Maybe product-liability litigation isn't an issue for the company, but the threat of a nasty labor matter is keeping the in-house counsel and senior management up at night. Or maybe the company doesn't have a current need for litigation services but could require future assistance in brand protection or an upcoming acquisition. In that case, the attorney would have created a positioning lead.

When you initiate contact, the goal of any Stage Two meeting is to build the relationship and come up with any kind of next step. BIG questions are far more conducive to achieving this objective.

Here are some examples of BIG questions:

- "How did you start this company?"

- "What's your background?"

- "How is the company organized?"

- "How have the recent changes in the economy affected you?"

- "What kind of planning goes on within your group?"

- "How do you decide whether you need outside assistance?"

- "Where do you see the company in the next three or four years?"

- "What are some of the projects you're working on currently?"

- "What are some of the challenges on your horizon?"

- "What do you think will be different about the way you do business in the next three or four years?"

- "What are your goals for the coming year?"

Of course, as in any game, personal style plays a major role in the approach you take. Some professionals will prefer to be more direct, while others will be less aggressive. Different styles work for different people. Timing and the stage of the SalesGame also play a major role in choosing the right questioning technique. More direct questions tend to work better in the latter stages of the SalesGame. For example, you need to be fairly direct in Stage Four (trial close) or Stage Five (final close) and ask "What's keeping us from working together?" Nevertheless, starting with wider areas of inquiry is a best practice that should improve your business-development performance.

Choose Three to Five Areas of Inquiry

Professionals who are effective at business development usually prepare for a meeting by identifying a few broad areas of inquiry to guide the conversation. In fact, planning questions is one of the differentiators that separates professionals who are good at business development from those who aren't. Developing areas of inquiry is the second best practice to improve questioning technique.

Note

Developing areas of inquiry should not be confused with scripting a meeting, which is rarely effective. No one can predict every twist and turn of a conversation any more than a soccer or football coach can predict the way a game will unfold.

Professionals often have limited time to prepare for a business-development meeting. For example, a consulting partner in an accounting firm might be called by an audit colleague to meet with a client who is already in the office and has a problem that needs to be discussed. Even during the short walk down the hall, however, the consulting partner can plan ahead by coming up with a few areas of inquiry to engage the client. This will enable the consulting partner to better understand the situation.

Use Areas of Inquiry to Get a Vision for the Meeting

In many sports—golf and basketball come to mind—one of the basics is to visualize the shot before you take it. I know from my own experience on the golf course that if I imagine something bad happening to a shot before I swing, nine times out of 10, that is exactly what happens. Conversely, if I imagine a positive result before the swing, good things are much more likely to occur. The same principle applies in the SalesGame. You need to get a vision—not a script—of the business-development meeting before you arrive at the meeting by determining three, four, or even five areas of inquiry that will engage the client or prospect and keep the conversation going. For my money, it's a lot easier to visualize a few areas of inquiry for a sales meeting than it is to visualize a three-point jump shot or a 190-yard three-iron shot over a swamp!

A valuable technique for visualizing the meeting is to think of a grid like the one shown in Figure 35.1. The top row of the grid should contain the areas of inquiry that will be pursued in the conversation. You will launch each of these areas of inquiry by asking an appropriate BIG question. You should plan the order in which you will introduce each area of inquiry. A best practice is to start with easier areas of inquiry, like historical or structural topics. Then you can move to more sensitive areas, such as determining needs or buying criteria.

> You need to get a vision—not a script—of the business-development meeting before you arrive at the meeting.

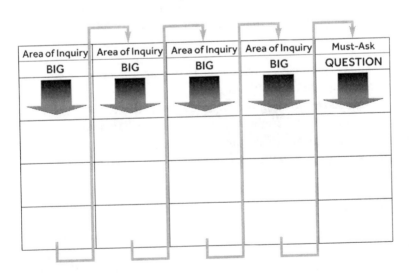

Figure 35.1 Questioning technique.

Tip

It's a good idea to write down a single word or short phrase from the BIG question to remember them and to ensure they cover the areas of inquiry in the preferred order during the meeting.

Start with Easier Areas of Inquiry

Chapter 34, "Questions: A Fundamental Tool in the SalesGame," discussed going from broad to narrow. That same concept applies to areas of inquiry as well. As you organize your areas of inquiry to develop a vision for the meeting, start with easier areas of inquiry before moving to those that might be harder. For example, it will be easier for someone to respond to an area of inquiry related to his or her background or that of the organization than one that centers around his or her buying criteria, which is much more direct.

Of course, there is something to be said for getting to the point. But starting a meeting with a question area that focuses on the service and buying criteria can immediately channel the discussion and limit your opportunity to build relationships and to better understand the underlying goals and objectives that make any service of value.

Clients and prospects tend to become guarded when they are asked narrow questions about buying criteria early in a conversation. When that happens, the meeting becomes more like a debate between people with different objectives. Obviously, professionals playing the SalesGame know that the key to success is working together to accomplish the same objectives—those of the client or prospect!

I once worked with a litigation partner who told me about an uncomfortable meeting he'd recently had. He had arranged a meeting with the lead in-house counsel for a mid-sized manufacturing firm. The litigation partner had met the in-house counsel several weeks before at an ABA conference, and they had gotten along well. The litigation partner wanted to explore the possibility of working with his new contact's company. In other words, he was initiating contact in Stage Two to qualify the lead. My client specialized in product-liability work and went immediately to an important but very specific question related to the use of outside counsel: "What criteria do you use to choose a firm you're going to engage for product liability cases?" This is not a bad question. It is an open-ended question. It would have been far worse if he had asked a closed-ended question, like, "Is rate structure your primary consideration when choosing a firm for product liability work?" And of course, you *do* need to ask a question about buying criteria at some point in the sales process. But this question would generally be asked during Stage Three of the SalesGame (Shaping the Service), after a need has been established, not Stage Two (Qualifying the Lead)—and certainly not in a first Stage Two meeting when the primary objective should be relationship building! Not surprisingly, my attorney client said that the meeting went south almost immediately. The in-house counsel became somewhat reticent to talk—almost as if he was worried that whatever he said could and would be used against him.

Even in a Stage Three meeting, opening the discussion by asking about buying criteria, the decision process, or any other very narrow or direct topic would probably not work well. Better to start with something easier, like, "What's been happening since the last time we talked?" That way, the client or prospect has a chance to get comfortable with the conversation. The key here is to plan your areas of inquiry so they set you up for the best outcome—and that includes having the prospect or client feel at ease throughout the flow of the meeting. Another key to doing this is using your initial questions within each area of inquiry to create a positive setup.

Identify the BIG Questions

I once worked with an accountant in China who was planning a meeting with the deputy general manager of a privately owned peanut manufacturer whom he had met at a seminar. The accountant was concerned that he would not have enough to talk about to keep the meeting going with this new contact. In a matter of minutes, we came up with four areas of inquiry for the discussion:

- Company history

- Organization/management structure

- Industry and competition

- Future plans/vision

We then converted each of these areas of inquiry into a BIG question:

- "How was the company started?"

- "How is the company organized?"

- "What is the peanut industry like in China?"

- "Where do you see the company in three or four years?"

His picture of the meeting looked like the chart in Figure 35.2.

Company history	Organization/ management structure	Industry and competition	Future plans/ vision
How was the company started?	How is the company organized?	What is the peanut industry like in China?	Where do you see the company in 3 or 4 years?
⬇	⬇	⬇	⬇

Figure 35.2 The questioning technique in action.

By investing a few minutes to identify the appropriate areas of inquiry, the accountant was able to visualize the grid and had a good idea of where he was going in the meeting. It was obvious from his smile that he was more confident about how he was going to handle the discussion.

Use the Ground Rule to Drill Down

As discussed, the Ground Rule is the fundamental selling skill that you use to play the SalesGame. As you may remember, Step 3 of the Ground Rule involves asking a question to keep the client talking and to control the direction of the meeting. You can use the Ground Rule to follow up the opening BIG question at the top of the grid to drill down—that is, to further explore the client or prospect's point of view in the same area of inquiry. You then continue to use the Ground Rule until you have all the information you need from the client or prospect to fully understand the situation. (See Figure 35.3.) The closer you are to the bottom of the grid—the end of a particular area of inquiry—the more likely you are to use closed-ended or checking questions to verify important facts. Of course, all these questions are only examples. They would be combined with agreement and comments. That way, it's a conversation, not an interrogation. But the flow of the conversation should follow a pattern similar to the one shown.

Company history	Organization/ management structure	Industry and competition	Future plans/ vision
How was the company started?	How is the company organized?	What is the peanut industry like in China?	Where do you see the company in 3 or 4 years?
AGREEMENT + What gave the owner the original idea?	AGREEMENT + How do you handle the sales function?	AGREEMENT + How do you hook up with the producers?	AGREEMENT + Where do you see this international market going?
AGREEMENT + How was it that you came to work with him?	AGREEMENT + How do you work with the farmers who produce the peanuts?	AGREEMENT + What does the competition look like?	AGREEMENT + How soon do you think you will be ready to go international?
AGREEMENT + How hard was it to get things going in view of government control?	AGREEMENT + What sort of accounting department do you have?	AGREEMENT + How aggressive have they been in competing with you?	AGREEMENT + What are you going to need to achieve those goals?
AGREEMENT + So you really were taking a chance on this?	AGREEMENT + So you could really use some help in that area?	AGREEMENT + Sounds to me like you're really the market leader. Right?	AGREEMENT + You're saying the biggest concern is raising capital then?

Figure 35.3 The questioning technique, using the Ground Rule to drill down.

Developing Questions for a Specific Meeting

In my work coaching many professionals, I've found that a good starting point is to write down every question they (or we—it's always better to collaborate) can think of. Chances are there will be a lot more than three or four questions. Usually, however, categories of questions will emerge. You can then choose the best question to start each area of inquiry and use other questions in the category to drill down. The last step in this process is to arrange the areas so they go from easy to hard, broad to narrow.

One issue that often comes up in workshops is how to balance the conversation if more than one professional is attending the meeting. This becomes more significant if one of the professionals is more senior or has a more well-known reputation than his or her colleague. In these situations, the conversation almost always focuses on the senior person in attendance for understandable reasons—that is, they have more experience, so the client or prospect will want to hear what that person has to say. Younger professionals are usually instructed to jump in as needed—for example, if the client or prospect asks a question that pertains to their area of expertise or if the senior professional asks them to talk about a particular issue. This is a difficult situation at best because younger professionals feel the pressure to shine when it's their moment in the sun. A better approach might be to come up with areas of inquiry and then assign each one to a professional involved in the meeting in an alternating pattern. For example, the senior professional would open the meeting and handle the first area of inquiry. Then, the junior professional would handle the next area, and so on.

Of course, this doesn't apply only to meetings where there is a senior and junior professional. It applies to any meeting when there are two or more professionals involved. Using this approach allows one professional to listen and observe while the other handles the BIG and drill down questions for one area of inquiry. Then the roles are reversed. I've used this technique many times and coached others to use it as well. It works like a charm to get everyone involved in the conversation, and clients and prospects never seem to notice what's happening.

Using POGO for Stage Two Meetings

Several years ago, I was working with the insurance industry team of a large law firm. One of the partners had recently rejoined the team after spending 10 years as the CEO of a national insurance company. To take advantage of his relationships and credibility in the industry, he was charged with initiating contact with prospect insurance company CEOs and setting up Stage Two meetings with them. This proved to be a very successful business-development initiative. He quickly realized that the most effective format and broad areas of inquiry for these meetings were the same, starting with the person, followed by the organization, and then delving into the company's goals and the obstacles to achieving them. This pattern, which follows the best practice of choosing areas of questioning that go from easy to hard, was the genesis of POGO, short for person, organization, goals, and obstacles.

Initial Stage Two meetings lend themselves especially well to the use of POGO. In Stage Two, you are mostly concerned with establishing a relationship. You want to learn as much as possible about the prospect, his or her organization, and the real issue(s)—the Heart of the Matter. Thus, your broad areas of inquiry in Stage Two should be aimed at the following:

- **Person (P):** Learning about the person. This helps to establish the personal relationship.

- **Organization (O):** Gaining background knowledge of the organization. This helps in establishing the relationship and understanding who has what role in the buying process.

- **Goals (G):** Learning about the vision of the client or prospect. This gives you a sense of which goals are the priority.

- **Obstacles (O):** Understanding the obstacles to achieving those goals.

Using the POGO approach is an extremely effective way to ensure a strong start in the sales process. It follows the best practices mentioned earlier—that is, it goes from broad to narrow and easy to hard and provides four broad areas of inquiry. Better yet, POGO is easy to remember, so it can be used even if you don't have adequate time to prepare.

Ask the Must-Ask Question

Asking the must-ask question is an easy practice to recommend, but is sometimes hard to implement. Throughout my career, I have watched professionals court a client or prospect for years without asking the must-ask question. As a result, the following occurs:

- Professionals waste their time—and that of the client or prospect—by delaying a decision that needs to be made.

- Professionals spend too much time selling to leads that have no real potential.

- Professionals fail to find out how to advance their cause—that is, move closer to a sale.

What Is a Must-Ask Question?

A must-ask question is one that will help you to identify where you stand or how you can advance your cause in the business-development process. This is why it is so critical and it is often difficult to ask. Earlier in the process, the must-ask question will yield useful information about qualifying the lead, which will help you to prioritize your leads. Later in the process, the must-ask question is more directly connected to your movement and can often yield a next step with an opportunity.

Regardless of where you are in the process, a must-ask question is something you should consider when planning a business-development meeting. But it's particularly important to ask this type of question in Stage Two.

In Stage Two, you are trying to find out if there is something you can help your client or prospect accomplish. In this scenario, then, the must-ask question is often something along the lines of, "What advice can you give me about the best way to position for an opportunity to work with ABC?" This will help you determine if you have a qualified lead, a positioning lead, or a lead not worth pursuing at all. Unfortunately, most professionals do not ask this question. Why? Because they fear rejection, the way a boy who fails to ask a girl on a date does.

This became apparent to me during one of my workshops. I was working with an attorney from Indianapolis who was preparing to meet with a client's in-house labor attorney about expanding his firm's representation in the labor area from regional to national in scope—a classic Stage Two meeting to initiate a discussion about additional services for a present client. We identified two goals for the meeting: to find out if there was any chance this expansion of service might happen and, if so, to find out the best way to approach it. We then hit on the must-ask question: "We've loved working for you over the last few years and would like to expand what we're doing from handling ABC in the Midwest to handling it nationally. What's your advice on how we might position for such an opportunity?" Finally, we role played. The attorney danced around this question for 15 minutes, but ended the simulation without ever asking it. Afterward, we critiqued the role play. Someone asked the attorney, "Why didn't you ask the must-ask question?" He said the must-ask question was one of those questions that "get stuck in your throat," like asking a girl for a date in high school. Everyone knew exactly what he was talking about!

Fortunately, the story had a happy ending. In the actual meeting, the lawyer asked the must-ask question. Afterward, a series of meetings took place with his contacts, the general counsel, and the human resources director. In the end, the firm expanded its representation from the Midwest to the East Coast and is now under consideration for work in other parts of the country.

Interestingly, asking the must-ask question is much more likely to open doors than to close them. I have found that most clients and prospects need you to ask this type of question before they will begin

> The must-ask question was one of those questions that "get stuck in your throat," like asking a girl for a date in high school.

to tell you what they want or share their concerns. If you don't ask a must-ask question, you may well miss opportunities or lose work to others who are more aggressive in their questioning technique.

Identifying the Must-Ask Question

So how do you identify the must-ask question? Typically, it depends on the stage of the sales process and the goal of the meeting. For example, if the opportunity is in Stage Four (trial close), the must-ask question might be, "What changes should we make to be sure we are on the same page as you?" In Stage Five, the must-ask question might be, "What's standing between us and getting the green light to start the work?" Table 36.1 provides examples of must-ask questions for each stage.

Table 36.1 Must-Ask Questions for Each Stage in the SalesGame

Stage	Goal	Must-Ask Questions
Stage One	Identify the lead	"I have really enjoyed meeting you and would love to meet with you one-on-one to learn more. How can we set that up?"
Stage Two	Qualify the lead	"What issues or challenges are you facing that we can help you with?"
		"What could we do that would really make a difference for you dealing with X issue?"
		"How might we position for an opportunity to work with ABC?"
		"What's the best way to stay on your radar screen?"
Stage Three	Shape the service	"How can we increase your comfort level that we've got the resources to work on this?"
		"Who should I connect with to make sure everyone on your team would be comfortable working with me?"
		"What can we do that would give us the best chance of being your choice for this project?"
Stage Four	Trial close	"If this sounds like what you're after, what do we need to do to move ahead?"
		"We can pick up the documents when we're out here next week or you can have them sent to our office. Which do you prefer?"
		"How can we change this package to make it better meet your needs?"
Stage Five	Final Close	"From what you say, we are in agreement on our objectives and approach and we'd very much like to start this project. How can we proceed?"
		"What's standing between us and starting the work?"
		"We'll put together an engagement letter and bring it out next week when we start. How does that sound?

(continues)

Table 36.1 Must-Ask Questions for Each Stage in the SalesGame

Stage	Goal	Must-Ask Questions
Stage Six	Ensure client satisfaction/ determine reason for loss	"What can we do to expand this relationship?" "What else can we help you with?" "What could we have done differently to have won this opportunity?" "What's the best way to stay on your radar for any future opportunities?"

Of course, this table contains only examples. The important point is that each and every business-development meeting has a must-ask question that you can use to advance your cause.

Tip

Often, professionals say a lead is "stale." In most cases, however, this is because the professional has not asked the must-ask question. Asking the must-ask question reveals whether there is a real opportunity to work with the prospect or client. If no opportunity exists, simply switch to positioning mode. Ask the same question again in a month, six months, or whatever time frame you establish at the close of the meeting.

There are two final key points to keep in mind as you prepare the must-ask question for any meeting. First, if you are working as part of a team, plan who will ask the must-ask question. Second, whether to ask the question is a game-time decision. You must use your own judgment as to whether to go for it and ask the question (or not). That call often depends on the tone and dialogue of the meeting. If you have a sense that it is not the right time to ask, it's OK to postpone the question until the next conversation to allow yourself to regroup. Don't delay too long, however. Asking the must-ask question is critical to determining whether you have a real opportunity.

Part Summary

Questions are an important tool for professionals in business-development meetings. Asking questions will be more effective if you start broad and easy, moving to narrower and harder questions as the meeting progresses. Using open-ended questions is one way to start broad. Open-ended questions work well particularly early in meetings because they have a low risk factor—that is, they do not suggest issues but explore them—and because they encourage the client or prospect to talk. Fortunately, this is something most clients and prospects like. As an added benefit, it enables you to learn more about their goals and ambitions, etc. In contrast, closed-ended questions are best used to verify information such as confirming a statement or checking to make sure you understand the client or prospect. You should use broad information gathering (BIG) questions early in the meeting—for example, "What led you to start this company?" When you start with questions about the specific service or buying criteria, the client or prospect will often become uncomfortable and reticent to share information because he or she feels pressured to buy.

To improve your questioning technique, prepare for meetings by identifying three to five areas of inquiry. This is important and useful even if you have only a few minutes to prepare for a meeting. Similar to questions, you can also make the prospect or client more comfortable by starting with easier areas of inquiry before moving to harder ones. Use areas of inquiry to develop a vision for the discussion, not to script it. Each of these areas of inquiry can be started by using a BIG question. You should plan the order in which you will introduce the areas of inquiry, moving from more comfortable topics to more sensitive areas—that is, broad to narrow, easy to hard. You can use the Ground Rule to explore each area of inquiry until you are satisfied you have the information you need. Then you should ask another BIG question to initiate a discussion of the next area of inquiry. Listing all questions in advance and then dividing them into three to five categories is a good way to plan. If you are in a meeting with more than one professional, alternate who handles each area of inquiry to provide balance. That way, no one dominates the conversation. For Stage Two meetings, use the mnemonic device POGO (short for person, organization goals, obstacles) to develop the most effective areas of inquiry, going from easy to hard.

Remember to plan a must-ask question. What this question is will differ from meeting to meeting, depending on which stage of the SalesGame you're in. For example, a must-ask question in Stage Two might be, "What's your advice on the best way to position for an opportunity to work with your company?" Many professionals find it difficult to ask must-ask questions because they fear they might not get the answer they want. However, these questions are critical because they help you prioritize leads and obtain the information you need to advance your cause.

Must-ask questions generate useful information on how to acquire a piece of business much more than they result in a negative response. Must-ask questions are particularly important in Stage Two and whenever a lead is stale because the client or prospect response tells you if you have a qualified lead, a positioning lead, or no lead at all. Whether to ask the must-ask question is a game-time decision, but doing so is critical if you want to learn how best to proceed in the business-development process.

Play On

In this part, you learned that the must-ask question is a key tool that, when used effectively, can yield information on how best to move ahead—a next step. In the SalesGame, these are called closes, and they are fundamental in planning and getting a next step, or closing. In the next part, you will see how every meeting has a close—a nextstep—and that most successful business developers plan two closes for every business-development meeting. You will also learn how to plan closes and what closes are most effective. Read on to incorporate this fundamental into your game!

Part 7

Closing: Establish Next Steps and Advance Your Cause

The Closing Process and Best Practices

Closing is a process much more than it is a single, specific event. Sure, the final score is what shows on the board when the buzzer goes off, but if you watch almost any game, you'll see that one team throughout is better at gaining the advantage, advancing, or even finishing the game off. Think about the game of football. Football is about advancing the ball down the field to an eventual touchdown to score. Getting the touchdown is almost always about the process. The teams that are most successful are the ones that consistently gain yardage, get first downs, get into the red zone (within 20 yards of the goal line), and get the ball across the goal line for a touchdown. They maintain possession of the ball and advance it down the field.

Now apply that same thought process to business development. A signed contract is your signal that the work has been sold (that is, it's your touchdown), but getting to that point is a process. You close (that is, you get a next step) to build relationships (that is, gain yardage). You close to move forward in the process once a need is recognized (that is, you get a first down). You continue to close to clearly understand the needs and how you might best work with the prospect (that is, you get more first downs). You close when you have a shared vision of the Scorecard to move into the trial close (that is, you move into the red zone). And you close to get across the goal line for the final close (that is, a touchdown). In short, the most successful business developers consistently and proactively close throughout the sales process. They maintain control (that is, they maintain possession of the ball) and consistently advance.

In the SalesGame, closing in its simplest form means getting a next step. It occurs when you reach agreement with the client or prospect on specific next steps to follow the current meeting or telephone call and it happens throughout all six stages. Closing may occur at any time in the meeting. That is, agreement on a next step may come early or late in the discussion. It's something you achieve by asking the right questions, and it is definitely easier to achieve if you prepare. Whether it is early in the process or late, face-to-face or on a telephone call, a formal presentation or an informal discussion, every meeting has a close!

> Whether it is early in the process or late, face-to-face or on a telephone call, a formal presentation or an informal discussion, every meeting has a close!

Although they may recognize the importance of closing as described here, many professionals are reluctant to close. Maybe they're afraid of rejection. Maybe they don't want to seem pushy. Whatever the reason, they can't seem to take that critical step. But any consultant, accountant, or attorney who has developed a book of business knows that closing is critical to achieving success. It can be used for many purposes:

- To determine the quality of the lead and thus be more efficient

- To learn if, how, and when to follow up

- To begin a proposal process

- To implement a strategy

- To make sure they know what will make the client enthusiastic

- To surface hidden objections

- To find the real decision-maker

- To find out what the client or prospect is *really* thinking

I once worked with an attorney, Mary, in Pennsylvania. She had been a lateral hire from a New York firm. One of Mary's clients at her previous firm was the in-house counsel with a major food franchiser and had become a good friend. She constantly called Mary with questions about various franchising issues because she found the partner at Mary's old firm to be relatively inaccessible. After a couple of months, several phone calls, and much free advice, the in-house counsel called Mary and began the discussion by saying, "You know, you probably should set up an account number for me." A week later, Mary asked me if this would have been a good time to close. I am not kidding.

Don't be like Mary. Embrace the close.

Unless you sell used cars or swampland in Florida, closing is not about using the right trick at some magical moment. Manipulating someone into agreeing to buy professional services doesn't work very well if the goal of the game is to end up with an enthusiastic client. Rather, closing is a process that ensures the client or prospect ends up with the best solution to his or her problem.

> Closing is a process that ensures the client or prospect ends up with the best solution to his or her problem.

If you want to improve at closing, your first step is to identify where you are in the SalesGame and what you need to ask for to move to the next stage. Then you need to apply the best practices that are discussed next to become more comfortable with and effective at closing, regardless of the type of close being used.

Best Practice #1: Be Prepared with Two Next Steps to Close Every Meeting

Early in the sales process, two types of next steps (that is, closes) are effective. The first is a *positioning close*—one that positions you for some future contact. The second is an *advancing close*—one that helps you move forward in the process.

A best practice is to plan at least two advancing closes for every meeting. An advancing close promotes forward movement in one of two ways:

- It enables you to build a new relationship with someone in the client or prospect organization or vice versa (that is, to introduce someone from the client or prospect organization to another person in your firm).

- It makes a Scorecard Factor real. For example, it makes a firm resource more tangible, as with demonstrating a unique software application.

It's particularly important to plan two advancing closes to conclude any meeting in Stages Two and Three. You do this in Stage Two so you can determine the potential of the client or prospect and positon for a future opportunity after a need has been recognized—that is, the lead becomes qualified. You do it in Stage Three to build relationships, develop a strategy, and differentiate your service. Of course, an advancing close might be used at any stage of the SalesGame, but Stages Two and Three are when the right advancing close can make all the difference between success and failure. Some examples of advancing closes that can promote forward movement include the following:

- Meeting with other decision-maker(s)

- Meeting with a superior

- Meeting with a subordinate

- Meeting with user(s)

- Meeting with influencers

- Arranging a meeting between the client or prospect and someone else (for example, another client with similar experiences or problems)

- Visiting their office or plant or having them visit yours

- Having a second meeting with your contact

- Meeting with someone else from your firm such as an industry or functional specialist, service personnel, etc.

- Demonstrating your product or service (for example, a computer application, estate plan, etc.)

- Conducting a survey to further define the situation

- Reviewing client records

- Reviewing previous work efforts (for example, past tax returns)

- Reviewing a draft of the engagement letter

- Reviewing a draft of a possible proposal

- Giving a presentation

- Reviewing the outline of a presentation

- Talking with those who will be in the audience for the presentation

You should use this list as a starting point. When I am working with my clients planning meetings, I find that determining options for closing is one of the most creative and fun parts of the process. Just as no two chess games are ever the same, neither are two closes. You must modify each close to the specific situation.

Much like any game, we all have our favorite way to play. Some golfers like to chip onto the green with a putter. Others prefer a wedge. When I am talking with clients and prospects, one of my favorite advancing closes is to conduct a survey. When interviewing client or prospect personnel as part of a survey, I build relationships and make a Scorecard Factor real. ("He does his homework!") I start working with the client or prospect as if I already had the engagement. That way, I provide value even during the sales process.

Regardless of your personal favorite, you will be more effective at closing if you prepare by identifying at least two next steps that will build a relationship, make a Scorecard Factor real, or both. For example, if an accountant is meeting with a CFO who is seeking a new firm to perform the company's audit, one of his or her two next steps might be to meet with the owner or to introduce the CFO to a firm IT expert. Meeting with the owner would build a relationship with the true decision-maker and determine whether it is really a qualified lead. Or, if problems exist in the IT area, a next step after meeting with the CFO might be to bring in an IT specialist from the firm. This would both build a new relationship (between the IT specialist and the CFO) and demonstrate the firm's expertise dealing with IT issues (a Scorecard Factor).

> You will be more effective at closing if you prepare by identifying at least two next steps that will build a relationship, make a Scorecard Factor real, or both.

In Stages Two and Six, you should have at least one positioning close—that is, another meeting with the same person—ready as an option for a next step. In both stages, odds are you will not have a qualified lead and will want to be ready to use a positioning close to establish some future contact. A positioning close might sound like this:

- "I'll give you a call in six weeks to see how you're coming with that IT project. How does that timing sound?" (Stage Two)

- "I've enjoyed working with you. I would like to stay in touch. How about I give you a call when spring finally gets here and we'll play a round of golf?" (Stage Six)

These positioning closes can be used if your attempt at advancing the cause is not accepted by the client or prospect or if you feel it's not the right time to advance the cause—for example, if there are budgetary constraints.

While a positioning close may not seem very aggressive and does not really advance your position in the SalesGame, it does keep the opportunity alive for another day. Plus, it's the right thing to do so you leave the meeting with at least some idea of what to do next.

Regardless of the type of close, the best practice remains the same: Be sure to prepare at least two next steps that could be used as a close. Will one of the closes that was prepared in advance always be the next step that emerges from the meeting with a client or prospect? Of course not. However, they will be used far more often than not. Either way, you will improve your game by building your confidence and avoiding less-desirable closes, like "Can you write me a proposal?" or, "I'll give you a call if something comes up."

Note

With some clients, referral sources, or even prospects, you may not need to establish a next step. That's because the next step will happen organically. This is the case if, for example, the prospect is a neighbor.

Best Practice #2: Set Up the Close with a Must-Ask Question

Chapter 36, "Ask the Must-Ask Question," discussed the importance of the must-ask question in qualifying the lead, surfacing objections, and prioritizing opportunities. It turns out, when you ask a must-ask question, you are actually asking for a close—a next step that advances the cause. Closing is not a distinct part of the business-development meeting but rather the result of a discussion that follows a game plan. This discussion starts with easier questions to build chemistry and comfort level and, depending on how the conversation progresses, leads to a must-ask question that sets up a close.

For example, a professional in a Stage Two meeting might ask, "What advice can you give me about the best way to position for an opportunity to work with you and ABC?" If the professional gets an answer that leads to some kind of actionable next step—for example, "You might want to meet with the CFO"—he or she can then proceed to establish the best way to implement this suggestion using the Ground Rule. If the client or prospect suggests something that's not actionable—for example, "If something comes up, we'll certainly give you a call!"—the professional can suggest one of the next steps that he or she came up with (refer to Best Practice #1) by saying something like, "I'd be happy to hear from you even if you just wanted to use me as a sounding board. In the meantime, I've often found it's beneficial to meet some of the other players in an organization. That way, when the right opportunity does come up, everyone's a bit more comfortable. I was thinking it might make sense for me to meet the CFO, just to put a face with a name. What do you think would be the best way to do that?"

Suggesting a next step with a must-ask question is helpful because it will give you an idea of where you stand. Even if you get a response you don't like—for example, "I don't think it's time to do that yet"—you can drop back to a positioning close, like arranging to contact the client or prospect again in a few months. If you use this best practice, then regardless of the outcome, you'll know you're playing the SalesGame well.

Best Practice #3: Avoid the Yes/No Question

Many years ago, I worked with a managing partner at an accounting firm in North Carolina who was a legendary rainmaker. One of his favorite sayings was, "I'll take a maybe forever. I just don't want to hear a no!" While I may not share his patience, I do agree with his basic premise. If you want to improve at closing, you should ask for the business or any next step in such a way that it minimizes the possibility of hearing a no. When a client or prospect says no, it is much harder to keep a dialogue going. Any future yes means a reversal of a position, which is always more difficult than changing a non-committal response.

The most reliable way to implement this best practice is to involve the client or prospect in choosing implementation alternatives for the next step. For example, if the next step is to meet with a decision-maker, you can involve the client or prospect in implementation alternatives by having him or her choose the time or place of the meeting. For example, you might say one of the following:

■ "As you say, I think it would be very beneficial for both of us to sit down with your CEO, Hank, to learn more about his thoughts on this issue. I'm open every day next week but Tuesday. What works for you?"

■ "Meeting with Hank makes a lot of sense. I'd like to get to know him and I'm sure he'll have an interesting perspective on this situation. You know him better than I do. What do you think he would prefer— meeting here at your offices or perhaps a lunch at Pasquale's?"

- "I think the next step here is to meet with Hank so he can share some of his thoughts on this issue. What's your advice on the best way to set that meeting up?"

Or, if the next step is to survey potential users of a service, such as an IT review or executive tax services, you might involve the client or prospect in implementation alternatives by saying something like the following:

- "I would really like to find out more about how some of the people who would be the users of this service view the situation. If I interview a cross section of four or five executives, it would really be useful. Who do you think would be the best people to talk to?"

- "I think it would be beneficial for both of us if we could get some background from some of the people who'll be using this service if you move ahead. A sample of four or five would work. What would be the best way to arrange 15-minute interviews with a representative sample of appropriate execs?"

Avoiding a yes/no question is not a technique or a trick to get the client or prospect to agree to work with you. It is simply a good way to keep the door open so you and your client or prospect can continue a dialogue. You don't want to end this dialogue prematurely by having the client or prospect become committed to an adversarial position, which is inherent when someone responds to a request to move ahead with a no. In the preceding examples, you would be at far greater risk of losing momentum with the client or prospect if you asked, "Can we meet with Hank?" or, "Could I do a survey of execs who would be using this service?"

> Avoiding a yes/no question... is simply a good way to keep the door open so you and your client or prospect can continue a dialogue.

Best Practice #4: Use the Ground Rule to Respond to a Rejection

When asked why they are reluctant to close, most professionals will say it's due mainly to a fear of rejection. Dealing with this fear is less difficult if you are prepared to handle a negative response when asking for a next step. The Ground Rule is an excellent tool to use in this situation because it enables you to explore the obstacles that are keeping the client or prospect from moving ahead in the sales process. One primary reason to avoid asking for a next step with a closed-ended question—that is, a yes/no question—is that you can't then use the Ground Rule to build agreement. After all, it is hard to agree with a no! The Ground Rule enables you to further explore the client or prospect's point of view. In this way, you can:

■ Make sure you know what will make the client enthusiastic.

■ Surface hidden objections.

■ Find the real decision-maker.

■ Find out what the client or prospect is *really* thinking.

Using the Ground Rule to respond to a rejected close is critical to your success in achieving your primary goal of ending up with an enthusiastic client. If you fail to explore why your attempt to close was rejected, you lose a wonderful opportunity to refine your approach to better meet the needs of the client or prospect.

By far, the most common rejection professionals encounter when they close by focusing on implementation alternatives is a client or prospect who says, "I want to think about this a little." Anyone who plays the SalesGame has heard this phrase many times. Fortunately, you can use the Ground Rule to respond to this comment. For example, you might say something like, "Hiring a new auditor is certainly an important decision. There are lots of moving parts. What issues are still on your mind?" This combination of agreement followed by an open-ended question does not necessarily mean you will obtain all the information you need or be suc-cessful in obtaining an enthusiastic client. It is really a matter of playing the game more effectively. The more effectively you play the SalesGame over hundreds of sales meetings during your career, the better the results you will achieve.

I once met with a managing partner of a Big Four accounting firm in Miami to discuss my research package. He gave me positive signals throughout the meeting. When I closed, I involved him in implementation alternatives by asking if he would be more interested in having the presen-tation in the morning or afternoon. He responded, "I never make a major decision without sleeping on it." I had a hard time buying the idea that this decision was "major." His desk cost more than the package I was offer-ing. Nevertheless, I expressed agreement that this decision was a major one and then asked what was on his mind. He repeated the same phrase: "I just never make a major decision without sleeping on it." I used the Ground Rule once more, only to receive the same response. Finally, I asked him what would be a good time to call him in the morning. Unfortunately, when I called the next morning—and in the days that followed—I couldn't get past the secretary. Although I was disappointed, at least I had the comfort of knowing I had played the game as well as possible given the situation.

Thankfully, there were many, many more meetings in which I tried this same technique and was rewarded with a signed contract. If you try your best close and use the Ground Rule to handle any rejection, you will be successful more often than not—and certainly more than you would be if they never asked the client or prospect what issues were still on his or her mind. Like Wayne Gretzky said, "You miss 100 percent of the shots you don't take."

Best Practice #5: Close as Soon as Possible

One of the most common misconceptions about closing—whether it is an advancing, positioning, trial, or final close—is that it always happens at the end of the meeting. While this may be true in a number of cases, you will be more effective at closing if you understand that the next step or close can occur at almost any point in a discussion with a client or prospect.

> The next step or close can occur at almost any point in a discussion with a client or prospect.

In Stages Two and Three, opportunities to make an advancing close may surface at any point in the discussion. The opportunity may be one you have identified in your preparation, as recommended in Best Practice #1, or it may be something that you did not anticipate. Either way, don't wait to take advantage of the opportunity. Establish a next step and continue the discussion with the comfort of knowing that additional contact with the client or prospect will follow. For example, suppose you're meeting with the CEO of a prospect company for a preliminary discussion about a particular issue. Early in the conversation, the CEO mentions that a meeting with the CFO would provide additional perspective on the problem at hand. You should take advantage of this opportunity and establish a next step by asking the best way to set up this follow-up meeting. Does the conversation with the CEO end because a next step has been established? Of course not! This could all take place in the first 10 minutes of an hour-long conversation. But you will feel much more at ease knowing you have mutual agreement for a next step in the process.

Note

When you establish a next step in the meeting, you can often identify one, two, or even three more next steps if you seize various opportunities as the discussion progresses. Be careful, though. In general, I find it is better to have only one or possibly two well-chosen next steps for each meeting to avoid rushing the process. When you do seize an opportunity to gain agreement on a next step, it should be a valid advancing close. That is, it should either build a relationship or make a Scorecard Factor real. Of course, at the conclusion of the conversation, you should summarize any next steps established during the meeting.

When moving to Stage Four, it's also important to launch your trial close at the earliest opportunity—as soon as you have a clear vision of the Scorecard. Otherwise, you risk putting the prospect or client off.

Years ago, I asked my father to watch a videotape I had made with a group of workshop participants. My father was in sales most of his life, so I always welcomed his counsel and advice. Halfway through, he sipped his martini, turned to me, and said, "You've already sold it. What are you trying to do now? Buy it back?" I replayed the video and saw exactly what he meant. I had clearly defined the heart of the matter and three important Scorecard Factors to shape the service. Yet I continued to talk about how good the service would be. Bad move.

Failing to launch a trial close as soon as you have a clear vision of the Scorecard is risky for two reasons. First, we have all been in conversations with a car or stereo salesman who keeps talking and talking about how good the deal is. No doubt, you became more suspicious of the deal the longer the guy talked. That's because the better something sounds, the more likely we are to distrust it. After all, we have all heard the phrase "If something sounds too good to be true, it probably is." (My son and daughter used to fall into this same trap when "selling" me on something they wanted my permission or my money to do.) Second, if you wait too long to make the trial close, you waste valuable time. This can come back to bite you later.

With regard to the second point, remember: You should not expect the client or prospect to accept your first trial close unless you are responding to a routine request from a client. In most cases when initiating with a client or prospect or responding to a prospect, the trial close is merely a tool to surface hidden objections and/or to better understand what the client or prospect really wants. By waiting too long to make a trial close or asking a must-ask question in any stage of the business-development process, you run the risk of the client or prospect rejecting the close and not having enough time to continue the dialogue. While the discussion could be continued at a later date, there is always a risk that it will not take place or start with the same foundation of agreement on the Scorecard.

So how do you know when to close? A trial close should be attempted as soon as you have agreement on the Scorecard. For an advancing close, you must take advantage of a good opportunity regardless of how early it is presented. You should also attempt an advancing or trial close if you start hearing implementation questions—that is, questions asked by the client or prospect that indicate he or she has moved beyond *if* and is thinking about *how*. Here are some examples of implementation questions:

- "How will my staff be kept up to speed on your progress?"

- "How long before we'll be able to see the results of your study?"

- "Who will have primary responsibility for coordination on your end?"

- "How will you make sure my staff knows what to do when you leave?"

If you start hearing questions like this after a productive discussion, the client or prospect is telling you it's time to move ahead. You should be thinking, "Close! Close!" Unfortunately, I have seen too many meetings in which professionals are asked one implementation question after another, but do not ask for the business or even a next step. Implementation questions are the most viable clues that you have that it's time to ask for a next step.

Best Practice #6: Avoid Writing Whenever Possible

I'll never forget visiting a Big Four accounting firm in its Chicago office at the end of what it called *Target Week*. During Target Week, each manager and partner was supposed to ask two clients or prospects for business. (Why they thought this was something to be done just once a year was beyond me.) On the wall of one hallway, they had placed large sheets of poster board with every partner and manager's name on it—well over 100 in total. Next to each name was a green, red, or yellow dot. A red dot meant the person had received a no, a green dot denoted he or she had obtained an engagement, and a yellow dot indicated that a proposal had been written. The dots were predominately yellow. This confirmed something I had always suspected: Proposals are an easy out. In the words of a frustrated managing partner, these professionals were "selling proposals, not work!"

An even better confirmation of my suspicion came from an unsolicited comment in a workshop I was doing for a law firm. A lateral hire who had been general counsel at a Fortune 500 company for several years shared his strategy for dealing with outside counsel seeking work. Over the years, he'd had many meetings in response to requests from high-level company executives who had friends or family who wanted to work with the organization. He said they usually came in and started talking about all the services they offered. After about 15 minutes, he'd ask them to write a proposal on all the things they could do for the company. He then said to the participants in my workshop, "They'd all get giddy over the opportunity to write a proposal for us. Of course, I'd never read any of the proposals. But it was a good way to get them out of my office."

As a next step, professionals often put something in writing. But writing is not only time-consuming, it also doesn't do much in terms of building relationships or making Scorecard Factors real. In particular, proposals are a deadly trap. They take a great deal of time to write and are frequently not read. But it's not just proposals. The director of a Washington, D.C. lobbying firm told me that after her first meeting with a prospect to discuss legislative assistance, she wrote a seven-page summary of key issues on Capitol Hill that affected the prospect. I asked her, "How long did you spend writing the summary?" Her response: "At least eight hours." A far better option would have been to arrange a meeting and discuss the same issues with the prospect and some of his key people. With this next step, she could have built relationships, better demonstrated her ability to collaborate and interact with the prospect, and saved herself valuable time. She also would not have given away written copies of her intellectual property, which could be sent to anyone.

The bottom line is that you should *not* include a writing assignment (and certainly not a proposal) as one of the two next steps you prepare in advance to close the meeting. I know proposals are sometimes required. As will be discussed in Chapter 41, "Stage Four: Close to Ensure Client Satisfaction and Surface Hidden Objections," you will play the SalesGame better and win more often if you avoid writing proposals as a next step. Instead, ask to review a draft of a proposal or presentation with the client or prospect. That *is* a legitimate next step.

> You will play the SalesGame better and win more often if you avoid writing proposals as a next step.

If a client or prospect asks you to write a proposal as a next step, use the Ground Rule to find out what client or prospect means by the word *proposal*. Try saying something like, "I'm really excited about this project! I'm not surprised that a summary of how we'd work with you is a part of the process. Some clients want everything in great detail, while others are looking for a one-page synopsis. What do you have in mind?" Defining what client or prospect is looking for when he or she asks for a proposal or presentation will save you a lot of time and probably increase your odds on winning the SalesGame.

Note

Notice the use of the word *summary* rather than *proposal* in the preceding sample phrasing. I've come to dislike the P words—that is, *proposal*, *presentation*, and *pitch*. They seem too one-sided rather than collaborative. I've always tried to use slightly different terminology, such as *engagement summary*, *work plan*, *discussion*, and *introductory meeting*. This is personal preference, but I've found most clients and prospects are receptive to this approach. Once again, this is a game, and we all have our own style of play.

I once worked with a group selling an internal controls review project for student financial aid to colleges and universities. We worked all morning, preparing for typical meetings. During the lunch break, three accountants in attendance went to a previously scheduled sales call at a nearby university. When they returned, they were ecstatic, and told the group what happened. First, they established good rapport. In doing so, they discovered that the head of student aid had been raised in the same small Minnesota town as one of the accountants—a stroke of luck. Next, they built the Scorecard and made a trial close all in one meeting. (This is very unusual but can happen if the right service is being offered at the right time.) After that, the VP of Student Affairs agreed with the trial close. He then asked them to write a proposal. As we had practiced in the morning, one of the accountants used the Ground Rule to find out what the VP had in mind. The VP replied, "I don't care what you write. Just don't make it longer than half a page!" By way of explanation, he turned to the file cabinet behind his desk, pulled out a green form labeled "Purchase Order," and pointed to a half-page section where he was required to enter a description of what he was purchasing! I have often wondered how many pages the accountants would have written in their proposal if they hadn't been prepared for just such a scenario.

Chapter

Stage One:
Close to Set Up Qualification

One of the most useful aspects of breaking down the SalesGame into six stages is that it allows you to measure your progress, not just your results. Before every sales contact with the client or prospect, you should recognize where you are in the sales process and identify the next steps that will move you ahead in the game.

This is easy in Stage One. You simply need to ask for an opportunity to talk in more depth about business with a lead. At this meeting, you can determine if you have a qualified or positioning lead. The latter is far more common, of course, when you are the one initiating contact.

Closing for Promotional Seminars

Almost all accounting, law, wealth-management, and consulting firms put on seminars in the hope of developing business, but very few of them make a concerted effort to close these marketing activities with a next step. Instead, five or six representatives from a firm typically attend a seminar with 20 or 30 participants to mingle with the attendees over coffee or cocktails. These discussions always involve some conversation about the business content of the session. Closing in this scenario usually means asking the client or prospect for a meeting to follow up on the material covered in the seminar.

One example from Boston demonstrates the importance of closing at firm seminars and other marketing activities. An attorney, Janette, approached me during a workshop for advice on following up on 250 leads she had developed after giving the same seminar for healthcare organizations in three different cities (Boston, New York, and Washington, D.C.). Obviously, Janette had hit on a hot-button topic to draw so many participants! To try to develop business, Janette sent a summary of her comments to each participant, followed by a couple of e-bulletins. She was frustrated, however, because only a few participants responded—and the handful who did represented less-desirable prospects. I suggested she contact attendees who represented the most attractive prospects using e-mail or some kind of business social networking. "I'm too busy," was her predictable response. The next time I talked to Janette, she had to be brief. "I have to catch a plane to San Francisco," she explained. I asked her the reason for the trip. You guessed it—she was going to put on another seminar! This unfortunate situation was made worse by the fact that there was a limited window of opportunity associated with the seminar topic. In the end, Janette developed very little business from this expensive investment of time. By putting in even a minimal amount of additional time to establish next steps with even 10 or 20 of the most desirable seminar attendees, she would have achieved much better results.

I am sure some of you will react by saying this approach would be way too pushy for you. Please don't misunderstand my suggestion. I am not saying you should try to close with everyone who attends a seminar. Rather, you should be more selective and try this close only with those attendees who meet the following criteria:

- They seem to have some genuine interest in the topic. Example of these attendees are people who come up after a seminar and ask questions or for a business card.

- They represent organizations with whom your firm would like to work.

- They have at least the potential for good chemistry.

Let's be honest: If a firm puts on a seminar, it's assumed that some of the attendees are interested. Otherwise, why would they attend? If you receive no response to a request for a follow-up conversation (common) or if the request is declined outright (rare), you know this probably is not the best prospect to pursue and should be a lower priority at best. Of course, the alternative is to simply wait for attendees to call if they are interested. Unfortunately, those who call may not be the ones you would most like on your client list, as happened with Janette.

> **Note**
>
> Not closing is fine if your goal is general image building. But it doesn't make a lot of sense if you want to proactively build the practice of your dreams. Isn't that why firms put on seminars in the first place?

Closing for Other Marketing Activities

The same applies to other types of marketing activities. You could close with trade groups, networking events, and even some social activities the same way as you would for a seminar. In these situations, the close is usually a matter of simply expressing interest in discussing a business or professional concern at some future point. I worked with one sage rainmaker whose protocol was to send an e-mail to each person he connected with at any networking activity, letting that person know he enjoyed meeting him or her and that he hoped to stay in touch. Those who responded went into his contact base. It was, as he said, "a good way to separate the wheat from the chaff."

If you are asking for a follow-up meeting with a contact from a Stage One activity, remember to sell the meeting, not the service. In other words, highlight some benefit that the client or prospect will gain by meeting even if they don't buy the service—for example, a discussion of how seminar content would affect their organization, exploring ways you and the client or prospect might be able to help each other, providing a sounding board for the future, etc. As discussed in Part 1, "An Overview of the SalesGame," you should never sell in a Stage One activity such as a trade, social, or civic function. Instead, use it to set up a Stage Two meeting.

Never sell in a Stage One activity such as a trade, social, or civic function. Instead, use it to set up a Stage Two meeting.

Stage Two: Close to Shape the Service or Position for Another Day

Stage Two is unique in the SalesGame in that it usually goes on for a period of time—often years. As a result, you must close in Stage Two with next steps that either advance the cause (that is, create a new relationship or make a potential Scorecard Factor real) or position for the future (for example, set up a meeting with the same person or people).

Positioning closes tend to be more informal. These are usually fun relationship-building activities, such as going to a ball game or having cocktails. Closes that advance the cause are usually more substantive, like conversations about the client or prospect's current situation. Certain next steps and closes can achieve both. For example, you might play a round of golf with a client or prospect and have others from your firm and/or your client or prospect's join in the activity.

Whether positioning or advancing the cause, next steps should create some value for the client or prospect. In the case of a positioning close, the value might simply be to provide a good time for the client or prospect. Or, if the objective is to advance the cause, the value might be to educate the client or prospect. In other words, in this stage, you shouldn't reach out to clients or prospects to ask if they're ready to buy. Rather, you're looking to bring value to each contact.

The Positioning Close

A positioning close is more likely to occur if you are initiating contact (Quadrant Three or Four in the sales matrix) than if you are responding.

To use a positioning close effectively, you must employ some form of system so you remember what you are supposed to do and when you are supposed to do it. This is made much easier with the proliferation of e-based tracking systems. For example, I maintain a list of prospects that's about 20 pages long and includes 80+ different firms. In truth, the vast majority of these firms are so low on my priority scale that I have not talked to them in a year or more—although I do send them e-letters once a month. Of course, this means I have lost some of these opportunities. But as in any game, you must make choices in the SalesGame and hope that the majority of them are right. Of the remaining clients and prospects on my list, five or six are in Stage Three, so I contact them relatively frequently to discuss next steps to advance the cause. The remaining prospects I reach out to by e-mail every month or two to set up a phone call to see how they are doing, what's going on in their world, and so on. Each of these calls ends with an agreement as to when I should call again. This is a positioning close. Assuming you do follow up in the agreed-upon time frame, it's like "putting a coin in a trust bank," as one sage partner from a law firm in Atlanta put it.

I'm frequently asked how long professionals should use the positioning close and stay in Stage Two. My answer is that it took me 17 years of positioning to acquire one of my most significant clients. That client is based in my hometown, making it a much easier commute than working in Japan or Moscow. I put a lot of coins in the trust bank over those 17 years. The other question I'm frequently asked is what professionals should do when a client or prospect doesn't respond to an e-mail or phone call that was set up as a next step in a previous contact—that is, there's "radio silence," as I like to say. The simple answer is keep following up.

I was once in Stage Three with a partner at an accounting firm who suddenly quit responding to my e-mails, even though we agreed on a time frame and a purpose for our next discussion. I continued to contact him with increasing time spans in between—for example a month, two months, etc. I tried leaving a couple of voicemails, also with no response. This went on for two years. I was convinced that I had done something wrong or that someone else had won the work. But eventually, when I made one of my regular phone calls to the partner, he answered the phone. He was extremely apologetic and told me that his wife had been ill. We worked together for five outstanding years after that.

While the reason for the radio silence may have been different, many professionals have had the same experience. It's hard to believe, but talking with someone who is offering professional services isn't always at the top of every client or prospect's priority list! Whether in business or in our personal lives, we all tend to think the worst in the absence of communication.

But establishing a next step earns you the right to follow up. Be persistent. In most cases, good things will happen. Professionals who identify and pursue high-quality prospects may use a combination of positioning closes and next steps to advance the cause for a long time to acquire the clients of their dreams.

> Establishing a next step earns you the right to follow up.

Closing to Advance the Cause in Stage Two

Next steps that advance the cause are those that either build a new relationship or make a potential Scorecard Factor real. That is, they answer the question, "Why should I use your firm?"

When you are responding in Stage Two, you are far more likely to use next steps that advance the cause because you probably have a qualified lead. However, next steps that advance the cause can and should be used even when you are initiating and you *don't* have a qualified lead.

If you do have a qualified lead, you might set up an in-depth discussion of exactly what the client or prospect wants to accomplish and start shaping the service. This is particularly important when responding to RFPs (Quadrant One in the sales matrix). As discussed in Part 2, "Best Practices for Setting Up the Game," you should try to come up with a creative close to follow up after the initial contact and avoid moving too quickly to writing a proposal. If, on the other hand, it's *not* a qualified lead, closing to advance the cause usually means creating a new relationship or providing an educational experience for the client or prospect.

In some cases, particularly if you are responding to a request from an existing client, the discussion will move through Stage Three (shape the service) and end with a trial close (Stage Four) that becomes the final close (Stage Five) when accepted. A good example would be a lawyer who regularly handles commercial loan work for a particular banker or an engineer who routinely provides traffic studies for a municipality. When the banker or municipality calls for assistance, the sale is usually consummated in one call. In these situations, closing really isn't a critical factor. As discussed, however, if you fail to recognize that the goal of the game is to get an enthusiastic client, not just to get work, it can become an issue. For example, you might take on the assignment without establishing the conditions of satisfaction (Stage Three) or launching a trial close (Stage Four) to make sure you know exactly what the client wants. In these situations, the most important close is the trial close, which summarizes your vision of the Scorecard to make sure you and the client are on the same page.

Get to the Decision-Maker

You should attempt an advancing close to meet with the decision-maker as soon as possible in Stage Two. You don't know if you *truly* have a qualified lead until you meet with the person who has the economic authority to hire you to solve a problem, take advantage of an opportunity, etc. This might require several meetings with someone who is not a decision-maker to build a relationship and create trust.

Of course, no one wants to feel like they are being circumvented to get to their boss. Nevertheless, one mistake that professionals frequently make is investing too much time selling to a user before they meet with the real decision-maker. In most cases, meeting with this decision-maker is necessary to advance to Stage Three. Only the decision-maker can tell you the true source of value—that is, what the decision-maker wants to accomplish from the service for which he or she is paying.

Even if your request to meet the decision-maker is rejected, you will learn a valuable piece of information: This is probably *not* a high-priority lead. What decision-maker wouldn't want to meet with someone who is providing an expensive and valuable service, to make sure the chemistry is good? Plus, you run the risk of getting the work but being unable to create an enthusiastic client because you don't know the decision-maker's criteria for excellent performance. While there are always exceptions, closing to get to the decision-maker should be a priority whether initiating or responding.

Don't Position When You Can Advance

Many professionals are not proactive enough when closing in Stage Two of the SalesGame. They use a positioning close when they should use an advancing close to build more relationships before the point of sale or to demonstrate selling points. I once positioned for 17 years to acquire a large accounting firm as a client. During that time, I used many advancing closes. I built relationships with several players at the organization, discussed business-development issues and potential solutions, etc. When the firm became a qualified lead, all those involved in the decision-making process knew who I was and what my credentials were. I have seen many professionals close a Stage Two contact by saying, "I'll call you in a month" when they could have suggested a luncheon to meet new people from the target organization or introduce new people from their own firm.

You should always prepare for a business-development meeting by identifying two next steps to advance your cause, even in Stage Two. You might not try to use either of these closes—and if you do, it might not be accepted.

In that case, you can always drop back to a positioning close—that is, gain agreement to meet again with the same person. Nevertheless, closing to advance the cause should be your primary objective.

Closing to advance the cause should be your primary objective.

Stage Three: Close to Build Relationships, Implement Strategy, and Differentiate

An advancing close to promote forward movement is most commonly used in Stage Three as you try to convert a qualified lead to an enthusiastic client. Based on my experience, there is no question that professionals who meet more often with clients and prospects in this stage of the SalesGame dramatically improve their chances of success. "Meet more, write less" has become almost a mantra for those who want to maximize their effectiveness when playing the SalesGame. The reasons are simple. The more you meet with clients and prospects, the more:

- You build chemistry with them

- Opportunity you have for in-depth discussions of needs and resources

- "Real" the value of working with you or your firm becomes (that is, you can demonstrate what it would be like to work with you)

- Information you will have to shape the service—that is, put together the right combination of features, benefits, and conditions of satisfaction—to meet prospect or client's needs and expectations and end up with an enthusiastic client

When you take the time to meet more often with clients and prospects, you send a message that you really want the opportunity to work together.

This is important! Based on my firm's research, when asked why they selected a specific professional, one of the top two or three reasons given by respondents was that they chose "the firm that wanted to work with us."

Relationships: The Key to Winning

When asked "Why did you hire the firm you work with?," the largest category of responses among 150,000 buyers of professional services was "Relationship." This category included responses like, "Good chemistry," "We just like them!," and similar comments. We all know there is no substitute for investing time to improve relationships, whether at home or at work. For my money, good relationships make up at least half the reason people buy professional services—and sometimes a lot more. It follows, then, that consideration and implementation of a strategy to build relationships ought to make up at least half of your selling effort. In short, you should move forward through advancing closes to create opportunities to interact with as many players in the client or prospect decision-making process as possible. This can be done in person or by phone. The former is preferable if travel is not too prohibitive. For example, I would certainly meet in person with a client or prospect near my home base in Detroit, whereas I would probably use the telephone to pursue an international opportunity (although on more than one occasion, I have invested my time and money for face-to-face meetings with qualified leads in Europe).

> Good relationships make up at least half the reason people buy professional services.

You should analyze this network of players as early as possible in the sales process. An approach for mapping this network is described in Chapter 2, "The Players: Who's Involved in the SalesGame?" It suggests you put a plus sign, minus sign, or zero by each player's name to indicate whether your relationship with that person is good, bad, or neutral or unknown, respectively. Anyone with a zero is an obvious opportunity for a possible next step—that is, an advancing close. Going for a trial close before there is a plus by the decision-maker's name just does not make sense. Most professionals realize that even if they do not obtain the engagement they are pursuing, using this approach enables them to build relationships with those who could be useful in the future. Even if they are currently only influencers or lower-level users, these individuals might leave the company or move up in the organization.

Implement a Strategy to Differentiate Your Service

Participants in my workshops often want to discuss how to build a strategy to differentiate themselves from their competitors. We have already defined strategy as "the artful or ingenious use of resources." In Stage Three, you should close in ways that use your resources to demonstrate to the client or prospect the reality of a Scorecard Factor—that is, to make it more tangible and understandable. A great rainmaker who was a partner at a Big Four firm used to say this in a slightly different way: "Don't talk about how you are going to give your prospects advice. Give them advice!"

> "Don't talk about how you are going to give your prospects advice. Give them advice!"

I have seen many examples of advancing closes that promote forward movement by implementing a strategy and differentiating a professional or firm. Closing in Stage Three is really where the fun takes place. In this stage, creativity plays a big part in determining the eventual outcome of competitive situations. Three examples drawn from the accounting, legal, and consulting professions should demonstrate how advancing closes can be used to differentiate a service, professional, or firm and build a winning strategy.

Example 1

Remember Ole? You read about him in Chapter 20, "Differentiating Your Service and Developing a Strategy." He was a partner in a Big Four firm in Denmark. Ole was in a Stage Three meeting with a prospect who wanted to expand his business internationally and was looking for a Big Four firm that could help him in this venture. The prospect, who was the CEO of his firm, told Ole that the company was going to begin operations in Minnesota in the near future—probably before they selected an accounting firm. Ole used an advancing close to promote forward movement. He suggested to the CEO that they arrange their next meeting late in the afternoon the following week. That way, they could engage in a telephone call with an industry expert in the Minneapolis office. Ole's close sounded something like this: "Regardless of whom you work with, you should be aware of some of the ins and outs of starting operations in the U.S. and specifically in Minnesota. I would like to involve my partner, Merle, who works in our Minneapolis office, in our next conversation to talk over some of those issues. Because of the time difference, we'll need to schedule it later in the day.

What afternoons look best for you next week?" The CEO could hardly refuse such an offer, and the meeting was arranged. As mentioned, the call was full of practical suggestions and advice, and eventually led to the prospect becoming a client.

This creative advancing close helped Ole's cause for three reasons:

- It differentiated Ole's firm. This differentiation was not based on something the firm had to offer that the competitors did not—all Big Four firms had offices in Minneapolis staffed with industry experts familiar with the issues at hand. Rather, differentiation occurred because Ole made this resource more tangible and real to the buyer.

- The close allowed for the creation of an additional relationship between Ole's firm and the prospect.

- The close was a good use of strategy, or "the artful or ingenious use of resources." In this case, the resource was the partner in Minneapolis with industry expertise.

Example 2

In Chapter 12, "Best Practices for Quadrant One: Responding to Prospects," you read about Carter, a partner at a law firm in Denver. The firm received an RFP from an international conglomerate that was looking for counsel to assist in building a dam in Wyoming. Carter called the prospect company and arranged a dinner when its representatives stopped over in Denver on their way back from Wyoming. At the dinner, one representative made it clear that he was concerned about wildlife issues that might arise when the plans for the dam were submitted to the government. Carter closed with a next step, arranging a phone call with a partner in the firm's Washington, D.C. office who was an alum of the National Fish and Wildlife Agency and was very familiar with the issues the prospect was facing.

This is another example of a great advancing close that promoted forward movement for Carter's firm in multiple ways:

- The close enabled the law firm to use a resource that was in fact different from what others had to offer—an alumnus of the appropriate government agency.

- The close allowed for the building of a relationship with another member of the law firm's team.

- It demonstrated Carter's listening skills and desire to be proactive in providing advice.

Again, do not talk to your prospects about how you are going to give them advice. Give them advice.

Example 3

An IT consulting firm in California was pursuing work from a movie chain operator who wanted to more quickly obtain information about the performance of various films in terms of box office and concession sales. Naomi, the director of the consulting firm, learned in her initial meeting with the client that part of the problem was getting local movie operators to input data promptly. Naomi recommended that she survey 10 to 20 of the operators as a next step to determine their reasons for their slow response to corporate requests for information. During the survey, a couple of non-IT factors causing the problem surfaced. Naomi shared these with the client, who immediately made the appropriate changes.

Using a survey as a next step or close advanced Naomi and her firm's cause for several reasons:

- It provided advice during the sales process.

- It enabled Naomi to build relationships not only with current users but also with potential buyers should they move up the corporate ladder or move to another theater chain.

- It was a great way to demonstrate the practicality of the advice her consulting firm could provide, thus making a Scorecard Factor real.

- It enabled Naomi to demonstrate what it would be like to use her firm on the project.

In all three examples, the professionals involved sent a clear message that they truly wanted their prospect's business—a significant buying criteria, as pointed out earlier. In other words, Ole, Carter, and Naomi closed with next steps that created value for their prospect by investing both their own and their firm's time even before they were awarded the engagement.

The three professionals could have moved more quickly to a trial close or a proposal, as most of their peers would have done. Instead, they opted for next steps that enhanced their chances of success. In other words, if professionals close more and meet more, they will write less and improve their winning percentage.

Better Understanding Means a More Enthusiastic Client

One of the most common mistakes that professionals make is to think they are being efficient by shortening the sales process—that is, jumping to the proposal or trial close stage as quickly as possible. But in reality, the best practice is to *extend* the process as long as is necessary to make sure you understand what it takes to convert the prospect into an enthusiastic client. Common sense and personal experience would suggest that the more time you spend with the client or prospect to shape the service, the better you will understand what it will take to create an enthusiastic buyer.

Although I understand the pressures that create this rush to a close, I am often frustrated by the unwillingness of professionals to use multiple advancing closes to set up additional, meaningful contacts with clients and prospects. One reason professionals give for this unwillingness is that clients and prospects are very busy people and don't want to spend time talking to professionals who are pursuing an opportunity to work with them. While this may be true in earlier stages of the business-development process, by the time you get to Stage Three, you are by definition dealing with a client or prospect who recognizes a need. In my experience, when people have a problem to solve or an opportunity to seize, they want to talk to those people who can assist them—particularly if they get value from the conversation rather than just listening to a pitch.

Research done by my own company supports this position. The most prevalent negative expressed by prospects was that professionals were "arrogant." That is, they offered solutions to the client or prospect before asking him or her to describe the problem. Even if you make the right recommendations, moving too quickly to describe the benefits that will result from using your services is annoying. Slow down! The key to success for professionals in business development is helping clients achieve their objectives. This is best done by coming up with advancing closes that promote forward movement by building relationships, defining the need, creating value, and sending a message that you really want to work with the client or prospect.

> The most prevalent negative expressed by prospects was that professionals were "arrogant."

Stage Four: Close to Ensure Client Satisfaction and Surface Hidden Objections

Trial close is used to describe Stage Four. It's also the type of close that needs to be used in this part of the sales process. The trial close is used in Stage Four to test for understanding. Does the service you are proposing best meet the needs of the client or prospect?

Written proposals in any form or format and the proverbial "beauty contest"—for example, when three or four firms are paraded in front of a panel of buyers—are the most common examples of a trial close, even though most professionals fail to realize that these activities are merely steps in the sales process, not the end of it. Consequently, they don't use Stage Four discussions to refine what they are offering. Rather, they treat proposals and presentations as a sort of "take it or leave it" offering to the prospect or client. A trial close should be part of any purchase, even when a client calls you to ask for additional assistance. You will remain in Stage Four until you feel confident that you share a vision of the Scorecard with the client or prospect.

Most professionals see the trial close in Stage Four as being the same as a final close. In fact, these two types of closes are extremely different. The trial close poses a question: "Do I really understand the core source of value—the Heart of the Matter—and the best way to address this from your point of view?" In essence, this involves summarizing the Scorecard verbally or in writing. The final close does not occur until you know the answer to this question is yes.

> The trial close poses a question: "Do I really understand the core source of value—the Heart of the Matter—and the best way to address this from your point of view?"

Don't be discouraged if your client or prospect does not agree with your initial summary of the Scorecard. If you handle the trial close correctly (that is, you don't ask for a final decision but do ask for a progress check), you will not only win more but end up with appreciative clients. Professionals who play the SalesGame should strive to extend the process in Stage Four. There are two techniques you can use as a trial close to extend the process and make sure you understand your client or prospect's needs. These are using a draft proposal and gaining permission to follow up after a presentation. Let's explore each of these further.

Use a Draft Proposal to Improve Your Success Rate

My company was once engaged to analyze 50 proposals for consulting services that were successful and 50 that were not. Our analysis would hopefully determine common threads that might be of use in the future. The client sent us the proposals and allowed us to interview the individuals who had developed them. One difference between the winners and the losers was apparent from the moment my receptionist brought them into my office. The stack of winners was about one-fifth as high as the stack of losers. Being a brilliant research scientist, I concluded that short sells better. After a month of analysis, only two other significant differences surfaced. First, the proposals that lost clearly used more boilerplate text—hence their length—and usually started with a recitation of why the firm would be a good choice instead of defining the client or prospect's problem. Second, 38 of the winners had been reviewed in draft form by someone in the client or prospect food chain, who gave advice as to what changes needed to be made.

Reviewing a draft of a proposal with a client is nothing more than a long trial close that tests the accuracy of your analysis of the client or prospect's situation and the likely efficacy of the corresponding service solution. If you ask buyers for feedback on whether you accurately captured their concerns, they will generally tell you. Buyers benefit if you perform well, so it is in their best interest to make sure you understand their needs. If the client or prospect does not want to provide feedback during the trial close, then you probably don't have a very good chance of obtaining the work. As I often say in workshops, "If your prospect doesn't want to help you, you're not going to win anyway!" Even if you *do* win the work, odds are that this type of client will be difficult to deal with for two reasons. First, it will be harder to create an enthusiastic client if you aren't sure of what they want. Second, if people don't want to collaborate with you on the front end, they probably won't be very collaborative when you need their input to perform the work.

Note

In addition to extending the sales process, asking the client or prospect to review a draft proposal allows you to be more confident that he or she will actually *read* the proposal. One study I saw found fewer than 50% of proposal recipients actually read them. It is difficult to discuss a draft if you have not read it!

I once went through three drafts of a proposal for a major project, receiving advice and making the appropriate revisions each time. Each time the prospect suggested a change, he took more ownership of the proposal, making sure it met his needs and those of his organization. When he requested a fourth revision, he said, "Let's not call this a proposal anymore. Let's think of it as an engagement letter."

Setting up the draft proposal as a trial close is very simple. Just tell the client or prospect the truth: "We've talked a great deal about your situation and how we might respond to it. Before we put together a proposal, I'd really like to prepare a draft for us to review to make sure we're on the same page. We could review it any time next week. Which day would be best for you?"

In some situations, you will not be able to use this technique to extend Stage Four. For example, like many municipalities both large and small, the bureaucracy in New York City limits prospective counsel for bond work to communicating in writing only. Moreover, any answers to questions posed by one vendor are shared with all the others. Many European governmental entities follow this same practice, as do some not-for-profits and educational institutions. Nevertheless, when you are playing the SalesGame, you should at least ask for the opportunity to review a draft. If your request is refused, at least you will not have to second-guess yourself if you are not successful in obtaining the work.

Gain Permission for Contact Beyond the Beauty Contest

Many workshop participants complain that they can't close when they are in a beauty contest—that is, when three or four firms are paraded in front of a panel of buyers. In such situations, it would be a rare occurrence for the panel to buy from one vendor before hearing from the others. Most panels want to talk among themselves about all the presentations. However, I discovered a way to extend Stage Four to enhance my chances of winning in just such a situation.

One day, as I made a presentation before one such panel of attorneys, it occurred to me that the panelists would likely be overwhelmed by information. After all, I was but one of four vendors they were hearing from that day. So I ended our discussion by saying the following: "My company recently interviewed three computer firms to establish who we should use to rebuild our database. As a buyer, I found it difficult to remember who said what. To make matters worse, questions were raised in the last presentation that I wished I could have asked the first two vendors. It might be beneficial for us to discuss any issues or questions you might have after today before you make a final decision. I would certainly appreciate the opportunity to talk further. Who would be the best person to follow up with?" Not surprisingly, they assigned this follow-up task to the least senior attorney on the panel. Even with this level of contact, however, I had an opportunity to continue the dialogue. When I called to follow up, I learned that the panel had several questions about how they should approach the task at hand. More phone calls followed. After almost a month and several refinements to the original service package, my company was rewarded with the assignment. Since then, I have recommended this technique to clients and used it several times myself. While it does not always lead to getting the work, this attempt to extend the trial close has rarely been rejected.

Use a Trial Close Even When You Know the Work Is Sold

You should use a trial close even if you feel sure you will be hired. The goal of the SalesGame is not to get the work, but to end up with an enthusiastic client. Summarizing the Scorecard and asking the client or prospect to confirm this shared vision of the project is an effective way to achieve this goal. This is particularly important if you are responding to a client request (Quadrant Two in the sales matrix), when the greatest danger is an easy sale.

You can and should use a trial close to extend Stage Four to be sure you really understand the client or prospect's conditions of satisfaction. You must still ask the client, "Do I really understand what you want to accomplish and your ideas as to the best way to do it?"

Remember back in Chapter 13, "Best Practices for Quadrant Two: Responding to Clients," when I told the story about calling my accounting firm to ask what the tax ramifications would be if I sold a piece of real estate? All I was looking for was a quick number. No in-depth analysis was required. Instead, several days later, I received a three-page letter, single-spaced, full of accounting lingo—but no estimate of what I would owe if I sold the property. Had the tax accountant done a trial close, she could have avoided irritating me (the client) by taking too long to respond, giving me a report that I did not want to read, and charging more than I wanted to pay for her opinion. That trial close might have sounded something like, "So, Larry, you want to know if you should consider this guy's offer based on how much you'd pay in taxes. You need to get back to him in a couple of days, so you want me to check this out before Tuesday and give you a call back with a rough idea. No report—you only want a verbal summary. I think that will take me just a couple of hours. Are we on the same page?"

> **Tip**
>
> The trial close can be used with more than just clients and prospects. I have recommended to a number of younger professionals—for example, associates at law firms and junior accountants and consultants—that they use this skill when taking assignments from more senior professionals. Certainly, these younger professionals do not have to sell their services, but they do need to end up with an enthusiastic user. The trial close is an excellent technique to help them accomplish this objective.

Use the Trial Close to Surface Hidden Objections

As with any form of closing in Stages Three or Four, asking to move ahead in the process will bring to the surface any undisclosed issues that might be working against you. These hidden objections are usually difficult to discuss. For example, perhaps the client or prospect wants to work with an older, more experienced accountant or favors a female attorney for certain kinds of litigation. I am sure the Equal Employment Opportunity

Commission might not like that these factors are considered in the buying process, but I have seen many examples of both (as well as others like them). If you fail to find and deal with these issues during the sales process—particularly when final agreement on the Scorecard is close—you will not fare well in competitive situations and run the risk of disappointing a client or prospect even if you do acquire the work. Once the objection has been surfaced, you can use the Ground Rule to respond to the issue at hand.

Chapter

Stage Five: Close to Start the Work or Position for Another Day

After you have described, revised, and gained agreement on the Scorecard, it's time to request permission to start the work—that is, to ask for the business. This is, in fact, the final close. It happens when a trial close is accepted. Obviously, this is going to take place in many different ways, depending on the type of sale.

Always Close, Even in Formal Situations

In a formal-proposal or competitive-bid situation, there may be no face-to-face opportunity for a final close. You simply submit your proposal (hopefully after having it reviewed by the client or prospect in draft form) and wait to hear when the decision has been made. In essence, the proposal is the trial close. If you receive the call and find you won the work, then you should close by asking to start the work. You should proceed with this step as soon as possible. For example, you might say something like this: "Thanks, Bob! That's great news. I'm delighted we won and appreciate all the help and support you gave us. I can come out with Renee and Tom next week to start planning this year's audit with your staff. We really need to have you there. What days look best for you?" The accountant in this example knows he will have substantial contact with the client from here out, so there is no reason to push for an immediate meeting to review why the firm was chosen. However, smart professionals will have such a discussion before too long so lessons can be learned from the success and performance criteria confirmed for an eventual assuring client enthusiasm (ACE) meeting.

With Some RFPs, Winning Is Just the Beginning

In situations when personal contact between the buyer and professional is prohibited before the proposal is submitted—for example, when responding to RFPs from some governmental entities—you must use a Stage Five close to go back to Stage Three or Four. Such a close might sound something like this: "We're delighted you've chosen us. This is a great opportunity, and we put a lot of effort into it. Before we start the project, we would really like an opportunity to sit down with you and your staff to work out some details so we're all on the same page. What would be the best way to set up this discussion?" In other words, now that the professional has the work, he or she must go back and make sure the service will be shaped in such a way as to create an enthusiastic client when the job is complete. I have often noted in workshops that in these situations, the sales process really starts when you win the competitive proposal. Without further relationship building and a dialogue to shape the service, you are at risk of acquiring the work only to end up with a client who is less than enthusiastic.

> Without further relationship building and a dialogue to shape the service, you are at risk of acquiring the work only to end up with a client who is less than enthusiastic.

Over the last several years, I have noticed a growing trend of companies sending out generic or blanket RFPs, particularly to law firms. These are often generated by the financial arm of the firm, such as the CFO or a purchasing department. The RFP typically lists several areas—for example, labor and employment, intellectual property, mergers and acquisitions, etc.—and asks the firm to provide its qualifications in each area. Needless to say, responding to these RFPs is extremely time-consuming because of all the information they require. At the end of the process, the winners are told they are on an approved list for one or more of the areas listed. I've observed, however, that in many cases, no actual work is forthcoming. My guess is that the *real* decision-maker—for example, the general counsel or someone on the legal staff—already has strong relationships with other attorneys and is not particularly pleased that someone from purchasing has attempted to usurp his or her authority in this arena.

Attorneys and other professionals should beware of these generic RFPs. If you absolutely must respond to one—after all, it can be hard to abstain from responding when a Fortune 500 company sends one of these RFPs out—you should do two things:

■ Try to get to know all the players, including those in the in-house legal staff, before you start writing your proposal. That way, if you *do* win, you'll have a better chance of getting some actual work because you will have started to build a relationship. You might also learn that you don't want to invest the time to respond given the low likelihood of getting any work.

■ If you win, you will jump right into Stage Five. That means you need to be proactive by reaching out to those with whom you might be working to determine what they really need and how they like to work with outside professionals.

Closing in Stage Five When You Lose

In formal-proposal situations, when the result of the competition is a loss, the close should establish a next step to determine the reasons for the unfavorable decision and how to position for the future. As obvious as this seems, I am frequently surprised by how few professionals close in this situation—that is, establish a next step. Asking for a meeting to debrief with the client or prospect when you have lost will always be of value. Such a meeting might do any of the following:

■ Create another opportunity with the same organization.

■ Teach you how to be more effective in a future opportunity.

■ Build a relationship with someone who could be a future lead.

■ Establish an image of respect for the buyer that can only help in the long run.

Closing in this situation follows the same principle as in any other stage. That is, you close to advance your position in the SalesGame. In this case, you are setting up a Stage Six meeting. The close on the telephone might sound something like this: "You know, Fred, we've always found it of great value to sit down face-to-face and learn more about how we could have done a better job on our end and what we might do to position for some future opportunity. I'd consider it most helpful if we could talk with you more about the whole process. I'd really like to take you to lunch next week and get your feedback. I'm open every day except Monday. What looks good for you?"

Stay Proactive, Even in Stage Five

Even in Stage Five, there are opportunities to extend the SalesGame with a next step that could advance your cause. I once worked with a partner named Wun Ming in an international accounting firm in China. She learned from an inside contact (her "coach") that her firm had submitted a proposal with a price structure that was not going to be competitive because it was based on the wrong assumptions. While one might correctly argue that this should have been uncovered in Stage Three or Four, sometimes we all find ourselves in a bad situation late in the game. Upon discovering the error, Wun Ming immediately worked her web of relationships. She found out that the prospect company's chairman was attending a large industry seminar that day. She jumped in her car, drove two hours, and arrived at the lunch break. She politely asked the chairman if they could talk. He listened patiently to what she had to say. He understood her position, wanted the best thing for his company, and agreed to wait for a revised proposal, which eventually carried the day. Sure, luck played a role in Wun Ming's success, but luck would not have mattered if she had not made the effort to extend the game in Stage Five. It reminded me of the time Isiah Thomas scored 16 points in the last 90 seconds of the game to bring his Detroit Pistons back from the brink and push a playoff game into overtime.

Recently, a workshop participant told me a story that clearly demonstrates why professionals must continue to reach out to the client or prospect in Stage Five. This person was a partner in an accounting firm and led a proposal effort in pursuit of a medium-sized manufacturer. The proposal process took place in September, with a decision to be made by mid-October. The decision date came and went, so the partner called the prospect to see what was up. The prospect said that other issues had arisen, so they hadn't had a chance to discuss the offers they'd received. The accounting firm partner asked when he should follow up and was told to call in mid-November. He did so, and it was the same story. There was still no decision. The same thing happened in mid-December and mid-January. When the partner called in mid-February, however, he got his answer. The prospect happily told him that his firm had won the engagement. When the partner asked what had led to this decision, the prospect told him he won because he was "the only one who kept calling."

The partner in this example played the game well not only because he stayed proactive in Stage Five, but because he continued to use positioning closes to gain agreement with the prospect to follow up in a given time frame. He put those coins in the trust bank and showed the prospect that he really wanted to work with the company.

When the Trial Close Is Accepted, Ask for the Business

Several years ago, I was in a discussion with a newly appointed marketing director with whom I had worked at his previous firm. He had landed a new position at a large, national law firm and was anxious to log some visible progress at his new employer's Los Angeles office. He wanted to use me to kick off a project aimed at developing business in the high-tech market. Previously, we had had several conversations about what he wanted to accomplish and his conditions of satisfaction. In other words, we had shaped the service. I had also summarized the Scorecard a couple of times, and each time the summary was met with agreement. Yet, no specific next step was offered. Finally, I said something like, "I understand the situation. You want to make your mark and get things going. So what happens now? What do we need to do to get this thing going?" When I asked how to move ahead, it was like someone turned on a faucet and water poured out. Dean proceeded to tell me exactly what he and I needed to do. We booked dates for an initial visit to Los Angeles and for the follow-up workshop. But Dean did not offer this information until I *asked for the business*. Of course, if I hadn't asked for the business, I might have obtained it at a later date anyway. But in this case, it was more beneficial for Dean to start the project as soon as possible than it was for me. In other words, asking for the business provided more value to the buyer than the seller.

I learned a lesson from this experience that you would do well to keep in mind as you play the SalesGame. If you do not ask for the business after the trial close has been accepted, you could be doing your client or prospect a disservice—not to mention wasting your own time. In my example, Dean wanted to demonstrate what an effective business-development effort could produce to enhance his image within his new firm. By delaying the project, however, he was at risk of missing an opportunity to make a difference and secure the goodwill of those to whom he reported. On the other side of the ledger, if I did not push a little after the trial close was accepted, I was at risk of losing the work to someone else who might have another way into the firm. At best, I would have been less efficient by taking the time to set up and make repeated calls to someone who already had agreed with the Scorecard we had developed together. If you truly believe you can offer a service that a client or prospect needs, then it is in everyone's best interest for you to ask for the business.

> If you truly believe you can offer a service that a
> client or prospect needs, then it is in everyone's best
> interest for you to ask for the business.

Maybe you've faced this same kind of situation. A client or prospect has talked to you about something he or she wants to accomplish. You have shaped the service. In some cases, you may even have developed a non-competitive proposal summarizing the project. And still you wait…and wait…and wait for the green light to begin work. In most cases, moving forward simply requires that you ask for the business.

In one of my workshops, I once worked with two partners from an accounting firm in Boston who had been chasing a special project for a real-estate developer. They had made repeated calls to find out the status of their non-competitive proposal, but each call was met with some delaying tactic. In our small group discussion, the partners wanted to work through this situation. It became obvious that they were in Stage Five but could not get the client to allow them to start the work. I asked them if they had ever simply said something like, "Gentlemen, we've been talking about this for six months. You want to develop that piece of property, and you're going to have to get a feasibility study done to share with your investors. We seem to be in complete agreement as to the best way to get the study done. We're excited about the project and want to be part of the team. What's standing between us and doing the work?" Of course, they had not been this direct. We talked about how to make the call and ease into a final close like the one I suggested. They made the call during a break in the workshop and the developer told them they were right. He told them they were his conscience reminding him to get in gear. They made arrangements to start the work immediately.

While I know this sounds too good to be true, it is only one of many examples of professionals failing to make the final close, particularly in sole-source or more informal situations. Even if it is a routine request, like in my case when I wanted my tax accountant to tell me how much I would owe the IRS if I sold a piece of property, you should follow the accepted trial close with a final close asking to start the work. In that example in Chapter 41, "Stage Four: Close to Ensure Client Satisfaction and Surface Hidden Objections," the trial close was, "So, Larry, you want to know if you should consider this guy's offer based on how much you'd pay in taxes.

You need to get back to him in a couple of days, so you want me to check this out before Tuesday and give you a call back with a rough idea. No report—you only want a verbal summary. I think that will take me just a couple of hours. Are we on the same page?" Assuming the answer was yes, the accountant should have gone on to a final close, with something like the following: "I'll get started on it this afternoon. I will call you Tuesday with what I find. What time works for you?"

It is important to recognize that you have the right—and maybe even the responsibility—to ask for permission to start the work if you have gone through the sales process and shaped your service to respond to the client or prospect's needs. How aggressive an attorney, wealth manager, accountant, or other professional is when making this final close is obviously a matter of style. But at this point, you really should not be overly concerned about being too pushy. Being pushy is more of a problem when you're making the transition from Stage Two to Stage Three, when you see a need but the client or prospect does not. If you and the client or prospect have moved through Stages One through Four, both of you should benefit from moving forward. If not, it means there is something that the client or prospect is not telling you. Asking for the business with a final close to gain permission to start the work will either move the process ahead, as in the earlier examples, or surface any remaining issues. I worked with a lobbyist in Washington, D.C., who used the final close with a non-profit organization. This surfaced a budgetary constraint that would go away in three months. She then knew exactly what the situation was, did not pester the non-profit with repeated calls, and, I am sure, reduced her own worry quotient considerably.

43

Chapter

Stage Six: Close to Create Future Qualified Leads

In the final stage of the SalesGame, you do one of two things:

- Talk with a client for whom you have completed at least one cycle of work—for example, after completing the audit, finishing depositions, or reviewing portfolio performance.

- Talk with a prospect who has chosen not to use your services at this time.

As discussed in Part 1, "An Overview of the SalesGame," no other stage is overlooked as often as Stage Six. This is most unfortunate because Stage Six provides an excellent opportunity to create leads for the future.

Closing in Stage Six usually takes the form of a positioning close. That is, you ask for a next step to maintain contact with a satisfied client or a prospect who has chosen not to use your services. An advancing close may also conclude Stage Six if the discussion with the client or prospect reveals a new opportunity to be of service.

Close with Enthusiastic Clients to Build Bridges for the Future

Ensuring client enthusiasm is a critical part of the SalesGame for three reasons:

- It is the only way you know you have achieved your goal—to create an enthusiastic client.

- A meeting to assure client enthusiasm (ACE) reinforces the value and good feelings that you have created during the engagement.

- It is an excellent opportunity to build leads for the future. In fact, most professionals find that at least half these meetings generate new business in the short run.

No professional religiously conducts client ACE meetings with every client he or she serves. As with most marketing activities, you need to set priorities so you can be as efficient and effective as possible with your use of time. Clearly, not all clients offer the same potential to develop work beyond the present engagement. For example, a labor and employment attorney would get far more benefit from an ACE meeting with a Fortune 500 client who is likely to use his or her services on a regular basis than a small client who had a one-off case. Of course, an ACE meeting could be beneficial in either case—for example, the small client might provide a referral or be bought by a larger company. (I once worked with an attorney in a small market who handled a piece of litigation for one such small client. One year later, said small client was acquired by a large conglomerate and generated almost half a million dollars in fees for the attorney. Sometimes even a blind squirrel finds an acorn!) But the payoff would likely be far greater with the larger client. When prioritizing opportunities for Stage Six meetings, you must consider the client's current and potential fees and leverage potential.

Each client ACE meeting should end with a positioning close or an advancing close to promote forward movement toward obtaining future work. The next step should either maintain the relationship with the current client or prospect or build a new relationship with someone else in the same company who could become a qualified lead. For example, when an accountant finishes a project to redesign an auto dealership's warranty review program, he or she should conduct an ACE meeting that would end with a positioning close, such as establishing a follow-up telephone call to see how the new warranty program is working or agreeing to go to a baseball game. This type of positioning close would keep the accountant on the client's radar screen, which is helpful if another opportunity arises.

While the primary purpose of a Stage Six meeting is not to sell but to assess the client's level of enthusiasm, these meetings do generate additional work about 50% of the time. As a managing partner of a law firm who conducted ACE meetings on a regular basis told his colleagues, "I'm there to make sure we're doing a great job. But if they open the door wide enough by asking if we do X service, I'll walk right through!"

> "I'm there to make sure we're doing a great job. But if they open the door wide enough by asking if we do X service, I'll walk right through!"

You can generate new opportunities in a Stage Six ACE meeting in a couple of ways. In some cases, the client will bring up something that leads to new work. One attorney I know who handled litigation for a company's operations in one region was asked at the end of an ACE meeting with the general counsel if his firm could extend its coverage to another region. The close in this case was to agree that the general counsel would set up a meeting with the appropriate people in the new region—a classic example of a close that advanced the cause. As another example, a director of a wealth-management company was pleasantly surprised when, at the end of an ACE meeting, the client said he had another "bucket" of money he wanted to add to his portfolio. In this case, the professional used a positioning close to set up another meeting with the client to see how to best allocate the new funds.

In other cases, the professional can generate new business opportunities by arriving at the ACE meeting with a game plan that includes an area of questioning and a next step. For example, a financial advisor might open an area of questioning focused on his client's long-term plans and suggest a meeting with a colleague who specializes in estate planning to advance the cause. There are many ways to use an ACE meeting to leverage a current client's enthusiasm, such as the following:

■ Meeting someone else in the organization who might benefit from your expertise

■ An introduction to someone at another organization who might have similar needs

■ An introduction to a third-party advisor who serves the same client

■ An invitation to attend an industry-association meeting with the client to build your network or even to make a joint presentation about the successful project

Next steps to advance the cause might be planned, such as the ones I just mentioned, or might develop organically out of the discussion. Either way, you should use an advancing close to promote forward movement when an opportunity presents itself.

Close with Lost Opportunities to Build Relationships and Position for the Future

Stage Six opportunities also include those situations when you have pursued a qualified lead but were not successful in your efforts. Conversations of this nature are often referred to as "reasons for loss meetings"—although I dislike referring to these situations as *losses*. As mentioned, I prefer to think of it the way a partner I knew in an accounting firm did: "We didn't lose. We just haven't won yet!" Nevertheless, there will likely be times in your career when situations such as the following occur:

■ A competitive proposal is awarded to another firm.

■ A client or prospect elects to use internal resources rather than an outside professional service firm.

■ A particular service is no longer needed because the transaction or deal goes away for some reason—for example, a merger falls through.

■ A client or prospect decides not to undertake a particular project at the current time—for example, the owner of a prosperous family business wants to wait to commence with succession planning.

In each of these cases, you are missing a wonderful opportunity to build relationships and develop leads if you fail to arrange a Stage Six discussion to learn what you might have done differently to change the outcome and close by asking for a next step to position for the future. Much like the close used with an enthusiastic client, a Stage Six meeting for a client or prospect who has decided *not* to use your services will usually take the form of a positioning close or, less often, an advancing close to promote forward movement.

After you conduct a Stage Six meeting to determine what happened with a lost opportunity, you need to close with a next step such as one of the following:

■ Establishing a time for a follow-up call with the same client or prospect contact

■ Arranging a meeting with the same client or prospect to discuss a different area of need

■ Meeting someone else in the organization who might provide insight as to how to be more effective in the future

■ Meeting with someone else in the organization who may have needs that your service could address

The first two next steps are positioning closes. The next two are advancing closes to promote movement. I used to work with a managing partner at an accounting firm who, in Stage Six meetings, always asked, "If we can't do this project for you, what *can* we do?" This question often led to a next step to pursue a new opportunity.

When dealing with blind or generic proposals, professionals often use a Stage Six meeting to open the door to new opportunities. I've often said that the only time you should pursue an RFP when you've had no previous contact with the issuer is if you are committed to arranging a Stage Six meeting to create opportunities for the future. Even if the rules of the game don't allow contact during the RFP process, they *do* allow contact after the process has been completed and a winner chosen. For example, an Irish accounting firm I worked with bid on the audit of a port authority even though they were quite certain they wouldn't acquire the work. They then followed up with a Stage Six meeting to talk about the process and uncovered many additional needs that would not be met by performing an audit. Over the next two years, the firm was able to acquire several consulting engagements to address these needs. Oh, and the profitability of the consulting work was far greater than that of the audit work!

In some cases, holding a Stage Six meeting with a prospect who decided not to buy may even generate new leads with other buyers. When I was selling research, I always tried to debrief with prospects who did not buy the package to learn what I might have done differently or how the package could be changed to make it more attractive. Surprisingly, prospects in many of these debriefings actually helped set up meetings with their competitors, who they thought could better use my service.

If I told the truth about my own business-development efforts, my prospect file contains many leads that arose from a lost opportunity, but that I did not follow up on as religiously as I should have. I will never forget a marketing director I worked with from a law firm in Birmingham, Alabama. I had developed a proposal and met face to face with the marketing committee, only to have them decide not to undertake any program at all for the time being. Nevertheless, the marketing director and I had started to develop a good relationship. I used a positioning close and talked to her again six months later, then six months after that, and so on.

Eventually, however, I became a bit lazy. I failed to follow up as we had agreed. A year later, I finally called her, only to learn that she had moved to another law firm, which her former employer refused to identify. I lost a potentially good lead for the future. We all make mistakes, of course, but the key is to at least ask for a next step and close, even in Stage Six with lost opportunities, to continue positioning for the future.

Part Summary

Closing is a process, not an event like obtaining a signed engagement letter. It occurs throughout the six stages each time you gain agreement with the client or prospect on a specific next step call. Every business-development meeting involves a close. Closing does not necessarily happen at the end of the meeting. Agreement on a next step might occur in the early, middle, or late stages of a business-development meeting. Closing is an important tool in the SalesGame because it can be used for many purposes, such as surfacing hidden objections and finding the real decision-maker.

Closing happens at every stage of the SalesGame and helps you identify the best ways to meet the client or prospect's needs. Regardless of what type of close you are making, you should remember six best practices to improve your closing skills:

- Prepare for every meeting by identifying two next steps that advance the cause.

- Set up the close with a must-ask question, like those discussed in Chapter 36, "Ask the Must-Ask Question." If the client or prospect responds to the must-ask question with something that's actionable, use that suggestion rather than the ones you prepared in advance.

- When asking for a next step, avoid a yes/no question. Instead, involve the client or prospect in choosing implementation alternatives.

- Use the Ground Rule to respond to a rejected close. This enables you to explore the obstacles keeping you from moving ahead in the SalesGame.

- Close as soon as possible. Don't wait until the end of the meeting. If an opportunity for an advancing close comes up early in the conversation, take advantage of it. You will be more comfortable and confident during the remainder of the conversation. You should also be sure to launch a trial close as soon as you have a clear vision of the client or prospect's Scorecard. This helps you avoid overselling and provides you with time to use the Ground Rule if you are rejected. If you're not sure when to close, listen for implementation questions. If the client or prospect asks an implementation question, it suggests he or she is deciding *how* to proceed, not whether he or she should move ahead.

- Avoid writing as a next step at any stage in the SalesGame. Writing is very time-consuming and rarely builds relationships or makes Scorecard Factors real. If you are asked to write a proposal, explore what the particular client or prospect means by this term. If a proposal is required as part of the buying process, ask to develop and review a draft proposal instead of submitting the final version, which is frequently not read.

Before every meeting, identify where you are in the sales process and determine the next step or close that will improve your chances of moving ahead. In Stage One, you should close or ask for a next step that will allow you to have a more in-depth discussion with your contact. In other words, connect with the client or prospect by e-mail, phone, social networking, etc. to express interest in arranging a future discussion to talk more about business. Never sell during any Stage One activity. Instead, close by setting up a next step. When setting up the next step, sell the meeting, not the service. You do not need to close with everyone you meet in Stage One marketing activities, only with those who share a mutual interest in a business topic, offer the potential for good chemistry, and represent a desirable target.

Closing in Stage Two takes two different forms: a positioning close or a close to advance the cause by building a new relationship or making a potential Scorecard Factor real. The positioning close is often effective in Stage Two because you can use it to stay in touch with a desirable client or prospect over a long period of time until he or she recognizes a need and becomes a qualified lead. A best practice is to mix next steps that position with those that advance the cause. Regardless of which type of close you are using, a next step should create value, even if only providing a good time for the client or prospect. A positioning close is more likely to occur when you initiate contact rather than when responding. Each time you use a positioning close to establish the next contact and follow up appropriately, it is like putting a coin in a trust bank. You will frequently use closes that advance the cause in Stage Two if you are responding to an opportunity with a new prospect either from a referral or an RFP. When you respond to clients in Stage Two, you may move through the stages quickly and get to Stage Five in one conversation. If so, it is important to use a trial close to make sure the service meets the client's expectations and to avoid an easy sale that might lead to an unhappy client. Try to advance your cause by arranging a meeting or phone call with the decision-maker as soon as appropriate in Stage Two. Only when you meet with the decision-maker and determine whether he or she has a recognized need will you truly have a qualified lead. Professionals often use a positioning close when they could be more proactive with a close that advances their cause. Stage Two often lasts over a long period of time. You can use this time to build relationships and demonstrate selling points before the lead becomes qualified.

In Stage Three, you are by definition dealing with a qualified lead, and should close to meet more often rather than less. Meeting more means you can develop chemistry, increase dialogue, better differentiate your firm, demonstrate the value of your services, and send a message you really want the work—a major buying criterion. Using advancing closes that promote forward movement by either building relationships or making Scorecard Factors more tangible is the key to better performance in this stage of the SalesGame. Building relationships is the most important consideration. Research shows that good chemistry is the most common reason clients or prospects choose a professional. You can differentiate your firm with advancing closes to make your resources more tangible, even when competitors offer the same service. Professionals often rush to a close—for example, writing a proposal or making a presentation—but extending the process is far more likely to lead to success.

Stage Four is the trial close. Here, you should ask if the service you are proposing meets the needs of the client or prospect. This question can be raised in a formal scenario, such as an oral presentation, or in an informal one, such as on a phone call with a client. Do not fear rejection when making a trial close. Each rejection is an opportunity to modify the service to be sure it meets the client or prospect's expectations. In fact, a best practice is to extend Stage Four by using a trial close to ensure the goal of the SalesGame is achieved—that is, to create an enthusiastic client. There are two techniques to extend Stage Four when dealing with a more formal proposal scenario. First, you can review a draft of a proposal with the client or prospect. This discussion is nothing more than a long trial close, testing the accuracy of your analysis of the client or prospect's situation and corresponding service solution. Each revision of the draft increases agreement between you and the client or prospect on the Scorecard and leads to a greater chance of success. Second, you can ask for another follow-up meeting or phone call at the end of an oral presentation. The purpose of this discussion is to review any questions that might arise after a client or prospect has heard from several different vendors. The follow-up discussion creates another opportunity for you to obtain feedback and modify your service package as necessary. You should use a trial close even if you are certain you will obtain an engagement—for example, if a client calls asking to expand the scope of work. By extending the conversation long enough to summarize the Scorecard and test your accuracy, you dramatically reduce the chances of having an easy sale lead to a dissatisfied client. A trial close also may be used by younger professionals when they are asked to do work by someone more senior. One of the most important reasons to use a trial close in any setting is that it brings to the surface any hidden objections—issues that the client or prospect is reluctant to discuss.

Stage Five is the final close. Here, you ask for a next step to start the work—that is, you ask for the business. It occurs only after you have qualified the lead, shaped the service, and made sure there is a shared vision of the Scorecard—that is, after your trial close has been accepted. An advancing close to promote movement may also occur in Stage Five if you learn new information that changes the way you should shape the service. The nature of the final close will depend on the situation. In more competitive situations, you should ask for a specific next step to start the work after you are awarded the engagement. If you are awarded an engagement in a situation where pre-proposal contact is prohibited, you should use the final close to go back to a Stage Three meeting to shape the service. If you fail to do this, you may acquire the work but end up with an unenthusiastic client. Many large companies now issue RFPs to cover several areas of service. These often result in a firm that wins and is put on an approved list but does not receive any actual work. To avoid this, you should close to develop relationships with users throughout the sales process—especially in Stage Five.

If you discover that you did not obtain a particular piece of work, you should use the final close to ask for a meeting to discuss ways to improve performance in the future and position for new opportunities. In more informal situations, you should ask for permission to start the work as soon as the trial close is accepted. Professionals often fear being too pushy in Stage Five and are reluctant to ask for the business even after the trial close has been accepted. But if you truly believe you have a service your client or prospect needs, then it is in everyone's best interest for you to ask for the business. Sometimes, the client or prospect will move ahead and grant permission to start the work only when asked to do so.

Ensuring client enthusiasm in Stage Six is important for several reasons, including making sure you have achieved your goal, reinforcing value from the engagement, and generating new leads. A positioning close—asking for a next step to maintain contact with a client—is the most common outcome of a Stage Six meeting. The primary purpose of an ACE (short for assuring client enthusiasm) meeting is to assess enthusiasm. However, an advancing close to promote forward movement may occur either by chance if you discover a new opportunity while you are assuring client enthusiasm or by plan if you prepare areas of questioning that could uncover potential needs. You must set priorities for ACE meetings and focus on those with the greatest potential to build the practice you desire. You should also debrief with clients and prospects who choose not to buy your services to learn what you might have done differently and be ready to close with a next step that either continues to position with the prospect (more common) or advances the cause for future opportunities. Because of time constraints and lack of interest, you may not always follow up on next steps established with clients or prospects who do not buy. The important point is to make sure to ask for a next step so you at least have the opportunity for another contact if you want to pursue the client or prospect in the future.

Now that you know all the fundamentals of the SalesGame, you are ready to put them all together to run a play. To win or be successful in any game, you must be able to effectively execute. Effective execution comes from practice (for example, scrimmages) and real-time action (that is, playing the game). Our advice is to practice and play often! To help you practice and play effectively, we have included some additional resources in Appendix A, "Marketing and Lead-Generation Activities" and Appendix B, "The Planning System." Appendix A shares some ideas on where to start—how to generate leads so you have an opportunity to play. Appendix B highlights a couple of tools for you to use to effectively prepare for meetings. In the end, we hope that the process, fundamentals, and tools help you build the practice of your dreams and achieve the goal of the game—enthusiastic clients!

Play On

Play On

Play On

Part 8

Appendixes

Marketing and Lead-Generation Activities

After 30-plus years working with thousands of professionals, I've learned that there is an almost infinite variety of ways to build relationships and develop leads—both of which occur in Stage One of the SalesGame. I've seen relationships that led to work developed from things as diverse as starting a hang-gliding club (in Wichita, Kansas, amazingly enough), to sending out holiday cards, to hosting "lunch and learns," to attending family weddings.

This appendix groups the many options into six major categories, as described in Chapter 4, "Stage One: Create and Identify Leads," to facilitate the discussion and management of these Stage One activities. The following list, which is organized into those six areas, is intended to help you generate some ideas of your own. (It is by no means a comprehensive list of all the options available; there are so many variations of basic themes—for example, sports activities—it would take an entire book to list them.)

Regardless of what type of Stage One activity you find interesting, there are some general guidelines that tend to differentiate what's successful from what is not. As in any game, there are always exceptions, but here are the principles that typically lead to success:

■ **One size does not fit all.** The type of Stage One activity that leads to success for any given professional depends on many factors—for example, level of professional advancement, type of personality, area or expertise, etc. Young professionals generally don't have a clear vision of the kind of business they want to develop nor enough experience to be an "expert," so they are more comfortable maintaining relationships with people they've already met, getting to know peers at the clients they serve, and so on. Some professionals have a gift for making small talk at cocktail hours and other semi-social events, while others are more comfortable writing articles or speaking on panels that help them become "famous." Attorneys who do appeal work might invest time in bar activities, while those who work in the automotive industry might be better served joining groups like the Original Equipment Suppliers Association (OESA).

- **Build relationships first.** All of the following activities work best if you remember that their purpose is to develop genuine relationships with those you meet. In some cases, such as staying in touch with college alumni, these relationships have already been established. Even in these situations, however, staying in touch with an alum who seems to be a likely source of business if there is not a genuine connection tends not to be very fruitful. In my experience, rarely if ever does any prospect or referral contact turn into a long-term, enjoyable source of work if no genuine relationship based on mutual compatibility and respect exists. For the record, I've worked on five continents, and this is as true in Shanghai as in Chicago, or in Dublin as in Detroit.

- **Start with vision.** As you gain experience and learn what type of work you most enjoy and want to pursue, your Stage One activities should become more defined, focusing on building relationships with those who can be most helpful to you. For example, an accountant who likes to work in the healthcare field might become active in the Hospital Financial Managers Association (HFMA) or an investment banker might find a group like the Association for Corporate Growth (ACG) to be a useful forum to meet potential clients and referral sources. Likewise, professionals who work with car dealers might write a column for a trade magazine that serves that market segment.

- **Find something to do that you enjoy.** Everyone tends to do better at things they find enjoyable than things they don't, and marketing activities are no exception. All the activities that follow take time, and all professionals are busy as they balance serving their present clients with trying to find new ones. The time you spend in Stage One activities will seem less like work and more like a break from the daily grind if you truly enjoy them. For example, it's better to be active in a church group or sports league than go to a civic club if the former is more enjoyable to you than the latter. If you do something you enjoy, you'll also be more likely to become a leader in the group, which will help you to gain more respect and build more relationships. Most importantly, you will be better able to build genuine relationships if you connect with others because you share a common interest with those you meet.

■ **Don't sell in Stage One activities.** Stage One activities are all about building relationships, not about selling work. After a relationship is established, you can move to Stage Two with an expression of interest in working with your new contact. A simple phrase like, "You know, we ought to get together to see if there might be some ways we could help one another" is usually enough to transition from Stage One to Stage Two. There are also many other ways to make this transition. The important point is to use a Stage One activity to set up a Stage Two meeting. Almost no one wants to be sold on a golf course or while watching a football game. Even something as inherently commercial as a trade association is a more effective forum for building relationships rather than selling. Let your contacts know you'd like to talk about business and they'll let you know if they're interested. In my experience, if professionals have even started to build a good relationship with their contact, about 99% of the time those contacts will respond positively to moving to Stage Two.

■ **Just do it.** Building relationships and creating opportunities through Stage One activities is the job of every professional who wants to build a career. Some professionals will invest more time in these activities than others because of a natural affinity for business development, but everyone who works for a professional-service firm needs to find some way to develop relationships with prospects and referral sources. Even if firm policy doesn't require professionals to engage in business development, it's always been clear to me that when it comes to compensation, promotion, partnership, and leadership, those who are active in business development are more successful than those who aren't. No one wants to make an employee a full partner who doesn't contribute to the long-term success of the firm. People who bring in business almost always receive more compensation, even if they are in a firm that supposedly uses a lock-step system that bases remuneration on number of years with the organization. Leadership positions in almost all firms are more likely to be earned by those who have demonstrated some success at business development. The bottom line for professionals is that they need to find something they can do to build relationships that can lead them to new business.

Examples of Stage One Marketing Activities

Following are several examples of Stage One marketing activities, divided into six main categories:

- Networking
- Prospecting
- Internal marketing
- Friends and family
- Promotional activities
- Present clients

Networking

- Start or maintain a list of contacts in a form that works for you.
- Get on LinkedIn.
- Stay in touch with high-school and college friends, regardless of their current career path.
- Be patient until your contacts advance in their careers so they have some knowledge or influence that might be useful. Then ask for advice, not business.
- Send holiday greeting cards.
- Send birthday greetings.
- Send congratulatory notes for promotions, new positions, family events, etc.
- Start or join a group of professionals that meets on a regular basis for lunch, breakfast, drinks, etc. and is made up of one representative from each relevant area like banking, law, insurance, wealth management, real estate, etc.
- Start or join a fantasy football or other sports league with relevant network contacts.
- Start or join a group of friends with a common, non-business interest like poker, softball, theater, symphony, spectator sports, etc.
- Find ways to collaborate with contacts so you can help them in their own business-development efforts and vice versa.

■ Use breakfasts, lunches, coffee, cocktails, etc. to cultivate and advance relationships.

■ Identify and prioritize time with contacts who are natural connectors.

■ Be a connector. Introduce people you believe will benefit from knowing each other.

Prospecting

■ Develop a list of prospects who fit your vision of practice.

■ Gather additional background information like postal and e-mail addresses.

■ Always sell the meeting, not the service. Offer something of value like ideas, updates on industry trends, contacts, etc., even if the prospect doesn't have any interest in your service.

■ Discuss your list with colleagues, networking contacts, and client contacts, or use LinkedIn to see if someone you know can arrange an introduction.

■ Send an electronic or paper newsletter for a couple of months before trying to make contact with people on your list.

■ Go to appropriate trade organizations at which your targets may be present and introduce yourself.

■ Develop a survey of interest to your target(s) and solicit their input with a promise to personally review results.

■ Use a third-party organization that specializes in prospecting calls to set up a meeting.

■ Send a letter stating you'll be calling and follow up as indicated.

■ Don't be stopped by the first objection, like, "I'm busy now" or "We're happy with our current provider." Use the Ground Rule to express understanding, mention another benefit, and ask again.

Internal Marketing

■ Get to know other professionals in your firm—that is, build a relationship—who have clients who could use your services.

■ Find out from your colleagues how they like to introduce and work with other professionals from the firm—for example, ask them how much they want to be involved in future communication.

■ Use a one-on-one meeting to review your internal colleagues' list of clients to learn about client personnel, preferences, and so on.

■ Provide ideas to your colleagues that they can use to bring value to their clients and make themselves and the firm look good.

■ Regularly attend appropriate practice groups that serve clients who could also use your services.

■ Ask the leader of an appropriate practice group if you can have two minutes to share something of value with team members—for example, a recent change in the law, an interesting engagement, or what have you.

■ Ask for an introduction to a colleague's clients in a social or semi-social setting *before* they need your services. (In other words, promise you won't make a pitch.)

Friends and Family

■ Make sure your friends know what you and your firm do…and how much you like doing it.

■ If friends and family members are in a position of influence at a prospect organization, express interest in getting together to see if there's a way you could help one another.

■ Arrange a social or sporting event to facilitate the meeting between a friend or family member and one of your enthusiastic clients.

■ If you're worried about damaging a friendship or family relationship by transitioning to business, let your friend or family member know about your concern, and that your first priority is the relationship.

■ When talking about business, don't ask for work. Instead, ask for advice.

Promotional Activities

■ Get involved in a civic, religious, or community organization in which you personally believe—for example, a not for profit, the local chamber of commerce, your parish, etc.

- Get involved in a sports league like softball, basketball, golf, or what have you that includes people you'd like to meet and may have some future influence or buying potential in the long term.

- Get involved in a trade or industry group that is consistent with your vision of practice.

- Get involved in your children's activities, like school committees, coaching or supporting sports teams, fundraising, and so on.

- Be a leader in all of the above, whether you're the person who starts the group, an officer, the head of a committee, a speaker, a panel member, or what have you.

- Write articles with key buzzwords on hot topics that will be picked up if someone searches for information on a related subject on the Internet.

- Write articles for a client or industry trade group's newsletter.

- Post relevant articles on LinkedIn or other social media.

Present Clients

- Conduct assuring client enthusiasm (ACE) meetings to make sure you have an enthusiastic client.

- Reach out on a regular basis—for example, quarterly—to clients who might need additional services.

- Make sure your clients know you'd like a referral by asking them to be a reference, getting excited about a new client, or telling them directly.

- When a client raves about your services, thank them and ask who else you should be talking to.

- Meet other players in the client organization who might need your services or be able to introduce you to others who do.

- Stay in touch with former client personnel with whom you have worked. They may move to a new or similar organization with a need for your services.

- Introduce colleagues with different skill sets to your clients before they need them so they know the resources are there.

- Get to know your clients on their home turf to meet their peers.

- Sponsor an event for clients to which they can bring their peers.

- Get to know the other professionals who serve your client—for example, accountants, attorneys, bankers, wealth advisors, real estate professionals, etc.

- Co-author an article or co-present at a trade or professional group with a client.

- Do a seminar, "lunch and learn," or presentation for your clients' clients.

The Planning System

As described in Part 1, "An Overview of the SalesGame," one of the best practices in planning is to follow a system. Our system combines the use of the Sales Planning Checklist and a Play Diagram, both of which are described in this appendix.

Following the Sales Planning Checklist

The Sales Planning Checklist will enable you to plan more effectively. The checklist is a tool to facilitate collaboration and generate ideas. It's a little like the list that college and pro quarterbacks wear on their wrist or the laminated cards that coaches carry on the sidelines.

Here's our Sales Planning Checklist:

1. **Set up the meeting.** How you do this depends on whether you are responding to an inquiry from a client or prospect or initiating contact yourself. If you are responding, be sure to gather the right information. If you are initiating, be sure to "sell the meeting."

2. **Identify the players in the game.** List client/prospect contacts who will be involved in the decision process. Note whether each person is a decision-maker, an influencer, a user, or a coach, and consider the strength of the relationship you have with each one. Remember, players in the game can often include outside advisors, family members, or others on a team that might be using your solution. Note them all—not just the ones who will be attending the meeting—and constantly monitor what you are doing to manage the network of relationships.

3.   **Define the purpose.** Decide what you want to accomplish as a result of the meeting. Your purpose will depend on your stage in the sales process and should help you identify what questions you want to ask and how to best facilitate the meeting.

4.   **Identify what you need to do *before* the meeting with the client or prospect.** This might include adding the client or prospect's name to your firm's tracking system, calling a referral source to thank them and gain information about the lead, gathering public information about the client or prospect, reviewing their website, rehearsing the discussion, and other steps.

5.   **Develop the Scorecard.** Regardless of where you are in the process, you want to think about what the Scorecard might look like in that moment. Considering the Scorecard will help you determine whether you need to ask more questions to uncover the Heart of the Matter and the Scorecard Factors or how you might get confirmation from the client or prospect based on your current understanding. Reviewing the Scorecard can also help you think about your own selling points and how to best position or strategize.

6.   **Develop open-ended questions.** Identify three or four areas of inquiry, and then start with broad information gathering (BIG) questions. Also, be sure to include a must-ask question.

7.   **Develop responses to objections and tough questions.** Going into each meeting, consider what objections may arise or what tough questions the client or prospect might ask you. Then, develop your response. To do this, use the Ground Rule.

8.   **Plan the best meeting opener.** First, identify areas for small talk. Then prepare the transition using the TEPE approach. Be sure to rehearse the transition out loud before the meeting.

9.   **Determine possible next steps for the close.** Remember the best practices for closing and always be prepared with two closes. A good advancing close makes a Scorecard Factor real or develops a relationship.

Tip

As you've probably noticed, this book has discussed the underlying concepts behind each of the steps in this checklist. If you need a refresher on any of these concepts, use the index at the back of the book to locate coverage of them in this book.

Creating a Play Diagram

I've noticed that some workshop participants become lost in the minutia when using the Sales Planning Checklist. They have a hard time seeing the big picture. To help with this, I started having them generate a Play Diagram. A Play Diagram is a tool to help you get the key points all down on one page. This makes it easier to develop a vision for the meeting, to see how you will start the meeting, and to identify where you want to go during the meeting. Figure B.1 shows an example of a blank Play Diagram.

As you can see, many of the nine points in the Sales Planning Checklist sync up with blanks on the Play Diagram (although not always in the same order). That means you can use the Sales Planning Checklist to fill out the Play Diagram. For example:

■ Use point 2 in the checklist to fill out the "Role in the buying process" line. On the Play Diagram, you will note with whom you are meeting, but you should always consider the connections with other players.

■ Use point 3 to fill out the "Stage in process" line.

■ Use point 5 to fill out the "Positive Scorecard Factors" line.

■ Use point 6 to fill out the "BIG Questions" and "Must-Ask Question" lines.

■ Use point 7 to fill out the "Anticipated Objection(s)" line.

■ Use point 8 to fill out the "Opening" line.

■ Use point 9 to fill out the "Closes/Possible Next Steps" line.

When you use the Sales Planning Checklist to create a Play Diagram, you follow two of the three best practices for preparation—having a system and writing things down. In this way, you can create a picture in your mind of the meeting you are going to conduct.

Note

As mentioned, I can't overstate the importance of collaboration—the last of the three best practices for preparation. Your Play Diagram will always be more useful if you assemble it with a colleague, a business-development professional, or even a friend or family member. After all, this isn't rocket science. Almost everyone can listen to the wording of a question or an iteration of the Ground Rule and know whether it sounds good or bad!

SalesGame   **Play Diagram**

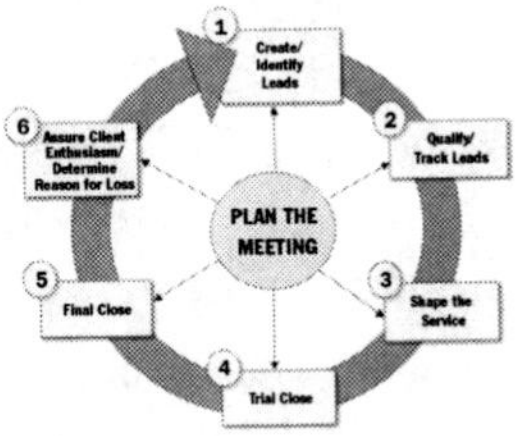

Meeting With: _____

Date of the Meeting: _____   **Stage in Process:** _____

Role in the "Buying Process" (Circle One):
       Decision Maker   Influencer   User   Coach

Opening - Transition Statement (Thanks, Express interest, Purpose, Easy question — TEPE):

B.I.G. (Broad Information Gathering) Questions (Consider Areas of Inquiry Based on Purpose):

1.

2.

3.

4.

"Must Ask" Question for This Meeting:

Closes/Possible Next Steps (to Maintain Contact and/or Advance Relationship—Identify at Least Two):

1.

2.

Anticipated Objection(s)/Tough Questions – Draft of "Ground Rule" Response

---

Positive Scorecard Factors (Positive "Selling Points")

1.

2.

3.

Copyright © 2015. SalesGame LLC. All Rights Reserved.

Figure B.1   A blank Play Diagram.

The Play Diagram was so effective for my workshop participants, I started using it in my own practice. I soon discovered that there are three collateral benefits to using this tool:

■ It shortens the planning process. You no longer get lost in the details. With the Play Diagram, you can keep the big picture in mind.

■ It's a great way to get multiple professionals involved in the same meeting on the same page, much like a football or basketball team.

■ It enables you to prepare on the fly on those occasions—and we all encounter them—when you don't have time to plan the way you would like.

With regard to the last point, I recently had one such experience. Due to plane delays, I had arrived in my client's city very late one night for an early breakfast meeting the next day. As I drove to the meeting, I thought about how I wanted to approach it. I found myself picturing the Play Diagram in my mind. Suddenly, I felt confident about how I wanted the meeting to go. Not surprisingly, the meeting went well! I've had many workshop alumni tell me they had the same experience. One caveat: Planning a meeting in your head like this only works if you use the Play Diagram to write down your thoughts on a regular basis. At least once a month seems to work well.

Execute Your Plan

One final point should be made about preparation. No matter how much or how well professionals prepare, part of what will dictate how well they play is how well they execute. At one time or another, all pro receivers drop passes, even though the coach drew up a perfect play. Likewise, I've made many mistakes executing my plan in business-development meetings. No one is perfect. Nevertheless, good preparation will always increase your chances of playing well!

A

ACE (assuring client enthusiasm)
    meetings, 65–67, 363–365
acquaintances. *See* friends and family
activities (Stage One), 335
advancing closes
    best practices, 321–324
    Stage Three, 345–347
    Stage Two, 339–341
agreement (Ground Rule), 206, 209–214
"all the same" objections (Ground
    Rule), 263
alternatives (Quadrant Four), 123
analyzing networks of relationships,
    16–17
apostles (clients), 8–9
areas of inquiry
    BIG questions, 305–307
    collaborating, 308–309
    developing, 303
    drilling down, 307–308
    Ground Rule, 307–308
    POGO, 309–310
    starting broad and easy, 305–306
    vision, 304
asking for business (Stage Four), 51–52
assuring client enthusiasm (ACE)
    meetings, 65–67, 363–365
attire, creating impressions, 272–274
awareness of resources (Quadrant
    Three), 117–118

B

being late (creating impressions), 275
benefits
    objections (Ground Rule), 235–237,
        247
    Scorecard Factors, 171–176
best practices
    closing
        advancing closes, 321–324
        Ground Rule, 326–328, 332
        must-ask questions, 324–325
        overview, 319–321
        positioning closes, 321–324
        rejection, 326–328
        setting up closes, 324–325
        when to close, 328–330
        writing proposals, 330–332
        yes/no questions, 325–326
    planning, 74–76
    Quadrant Four, 125
    questions, 295–296
bidding (Stage Five), 355
BIG (broad information gathering)
    questions
    areas of inquiry, 305–307
    overview, 300–301
broad and easy
    areas of inquiry, 305–306
    questions, 296

building (*continued*)

  practice, selling work comparison, 8

  rapport

    greetings, 278

    introductions, 278

    overview, 277

    simplicity, 278–279

    time, 279–280

  relationships

    closing, 344

    listening, 7–8

    penetrate and radiate strategy, 17

    positioning, 6

    positioning leads, 38–39

    Quadrant One, 104–106

    Stage One, 23–24

    Stage Three, 344

    stages of the SalesGame. *See* stages of the SalesGame

business, asking for, 51–52

business-development process. *See* stages of the SalesGame

C

calling (Stage Two), 36

checking questions, 218, 299

checklists (Sales Planning Checklist), 383–384

choosing right situations (Quadrant Four), 120–123, 133–134

clarity (Scorecard), 149–150

clients. *See also* **prospects**

  ACE meetings, 65–67, 363–365

  analyzing networks of relationships, 16–17

  apostles, 8–9

  coaches, 15–16

  connecting (Ground Rule), 211–214

  decision-makers

    overview, 13

    Quadrant Two, 111–113

    qualified leads, 6, 340

    Stage Three, 45–46

    Stage Two, 340

enthusiasm

  ACE meetings, 65–67, 363–365

  assuring. *See* Stage Six

  closing, 348, 352–353

  goals, 4–5

  Stage Four, 352–353

  Stage Three, 348

getting information

  marketing, 97–98

  next steps, 100–102

  Quadrant One, 95–102

  Quadrant Two, 110–111

  recognized needs, 98–99

  referrals, 97–98

  time frame, 99–100

  who is calling, 96–97

Heart of the Matter

  overview, 157

  Quadrant Four, 164–170

  Quadrant One, 160–164

  Quadrant Three, 164–170

  Quadrant Two, 111–113, 160–164

  refining (Ground Rule), 223–226

  Scorecard, 147–149, 151

  services/value comparison, 158–160

  Stage Three, 43–48

  value, defined, 157–158

influencers, 14–15

initiating contact (Quadrant Three)

  awareness of resources, 117–118

  cross-selling, 86, 116–117

  cross-serving, 116–117

  facilitated self-discovery, 118

  goals, 88–90

  Heart of the Matter, 164–170

  importance of, 90–91

  issues, 116–117

  next steps, 88–90

  overview, 86–87, 115–116

  products, 116–117

  Scorecard, 164–170

  value statements, 118

loss. *See* Stage Six

objectives. *See* Heart of the Matter

players overview, 11–12
present clients (Stage One), 381–382
questions, interrogating, 219
responding (Quadrant Two)
    decision-makers, 111–113
    getting information, 110–111
    Heart of the Matter, 111–113,
        160–164
    overview, 86, 109
    recognized needs, 87–88
    responding quickly, 110–111
    Scorecard, 160–164
satisfaction, 8–9
    conditions of satisfaction, 171–176
    objections (Ground Rule), 251–253
Scorecard. See Scorecard
sole-source clients (Scorecard Factors),
    178–179
Stage Six (assuring enthusiasm)
    ACE meetings, 65–67, 363–365
    closing overview, 363
    following up after loss, 67–69,
        366–368
    Ground Rule, 203
    must-ask questions, 313–314
    overview, 63–64
    positioning for future, 69–71,
        366–368
    Scorecard, 154
thanking (TEPE), 283
users, 14
words (Ground Rule), 212–213
closed-ended questions, 240, 297–300
closing
    advancing closes
        best practices, 321–324
        Stage Three, 345–347
        Stage Two, 339–341
    best practices
        advancing closes, 321–324
        Ground Rule, 326–328, 332
        must-ask questions, 324–325
        overview, 319–321
        positioning closes, 321–324
        rejection, 326–328

setting up closes, 324–325
when to close, 328–330
writing proposals, 330–332
yes/no questions, 325–326
continuing
    Stage Five, 59–61, 358–361
    Stage Four, 352
creative closes (Quadrant One),
    102–104
final close. See Stage Five
positioning closes
    best practices, 321–324
    Stage Two, 337–341
positioning for future, 69–71, 366–368
Stage Five (final close)
    competitive bids, 355
    confirming financial arrangement,
        61–62
    continuing to close, 59–61, 358–361
    formal bids, 355
    Ground Rule, 203
    identifying obstacles, 58–59
    losing, 357
    must-ask questions, 313–314
    overview, 57–58, 355
    RFPs, 356–357
    Scorecard, 154
Stage Four (trial close)
    asking for business, 51–52
    client enthusiasm, 352–353
    continuing contact, 352
    continuing to close, 352
    draft proposals, 350–351
    extending, 52–55
    Ground Rule, 203
    hidden objections, 353–354
    must-ask questions, 313–314
    overview, 49–51, 349–350
    Scorecard, 49, 51–52, 153
Stage One
    marketing activities, 335
    overview, 333
    seminars, 333–335
Stage Six, 363

closing (*continued*)

Stage Three
advancing closes, 345–347
building relationships, 344
client enthusiasm, 348
differentiating services, 345–347
overview, 343–344
Stage Two
advancing closes, 339–341
decision-makers, 340
overview, 337
positioning closes, 337–341
trial close. *See* Stage Four
clothing, creating impressions, 272–274
coaches, 15–16
collaborating
areas of inquiry, 308–309
planning, 75
competitive bids (Stage Five), 355
conditions of satisfaction (Scorecard
Factors), 171–176
confidence (creating impressions), 274
confirming/verifying
financial arrangement (Stage Five),
61–62
questions, 299
connecting with clients/prospects
(Ground Rule), 211–214
contact
continuing (Stage Four), 352
initiating. *See* initiating contact
contacts (Quadrant Four), 130–133
continuing
closing
Stage Five, 59–61, 358–361
Stage Four, 352
contact (Stage Four), 352
cost. *See* price
coverage gaps (objections), 249–251
creating
impressions
being late, 275
confidence, 274
dress, 272–274

overview, 271–272
punctuality, 274–275
leads (Stage One)
Stage One, 28–29
building relationships, 23–24
closing, 333–335
friends and family, 380
Ground Rule, 203
initiating contact, 29–31
internal marketing, 379–380
marketing activities, 335
must-ask questions, 313–314
networking, 378–379
not selling, 26–28, 35
overview, 21–23
present clients, 381–382
principles, 375–377
promotional activities, 380–381
prospecting, 379
Scorecard, 153
sell the meeting, not the service, 31
seminars, 333–335
success, 375–377
vision of practice, 24–26
creative closes (Quadrant One), 102–104
cross-selling (Quadrant Three), 86,
116–117
cross-serving (Quadrant Three), 116–117
current clients (Stage One), 381–382

D

danger zone (Ground Rule), 218
decision-makers
overview, 13
Quadrant Two, 111–113
qualified leads, 6, 340
Stage Three, 45–46
Stage Two, 340
definable groups (Quadrant Four),
122–123
depth (objections), 260
developing areas of inquiry, 303
diagram (Play Diagram), 385–387

differentiating services
  honesty, 192–193
  long term, 188–189
  negative Scorecard Factors, 189–191
  objections, 190
  overview, 183–184
  power of three, 186–187
  responsibility, 192–193
  Stage Three, 345–347
  starting early, 184–186
  tangibility, 187–188
distance (objections), 259–260
don't sell approach, 26–28, 35
dress, creating impressions, 272–274
drilling down (areas of inquiry), 307–308

E
emotions (Ground Rule), 206–207
ending
  TEPE, 287–289
  with questions, 219–221
enthusiasm (clients)
  ACE meetings, 65–67, 363–365
  assuring. See Stage Six
  closing, 348, 352–353
  goals, 4–5
  Stage Four, 352–353
  Stage Six (assuring enthusiasm)
    ACE meetings, 65–67, 363–365
    closing overview, 363
    following up after loss, 67–69,
      366–368
    Ground Rule, 203
    must-ask questions, 313–314
    overview, 63–64
    positioning for future, 69–71,
      366–368
    Scorecard, 154
  Stage Three, 348
executing plan, 387
existing clients (Stage One), 381–382
experience (objections), 261–262
exploring opportunities (Stage Two),
  34–35

expressing interest
  Stage Two, 33
  TEPE, 283–285
extending (Stage Four), 52–55

F
facilitated self-discovery (Quadrant
  Three), 118
Factors (Scorecard Factors)
  benefits, 171–176
  conditions of satisfaction, 171–176
  features, 171–176
  Ground Rule, 224–225, 227–229
  hard factors, 173
  identifying, 176–177
  negative factors, 189–191
  number, 181–182
  overview, 147–149
  RFPs, 177–178
  selling points, 179–180
  size, 151
  soft factors, 173
  sole-source clients, 178–179
  style, 180
family. See friends and family
features (Scorecard Factors), 171–176
feeding back (Ground Rule), 209–214
feelings (Ground Rule), 206–207
files (Scorecard), 193
final close (Stage Five)
  competitive bids, 355
  confirming financial arrangement,
    61–62
  continuing to close, 59–61, 358–361
  formal bids, 355
  Ground Rule, 203
  identifying obstacles, 58–59
  losing, 357
  must-ask questions, 313–314
  overview, 57–58, 355
  RFPs, 356–357
  Scorecard, 154
financial arrangement. See price

focus (Scorecard), 149–150

following up
    after loss, 67–69, 366–368
    Quadrant Four, 128–129, 136

formal bids (Stage Five), 355

four quadrants. *See* quadrants

frame of reference (objections), 241–245

friends and family
    Quadrant Four, 137–140
    Quadrant One, 106–107
    Stage One, 380

fun (Scorecard), 154

future
    positioning for, 69–71, 366–368
    Scorecard, 149–150

G

gaps in coverage (objections), 249–251

getting information
    BIG (broad information gathering)
        questions
        areas of inquiry, 305–307
        overview, 300–301
    Quadrant One
        marketing, 97–98
        next steps, 100–102
        overview, 95–96
        recognized needs, 98–99
        referrals, 97–98
        time frame, 99–100
        who is calling, 96–97
    Quadrant Two, 110–111

goals
    client enthusiasm, 4–5
    overview, 3–4
    POGO (person, organization, goals,
        obstacles), 309–310
    Quadrant Four, 88–90
    Quadrant Three, 88–90

greetings (building rapport), 278

Ground Rule
    agreement, 206, 209–214
    areas of inquiry, 307–308
    checking questions, 218

closing best practices, 326–328, 332

connecting (clients/prospects), 211–214

danger zone, 218

feelings, 206–207

Heart of the Matter, refining, 223–226

objections
    closed-ended questions, 240
    depth, 260
    distance, 259–260
    experience, 261–262
    frame of reference, 241–245
    gaps in coverage, 249–251
    identifying, 232–235
    new areas, 262
    offsetting benefits, 235–237, 247
    overview, 231–232
    price. *See* price
    questions, 255–258
    rule of three, 257–258
    satisfaction, 251–253
    scope of service, 245–247
    strategy, 237–238
    "you're all the same", 263
    overview, 199–200
    practicing, 221–222
    providing information, 215–218
    questions
        closed-ended, 240
        ending with, 219–221
        interrogating clients, prospects, 219
        open-ended, 221
    Scorecard Factors, 224–225, 227–229
    smiling, 213–214
    Stage Five, 203
    Stage Four, 203
    Stage One, 203
    Stage Six, 203
    Stage Three, 203
    Stage Two, 203
    value, 200–203
        feeding back, 209–214
        listening, 205–207
    words (clients/prospects), 212–213

groups (Quadrant Four), 122–123

H

hard factors (Scorecard Factors), 173
Heart of the Matter
    overview, 157
    Quadrant Four, 164–170
    Quadrant One, 160–164
    Quadrant Three, 164–170
    Quadrant Two, 111–113, 160–164
    refining (Ground Rule), 223–226
    Scorecard
        overview, 147–149
        size, 151
    services/value comparison, 158–160
    Stage Three, 43–48
    value, defined, 157–158
hidden objections (closing), 353–354
honesty (differentiating services), 192–193

I

identifying
    leads (Stage One)
        building relationships, 23–24
        closing, 333–335
        creating leads, 28–29
        friends and family, 380
        Ground Rule, 203
        initiating contact, 29–31
        internal marketing, 379–380
        marketing activities, 335
        must-ask questions, 313–314
        networking, 378–379
        not selling, 26–28, 35
        overview, 21–23
        present clients, 381–382
        principles, 375–377
        promotional activities, 380–381
        prospecting, 379
        Scorecard, 153
        sell the meeting, not the service, 31
        seminars, 333–335
        success, 375–377
        vision of practice, 24–26
    objections (Ground Rule), 232–235

obstacles (Stage Five), 58–59
Scorecard Factors, 176–177
importance of
    Quadrant Four, 90–91
    Quadrant Three, 90–91
impressions, creating
    being late, 275
    confidence, 274
    dress, 272–274
    overview, 271–272
    punctuality, 274–275
influencers, 14–15
information
    BIG (broad information gathering)
        questions
        areas of inquiry, 305–307
        overview, 300–301
    Quadrant One
        marketing, 97–98
        next steps, 100–102
        overview, 95–96
        recognized needs, 98–99
        referrals, 97–98
        time frame, 99–100
        who is calling, 96–97
    Quadrant Two, 110–111
    getting information
        providing (Ground Rule), 215–218
information gathering. See getting
    information
initiating contact
    clients (Quadrant Three)
        awareness of resources, 117–118
        cross-selling, 86, 116–117
        cross-serving, 116–117
        facilitated self-discovery, 118
        goals, 88–90
        Heart of the Matter, 164–170
        importance of, 90–91
        issues, 116–117
        next steps, 88–90
        overview, 86–87, 115–116
        products, 116–117
        Scorecard, 164–170
        value statements, 118

initiating contact (*continued*)
  prospects (Quadrant Four)
    alternatives, 123
    best practices, 125
    choosing right situations, 120–123,
      133–134
    contacts, 130–133
    definable groups, 122–123
    following up, 128–129, 136
    friends and family, 137–140
    goals, 88–90
    Heart of the Matter, 164–170
    importance of, 90–91
    initiating contact, 136
    last resort, 123
    next steps, 88–90
    objections, 126–128, 136
    overview, 86–87, 119
    Scorecard, 164–170
    sell the meeting, not the service,
      123–124, 134–135
    social media, 120
    unique services, 121
  Stage One, 29–31
interest, expressing
  Stage Two, 33
  TEPE, 283–285
internal marketing (Stage One), 379–380
introductions (building rapport), 278
issues (Quadrant Three), 116–117

L

last resort (Quadrant Four), 123
lateness (creating impressions), 275
leads
  continuing contact (Stage Four), 352
  creating/identifying (Stage One)
    building relationships, 23–24
    closing, 333–335
    creating leads, 28–29
    friends and family, 380
    Ground Rule, 203
    initiating contact, 29–31

    internal marketing, 379–380
    marketing activities, 335
    must-ask questions, 313–314
    networking, 378–379
    not selling, 26–28, 35
    overview, 21–23
    present clients, 381–382
    principles, 375–377
    promotional activities, 380–381
    prospecting, 379
    Scorecard, 153
    sell the meeting, not the service, 31
    seminars, 333–335
    success, 375–377
    vision of practice, 24–26
  initiating contact
    Quadrant Four, 136
    Stage One, 29–31
  positioning closes
    best practices, 321–324
    Stage Two, 337–341
  qualified leads (decision-makers), 6,
    340
  qualifying and tracking leads (Stage
    Two)
    advancing closes, 339–341
    building relationships, 38–39
    decision-makers, 340
    exploring opportunities, 34–35
    expressing interest, 33
    Ground Rule, 203
    long-term commitment, 39–41
    meetings, 36
    must-ask questions, 313–314
    not selling, 26–28, 35
    overview, 33–34, 41, 337
    positioning closes, 337–341
    positioning leads/qualified leads
      comparison, 37
    quadrants. *See* quadrants
    recognized needs, 87–88
    Scorecard, 153
    skipping to Stage Five, 111–113
    telephone, 36

listening
building relationships, 7–8
Ground Rule
feeding back, 209–214
value, 205–207
instead of selling, 35
long term
commitment (Stage Two), 39–41
differentiating services, 188–189
strategy, 188–189
losing
clients. *See* Stage Six
following up after, 67–69, 366–368
Stage Five, 357
Stage Six (assuring enthusiasm)
ACE meetings, 65–67, 363–365
closing overview, 363
following up after loss, 67–69,
366–368
Ground Rule, 203
must-ask questions, 313–314
overview, 63–64
positioning for future, 69–71,
366–368
Scorecard, 154

M

marketing
Quadrant One, 97–98
Stage One (creating and identifying
leads)
building relationships, 23–24
closing, 333–335
creating leads, 28–29
friends and family, 380
Ground Rule, 203
initiating contact, 29–31
internal marketing, 379–380
marketing activities, 335
must-ask questions, 313–314
networking, 378–379
not selling, 26–28, 35
overview, 21–23

present clients, 381–382
principles, 375–377
promotional activities, 380–381
prospecting, 379
Scorecard, 153
sell the meeting, not the service, 31
seminars, 333–335
success, 375–377
vision of practice, 24–26
matrix. *See* quadrants
meet more, write less approach, 46–48
meetings
ACE meetings, 65–67, 363–365
sell the meeting, not the service, 31,
123–124, 134–135
Stage Two, 36
transitioning to business. *See*
transitioning to business
MEGO (my eyes glaze over), 282
must-ask questions
closing best practices, 324–325
overview, 311–312
six stages of the SalesGame, 313–314
my eyes glaze over (MEGO), 282

N

needs, recognized, 87–88, 98–99
negative Scorecard Factors, 189–191,
237–238
networks
analyzing, 16–17
Stage One, 378–379
new areas (objections), 262
next steps
Quadrant Four, 88–90
Quadrant One, 100–102
Quadrant Three, 88–90
not selling, 26–28, 35
number
power of three, 186–187
Scorecard Factors, 181–182

O

objections
  differentiating services, 190
  Ground Rule
    closed-ended questions, 240
    depth, 260
    distance, 259–260
    experience, 261–262
    frame of reference, 241–245
    gaps in coverage, 249–251
    identifying, 232–235
    new areas, 262
    offsetting benefits, 235–237, 247
    overview, 231–232
    price. *See* price
    questions, 255–258
    rule of three, 257–258
    satisfaction, 251–253
    scope of service, 245–247
    strategy, 237–238
    "you're all the same", 263
  hidden objections (Stage Four), 353–354
  price
    closed-ended questions, 240
    frame of reference, 241–245
    offsetting benefits, 247
    overview, 239–241
    scope of service, 245–247
  Quadrant Four, 126–128, 136
  strategy, 190
objectives, clients/prospects (Heart of the Matter)
  overview, 157
  Quadrant Four, 164–170
  Quadrant One, 160–164
  Quadrant Three, 164–170
  Quadrant Two, 111–113, 160–164
  refining (Ground Rule), 223–226
  Scorecard
    overview, 147–149
    size, 151
  services/value comparison, 158–160
  Stage Three, 43–48
  value, defined, 157–158

obstacles
  identifying (Stage Five), 58–59
  POGO (person, organization, goals, obstacles), 309–310
offsetting benefits (objections), 235–237, 247
open-ended questions, 221, 287–289, 297–299
opportunities, exploring, 34–35
organization (POGO), 309–310
penetrate and radiate strategy (building relationships), 17
permanent file (Scorecard), 193
person, organization, goals, obstacles (POGO), 309–310
phone calls (Stage Two), 36
planning
  best practices, 74–76
  collaborating, 75
  systems, 75
    executing, 387
    Play Diagram, 385–387
    Sales Planning Checklist, 383–384
  transitioning to business, 281–282, 290–291
  will to prepare, 73–74
  writing down ideas, 75
Play Diagram, 385–387
players
  analyzing networks of relationships, 16–17
  coaches, 15–16
  decision-makers
    overview, 13
    Quadrant Two, 111–113
    qualified leads, 6, 340
    Stage Three, 45–46
    Stage Two, 340
  influencers, 14–15
  overview, 11–12
  transitioning, 12
  users, 14
POGO (person, organization, goals, obstacles), 309–310

positioning
building relationships, 6
for futre, 69–71, 366–368
positioning closes
best practices, 321–324
Stage Two, 337–341
positioning leads, qualified leads
comparison, 37
power of three, 186–187
practice
building/selling work comparison, 8
vision (Stage One), 24–26
practicing
Ground Rule, 221–222
TEPE, 289–290
preparing. See planning
present clients (Stage One), 381–382
price
confirming (Stage Five), 61–62
objections
closed-ended questions, 240
frame of reference, 241–245
offsetting benefits, 247
overview, 239–241
scope of service, 245–247
principles (Stage One), 375–377
products (Quadrant Three), 116–117
promotional activities (Stage One),
380–381
proposals
closing, 330–332
Stage Four, 350–351
prospects. See also clients
connecting (Ground Rule), 211–214
Heart of the Matter
overview, 157
Quadrant Four, 164–170
Quadrant One, 160–164
Quadrant Three, 164–170
Quadrant Two, 111–113, 160–164
refining (Ground Rule), 223–226
Scorecard, 147–149, 151
services/value comparison, 158–160
Stage Three, 43–48
value, defined, 157–158

initiating contact (Quadrant Four)
alternatives, 123
best practices, 125
choosing right situations, 120–123,
133–134
contacts, 130–133
definable groups, 122–123
following up, 128–129, 136
friends and family, 137–140
goals, 88–90
Heart of the Matter, 164–170
importance of, 90–91
initiating contact, 136
last resort, 123
next steps, 88–90
objections, 126–128, 136
overview, 86–87, 119
Scorecard, 164–170
sell the meeting, not the service,
123–124, 134–135
social media, 120
unique services, 121
objectives. See Heart of the Matter
players. See players
questions (interrogating), 219
responding. See Quadrant One
Scorecard. See Scorecard
Stage One, 379
words (Ground Rule), 212–213
providing information(Ground Rule),
215–218
punctuality (creating impressions),
274–275
purpose, stating (TEPE), 285–287

Q

Quadrant Four
alternatives, 123
best practices, 125
choosing right situations, 120–123,
133–134
contacts, 130–133
definable groups, 122–123
following up, 128–129, 136

Quadrant Four (*continued*)
    friends and family, 137–140
    goals, 88–90
    Heart of the Matter, 164–170
    importance of, 90–91
    initiating contact, 136
    last resort, 123
    next steps, 88–90
    objections, 126–128, 136
    overview, 86–87, 119
    Scorecard, 164–170
    sell the meeting, not the service, 123–124, 134–135
    social media, 120
    unique services, 121
Quadrant One
    blind requests for services, 95
    building relationships first, 104–106
    creative closes, 102–104
    friends and family, 106–107
    getting information
        marketing, 97–98
        next steps, 100–102
        overview, 95–96
        recognized needs, 98–99
        referrals, 97–98
        time frame, 99–100
        who is calling, 96–97
    Heart of the Matter, 160–164
    overview, 86, 93
    recognized needs, 87–88
    responding quickly, 94–95
    Scorecard, 160–164
Quadrant Three
    awareness of resources, 117–118
    cross-selling, 86, 116–117
    cross-serving, 116–117
    facilitated self-discovery, 118
    goals, 88–90
    Heart of the Matter, 164–170
    importance of, 90–91
    issues, 116–117
    next steps, 88–90
    overview, 86–87, 115–116

    products, 116–117
    Scorecard, 164–170
    value statements, 118
Quadrant Two
    decision-makers, 111–113
    getting information, 110–111
    Heart of the Matter, 111–113, 160–164
    overview, 86, 109
    recognized needs, 87–88
    responding quickly, 110–111
    Scorecard, 160–164
quadrants
    overview, 83–87
    Quadrant Four
        alternatives, 123
        best practices, 125
        choosing right situations, 120–123, 133–134
        contacts, 130–133
        definable groups, 122–123
        following up, 128–129, 136
        friends and family, 137–140
        goals, 88–90
        Heart of the Matter, 164–170
        importance of, 90–91
        initiating contact, 136
        last resort, 123
        next steps, 88–90
        objections, 126–128, 136
        overview, 86–87, 119
        Scorecard, 164–170
        sell the meeting, not the service, 123–124, 134–135
        social media, 120
        unique services, 121
    Quadrant One. *See* Quadrant One
    Quadrant Three
        awareness of resources, 117–118
        cross-selling, 86, 116–117
        cross-serving, 116–117
        facilitated self-discovery, 118
        goals, 88–90
        Heart of the Matter, 164–170
        importance of, 90–91

issues, 116–117
next steps, 88–90
overview, 86–87, 115–116
products, 116–117
Scorecard, 164–170
value statements, 118
Quadrant Two
decision-makers, 111–113
getting information, 110–111
Heart of the Matter, 111–113,
160–164
overview, 86, 109
recognized needs, 87–88
responding quickly, 110–111
Scorecard, 160–164
qualified leads
decision-makers, 6, 340
positioning leads comparison, 37
qualifying leads (Stage Two)
advancing closes, 339–341
building relationships, 38–39
decision-makers, 340
exploring opportunities, 34–35
expressing interest, 33
Ground Rule, 203
long-term commitment, 39–41
meetings, 36
must-ask questions, 313–314
not selling, 26–28, 35
overview, 33–34, 41, 337
positioning closes, 337–341
positioning leads/qualified leads
comparison, 37
quadrants. *See* quadrants
recognized needs, 87–88
Scorecard, 153
skipping to Stage Five, 111–113
telephone, 36
quality/value comparison, 9–10
questions
areas of inquiry
BIG questions, 305–307
collaborating, 308–309
developing, 303

drilling down, 307–308
Ground Rule, 307–308
POGO, 309–310
starting broad and easy, 305–306
vision, 304
best practices, 295–296, 325–326
BIG (broad information gathering)
questions
areas of inquiry, 305–307
overview, 300–301
checking questions, 218, 299
closed-ended, 240, 297–300
confirming/verifying, 299
ending with, 219–221
Ground Rule
areas of inquiry, 307–308
checking questions, 218
closed-ended questions, 240
interrogating clients, prospects, 219
objections, 255–258
must-ask
closing best practices, 324–325
overview, 311–312
six stages of the SalesGame,
313–314
open-ended questions, 221, 287–289,
297–299
starting broad and easy, 296
yes/no questions, 325–326

R
rapport, building
greetings, 278
introductions, 278
overview, 277
simplicity, 278–279
time, 279–280
**recognized needs, 87–88 (Quadrant
One), 98–99**
referrals (Quadrant One), 97–98
**refining Heart of the Matter (Ground
Rule), 223–226**
**rejection (closing best practices),
326–328**

relationships

analyzing networks, 16–17

building

closing, 344

listening, 7–8

penetrate and radiate strategy, 17

positioning, 6

positioning leads, 38–39

Quadrant One, 104–106

Stage One, 23–24

Stage Three, 344

stages of the SalesGame. *See* stages of the SalesGame

relatives. *See* **friends and family**

requests (blind requests for services), 95

resources (Quadrant Three), 117–118

responding

clients (Quadrant Two)

decision-makers, 111–113

getting information, 110–111

Heart of the Matter, 111–113, 160–164

overview, 86, 109

recognized needs, 87–88

responding quickly, 110–111

Scorecard, 160–164

prospects. *See* Quadrant One

responsibility (differentiating services), 192–193

RFPs

Scorecard Factors, 177–178

Stage Five, 356–357

rule of three (objections), 257–258

rules

Ground Rule. *See* Ground Rule

rule of three (objections), 257–258

running late (creating impressions), 275

S

sales matrix

overview, 83–87

Quadrant Four

alternatives, 123

best practices, 125

choosing right situations, 120–123, 133–134

contacts, 130–133

definable groups, 122–123

following up, 128–129, 136

friends and family, 137–140

goals, 88–90

Heart of the Matter, 164–170

importance of, 90–91

initiating contact, 136

last resort, 123

next steps, 88–90

objections, 126–128, 136

overview, 86–87, 119

Scorecard, 164–170

sell the meeting, not the service, 123–124, 134–135

social media, 120

unique services, 121

Quadrant One. *See* Quadrant One

Quadrant Three

awareness of resources, 117–118

cross-selling, 86, 116–117

cross-serving, 116–117

facilitated self-discovery, 118

goals, 88–90

Heart of the Matter, 164–170

importance of, 90–91

issues, 116–117

next steps, 88–90

overview, 86–87, 115–116

products, 116–117

Scorecard, 164–170

value statements, 118

Quadrant Two

decision-makers, 111–113

getting information, 110–111

Heart of the Matter, 111–113, 160–164

overview, 86, 109

recognized needs, 87–88

responding quickly, 110–111

Scorecard, 160–164

Sales Planning Checklist, 383–384

SalesGame. *See* stages of the SalesGame
satisfaction (clients), 8–9
  conditions of satisfaction, 171–176
  objections (Ground Rule), 251–253
scope of service (objections), 245–247
Scorecard
  clarity, 149–150
  differentiating services
    honesty, 192–193
    long term, 188–189
    negative Scorecard Factors, 189–191
    objections, 190
    overview, 183–184
    power of three, 186–187
    responsibility, 192–193
    starting early, 184–186
    tangibility, 187–188
  focus, 149–150
  fun, 154
  future, 149–150
  Heart of the Matter
    overview, 147–149, 157
    Quadrant Four, 164–170
    Quadrant One, 160–164
    Quadrant Three, 164–170
    Quadrant Two, 160–164
    services/value comparison, 158–160
    size, 151
    value, defined, 157–158
  permanent file, 193
Scorecard Factors
  benefits, 171–176
  conditions of satisfaction, 171–176
  features, 171–176
  Ground Rule, 224–225, 227–229
  hard factors, 173
  identifying, 176–177
  negative factors, 189–191
  number, 181–182
  overview, 147–149
  RFPs, 177–178
  selling points, 179–180
  size, 151
  soft factors, 173

  sole-source clients, 178–179
  style, 180
service tangibility, 155–156
size, 150–151
Stage Five, 154
Stage Four, 49, 51–52, 153
Stage One, 153
Stage Six, 154
Stage Three, 43, 153
Stage Two, 153
strategy
  honesty, 192–193
  long term, 188–189
  negative Scorecard Factors, 189–191,
    237–238
  objections, 190
  overview, 183–184
  power of three, 186–187
  responsibility, 192–193
  starting early, 184–186
  tangibility, 187–188
Scorecard Factors
  benefits, 171–176
  conditions of satisfaction, 171–176
  features, 171–176
  Ground Rule, 224–225, 227–229
  hard factors, 173
  identifying, 176–177
  negative factors, 189–191
  number, 181–182
  overview, 147–149
  RFPs, 177–178
  selling points, 179–180
  size, 151
  soft factors, 173
  sole-source clients, 178–179
  style, 180
self-discovery (Quadrant Three), 118
selling
  cross-selling (Quadrant Three), 86,
    116–117
  cross-serving (Quadrant Three),
    116–117
  listening instead of, 35

selling (*continued*)

not selling (Stage One), 26–28, 35

sell the meeting, not the service, 31, 123–124, 134–135

work, building practice comparison, 8

selling points (Scorecard Factors), 179–180

seminars (Stage One), 333–335

services

blind requests for services, 95

cross-serving, 116–117

differentiating

honesty, 192–193

long term, 188–189

negative Scorecard Factors, 189–191

objections, 190

overview, 183–184

power of three, 186–187

responsibility, 192–193

Stage Three, 345–347

starting early, 184–186

tangibility, 187–188

Heart of the Matter (value comparison), 158–160

scope (objections), 245–247

sell the meeting, not the service, 31, 123–124, 134–135

shaping (Stage Three)

advancing closes, 345–347

building relationships, 344

client enthusiasm, 348

decision-makers, 45–46

differentiating services, 345–347

Ground Rule, 203

Heart of the Matter, 43, 45–46, 48

meet more, write less approach, 46–48

must-ask questions, 313–314

overview, 43–45, 343–344

Quadrant Two, 111–113

Scorecard, 43, 153

tangibility (Scorecard), 155–156

unique services, 121

setting up closes (best practices), 324–325

shaping the service (Stage Three)

advancing closes, 345–347

building relationships, 344

client enthusiasm, 348

decision-makers, 45–46

differentiating services, 345–347

Ground Rule, 203

Heart of the Matter, 43, 45–46, 48

meet more, write less approach, 46–48

must-ask questions, 313–314

overview, 43–45, 343–344

Quadrant Two, 111–113

Scorecard, 43, 153

simplicity (building rapport), 278–279

six stages of the SalesGame. *See* stages of the SalesGame

size (Scorecard), 150–151

skipping stages, 111–113

smiling (Ground Rule), 213–214

social media (Quadrant Four), 120

soft factors (Scorecard Factors), 173

sole-source clients (Scorecard Factors), 178–179

source of value (Heart of the Matter)

overview, 157

Quadrant Four, 164–170

Quadrant One, 160–164

Quadrant Three, 164–170

Quadrant Two, 111–113, 160–164

refining (Ground Rule), 223–226

Scorecard

overview, 147–149

size, 151

services/value comparison, 158–160

Stage Three, 43–48

value, defined, 157–158

speed, responding

Quadrant One, 94–95

Quadrant Two, 110–111

Stage Five (final close)

competitive bids, 355

confirming financial arrangement, 61–62

continuing to close, 59–61, 358–361

formal bids, 355

Ground Rule, 203
identifying obstacles, 58–59
losing, 357
must-ask questions, 313–314
overview, 57–58, 355
RFPs, 356–357
Scorecard, 154
Stage Four (trial close)
asking for business, 51–52
client enthusiasm, 352–353
continuing contact, 352
continuing to close, 352
draft proposals, 350–351
extending, 52–55
Ground Rule, 203
hidden objections, 353–354
must-ask questions, 313–314
overview, 49–51, 349–350
Scorecard, 49, 51–52, 153
Stage One (creating and identifying leads)
building relationships, 23–24
closing, 333–335
creating leads, 28–29
friends and family, 380
Ground Rule, 203
initiating contact, 29–31
internal marketing, 379–380
marketing activities, 335
must-ask questions, 313–314
networking, 378–379
not selling, 26–28, 35
overview, 21–23
present clients, 381–382
principles, 375–377
promotional activities, 380–381
prospecting, 379
Scorecard, 153
sell the meeting, not the service, 31
seminars, 333–335
success, 375–377
vision of practice, 24–26
Stage Six (assuring enthusiasm)
ACE meetings, 65–67, 363–365
closing overview, 363

following up after loss, 67–69, 366–368
Ground Rule, 203
must-ask questions, 313–314
overview, 63–64
positioning for future, 69–71, 366–368
Scorecard, 154
Stage Three (shaping the service)
advancing closes, 345–347
building relationships, 344
client enthusiasm, 348
decision-makers, 45–46
differentiating services, 345–347
Ground Rule, 203
Heart of the Matter, 43, 45–46, 48
meet more, write less approach, 46–48
must-ask questions, 313–314
overview, 43–45, 343–344
Quadrant Two, 111–113
Scorecard, 43, 153
Stage Two (qualifying and tracking leads)
advancing closes, 339–341
building relationships, 38–39
decision-makers, 340
exploring opportunities, 34–35
expressing interest, 33
Ground Rule, 203
long-term commitment, 39–41
meetings, 36
must-ask questions, 313–314
not selling, 26–28, 35
overview, 33–34, 41, 337
positioning closes, 337–341
positioning leads/qualified leads comparison, 37
Quadrant Four
alternatives, 123
best practices, 125
choosing right situations, 120–123, 133–134
contacts, 130–133
definable groups, 122–123
following up, 128–129, 136
friends and family, 137–140
goals, 88–90

Stage Two (qualifying and tracking leads)
(*continued*)
  Heart of the Matter, 164–170
  importance of, 90–91
  initiating contact, 136
  last resort, 123
  next steps, 88–90
  objections, 126–128, 136
  overview, 86–87, 119
  Scorecard, 164–170
  sell the meeting, not the service,
    123–124, 134–135
  social media, 120
  unique services, 121
Quadrant One. *See* Quadrant One
Quadrant Three
  awareness of resources, 117–118
  cross-selling, 86, 116–117
  cross-serving, 116–117
  facilitated self-discovery, 118
  goals, 88–90
  Heart of the Matter, 164–170
  importance of, 90–91
  issues, 116–117
  next steps, 88–90
  overview, 86–87, 115–116
  products, 116–117
  Scorecard, 164–170
  value statements, 118
Quadrant Two
  decision-makers, 111–113
  getting information, 110–111
  Heart of the Matter, 111–113,
    160–164
  overview, 86, 109
  recognized needs, 87–88
  responding quickly, 110–111
  Scorecard, 160–164
quadrants overview, 83–87
recognized needs, 87–88
Scorecard, 153
skipping to Stage Five, 111–113
telephone, 36

stages of the SalesGame
  overview, 19–20, 31
  skipping stages, 111–113
Stage Five (final close)
  competitive bids, 355
  confirming financial arrangement,
    61–62
  continuing to close, 59–61, 358–361
  formal bids, 355
  Ground Rule, 203
  identifying obstacles, 58–59
  losing, 357
  must-ask questions, 313–314
  overview, 57–58, 355
  RFPs, 356–357
  Scorecard, 154
Stage Four (trial close)
  asking for business, 51–52
  client enthusiasm, 352–353
  continuing contact, 352
  continuing to close, 352
  draft proposals, 350–351
  extending, 52–55
  Ground Rule, 203
  hidden objections, 353–354
  must-ask questions, 313–314
  overview, 49–51, 349–350
  Scorecard, 49, 51–52, 153
Stage One (creating and identifying
  leads)
  building relationships, 23–24
  closing, 333–335
  creating leads, 28–29
  friends and family, 380
  Ground Rule, 203
  initiating contact, 29–31
  internal marketing, 379–380
  marketing activities, 335
  must-ask questions, 313–314
  networking, 378–379
  not selling, 26–28, 35
  overview, 21–23
  present clients, 381–382
  principles, 375–377

promotional activities, 380–381
prospecting, 379
Scorecard, 153
sell the meeting, not the service, 31
seminars, 333–335
success, 375–377
vision of practice, 24–26
Stage Six (assuring enthusiasm)
ACE meetings, 65–67, 363–365
closing overview, 363
following up after loss, 67–69,
366–368
Ground Rule, 203
must-ask questions, 313–314
overview, 63–64
positioning for future, 69–71,
366–368
Scorecard, 154
Stage Three (shaping the service)
advancing closes, 345–347
building relationships, 344
client enthusiasm, 348
decision-makers, 45–46
differentiating services, 345–347
Ground Rule, 203
Heart of the Matter, 43, 45–46, 48
meet more, write less approach,
46–48
must-ask questions, 313–314
overview, 43–45, 343–344
Quadrant Two, 111–113
Scorecard, 43, 153
Scorecard, 43, 153
Stage Two (qualifying and tracking leads)
advancing closes, 339–341
building relationships, 38–39
decision-makers, 340
exploring opportunities, 34–35
expressing interest, 33
Ground Rule, 203
long-term commitment, 39–41
meetings, 36
must-ask questions, 313–314
not selling, 26–28, 35
overview, 33–34, 41, 337

positioning closes, 337–341
positioning leads/qualified leads
comparison, 37
quadrants. *See* quadrants
recognized needs, 87–88
Scorecard, 153
skipping to Stage Five, 111–113
telephone, 36
starting
broad and easy
areas of inquiry, 305–306
questions, 296
early (differentiating services), 184–186
stating purpose (TEPE), 285–287
steps (next steps)
Quadrant Four, 88–90
Quadrant One, 100–102
Quadrant Three, 88–90
strategy
objections (Ground Rule), 237–238
Scorecard
honesty, 192–193
long term, 188–189
negative Scorecard Factors, 189–191,
237–238
objections, 190
overview, 183–184
power of three, 186–187
responsibility, 192–193
starting early, 184–186
tangibility, 187–188
style (Scorecard Factors), 180
success (Stage One), 375–377
systems (planning), 75
executing, 387
Play Diagram, 385–387
Sales Planning Checklist, 383–384

T

tangibility
services
differentiating, 187–188
Scorecard, 155–156
strategy, 187–188

tardiness (creating impressions), 275
telephone (Stage Two), 36
TEPE (transitioning to business)
    ending, 287–289
    expressing interest, 283–285
    open-ended questions, 287–289
    overview, 283
    practicing, 289–290
    stating purpose, 285–287
    thanking clients, 283
thanking clients (TEPE), 283
time
    building rapport, 279–280
    closing best practices, 328–330
    extending Stage Four, 52–55
    long term
        commitment (Stage Two), 39–41
        differentiating services, 188–189
        strategy, 188–189
    punctuality (creating impressions),
        274–275
    responding quickly
        Quadrant One, 94–95
        Quadrant Two, 110–111
    starting early
        differentiating services, 184–186
        strategy, 184–186
    time frame (Quadrant One), 99–100
time frame (Quadrant One), 99–100
tips. See best practices
tracking leads (Stage Two)
    advancing closes, 339–341
    building relationships, 38–39
    decision-makers, 340
    exploring opportunities, 34–35
    expressing interest, 33
    Ground Rule, 203
    long-term commitment, 39–41
    meetings, 36
    must-ask questions, 313–314
    not selling, 26–28, 35
    overview, 33–34, 41, 337
    positioning closes, 337–341

positioning leads/qualified leads
    comparison, 37
quadrants. See quadrants
recognized needs, 87–88
Scorecard, 153
skipping to Stage Five, 111–113
telephone, 36
transitioning players, 12
transitioning to business
    planning, 281–282, 290–291
    TEPE
        ending, 287–289
        expressing interest, 283–285
        open-ended questions, 287–289
        overview, 283
        practicing, 289–290
        stating purpose, 285–287
        thanking clients, 283
    value propositions, 282
trial close (Stage Four)
    asking for business, 51–52
    client enthusiasm, 352–353
    continuing contact, 352
    continuing to close, 352
    draft proposals, 350–351
    extending, 52–55
    Ground Rule, 203
    hidden objections, 353–354
    must-ask questions, 313–314
    overview, 49–51, 349–350
    Scorecard, 49, 51–52, 153

U–V

unique services (Quadrant Four), 121
users, 14
value
    Ground Rule, 200–203, 205–207
    Heart of the Matter
        overview, 157
        Quadrant Four, 164–170
        Quadrant One, 160–164
        Quadrant Three, 164–170
        Quadrant Two, 111–113, 160–164

refining (Ground Rule), 223–226

Scorecard, 147–149, 151

services/value comparison, 158–160

Stage Three, 43–48

value, defined, 157–158

listening, 205–207

quality comparison, 9–10

source of. *See* Heart of the Matter

value propositions (transitioning to business), 282

value statements (Quadrant Three), 118

value propositions (transitioning to business), 282

value statements (Quadrant Three), 118

verifying/confirming

financial arrangement (Stage Five), 61–62

questions, 299

vision

areas of inquiry, 304

practice (Stage One), 24–26

W–Y

wardrobe, creating impressions, 272–274

who is calling (Quadrant One), 96–97

will to prepare, 73–74

words of clients/prospects (Ground Rule), 212–213

work, selling/building practice comparison, 8

writing

proposals (closing best practices), 330–332

ideas (planning), 75

yes/no questions, 325–326

"you're all the same" objections (Ground Rule), 263